STATE INCOME DIFFERENTIALS, 1919-1954

STATE INCOME DIFFERENTIALS 1919-1954

Frank A. Hanna

DUKE UNIVERSITY PRESS, *DURHAM, N. C., 1959*

CAMBRIDGE UNIVERSITY PRESS, LONDON, N.W. 1, ENGLAND

LIBRARY OF CONGRESS CATALOG CARD NUMBER 59-11765

PRINTED IN THE UNITED STATES OF AMERICA
BY THE SEEMAN PRINTERY, DURHAM, N. C.

To

NORA

The publication of this book was assisted by a grant to the Duke University Press by the Ford Foundation.

PREFACE

MANY OF the possible approaches to income differentials among states or regions appear fruitful for one or more purposes. What might be called the reportorial approach, the provision of estimates of the amounts of income in each state and region, is basic to the other fruitful approaches. Estimates which are sufficiently reliable for most purposes are provided by the National Income Division of the U. S. Department of Commerce (*Personal Income by States since 1929,* Washington, 1956) for each of the states except Alaska. The pioneering estimates prepared by Maurice Leven for 1919-1921 (*Income in the Various States, Its Sources and Distribution, 1919, 1920, and 1921,* New York, 1925) extend the period for which state income data are available. The official estimates for some of the states have been distributed by county, usually by research workers within the state.

Another approach uses all of the available statistical data and other information in an effort to describe for a particular region its economic characteristics and the changes in these characteristics. Examples of such studies are *The Economic Resources and Policies of the South* (New York, 1951) by Calvin B. Hoover and B. U. Ratchford, and *The Economics of New England* (Cambridge, 1952) by Seymour E. Harris. Aggregate and per capita incomes, because they are both all-inclusive and unduplicated measures, have a prominent, though by no means an exclusive, place in such studies.

Regional differences have also been approached through the construction of theoretical models which seek to account for their causes. Most of these models are based on European experience and are concerned with income differences only indirectly. The more recent regional models, and particularly those concerned with income differences in the United States, are discussed in *Regional Income: Studies in Income and Wealth* (Princeton, 1957). These discussions contain or suggest reasonable hypotheses which might, if data were available to test them, open up additional ways to further our knowledge of regional income differences.

Another approach seeks to analyze the observed state and regional differences in terms of sets of "fundamental" or "universal" elements or forces, such as skills or industries, especially those for which there is likely to be a continuing supply of data. This approach is adopted here. Several considerations favored its adoption.

First, it is an essential first step in understanding the characteristics of the state or regional differentials which are the subject of study. To the extent that the characteristics of the differentials and the patterns of their behavior in the presence of cyclical and secular forces can be determined and statistically tested, such an analysis will provide criteria for, and thus help to focus, many special-purpose analyses in which regional differentials are a variable.

Secondly, such an analysis provides a further test of the validity of the annual estimates of state income, the statistical series basic for most regional studies. One appraisal of this series is provided in the report of the National Accounts Review Committee of the National Bureau of Economic Research in *The National Economic Accounts of the United States* (Hearings before the Subcommittee on Economic Statistics of the Joint Economic Committee, October 29 and 30, 1957, 85th Congress, 1st Session; especially chapter 9). This appraisal is largely in terms of the suitability of the concepts used for generally recognized purposes, such as estimating the market potential of small areas. It also deals with the quantity and characteristics of the data available for constructing the state estimates. The studies here, since they concentrate on the pattterns of and the regularities in the behavior of the state estimates, are oriented toward an appraisal of the data as variables in economic analyses. However, the concentration on patterns helped to isolate instances in which departures from the patterns appear to be traceable to the characteristics of the estimates rather than to differences in the behavior of the forces being estimated. For the most part these instances relate to areas already known to be weak—to agricultural income and to other nonwage components of income.

Finally, in addition to an intensive analysis of the state income estimates, it also seemed desirable to examine carefully all the major bodies of primary statistical data for states, such as the data provided by the various censuses, for illumination of many aspects of the state income differentials. The approach adopted here can both accommodate such data and provide some criteria for allocating analytical resources among the diverse bodies of data. Some use is made of independent data in ascertaining and testing the interrelationships among the changes in regional and national income components and totals. The chapters dealing with earnings differentials and with demographic factors rely most heavily upon these bodies of primary data.

What are some of the more familiar variables which may help us understand the observed differences in state per capita incomes? Occupation and industrial attachment rank high among the sets of such explanatory variables. These two sets of variables are, of course, interrelated. Occupation tends to reflect, though not precisely, the educational attainment, the skills, the age, the health, and other personal characteristics of the residents of the various states. In substance, occupation reflects the supply of skills by which the nation's work is done and income is created. On the other hand, the farms, mines, factories, stores, and offices in which these skills are employed are classified for most analytical purposes by their industrial characteristics. Industry, consequently, tends to reflect the current demand for various skills.

Together, occupation and industrial attachment, the latter to a lesser extent, provide meaningful classification of the recipients of wages and salaries, of proprietors' income, and of most transfer payments. Only the flow of property income is not directly connected with these characteristics. The principal bodies of state data by occupation and by industry have been subjected to extensive analyses, and, insofar as data permit, these analyses have been supplemented by analyses of associated variables such as age, participation in the labor force, urbanization, and sex. Since all of these variables are interrelated, much of their explanatory value is also reflected by occupation and/or industry. Consequently, the interest in these variables is of a somewhat different order.

There are findings, for example, that the 1949 earnings of women are lower than those of men in almost every occupation and that the occupations in which women are more prevalent are the lower-paying occupations both in each of the states and in the nation (chapter 5). While these findings are of interest, they contribute little to the explanation of state earnings differentials. On the contrary, they raise a number of new questions which go beyond the scope of this study. One example should suffice: Do the lower occupational earnings of women reflect differences in skill, perhaps because of an average work-life shorter than that of men, or do they reflect simply lower pay than men would receive for a specific job? There are no data which will permit direct answers to these questions. As a matter of procedure, had data been available which would have permitted distinguishing degrees of skill within an occupational category, a more promising way to use such data would have been to create new occupational categories which reflected these differences.

This example of the earnings differences between men and women is mentioned because of its obvious parallel to the earnings differences between whites and nonwhites. The differences among races are not analyzed in this volume. Had data been available to support such an analysis, one probably would have been made, just as some resources were devoted to analyzing the male-female differentials. It is doubtful, however, whether such an analysis would have contributed substantially to the explanation of state income differentials. To the extent that Negroes tend to concentrate in the lower-paying occupations or tend to be among the less skilled within a given occupation, then the analysis of occupational earnings differentials gives full weight to these important attributes of Negro earnings. Somewhat more precise and more detailed data than are now available even at the national level, however, would be needed to measure the extent to which variation in remuneration for a given level of performance is associated with color, race, sex, age, or similar personal characteristics.

In addition to "explanatory" variables, such as occupation and industrial attachment, much attention has been accorded to the changes in the state income differentials and how these differentials are related to the level of income and to its many structural aspects. Cyclical and secular factors, particularly, have been examined intensively with a view to uncovering their relationship to changes in state differentials.

The patterns of change in state per capita incomes during recent decades, the concern of much of this volume, should provide background materials that are needed to interpret, appraise, and provide perspective for the specific and detailed studies of particular areas, such as those often conducted by the development or planning commission of a state or the chamber of commerce of a metropolitan area. To facilitate the use of the volume in local studies, the results are presented for each of the 48 states individually, although similarities among groups of contiguous states are pointed out. The study relates to a period which ended before Alaska and Hawaii became states.

ACKNOWLEDGMENTS

An empirical study of this kind requires the participation and co-operation of many persons. The help given by some has been specific enough that their contributions are mentioned in the text; that given by others has been more general. I wish to acknowledge here their help and to express my appreciation for it.

The comments and discussions which have grown out of the publication of earlier versions of some of the materials have affected my thinking about many of the issues and have, I hope, helped to improve their treatment here. My thanks are due to the editors of the *Review of Economics and Statistics,* the *Southern Economic Journal,* and the *Bulletin of the International Statistical Institute,* for permission to draw freely upon materials which I first presented in their pages. Similarly, I am indebted to the National Bureau of Economic Research for permission to draw upon my article in volume 21 of *Studies in Income and Wealth, Regional Income.*

Charles F. Schwartz and Robert E. Graham, Jr. of the National Income Division were generous and co-operative in making unpublished materials available and in helping me in other ways. In many instances so much work was required on their part that it would not have been unreasonable for them to decline. Maxwell R. Conklin, Harvey Kailin, and Herman P. Miller were particularly helpful in arranging for special tabulations of census data in a form that was most useful to me.

Charles M. Tiebout, now at the University of California at Los Angeles, and Richard F. Muth, Resources for the Future, read the entire manuscript. One or more chapters were read by Howard G. Schaller, Tulane University; Edwin Mansfield, Carnegie Institute of Technology; Lowell DeWitt Ashby, University of North Carolina; and Brinley Thomas, University College, Cardiff. For their comments I am most grateful. Any remaining errors are my responsibility alone.

Rena B. Webster supervised the computations and the preparation of the many tables which appear in this volume. The charts were drawn by Norman Perry. The manuscript was edited and the index was prepared by Julia Negley.

This volume is the final report of the Study of Differences in State Per Capita Incomes, which was supported jointly by Duke University and The Rockefeller Foundation.

F. A. H.

June 1959

The comments and discussions which have grown out of the publication of earlier versions of some of the materials have affected my thinking about many of the issues and have, I hope, helped to improve their treatment here. My thanks are due to the editors of the *Review of Economics and Statistics*, the *Southern Economic Journal*, and the *Bulletin of the International Statistical Institute* for permission to draw freely upon materials which I first presented in their pages. Similarly, I am indebted to the National Bureau of Economic Research for permission to draw upon my article in volume 21 of *Studies in Income and Wealth*, *Regional Income*.

Charles F. Schwartz and Robert E. Graham, Jr. of the National Income Division were generous and cooperative in making unpublished materials available and in helping me in other ways. In many instances so much work was required on their part that it would not have been unreasonable for them to decline. Maxwell R. Conklin, Harvey Kailin, and Herman P. Miller were particularly helpful in arranging for special tabulations of census data in a form that was most useful to me.

Charles M. Tiebout, now at the University of California at Los Angeles, and Richard F. Muth, Resources for the Future, read the entire manuscript. One or more chapters were read by Howard G. Schaller, Tulane University; Edwin Mansfield, Carnegie Institute of Technology; Lowell DeWitt Ashby, University of North Carolina; and Brinley Thomas, University College, Cardiff. For their comments I am most grateful. Any remaining errors are my responsibility alone.

Rena E. Weiss supervised the computations and the preparation of the many tables which appear in this volume. The charts were drawn by Norman Perry. The manuscript was edited and the index was prepared by Julia Naylor.

This volume is the final report of the Study of Differences in State Per Capita Incomes, which was supported jointly by Duke University and The Rockefeller Foundation.

F. A. H.

June 1959

CONTENTS

TABLES

CHARTS

STATE INCOME DIFFERENTIALS, 1919-1954

Chapter 1

INTRODUCTION AND SUMMARY

THE LARGE differences among state personal incomes, even after adjustment for differences in state populations, have persisted since 1919. These large and persistent differences among states raise many questions that are of more than passing interest to all who are concerned with the development of resources in particular areas.

To what extent has the increase or decrease in per capita personal income at the national level been reflected in each of the states? Does each of the states experience the same dollar increase or decrease? Or do the dollar incomes in some states tend to fluctuate more than in others? If there are differences in dollar amounts, is there some tendency for the state incomes to increase or decrease proportionally, so that they have about the same percentage increases or decreases? If there are differences in the responses of particular states to changes in the national level of per capita income, are these differences associated with the level of income during some previous period, with the industrial composition of the states' economies, or with some set of unchanging and unchangeable geographical characteristics, such as average rainfall or the distance from a seaport?

When the level of personal income changes, do some states experience more and some less fluctuation in their per capita personal incomes? If so, do the states that are more sensitive to changes at the national level tend to have distinct industrial characteristics? Is there evidence that some states are growing faster than others over the recent period?

The answers to such questions provide the starting point for understanding state income differentials. A knowledge of the patterns of change in state per capita incomes during recent decades is essential if meaningful results are to come from the more specific and detailed studies of particular areas, such as those that might be conducted by the development or planning commission of a state or the chamber of commerce of a metropolitan area. Typically, it is not enough to know that per capita income in an area has increased. Also needed is some basis for appraising such a fact—for example, a knowledge of whether other areas with similar characteristics have increased more or less than the area under study. If the available data on state per capita personal income since 1919 are to provide such background material, they must be analyzed with a view to uncovering and testing these patterns.

This study is concerned with all of the differences among the state per capita personal incomes. The search is for the general patterns of change in these differences. While interest in the level or change in individual state per capita personal income is not ignored, greater attention is accorded the contributions of individual states to the pattern of change in state differentials. Moreover, there has been no attempt to group states into regions, although the similarity of several states with respect to some one characteristic often is pointed out.

The 48 states of the United States have been adopted as the basic geographic unit for study.[1] More data are available for the states than for any other geographic unit, an important reason, though not the principal one, for adopting the state as the geographic unit. The fact that data have been compiled by states stems from reasons which make the state boundaries a meaningful and useful device for delineating geographic areas. In the United States the state is sovereign, and the federal government derives its sovereignty from the states. Each state has a complete governmental framework, paralleling that of the federal government, complete with governor, legislature, and courts. Although the Constitution prohibits states from levying imposts and duties and thus erecting economic barriers to free trade among residents of the several states, it reserves large areas of economic responsibilty to the states. Among other powers, a state has general taxing power and is responsible for many of the improvements within its borders. Even though a state government may be virtually powerless to affect directly the direction and extent of its economic development, whatever development does take place within its borders will color many of the state government's activities. For this

[1] The District of Columbia is not treated as a state and consequently is excluded from most measures presented in this study. The District of Columbia is included in tables showing data for individual states. However, when means, standard deviations, and other statistical measures relating to all of the 48 states are computed, the District of Columbia is excluded. This treatment follows from the fact that the District has the characteristics of a city rather than of a state, is closely circumscribed in area, and its extremely high per capita income is greatly affected—one might almost say determined—by the Congress through its annual appropriations and the fixing of federal employee pay scales. This study was completed before Alaska became a state.

reason a state government needs knowledge of the economic activities within its boundaries. The states thus would be worthy of attention even though as many data were available for other subdivisions of the nation.

State boundaries have been stable for several decades and are well known. Most economic activity can be located unambiguously with respect to them. With the minor exception of the area within the District of Columbia, all of the area within the nation is assigned to the states.

There are many ways in which the economic activity of a state may be measured. The most comprehensive statistical measure for which data are available is personal income. The state personal income estimates provided by the National Income Division for 1929-1954 include all income flows arising out of current economic activity, and transfer payments from government and business, received by the residents of a state during a calendar year.[2] These state estimates of personal income and of the principal components of personal income, on a per capita basis, form the chief basis for most of the analyses.

These estimates, which are available only for the years since 1929, have been supplemented by the Leven estimates of "current income" for 1919-1921.[3] The Leven estimates are not strictly comparable with the official estimates for the years since 1929, and probably are less reliable. However, they provide a useful indication of state income differentials during the earlier period and thus permit many analyses to cover an additional decade.

Summary

The remainder of this chapter is devoted to a description of the analyses of state per capita personal income differentials to be undertaken in this book, the methods used, and a summary of the principal findings. The purpose of summarizing the principal findings at this point is twofold: First, an early statement of the principal findings should make it

[2] The following definition of personal income is provided by the *National Income Supplement to the Survey of Current Business, 1954 Edition,* Department of Commerce, 1954, p. 58: "Personal Income is the current income received by persons from all sources, inclusive of transfers from government and business, but exclusive of transfers among persons. Not only individuals (including owners of unincorporated enterprises) but nonprofit institutions, private trust funds, and private pension, health, and welfare funds are classified as 'persons.' Personal income is measured on a before-tax basis, as the sum of wages and salary disbursements, other labor income, proprietors' and rental income, interest and dividends, and transfer payments, minus personal contributions for social insurance." The state per capita personal incomes used in this study are those given in Charles F. Schwartz and Robert E. Graham, Jr., "Personal Income by States, 1929-1954," *Survey of Current Business,* September 1955, pp. 12-22, 32.

[3] Maurice Leven, *Income in the Various States, Its Sources and Distribution, 1919, 1920, and 1921,* New York, 1925.

easier to follow the detailed arguments in the later chapters. Secondly, the summary may suffice for those whose interests are concentrated on a particular area of investigation but who would also like some knowledge of related findings without having to deal with a technical analysis of them. To precede the detailed arguments with such a summary statement, however, involves some risks.

The search for patterns of state per capita personal income differentials often leads to comparisons of each of the states with each of the other states and the extensive use of technical devices to provide a statistical summary of these manifold comparisons. A general statement of statistical results in terms of tendencies or averages ignores the many exceptions typically found in a statistical investigation. When these exceptions are of consequence to a particular problem, they must be taken into account. Yet if a summary is really to summarize, attention must be directed to its general characteristics rather than to the exceptions which appear to have only limited application. Consequently the summary material in this chapter reflects, to a greater extent than he would like, the author's interpretation of the findings, and these findings are sometimes controversial. Subsequent chapters provide, although in somewhat more technical terms, a detailed account of the investigations on which these findings and their limitations are based.

Income changes

Although per capita personal income in the United States has varied from $373 in 1933 to $1,788 in 1953, and these changes in income level have been accompanied by differential changes among the states, the rank order of the states has not changed greatly. The state ranks for 1919 tend to be the ranks in 1929, 1939, 1949, and 1954.

In dollar terms the changes in the higher-income states have been larger than in the lower-income states. In percentage terms, however, the lower-income states have experienced larger income changes.

The period from 1929 to 1954, although it includes the great depression of 1929-1933, is characterized largely by rising income, both in current and constant dollars. The dollar differences between state per capita incomes tend to move with the income level and were greater in 1953 than for any other year for which data are available.

There has been a pronounced narrowing of relative interstate differentials.[4] Starting at a level of 37 to 41 percent during 1929-1932, the

[4] Relative interstate dispersion is measured by the coefficient of variation, one of the principal measures of relative dispersion. The coefficient of variation is the standard deviation expressed as a percentage of the mean.

relative interstate dispersion decreased steadily through 1945 and has varied within the narrow range of 21 to 24 percent since then. Relative interstate dispersion tends to move inversely with the level of income, and the upward drift of personal income during the period would account for some of the decrease in the dispersion. The decrease in the relative interstate dispersion, particularly during the earlier part of the period, is too great to be attributed entirely to this inverse relationship.

When the state per capita personal incomes are expressed as relatives of the national one, the state relatives contain adjustments both for state differences in population and for changes in the level of national per capita income. There is some tendency for the relatives of the lower-income states to follow the cyclical pattern of income changes—that is, for the relatives to decrease when national per capita income decreases and to increase when the income level increases, and for the relatives of the upper-income states to follow a contracyclical course. There are, however, many deviations from these patterns. For example, the relatives of all of the lower-income states did not reach the trough of the great depression of 1929-1933 during the same year. Similar deviations from the general pattern are found among the upper-income states and during the wartime peak. There are also large interstate differences in the cyclical amplitude of the year-to-year changes of the state relatives; the larger amplitudes are found most often among the lower-income farm states, and the smaller amplitudes among the upper-income states.

That the states respond to cyclical changes in the national per capita income with varying intensities and even in differing directions can be seen clearly in the charts and tables of the state income relatives (chapter 2). The presence of these cyclical responses makes it difficult to isolate and measure trend elements, particularly since the period following the great depression of 1929-1933 has been one of generally rising income. The upward trend in national per capita income has been broken since 1933 only by the short-lived and minor recessions in 1937-1938, 1948-1949, and 1953-1954. Consequently, it is difficult to say whether an upward or downward drift in the state relatives reflects a differential trend or whether it reflects mainly the state's particular pattern of response to cyclical changes in the national per capita income.

The pattern of the cyclical responses of the state relatives to changes in national per capita personal income indicates why the interstate coefficients of variation tend to move contracyclically. During periods of contraction the state relatives of the lower-income states tend to become even smaller and thus to depart more from the national average (of 100 percent). Similarly, there is a tendency for the relatives of the upper-income states, which already exceed 100 percent, to become larger and thus farther from the mean. Thus during periods of contraction both ends of the distribution of state relatives become farther removed from the mean. During periods of rising income there are reverse tendencies.

The fact that the coefficients of variation move contracyclically leads to the expectation of some regression of the state per capita incomes toward their mean as income increases. When the state per capita incomes of one year are regressed on those of an earlier year, one measurement of the extent of this regression is possible. Extensive work based on the 1929-1949 state income payments series (which was replaced in 1955 by the state personal income series) and some experimentation with the 1929-1954 personal income data indicate that a linear regression line fits the data fairly well. However, the distribution of states around such a line suggested that a slightly better fit might be provided by a line that was curved slightly—a line which started somewhat below the straight line, increased somewhat more rapidly to somewhere within the third quartile, and then turned downward so that at the upper extreme of the observed data it occupied a position which was about the same as or slightly below the straight line. Attempts to fit such a curved line were not rewarding. The differences between the linear and curved regression lines typically are less than the differences between either of these lines and a line describing proportional changes (that is, a line passing through the origin and the means of the two distributions). Thus the linear regression line for a pair of years, such as 1929 and 1953, describes the change in the income of a particular state as a function of both the level of the state's income and of the change in the national per capita income level, while a line of proportional change treats the change in a state as a function only of the changes in national income. The linear regression thus appears to be superior for describing the general pattern of state per capita income changes. Since the statement "New York's personal income during the 1929-1953 period regressed toward the mean more than did the average of all states" takes account of the general pattern, it is perhaps more meaningful than "New York's per capita personal income increased less from 1929 to 1953 than did the per capita income of the nation."

Cyclical and secular changes

The behavior of the interstate coefficients of variation, the state income relatives, and the regression coefficients points to the different behavior of the states with regard to changes in the level of national per capita personal income. None of these statistical devices, however, is suitable for a precise measurement of the cyclical responses of a particular state, nor for eliminating the cyclical influence so that some estimate of any remaining trend elements may be made. To overcome these deficiences, a sensitivity index is computed for each state. The state sensitivity index indicates the percentage change in the state's per capita personal income that is expected to accompany a one-percent change in the per capita personal income of the nation (chapter 3). When systematic changes over the 1929-1954 period are important, the sensitivity index is taken net of these influences, and these systematic changes are gathered into a time-factor index.

For all but a half-dozen farm states these sensitivity and time-factor indexes, together with a knowledge of the change in the level of national per capita personal income, provide a reasonably good description of how a state's per capita personal income has changed over the period. The technical deficiencies of these indexes, combined with the fact that the 1929-1954 period was more heavily weighted by increases in income than by decreases, make the separation of cyclical and secular forces provided by the indexes less precise than is desirable. Despite these limitations the indexes appear, on balance, to provide a reasonably good estimate of the pattern of cyclical behavior of each state, one that is perhaps as good as any that can be derived from the data. A time-factor index is an indication that there is some set of systematic factors in addition to the factors reflected by the sensitivity index. Whether these systematic factors can be identified only with those cumulative and irreversible forces which are customarily associated with a trend must be determined on other grounds. The absence of a significant time-factor index indicates a need to subject an apparent trend to close scrutiny before accepting it as fact.

When the states are arrayed by their average 1929-1954 per capita incomes and the array divided into quartiles, the states in the highest income quartile tend to have sensitivity indexes of less than unity, those in the next quartile to have indexes which approximate unity, and those in the two lowest quartiles to have indexes which are above unity. Thus there is an inverse relationship between a state's income level and its sensitivity to cyclical changes in national per capita income. The time-factor indexes tend to be positive, larger, and more frequent in the lowest quartile, and three of the four negative time-factor indexes are found in the highest quartile. However, Delaware, the state with the highest average 1929-1954 income and the lowest sensitivity index, has a positive time-factor index.

Some measure of the extent to which the sensitivity and time-factor indexes reflect the forces which make for income changes within the states is afforded by comparing the difference between the state's per capita personal income as estimated by the National Income Division and as adjusted on the basis of the two indexes. This difference, expressed as a percentage of the adjusted income, has been labeled as "estimating error," although the irregular elements in a state's income are included in it. About 80 percent of the estimating errors (for each state and each year) are less than 6 percent and about 63 percent are less than 4 percent of the adjusted per capita incomes. Most of the extreme estimating errors are found in a few farm states: the Dakotas, Nebraska, Idaho, and Mississippi. When the estimating errors for a state are averaged over the 26 years, and these five farm states with extreme errors are omitted, there does not seem to be much association between the size of a state's per capita income and the size of its average estimating error.

The use of the sensitivity and time-factor indexes to adjust the personal income series by removing, successively, the effects of random or irregular elements such as calamities, strikes, and weather and then the systematic elements which are associated with time provide additional insight into the forces which make for the observed patterns of change. When both the irregular and time-associated elements are removed, so that only the elements associated with the sensitivity index remain, an adjusted state series is obtained which shows clearly the "accordion effect" of the inverse relationship between income level and relative interstate dispersion. The relative interstate dispersion of this adjusted series increases with every decrease in income level and decreases with every increase in income level, although the magnitude of the changes in dispersion is not as great as those in the unadjusted series. When only the irregular forces are removed, the resulting state series continues to show a perfect concordance between a change in national income level and a change in the opposite direction of the relative interstate dispersion, and the magnitude of change in the relative interstate dispersion approximates that of the unadjusted series. By adjusting the series to remove all of the elements except those associated with the time-factor index, then comparing the relative interstate dispersion of this series with that of a series which contains only the elements included in the sensitivity index, some notion of the relative effect of the two factors can be obtained. Such a comparison indicates that roughly two-thirds of the observed decrease in the relative interstate dispersion from 1932-1934 to 1952-1954 is due to elements associated with the sensitivity indexes and about one-third to the systematic elements associated with time.

Since per capita personal income for a few of the farm states had irregular elements so large that the validity of their sensitivity and time-factor indexes is doubtful, the indexes have been computed separately for per capita farm and nonfarm income.

On a national level the year-to-year changes in farm income tend to follow those of personal income, though the rates of change are larger for farm income and there are some important differences in timing. The increase in farm income in 1933 preceded by one year the increase in personal income; there was a sharp but short-lived farm-income recession in 1936; and farm income started decreasing in 1952, thus anticipating by two years the decrease in personal income. Since 1947 the farm-income and personal-income series have diverged, perhaps as the result of a continuation of the long-term decline in the importance of agriculture. The direction of the year-to-year change in state farm income often diverges from that of the nation. For example, in 1947 and 1950, years in which farm income was increasing, farm income decreased in one-half of the states. The state-national differences in the direction of farm-income changes reflect an irregular element large enough to obscure, if not destroy, any regular state-national pattern such as the sensitivity and time-factor indexes are designed to reflect. These differences also give rise to exceedingly large estimating errors; for 34 states the estimating errors exceed 15 percent in five or more years.

Farm income thus may be viewed as one of the irregular influences which disturb the personal-income sensitivity and time-factor indexes and give rise to personal-income estimating errors. The effect of including such an irregular element in personal income will depend in part upon how large a proportion farm income is of personal income, but even when the farm-income share of personal income is quite small it can still be disturbing.

It is possible to obtain an estimate of state per capita nonfarm income by subtracting per capita farm income from per capita personal income. Such a computation, however, does not remove the effects of the erratic changes in farm income on the remaining per capita nonfarm income. The farm- and nonfarm-income components are interrelated by numerous transactions, and there is no easy statistical device by which the effects of one can be isolated and removed from the other. Thus, sensitivity and time-factor indexes based on nonfarm income are free only of the direct effects of rapid changes in farm income; the indexes will still contain many of the indirect effects of these changes on the state's economy.

Except for the states deriving a large share of their income from farms, the differences between the nonfarm- and personal-income sensitivity and time-factor indexes are not large. Time-factor indexes based on nonfarm income are significant in more states than are those based on personal income, and for those states with significant time-factor indexes for both series the nonfarm indexes tend to be larger. Except for North Dakota and Mississippi, the removal of the farm-income component of personal income, although the indirect effects of a rapidly changing farm income are not removed, is sufficient to limit the estimating errors to a reasonable size. Most of the extreme errors which remain are concentrated in the war years, a period when war mobilization gave rise to irregular forces of considerable magnitude. For most states the difference in the average estimating errors based on nonfarm and personal incomes is small.

What can be said about the relative trends in the various states when the results of the analyses of the state relatives and of the sensitivity and time-factor indexes are pooled? As mentioned earlier, the state relatives are a mixture of cyclical and trend elements, so that a direct interpretation of them is hazardous. The sensitivity index, while designed to reflect only cyclical influences, may not perform this function precisely during periods in which most of the income changes are in one direction. To the extent that trend elements are caught up by the sensitivity index, the time-factor indexes will be affected. This deficiency can have two effects: it can affect the size of the time-factor index and thus reduce further its usefulness as a measure of trend, or it can make a trend insignificant by the usual statistical tests of significance. Moreover, conceptual difficulties discourage the direct use of the time-factor index as a measure of trend.

In the face of these difficulties, considerable subjective judgment is required even to select the states in which a significant trend exists. It does not seem possible on the basis of the 1929-1954 data to provide measures of these trends. The time-associated elements in a few states are so marked that there can be little doubt that the cumulative and irreversible forces usually associated with secular trend are at work. Thus it can be said that New York had a downward trend and the Carolinas an upward trend in per capita incomes during the 1929-1954 period. The difficulty encountered in dealing with the data for many states is illustrated by the Delaware data. The Delaware relatives show a precipitous decrease from a level of about 165 percent in 1939-1940 to about 124 percent in 1944-1948, and although they recovered slightly thereafter, the 1951-1954 relatives are about 7 percentage points below their 1929-1932 level. The Delaware time-factor index is + 1.0, indicating an increase of 1.0 percent per year which is not accounted for by the state's sensitivity index. The decrease in the Delaware relatives is traceable to the property-income component of Delaware's personal income. Property income as a share of the national personal income has decreased from about 22-24 percent during 1929-1933 to about 11-12 percent during 1946-1954, and Delaware's per capita property income has decreased relative to that of the nation. Delaware's relatives for all other income components have increased. Thus a decision as to whether Delaware's per capita personal income has undergone secular change, whether the direction of this change is up or down, and whether these changes are likely to grow, diminish, or merely persist in the future, requires additional knowledge concerning the probable changes in particular income sources and in particular industries.

The failure of the sensitivity analysis to yield a significant time-factor index for a state is not conclusive evidence that a trend does not exist. However, the absence of a significant time-factor does raise the question of whether an apparent trend in a state's relatives is the product of cyclical factors or of irregular deviations. Adequate answers to such a question require a detailed investigation of a state's economy and are beyond the scope of this study. With the exception of Delaware, the states with significant time-factor indexes also tend to have relatives which display a trend of considerable magnitude; states without significant time-factor indexes tend to have relatives which show little or no trend. A significant time-factor index usually may thus be taken as an indication of the existence of a relative trend.[5] The direction of the trend can be known with confidence only after a detailed investigation of the state's income sources, as the data for Delaware show, and neither the time-factor index nor the state relatives are capable of providing a reliable measure of the trend's magnitude.

Income components

The differential behavior of the state per capita income components both provides a key to an understanding of the interrelationships among the components and affords some insight into the sources of the observed differences in state per capita personal income.

[5] The states with significant positive time-factor indexes, based on per capita nonfarm income, are: Alabama, Delaware, Florida, Georgia, Idaho, Kentucky, Louisiana, Minnesota, Montana, Nevada, New Mexico, North Carolina, North Dakota, South Carolina, South Dakota, Tennessee, Texas, Virginia, and Wyoming. Those with negative time-factor indexes are Illinois, New York, and Pennsylvania.

Four component flows of personal income are treated: labor income, property income, proprietors' income, and transfer payments. The farm and nonfarm subcomponents of proprietors' income are also accorded some attention.

The per capita amounts of labor income, property income, and transfer payments tend to be larger in the states with the larger per capita personal incomes during the 1929-1954 period (chapter 4). The nonfarm subcomponent of proprietors' income is also directly related to per capita personal income, but per capita farm proprietors' income tends to be larger in the states with the smaller per capita personal incomes; as a consequence of these opposing relationships, there is no significant relationship between the state per capita proprietors'-income component and personal income.

The relative interstate dispersion of the average 1929-1954 components is highest for property income. The state distribution of the farm proprietors' subcomponent, however, is more disperse than any one of the components. For transfer payments the relative interstate dispersion is lower than it is for per capita personal income, the sum of the four components. When labor and proprietors' income or property and proprietors' income are combined, the combination has less relative interstate dispersion than either of the components included in the combination. This is traceable to a strong inverse correlation between the combination's constituent components—for example, to the tendency for labor and property income to be higher in the states with lower proprietors' income. Although there is a significant tendency for both labor and property income to be higher in the states with higher per capita incomes, there is no significant tendency for the higher per capita property incomes to be found in the states with the higher per capita labor incomes, and the relative interstate dispersion of the labor and property income combination is less than that of property income but more than that of labor income. A similar situation is found in each of the combinations of transfer payments with another component; the combination has more relative interstate dispersion than transfer payments alone but less than that of the component with which transfer payments is combined.

A combination of three components has more relative interstate dispersion than does per capita personal income, which may be viewed as a combination of all four components, if the three-component combination includes both labor and property income, but less relative interstate dispersion if only one of these components is included in the combination.

The relative interstate dispersion of labor income, of property income, and of transfer payments decreases from 1929-1933 to 1950-1954, but for only the property-income component do the coefficients of relative interstate dispersion trace a course similar to those for per capita personal income. The relative interstate dispersion of proprietors' income, which was largest in 1948 and for 1950-1954 was well above that of the 1929-1933 period, is the result of opposing trends in its farm and nonfarm subcomponents. The relative interstate dispersion has been larger and has varied more from year to year for per capita farm proprietors' income than for any of the other components or subcomponents. Over the 1929-1954 period the relative interstate dispersion of farm proprietors' income has shown a marked tendency to increase, while that of nonfarm proprietors' income has decreased.

All of the combinations of two per capita components tend to have decreasing relative interstate dispersions from 1929-1954. The relative interstate dispersions of the combinations of proprietors' income with labor and with property income were decreasing and were smaller than the dispersion of either labor income (except in 1935) or property income throughout the period, and were less than those of proprietors' income after 1941.

The combinations of three components which consist of per capita personal income less labor income, or per capita personal income less property income, tend to have less relative interstate dispersion than does per capita personal income. When proprietors' income or transfer payments are omitted from personal income, the resulting three-component combination tends to be relatively more disperse than is personal income. The omission of transfer payments from personal income affects the coefficients of relative interstate dispersion by a maximum of 0.8 percentage points, and the coefficients were unaffected in 1935 and from 1941 to 1944. In 1938 and 1940 the omission of transfer payments left a three-component combination which was slightly less disperse than was per capita personal income, indicating that in these two years the interstate distribution of transfer payments tended to accentuate the interstate differences in other components. All of the three-component combinations show decreasing relative interstate dispersion over the period, the decrease being least marked in the combination which omits property income.

With the exception of proprietors' income, its farm subcomponent, and its combination with transfer payments, the inverse relationship between changes in relative interstate dispersion and the changes in the level of income, called the "accordion effect" when per capita personal income was discussed, is present in all of the components and their combinations. Proprietors' income, on the other hand, tends to have more relative interstate dispersion when its per capita amount is higher.

After the influence of year-to-year changes in a per capita component is taken into account, the remaining relationship between the upward drift in the per capita components and their relative interstate dispersion is significant for all of the single components except labor income, as well as for the proprietors' income subcomponent, and is direct for all of them except property income.[6] Among the two- and three-component combinations such a significant relationship is found only for the combination of proprietors' income and transfer payments (direct) and for the combination of property income and transfer payments (inverse).

The interstate distribution of property income, taken alone or in combination with transfer payments, is thus the only component which shows a tendency to become relatively less disperse over the period to a greater degree than can be accounted for by the changes in its level. The marked tendency for the relative interstate dispersion of per capita personal income to decrease thus stems largely from the changes in the interstate distribution of per capita property income while its relative importance as a source of income decreased from 1929 to 1954.

When for the entire 1929-1954 period a component is expressed as a percentage of personal income rather than in terms of its absolute amount, the relative interstate dispersion of these percentages is smaller for all components except proprietors' income and its farm subcomponent. For this period, state farm proprietors' income accounts for from less than 1 to more than 30 percent of state personal income.

On a national basis the most marked change in the percentage distribution of personal income among the components is in property income, which decreased from a level of 22-24 percent in 1929-1933 to about 11-12 percent in 1946-1954. Preliminary data for 1939-1951 suggest that there was little year-to-year change in the relative interstate dispersion of the percentage components other than the property-income component. The relative interstate dispersion for property income decreased from 39 percent in 1939 to 22-23 percent in 1946-1951.

Occupational earnings

The 1949 data on money wage and salary earnings collected in the *Census of Population, 1950* provide an opportunity to analyze state earning

[6] This statement is based on the coefficients of partial determination between the logarithms of interstate coefficients of variation and time, after the effects of the level of the specified income component are taken into account.

differentials in terms of the state occupational structures (chapter 5). During the 1929-1954 period wages and salaries were from three-fifths to two-thirds of personal income.[7]

The population-census data on earnings yield national average earnings which are about 13 percent below the estimates of the National Income Division after the latter have been adjusted to make them as nearly comparable as possible with the money-income concepts used in the census.[8] Moreover, the census data tend to underestimate the earnings in high-earning states to a greater extent than the earnings of low-earning states; thus there is a systematic bias in the census data for states. The implications of this bias are not fully understood, but one obvious effect is that the earnings reported in the census have less interstate dispersion than do those estimated by the National Income Division. There are many small differences, but few large ones, in the state ranks for the two distributions. Methods of adjusting for these differences have not been found, so that if the census data are to be analyzed, they will have to be analyzed without adjustment. Consequently the analytical results can be looked upon only as first approximations.

On a national basis the average annual earnings of private wage and salary workers and government employees vary by occupation from a low of $488 among private household laundresses who live out to a high of $7,335 among airplane pilots and navigators. A state which has relatively more of its experienced labor force engaged in the higher-paid occupations would be expected to have a higher average earning. To obtain a measure of the state average earning that would be expected if occupational composition were the only difference among states, there has been computed for each state an earning figure which is based on the national rates for each occupation and the state's occupational distribution of its experienced labor force. Since identical occupational earning rates have been used for every state—only the occupational composition of the states has been allowed to vary—the computed earning figure is called the state's rate-constant earning. The difference between two state's rate-

[7] Wages and salaries differ from the labor-income component (treated in chapter 4) by including the personal contributions to social insurance and excluding "other labor income." Other labor income consists of compensation for injuries, employer contributions to private pension and welfare funds, pay of military reservists, directors' fees, jury and witness fees, and similar minor items. When other labor income exceeds personal contributions for social insurance, as it does for the years other than those from 1941 to 1946, labor income exceeds wages and salaries.

[8] These adjustments consisted of subtracting the sum of farm wages paid in kind and military wages and salaries from the National Income Division's estimates of wage and salary disbursements. Nonfarm wages paid in kind also should have been subtracted, but an estimate of their magnitude is not available.

constant earnings provides a measure of the difference in their occupational compositions.[9]

Nineteen states have rate-constant earnings that exceed the national average and thus may be said to have favorable occupational compositions. Most of these states are in the Middle Atlantic or East North Central divisions and have large metropolitan centers or, like Connecticut, are located in heavily populated and industrialized areas. The most unfavorable occupational compositions are found among Southern states. Five states—Arkansas, Georgia, North Carolina, Mississippi, and South Carolina—have occupational compositions which depart from the national average composition by more than 10 percent.

The state differences in male occupational earnings follow closely those found for all workers, and the differences in a state's male and all-worker composition tend to be small (about 1.5 percentage points).

The 1949 average earning reported for females was about 57 percent of that for males, and the level of female earnings was lower than that of males in every state, ranging from 51 percent in Delaware to 64 percent in North Carolina. The absolute size of the state differences in occupational composition tends to be larger for females than for male wage and salary workers. In most states, however, the occupational composition for females is more favorable than for males.

The reported female earnings by state tend to vary directly with state reported male earnings, and the association is close enough to be described adequately by linear regression. For the states outside the South and for Kentucky and West Virginia, the association between the state rate-constant earnings for males and females is also linear. Within the South the association between male and female rate-constant earnings is not as strong as for the non-South, and while it can be described about as well by a straight as by a curved line, the level of female rate-constant earnings compared to that for males is about $100 lower than would be expected from the relationship found for states in the non-South. The relatively unfavorable occupational composition of the females in the

[9] The occupational earning rates were computed from a tabulation based on a 3.3-percent sample of the population and are subject to some sampling error. The lower limit of the top open-end class is relatively low ($10,000), and it was necessary to estimate the average earning in this class from other data. The numbers in the experienced labor force were used in obtaining the rate-constant earnings; the numbers of private wage and salary workers and government employees with 1949 earnings were used in obtaining the national average occupational earning; and the numbers of persons reporting wage and salary income in 1949 were used in obtaining the state reported earnings. Consequently there are minor differences in the national averages of the state reported earnings, occupational earnings, and state rate-constant earnings (chapter 5). The similarity of these rate-constant earnings to constant-weight index numbers is readily apparent.

South is traceable, in part, to the disproportionate numbers engaged in private household work, perhaps a reflection of the large numbers of Negroes in the South; but, in part, it must be attributed to the interaction of such circumstances as a large rural population, a low female participation in the labor force, and a lack of employment opportunities for females in the better-paid occupations.

A favorable occupational composition can be the result of a concentration of workers within one or two of the higher-rate major-occupational groups (that is, a favorable group composition), or of a concentration of workers in the higher-earning detailed occupations within each major group accompanied by an average distribution among the major groups (that is, a favorable within-group composition). It is not clear which of these two elements is the stronger. The tendency for the within-group composition to be predominantly in one direction is strongest in the states in the lowest income quartile, is present but weaker in the highest quartile, and is almost nonexistent in the central quartiles. This tendency appears to be slightly stronger for all wage and salary workers than for either male or female wage and salary workers. On the other hand, there are a number of examples in which a heavy concentration of workers in a particular major group appears to have determined the favorableness or unfavorableness of a state's occupational composition.

There is a strong tendency for a state with an unfavorable occupational composition to have earning rates below the national average for its particular occupational composition, and for a state with a favorable occupational composition to have earning rates above the national average.

The next section deals with the effects of industrial composition on interstate earning differentials. The same statistical methods are used, and the *Census of Population, 1950,* which is the basis of the analysis of interstate differentials in occupational composition, is the only body of available data which covers all industries. Consequently, a summary of the occupational composition is delayed until comparative data are available for industrial composition.

Industrial earnings

For three industrial segments—manufactures, wholesale trade, and government—there are detailed data suitable for analyzing interstate earning differentials in terms of industrial composition (chapter 6). The data for manufactures relate to the average hourly earnings of production workers in 458 detailed industries for 1947; those for wholesale trade to the average annual earnings of employees in 244 kinds of businesses; and those for government to the average annual earnings of employees in three industries—federal, state and local government education, and other state and local government—in 1939 and 1952. In addition, the population-census earning data for 1949 used in the analysis of interstate differences in occupational composition permit classification of annual earnings into 146 industrial categories. For each of these bodies of data it is possible to compute state rate-constant earnings by methods similar to those used in analyzing occupational composition, and then to analyze the interstate relationship of the rate-constant earnings to those reported. The state distributions of the wage and salary receipts for each industrial segment prepared by the National Income Division for the years 1929, 1933, and 1939 to 1951 provide the basis for appraising the year-to-year changes in the interstate distribution of industrial earnings.

Within manufactures the most favorable compositions are found in the East North Central and Middle Atlantic states and the most unfavorable compositions in the Southern states. The rate-constant earnings range from 12 percent above reported earnings in Michigan to 19 percent below reported earnings in North Carolina. When the states are grouped into the nine census regions, it is found that the differences in major-group composition contribute more than the compositional differences within the major groups to regional differences in rate-constant earnings.

The interindustry dispersion in wholesale-trade earnings is larger than it is for manufactures, although the interstate differences are of about the same order. Rate-constant earnings are from 12 percent above to 19 percent below reported earnings, the more favorable compositions being found chiefly along the Eastern seaboard and in states which have large metropolitan centers. The differences both between and within the major kind-of-business groups for wholesale trade, unlike manufactures, contribute to the compositional differences among the nine census regions.

The interest in the state distribution of government-employee earnings centers more in whether there is evidence that the federal government, particularly, has tried to set its pay-scales and locate its activities in such a way as to reduce the interstate differences in per capita incomes. Such evidence could not be found. The fact that the data can be classified by only three industrial categories is a serious limitation on this type of analysis. Largely because of the limited number of categories, the interstate range of rate-constant earnings is only 13 to 20 percent of the interstate range of reported earnings. There is a well-marked tendency for government earnings in 1939 and 1952 to increase more in the states with the lower earnings in 1939. In both years government earnings tend to be higher in the states with higher earnings from nongovernmental sources.

The population-census earnings for 1949 are less suitable for analyzing interstate industrial differentials than they were for analyzing occupational differentials. An industrial category contains both wage and salary and self-employed workers more often than does an occupational category. Only for the farm industries was it possible to adjust the data so as to exclude the self-employed.

The interstate range of rate-constant earnings is only about one-third that of reported earnings, partly because the entire range of industrial activity is classified into too few industrial categories, and partly because the interindustry range of average earnings is smaller than the inter-occupation range.

There is a marked tendency for a state with an industrial composition that is favorable in one set of industrial earning data to have a favorable composition in the other sets of data. However, the population-census and detailed census data relate to different years, and little confidence can be placed in the few observed differences between them.

Although 458 industries are recognized in the manufactures census and only 59 in the population census, the percentages by which rate-constant earnings differ from the reported earnings tend to be similar in both distributions. They differ enough, however, to change the classification based on the industrial composition of manufacturing industries from unfavorable to favorable in eight states and in the opposite direction in another state. The similarity of the results from the two bodies of manufactures data is consistent with the finding, based on the manufactures-census data, that the differences in major-group composition are more effective than differences in the composition within groups in determining the favorableness of a region's composition.

The 244 kinds of business in the business census are telescoped into 10 categories in the population census. Since it was found that differences both among major groups and within them contributed to a region's wholesale-trade composition, one effect of telescoping categories is to cover up much of the compositional differences among states. In no state do the population-census rate-constant earnings differ from reported earnings by more than four percent.

Many government employees are scattered among nongovernmental categories in the population census so that the census government industries are not comparable with those for 1939 and 1952. Nevertheless, the favorableness of a state's composition was seldom different in the two series.

The rate-constant earnings for many of the major groups within the population-census industries can be used to gain some notion of whether the major-group composition or the composition within major groups is more important in determining the favorableness (or unfavorableness) of a state's composition. There is no state in which the composition within every major group is favorable (or unfavorable). However, when the states are arrayed from most favorable to most unfavorable composition, the states near the ends of the array tend to have within-group compositions which differ from the national composition predominantly in the direction of the state's composition. In the states near the center of such an array there are about an equal number of groups with favorable and with unfavorable within-group composition.

Reliable measures of the year-to-year changes in a state's composition cannot be obtained by comparing the population census with the manufactures or the wholesale-trade census, since there are differences both in industrial classification and reliability of earnings data. The industrial distribution of wages and salaries among 12 broad categories, as estimated by the National Income Division for 1929, 1933, and annually from 1939 to 1951, provides material pertinent to the question of the stability of industrial composition. Based on the average 1939-1951 industrial distribution of wages and salaries, mining has the most relative interstate dispersion, followed by agriculture and manufactures. The least relative interstate dispersion is in the trade and service industries.

The tendency for the relative interstate dispersion of all wages and salaries to decrease from 1929 to 1951 is also found in the manufacturing, transportation, and communication industries. An upward trend is noted for the power industry. The other industries display no pronounced trend; the shifts in importance of industries occasioned by the war effort perhaps account for the year-to-year shifts in their relative interstate dispersion. The reduction in the relative interstate dispersion of per capita wages and salaries apparently is the result more of selective wage-equalizing shifts within the 12 broad industrial groups than of an increasing similarity of the state industrial compositions.

Composition and earning rates

There is a significant tendency for states with unfavorable compositions in manufactures, wholesale trade, and the population-census industries and occupations, but not for government, to have earning rates below the national average for their industries or occupations and, conversely, for states with favorable compositions to have above-average earning rates. When the government industries are excluded, some 25 of the states differ from the national average composition and earning rate in the same direction in every set of data. This relationship between composition and earning rates has practical consequences relevant to the attempt to gauge the importance of composition in accounting statistically for the observed differences in interstate earnings (chapters 5 and 6).

The differences between reported and rate-constant earnings for a state provide a basis for judging whether earning rates on the average are above or below those of the nation for the particular industries found in the state. Since the percentage differences between reported and rate-constant earnings provide a valid and valuable comparison of state with national rates for the particular industrial composition found within the state, they are shown by state in each of the tables relating to rate-constant earnings. However, they are not comparable among states and cannot be used to assay the relative importance of composition and rates in accounting for the observed state earning differentials.

The size of the rate-constant earning, and the size of its difference from the reported earning, are affected by the number of significantly different industrial categories used in computing the rate-constant earning. When the categories are so broad that they contain most of the variation in earning rates, the differences among the state rate-constant earnings will reflect only the residual variation among the broad categories. In such a case the difference between the rate-constant and reported earnings will be larger than if more detailed categories which have significantly different earning rates can be used. Too, the state industrial compositions differ, both when detailed and when broad categories are used. Since the industrial composition of the state enters into rate-constant earnings, the base to which the percentage difference attributable to earning rates is computed, the percentages are not comparable among states.

This lack of comparability among states can be overcome by computing for each state a nationally weighted composition-constant earning. This computation requires the weighting of state-specific industrial earnings by the relative numbers in the industry in the nation. Only for manufactures will the available data permit even an approximation of nationally weighted composition-constant earnings for the states. However, nationally weighted composition-constant earnings facilitate the assaying of the importance of rates relative to composition only when there is no correlation between the differences, reported minus rate-constant earnings and reported minus nationally weighted composition-constant earnings. Although the state-weighted composition-constant earnings differ by an unknown amount from the nationally-weighted ones, there is probably enough correspondence between them to indicate the existence of sufficient correlation to limit the usefulness of nationally weighted composition-constant earnings.

A one-sided test of the importance of the state compositional differentials is available (appendix B). The ratio of the interstate variation of rate-constant earnings to that of reported earnings provides a measure of the "independent effect" of composition on observed interstate differences in earnings. For the population-census industries and occupations this amounts to 9 or 10 percent; for wholesale trade and manufactures it is 27 and 32 percent. These percentages indicate that a statistically significant proportion of the total interstate variation in earnings is accounted for by interstate differences in composition. The corresponding percentages for government industries in 1939 and 1952 are not significant.

Many of the influences which help to determine earning levels are correlated with composition. These influences are difficult to specify, although it seems reasonable that they include some of the effects of the observed association between earning rates and composition. When state observed earnings and state rate-constant earnings are correlated, the coefficient of determination (r^2) provides a measure of the total statistical explanatory power, which includes both the independent and associated effects, of interstate differences in composition. Thus measured, composition is capable of accounting for up to 70 percent of total interstate variation in earnings for the industries other than government. By the same measure, occupational composition can account for up to more than 80 percent.

Demographic factors

The use of the total population in the computation of per capita income presumes that there are no important differences among states in the characteristics of their populations by age, education, marital status, crude fertility rates, and participation in the labor force. For the period covered by this study, data on these characteristics are available only for the four decennial census years, 1920, 1930, 1940, and 1950.

The direct effects of substituting for total population another variant of the state population in the denominator of the per capita income computation are examined for four decennial census years (chapter 7). The variants used are the populations which consist of persons 15 years old and older, persons 20 years old and older, persons from 20 to 64 years old, persons in the total labor force, and persons in the employed labor force.

These age groups were selected as those which do or can participate most directly in income production. The persons not in these age groups tend to be either too young or too old to participate fully in productive activities. Other variants could be designed which would exclude other persons who are prevented for one or another reason from full participation in income production, but the age criteria appear to account for the principal demographic factors in state per capita income differentials or are closely associated with the other important criteria.

The states with relatively larger percentages of their populations in the three age groups considered tend to be located in the Northeast and along the Pacific Coast, while the states with the larger proportions of their populations among those under 15 years old, those under 20, or those over 64 years old tend to be located in the Southern and Mountain states. The states with the larger percentages of their total population under 15 years old tend to be the states with the larger percentages under 20 years old, or under 20 years old and 65 years old or older. They also tend to have larger percentages of their populations outside the labor force.

The composition of the state populations is becoming more alike with respect to three age-distribution and two labor-force criteria. Over the 30-year period 1920-1950, the interstate dispersion of the percentage differences from the national average composition have decreased from 25 to 33 percent, with the largest decrease being recorded for persons 20 to 64 years of age.

Were only persons 15 years old and older in a state considered the appropriate population to use in computing "per capita" income, the "per capita" income of each of the states would be higher. The relative differences among states would not be the same, however, since persons 15 years old and older are a larger percentage of the population in some states than in others. When "per capita" incomes are computed for each of the five variant populations, their relative interstate dispersions are from 13 to 23 percent below those for the per capita incomes computed for the total population. The largest percentage differences in the relative interstate dispersions are for 1950. The tendency for the lower-income states to have the smaller percentages of their total populations in the more productive age groups and the tendency for these same lower-income states to have had the larger relative increases in per capita income, particularly since 1930, both contribute to this result.

A tendency for income to increase with city size has been noted repeatedly and has led to the suggestion that income differentials might be explained by the regional distribution of cities of various sizes. The income data collected in the *Census of Population, 1950* provide the opportunity to investigate intercity income differences in detail.

When the median incomes for each of the cities in a particular size class, as measured by number of inhabitants, are averaged, the averages tend to increase with an increase in city size. This relationship is accompanied, however, by a large dispersion within each of the city-size classes. Consequently, only four or five broad classes can be used if the income differences among city-size classes are to be statistically significant.[10]

Moreover, the interregional differences among mean median incomes tend to be larger than the interclass differences. The dispersion within region and city-size class, while smaller than in the city-size class for all regions combined, remains large. Thus, the regional differences do not account for the dispersion of city median incomes within a national city-size class. Region is a signficant classification of the median incomes of cities of similar size.

When the sources of intraclass dispersion are investigated in terms of labor-force participation, educational attainments, family status, and whether manufactures is the prevalent source of employment, it is found that the interregional range with respect to these characteristics tends to be larger than the range among city-size classes.

Apparently the forces which determine a city's income level are as much an agglomeration as are those which determine a state's income level. As a consequence, an explanation of state differentials in terms of city-size composition would be largely a mechanical explanation and would not aid materially in identifying and isolating the economic forces which give rise to state income differentials. The large intraclass dispersion, coupled with the significant differences among regions of the mean median incomes of cities of similar size, is sufficient to discourage the attempt to use the relation between city size and income to derive even a mechanical explanation of state income differentials.

[10] The classes with 1949 mean median incomes which differ significantly are: 2,500-9,999; 10,000-249,999; 250,000-499,999; and 500,000 or more inhabitants. Alternatively, a break at 175,000 rather than at 250,000 inhabitants provides statistically significant differences.

Chapter 2

PATTERNS OF DIFFERENTIAL CHANGE

THE CHANGES in state per capita personal incomes are much like the changes in their average, the per capita personal income of the United States. Yet there are differences among the states. Some change more, others less, than their average. The year-to-year differential changes tend to be small, and it would be easy to conclude that many of them are inconsequential. Yet some differentials may cumulate and over a period of years become large enough to be important. Consequently this study is opened with an examination of these changes with a view to uncovering their broad patterns. Do the states at the lower-income levels experience as large absolute or relative changes as those with higher incomes? Are these changes about the same when national income is increasing as when it is decreasing? Is there evidence that the poor states are becoming poorer, or are all of the states becoming more alike? Answers to such questions, even though tentative and lacking in detail, are indispensable guides to more detailed analyses of some of the sources of state income differentials.

STATE ESTIMATES

The earliest estimates of state incomes are those provided by Leven for 1919-1921.[1] Though deficient in many respects, these estimates provide useful indicators of state income levels for the years immediately following World War I. For the years 1929-1954 there are official estimates prepared by the National Income Division of the Department of Commerce.[2] Their recently revised and reworked series on state per capita personal income will be the chief series used in this study (table 1).

[1] Maurice Leven, *Income in the Various States, Its Sources and Distribution, 1919, 1920, and 1921*, New York, 1925. The state incomes were obtained by allocating the national estimates for these years prepared by W. I. King.

[2] The official estimates of state incomes were initiated in Robert R. Nathan and John L. Martin, *State Income Payments, 1929-37*, Department of Commerce, 1939. The state

TABLE 1

PER CAPITA PERSONAL INCOME, 1929-1954, BY STATE AND YEAR
(Dollars per capita)

State	1929	1930	1931	1932	1933	1934	1935	1936	1937	1938	1939
New England											
Maine	601	575	491	379	374	413	428	500	505	470	493
New Hampshire	690	648	560	430	419	477	495	536	565	534	559
Vermont	627	569	468	360	339	370	409	462	478	452	480
Massachusetts	913	844	767	622	570	616	646	718	735	677	727
Rhode Island	871	787	712	576	561	596	639	706	723	670	713
Connecticut	1,029	926	805	621	587	654	704	804	859	769	834
Middle Atlantic											
New York	1,159	1,043	886	681	634	684	723	810	839	792	825
New Jersey	931	859	745	592	529	578	628	713	750	700	751
Pennsylvania	775	716	602	451	421	482	517	599	634	562	599
East North Central											
Ohio	781	671	568	404	390	457	519	597	651	565	619
Indiana	612	519	439	311	297	357	419	480	545	474	519
Illinois	957	816	675	489	442	508	575	652	731	650	705
Michigan	793	659	540	394	349	452	528	616	682	572	624
Wisconsin	682	595	474	364	336	380	463	519	553	512	517
West North Central											
Minnesota	598	552	458	363	311	358	447	470	535	494	517
Iowa	577	507	398	295	254	268	417	387	508	455	469
Missouri	628	569	495	368	338	368	422	468	508	478	506
North Dakota	375	305	182	176	145	177	266	229	319	278	314
South Dakota	417	358	239	188	129	179	300	240	319	316	340
Nebraska	590	517	410	306	276	255	401	390	409	402	395
Kansas	535	468	399	268	251	285	357	381	421	382	380
South Atlantic											
Delaware	1,017	849	769	588	565	628	690	850	929	782	916
Maryland	777	719	640	511	465	521	545	617	664	633	661
D. C.	1,273	1,262	1,198	1,051	900	921	974	1,095	1,162	1,096	1,117
Virginia	435	384	368	282	283	314	345	386	417	387	422
West Virginia	462	411	358	258	260	311	337	389	416	371	387
North Carolina	334	293	248	187	207	245	269	295	321	296	316
South Carolina	270	241	204	157	174	205	226	253	267	249	273
Georgia	350	308	256	199	204	240	267	301	311	290	310
Florida	521	464	395	314	284	339	367	440	476	452	486
East South Central											
Kentucky	391	325	289	210	205	229	262	290	334	292	303
Tennessee	377	325	275	197	204	240	260	300	328	298	308
Alabama	324	266	222	161	165	205	215	248	262	243	250
Mississippi	285	203	174	126	131	165	175	222	220	200	205
West South Central											
Arkansas	305	223	209	155	155	177	201	239	247	226	242
Louisiana	415	358	318	239	226	260	286	325	348	346	357
Oklahoma	454	368	299	216	222	247	293	317	369	343	345
Texas	478	411	346	262	253	284	318	363	408	396	409
Mountain											
Montana	595	503	383	337	299	361	473	477	513	514	530
Idaho	503	497	370	270	228	378	393	461	418	421	434
Wyoming	677	584	476	374	365	403	489	542	601	553	585
Colorado	637	580	474	356	355	369	442	538	531	507	516
New Mexico	407	333	287	209	209	243	286	333	354	333	352
Arizona	591	514	424	315	300	353	406	454	492	468	477
Utah	559	505	378	309	300	314	392	465	450	450	462
Nevada	878	826	649	542	500	531	650	822	748	762	841
Pacific											
Washington	750	665	538	403	378	439	489	568	600	586	617
Oregon	683	620	513	384	363	439	464	554	564	544	582
California	995	889	746	574	541	592	651	760	786	764	775
United States[a]	703	621	526	398	373	421	470	531	570	524	553

(Continued on next page)

TABLE 1 (Continued)

PER CAPITA PERSONAL INCOME, 1929-1954, BY STATE AND YEAR
(Dollars per capita)

State	1940	1941	1942	1943	1944	1945	1946	1947
New England								
Maine	523	626	850	1,087	1,091	1,067	1,117	1,150
New Hampshire	579	707	849	967	1,048	1,106	1,145	1,208
Vermont	507	629	757	902	930	1,013	1,058	1,099
Massachusetts	784	902	1,074	1,261	1,300	1,351	1,398	1,434
Rhode Island	743	921	1,134	1,184	1,261	1,267	1,349	1,436
Connecticut	917	1,142	1,417	1,590	1,601	1,568	1,578	1,693
Middle Atlantic								
New York	870	995	1,169	1,379	1,536	1,644	1,691	1,715
New Jersey	822	960	1,170	1,432	1,563	1,591	1,529	1,570
Pennsylvania	648	771	942	1,133	1,240	1,268	1,273	1,348
East North Central								
Ohio	665	829	1,028	1,259	1,322	1,349	1,311	1,412
Indiana	553	726	913	1,132	1,198	1,248	1,193	1,303
Illinois	754	895	1,039	1,258	1,392	1,470	1,530	1,636
Michigan	679	827	1,047	1,347	1,387	1,319	1,318	1,454
Wisconsin	554	675	872	1,053	1,115	1,186	1,209	1,294
West North Central								
Minnesota	526	617	796	935	998	1,100	1,174	1,256
Iowa	501	607	825	995	984	1,069	1,207	1,190
Missouri	524	646	809	962	1,073	1,134	1,186	1,221
North Dakota	350	522	654	927	1,002	1,009	1,046	1,446
South Dakota	359	470	742	816	950	1,047	1,083	1,232
Nebraska	439	548	811	993	1,072	1,163	1,151	1,243
Kansas	426	552	849	1,034	1,164	1,159	1,116	1,288
South Atlantic								
Delaware	1,004	1,141	1,267	1,438	1,483	1,507	1,533	1,634
Maryland	712	873	1,120	1,292	1,331	1,318	1,313	1,350
D. C.	1,170	1,205	1,364	1,508	1,561	1,635	1,680	1,748
Virginia	466	581	782	839	898	946	990	1,002
West Virginia	407	495	613	738	822	890	921	1,029
North Carolina	328	426	575	691	765	821	858	894
South Carolina	307	392	540	639	724	743	763	779
Georgia	340	424	571	725	835	882	844	884
Florida	513	597	769	985	1,090	1,151	1,137	1,143
East South Central								
Kentucky	320	392	533	689	759	794	811	850
Tennessee	339	433	555	717	856	902	856	876
Alabama	282	375	515	651	735	780	744	794
Mississippi	218	313	440	528	627	627	605	662
West South Central								
Arkansas	256	338	471	541	672	722	729	719
Louisiana	363	449	593	784	879	892	829	881
Oklahoma	373	434	624	774	944	967	939	1,015
Texas	432	524	712	931	1,038	1,051	1,028	1,128
Mountain								
Montana	570	715	896	1,128	1,168	1,191	1,278	1,457
Idaho	464	594	904	1,004	1,080	1,114	1,169	1,251
Wyoming	608	783	944	1,142	1,229	1,258	1,340	1,488
Colorado	546	648	891	1,030	1,063	1,183	1,195	1,338
New Mexico	375	471	628	758	869	926	906	988
Arizona	497	628	898	986	1,036	1,107	1,083	1,149
Utah	487	603	890	1,132	1,058	1,128	1,094	1,178
Nevada	876	975	1,547	1,493	1,477	1,585	1,717	1,732
Pacific								
Washington	662	871	1,203	1,473	1,535	1,425	1,395	1,497
Oregon	623	838	1,140	1,401	1,415	1,381	1,396	1,518
California	840	1,009	1,281	1,540	1,582	1,580	1,654	1,678
United States[a]	592	716	906	1,099	1,192	1,231	1,247	1,313

(Continued on next page)

TABLE 1 (Continued)

PER CAPITA PERSONAL INCOME, 1929-1954, BY STATE AND YEAR
(Dollars per capita)

State	1948	1949	1950	1951	1952	1953	1954	Average 1929–1954
New England								
Maine	1,229	1,175	1,192	1,323	1,485	1,501	1,492	851
New Hampshire	1,269	1,244	1,323	1,491	1,531	1,560	1,605	906
Vermont	1,170	1,122	1,177	1,310	1,361	1,400	1,408	802
Massachusetts	1,513	1,490	1,660	1,835	1,887	1,928	1,922	1,137
Rhode Island	1,513	1,464	1,629	1,769	1,808	1,842	1,823	1,104
Connecticut	1,752	1,699	1,903	2,191	2,323	2,423	2,361	1,337
Middle Atlantic								
New York	1,798	1,756	1,879	2,006	2,077	2,150	2,163	1,304
New Jersey	1,650	1,622	1,796	2,001	2,107	2,239	2,219	1,233
Pennsylvania	1,446	1,422	1,566	1,747	1,835	1,893	1,785	1,026
East North Central								
Ohio	1,552	1,472	1,616	1,855	1,926	2,050	1,983	1,071
Indiana	1,440	1,364	1,522	1,702	1,768	1,936	1,834	954
Illinois	1,809	1,690	1,826	2,013	2,081	2,168	2,155	1,189
Michigan	1,542	1,504	1,684	1,860	1,941	2,124	2,017	1,087
Wisconsin	1,402	1,361	1,460	1,694	1,726	1,762	1,706	941
West North Central								
Minnesota	1,404	1,298	1,392	1,524	1,558	1,624	1,644	883
Iowa	1,547	1,320	1,442	1,550	1,593	1,539	1,667	868
Missouri	1,384	1,344	1,444	1,566	1,671	1,732	1,747	907
North Dakota	1,383	1,136	1,255	1,310	1,193	1,183	1,186	706
South Dakota	1,451	1,094	1,220	1,416	1,222	1,311	1,332	722
Nebraska	1,463	1,305	1,468	1,548	1,624	1,554	1,635	860
Kansas	1,277	1,245	1,378	1,516	1,719	1,653	1,689	854
South Atlantic								
Delaware	1,766	1,896	2,150	2,270	2,355	2,448	2,372	1,340
Maryland	1,458	1,453	1,590	1,773	1,889	1,979	1,940	1,082
D. C.	1,905	2,078	2,191	2,304	2,339	2,241	2,220	1,508
Virginia	1,112	1,101	1,215	1,373	1,446	1,473	1,480	759
West Virginia	1,146	1,062	1,098	1,220	1,274	1,285	1,232	700
North Carolina	944	919	1,011	1,118	1,145	1,181	1,190	611
South Carolina	879	838	877	1,045	1,108	1,122	1,063	551
Georgia	948	932	1,017	1,146	1,208	1,270	1,237	627
Florida	1,184	1,203	1,305	1,382	1,467	1,585	1,610	833
East South Central								
Kentucky	965	921	960	1,127	1,193	1,235	1,216	611
Tennessee	935	925	997	1,085	1,132	1,225	1,212	621
Alabama	856	810	868	994	1,077	1,121	1,091	548
Mississippi	753	667	729	793	844	878	873	449
West South Central								
Arkansas	847	780	802	906	948	981	979	503
Louisiana	1,002	1,059	1,089	1,178	1,241	1,304	1,302	666
Oklahoma	1,130	1,155	1,127	1,237	1,360	1,439	1,466	710
Texas	1,188	1,283	1,341	1,460	1,518	1,555	1,574	796
Mountain								
Montana	1,598	1,390	1,602	1,756	1,673	1,768	1,729	961
Idaho	1,281	1,239	1,275	1,438	1,549	1,475	1,433	832
Wyoming	1,554	1,588	1,622	1,886	1,830	1,843	1,779	1,021
Colorado	1,394	1,385	1,449	1,739	1,809	1,750	1,686	939
New Mexico	1,076	1,113	1,165	1,292	1,348	1,379	1,387	693
Arizona	1,216	1,245	1,295	1,555	1,639	1,597	1,582	858
Utah	1,219	1,224	1,281	1,453	1,486	1,503	1,483	839
Nevada	1,750	1,758	1,938	2,189	2,344	2,390	2,414	1,305
Pacific								
Washington	1,600	1,587	1,677	1,806	1,905	1,960	1,949	1,099
Oregon	1,609	1,562	1,607	1,749	1,814	1,794	1,757	1,051
California	1,750	1,725	1,850	2,055	2,138	2,194	2,162	1,274
United States[a]	1,417	1,378	1,487	1,646	1,720	1,788	1,768	966

[a]Excludes the District of Columbia.
Source: Charles F. Schwartz and Robert E. Graham, Jr., "Personal Income by States, 1929-54," *Survey of Current Business* (September 1955).

An exact description of the state personal income series is readily available in official publications and need not be repeated here. Since an understanding of the main outlines of the conceptual framework underlying these data is fundamental to understanding this study, some characterization of the series is in order. The estimates cover all income flows received by residents of a state during the current year. These income flows include the wages and salaries and certain supplements to them such as employers' contributions to pension and welfare funds, proprietors' income from all forms of self-employment, net rental income, dividends, and interest paid directly to individuals in cash or in kind. These payments are counted during the year in which they are received—that is, they are on a cash rather than an accrual basis. Also included are "transfers" from governments and business (that is, gifts or payments not arising out of the recipient's contribution to current productive activities). Transfers among persons are excluded, however, since they would be of consequence in the state data only when the transferor and transferee reside in different states. Certain benefits which accrue to individuals either in their personal capacities or as members of society but which are not received personally are also included. Thus the income of nonprofit institutions and the net rental value of owner-occupied homes are also included. Employee contributions to social security, government retirement, and other social insurance programs are excluded since personal income is on a cash rather than an accrual basis. Income taxes and other direct taxes are not deducted, however, even though they may be withheld by the employer.

These definitions substantially achieve the avowed intent to make the personal income series "the most comprehensive available record of differences among States in economic structure and change."[3] The National

---

income payments series was carried forward annually through 1953, with the estimates usually published in the August issues of the *Survey of Current Business*. A revised series that is conceptually comparable with personal income, a series which has been a part of the national income and product accounts since 1947, was inaugurated in Charles F. Schwartz and Robert E. Graham, Jr., "Personal Income by States, 1929-54," *Survey of Current Business,* September 1955, pp. 12-22 and 32. The principal conceptual difference between the state personal income and state income payments series is that the former includes the net rental value of owner-occupied dwellings, the value of food and clothing furnished members of the armed forces stationed in the United States, a broader coverage of income in kind, and the contribution of employers to pension and welfare funds. A detailed description of the differences will be provided by "a comprehensive bulletin on State personal income" scheduled for publication as a supplement to the *Survey of Current Business* in 1957. The state personal income series also "incorporate a complete reworking of the statistics back to 1929."

[3] It should be recognized, however, that some flows are omitted from personal income. Current practice is to exclude all capital gains from the national income accounts. To the

Income Division per capita estimates are used here without adjustment. The per capita series, which incorporates a crude adjustment for differences in the size of the various states, is used in preference to the total personal income series in most of the computations.[4]

The order of the states in the general tables in this volume follows the familiar regional classification of the Bureau of the Census. While the divisional names are given as an aid to finding data for a particular state, there has been no attempt to provide summary figures for these regional groupings. Emphasis throughout the volume is on the states; while groups of states often appear to show similarities, no effort has been made to pursue this facet of state income figures.[5]

The "current income" concept used by Leven in preparing state estimates for 1919-1921 differs in several particulars from the personal income concept.[6] The principal ones are that the Leven estimates include the net rental value of farm homes; the value of product from urban cows, gardens, and poultry; and the value of land sold by farmers for urban uses, but exclude changes in business inventories. Apparently, estimates were made for the latter, which include all inflationary changes in values, and they are presented in combination with capital gains and losses, whether realized or not, on all property. Consequently, changes in inventories are excluded from the totals used. The imputed net rental value of owner-occupied urban and farm homes was 2 to 3 percent of current income; while the total for the rental value of farm homes is not shown separately, it probably did not exceed 1 to 2 percent of the national totals. The extent of the state biases introduced by these differences is hard to appraise, but it seems clear that there is some tendency

extent that these gains arise from the revaluation of existing assets their exclusion, though controversial, appears to be well founded. The increase in income tax rates during recent years has put a premium on receiving income as *de jure,* if not *de facto,* capital gains. See Lawrence H. Seltzer, *The Nature and Tax Treatment of Capital Gains and Losses,* New York, 1951. Corporate profits which are realized by stockholders as capital gains thus may never be included in personal income.

[4] For 1941-1947 the population figures used were estimated by the National Income Division by adding to the midyear estimate of the civilian population prepared by the Bureau of the Census an estimate of the number of military personnel in each state (derived from monthly or quarterly information supplied by the armed services). For other years the state estimates of midyear population prepared by the Bureau of the Census are used. The per capita computations are made and published by the National Income Division.

[5] See Morris B. Ullman and Robert C. Klove, "The Geographic Area in Regional Economic Research" in *Studies in Income and Wealth,* 21 (Princeton, 1957), 87-109.

[6] Leven also presents estimates for "total income." These include, in addition to the items in "current income," capital gains and losses and an imputed interest on the value of durable consumption goods in the hands of consumers. *Op. cit.,* p. 261 n.

for them to offset one another. Inclusion of the rental value of farm homes would favor agricultural states; the product of urban cows, gardens, and poultry would tend to be more prevalent in small urban communities; and the value of farm land transferred to urban uses would tend to be greater in states containing expanding metropolitan centers.

That less reliability attaches to the estimates for 1919-1921 seems indicated both by the conceptual differences between the Leven and National Income Division estimates and by the fact that Leven was forced to rely on more fragmentary and less refined data without an opportunity to review and revise his estimates as new statistical series, which permitted more sophisticated estimating relationships, became available. Consequently, the analyses in this volume are carried out chiefly in terms of the National Income Division estimates for 1929-1954. Leven's estimates are then compared with the relationships ascertained from the more recent series. In this way the Leven estimates can be used to lend historical perspective to the relationships based on official estimates, with the conceptual and statistical differences between the two series minimized.

The state per capita income estimates are in current dollars. Nowhere in this study is an attempt to reduce them to a constant dollar or a "real" basis. Rather, state data will often be expressed in relatives of the national average. These relatives will be identical with those that would be computed from constant dollar figures obtained by applying a uniform adjustment to each of the states.[7] Although a series of state price indexes is available for most of the period covered, the interstate differences in these indexes tend to be inconsequential to the types of analyses made here.[8]

The period 1929-1954 has been dominated by increasing per capita personal incomes (chart 1). Decreases have been recorded in only 7 of the 25 year-to-year changes, and 4 of these decreases occurred during the great depression, 1929-1933. Since then short-lived and moderate decreases have occurred only for 1937-1938, 1948-1949, and 1953-1954 (table 2). Ten of the changes from the previous year are larger than 10 percent, and of these four are larger than 20 percent. The larger year-to-year changes

[7] The state per capita income relatives—i.e., the state per capita income expressed as a percentage of the corresponding United States per capita income—are unaffected when both the numerator and denominator are multiplied by a constant—i.e., the reciprocal of a specific price index.

[8] See Abner Hurwitz and Carlyle P. Stallings, "Interregional Differentials in Per Capita Real Income Changes," in *Studies in Income and Wealth,* 21 (Princeton, 1957), 195-265.

occurred during the great depression, World War II, and the Korean affair.

The range, in absolute terms, of annual per capita personal incomes is $1,415, from $373 in 1933 to $1,788 in 1953. The interstate range of in-

CHART 1

PER CAPITA PERSONAL INCOME, UNITED STATES, 1929-1954

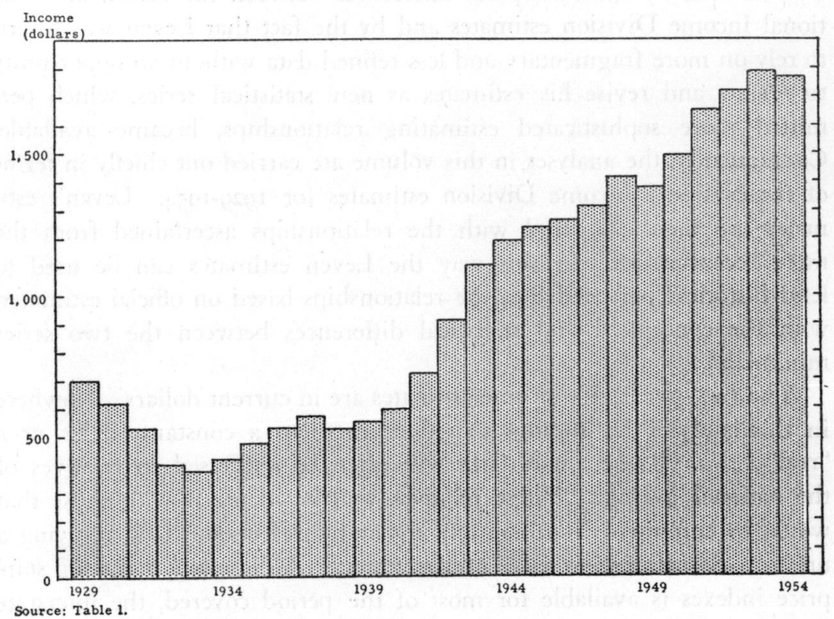

Source: Table 1.

TABLE 2

CHANGES IN PER CAPITA PERSONAL INCOME, 1929-1954

Year	Per capita personal income	Percentage change from previous year	Year	Per capita personal income	Percentage change from previous year
1929	$703		1942	$ 906	26.5
1930	621	−11.7	1943	1,099	21.3
1931	526	−15.3	1944	1,192	8.5
1932	398	−24.3	1945	1,231	3.3
1933	373	− 6.3	1946	1,247	1.3
1934	421	12.9	1947	1,313	5.3
1935	470	11.6	1948	1,417	7.9
1936	531	13.0	1949	1,378	− 2.8
1937	570	7.3	1950	1,487	7.9
1938	524	− 8.1	1951	1,646	10.7
1939	553	5.5	1952	1,720	4.5
1940	592	7.1	1953	1,788	4.0
1941	716	20.9	1954	1,768	− 1.1

Source: table 1.

comes exceeds $1,415 only during 1950-1954 and is largest ($1,570) in 1953. The relative range (that is, the absolute range divided by the mean) over the years (1.46) is somewhat larger than the 1929-1954 average relative interstate range (0.92).[9] The annual relative interstate ranges vary from a high of 1.38 in 1932 to a low of 0.74 in 1948. The interstate range exceeds the average per capita personal income every year from 1929 to 1942 and is smaller thereafter.

COEFFICIENTS OF VARIATION

A superficial examination of the state per capita incomes (in table 1) is sufficient to note that despite differential changes from one year to another the rank order of the states is not changed greatly.[10] South Carolina's income in current dollars, for example, has increased by $793 from $270 in 1929 to $1,063 in 1954. Yet it had the lowest income of any of the states in 1929 and third from the lowest in 1954. On the other hand, Connecticut's income increased by $1,332 from $1,029 in 1929 to $2,361 in 1954. It was next to the highest in income in 1929 and third from the highest in 1954. The incomes of the upper-income states have increased more in dollar amounts and less in percentage terms than those of the lower-income states.

A somewhat better picture of the behavior of the interstate differentials can be obtained by comparing their standard deviations for each of the years (table 3). When the state incomes are weighted by their populations, there is a marked tendency for the standard deviations to follow the changes in the weighted mean state per capita income (that is, the national per capita income), although the magnitude of the changes in the standard deviations is lessened somewhat, especially during the more recent years.

There is a pronounced tendency for the interstate coefficient of variation,[11] one of the principal measures of relative dispersion, to decrease with an increase in income and to increase with a decrease in income. Since the period is one of increasing income, there is a tendency for the coefficients of variation to decrease, from the earlier to the latter part of

[9] The mean per capita personal income for 1929-1954 is $972. This figure is computed by taking a simple average of the annual per capita figures. It is equivalent to totaling the annual incomes and dividing this sum by the sum of the midyear population estimates for the United States.

[10] The coefficients of rank correlation between the 1929 and the 1939, 1949, and 1954 state per capita incomes are from .94 to .98; those between 1919 and the 1929, 1939, 1949, and 1954 state per capita incomes are from .86 to .92.

[11] The coefficient of variation is the standard deviation expressed as a percentage of the mean. The state per capita incomes used in these computations have been weighted by the state's midyear population.

TABLE 3

MEANS AND DISPERSION OF STATE PER CAPITA PERSONAL INCOME, 1919-1921 AND 1929-1954, BY YEAR

Year	Mean	Standard deviation	Coefficient of variation	Year	Mean	Standard deviation	Coefficient of variation
1919	$ 613	$169	27.6	1944	$1,192	$281	23.6
1920	660	219	33.1	1945	1,231	279	22.7
1921	549	205	37.3	1946	1,247	295	23.6
				1947	1,313	297	22.6
Average 1919-21	607	196	32.2	1948	1,417	303	21.4
1929	703	259	36.9	1949	1,378	291	21.2
1930	621	242	38.9	1950	1,487	324	21.8
1931	526	208	39.5	1951	1,646	350	21.3
1932	398	163	41.0	1952	1,720	360	20.9
1933	373	147	39.4	1953	1,788	379	21.2
1934	421	155	36.9	1954	1,768	368	20.8
1935	470	158	33.7				
1936	531	183	34.4	Average 1929-54	966	246	25.5
1937	570	186	32.6				
1938	524	172	32.9				
1939	553	183	33.1				
1940	592	196	33.1				
1941	716	219	30.6				
1942	906	244	26.9				
1943	1,099	283	25.8				

Source: 1919-1921, Leven, *op. cit.;* 1929-1954, *Survey of Current Business* (Sept. 1955). The District of Columbia is excluded. The midyear populations of the states were used as weights.

the period. Starting at a level of 37-41 percent during 1929-1932, the coefficients have decreased steadily through 1945. From 1944 to 1954 they have varied within the narrow range of 21-24 percent. In the relative terms provided by the coefficients of variation, there has been a pronounced narrowing of interstate differentials.

The decrease in the interstate coefficients of variation during the 1929-1954 period apparently is a function of both increasing income and time.[12]

[12] The coefficient of determination between the logarithms of the weighted coefficients of variation and the weighted logarithms of national per capita personal incomes for 1929-1954 is .92. When time (year minus 1941) is added as an independent variable and multiple correlation is used, a coefficient of multiple determination of .97 is obtained. This is a significant improvement (at the .01 significance level) over the coefficient of simple determination. However, an examination of the deviations from the simple regression line between the coefficients of variation and income indicates that much of the downward trend occurred during the first half of the period; in fact, the deviations for 1951-1954 are positive. The use of logarithms, rather than percentage changes from the previous year, introduces an element of autocorrelation into these coefficients. This element of autocorrelation is unavoidable if time is to be retained as an effective variable, and it seems less objectionable than giving full weight to the irregular and transitory elements which result from the use of a constantly changing base in computing the percentage changes from the previous year. The constantly changing base is particularly objectionable during an inflationary period, since the dollar-income amounts will contain all the changes in the unit of value, while the coefficients of variation, which are expressed in terms of percentages of the weighted mean state per capita income, are relatively free from this effect. The coefficients of partial determination between the coefficients of variation and

The fact that the coefficients of variation fluctuate within very narrow limits after 1943 would indicate, however, that these functions were more pronounced during the earlier than during the later part of the 1929-1954 period. Moreover, the coefficients of variation for the 1919-1921 period do not differ greatly or consistently from those of years in the 1930's having approximately the same income levels. If there was a marked change in the coefficients of variation which is not explained by the changes in the level of income, it occurred during the 1930's.

State Relatives

In reviewing the changes in the dollar amounts of state per capita incomes, the lack of some standard by which to judge the behavior of a particular state becomes evident, and is especially noticeable since all of the states tend to change in the same direction. The differential behavior of the states thus shows up, not in differing directions, but in larger or smaller changes in the same direction. By expressing each of the state per capita incomes as a percentage of the national per capita income for the same year, state income relatives are obtained (table 4). These relatives facilitate comparisons among the states. An increase in the income relative for Maine indicates that Maine's income increased more (or decreased less) than did the weighted average income of all states. It requires further computation to show whether Maine's or Georgia's per capita income increased comparatively more during this period.

By transforming the per capita incomes to state relatives, two types of adjustments are incorporated in the series: First, the differences in the size of the states, as represented by their populations, are taken into account. Secondly, the changes over time in the national per capita income level are taken into account. The latter adjustment corrects for both changes in the general price level and in the general level of production. In dealing with these state income relatives, it must be remembered that both inflationary and production changes affect various commodities and industries differentially. While percentage changes in a state that followed exactly the percentage changes in the national per capita income would leave the state relatives unchanged, there is no presumption that the state and national price and productivity changes should be the same.

There is a well-marked inverse relationship between a state's 1929-

---

income, holding the effects of time constant (—.56), and with time, holding the effects of income constant (—.59), are approximately equal.

TABLE 4

State Relatives of United States Per Capita Personal Income, 1919-1921 and 1929-1954, by Year

(A state relative is the state's per capita personal income expressed as a percentage of the United States' per capita personal income.)

State	1919	1920	1921	Average 1919–1921	1929	1930	1931	1932
New England								
Maine	88.0	93.8	99.1	93.6	85.5	92.2	92.8	94.5
New Hampshire	94.1	102.6	105.1	100.6	98.2	103.8	105.9	107.2
Vermont	82.9	91.7	93.5	89.4	89.2	91.2	88.5	89.8
Massachusetts	127.8	141.8	141.7	137.1	129.9	135.3	145.0	155.1
Rhode Island	119.5	130.1	136.7	128.8	123.9	126.1	134.6	143.6
Connecticut	115.2	125.4	115.4	118.7	146.4	148.4	152.2	154.9
Middle Atlantic								
New York	146.1	152.9	167.2	155.4	164.9	167.2	167.5	169.8
New Jersey	118.4	123.3	125.6	122.4	132.4	137.7	140.8	147.6
Pennsylvania	107.8	116.2	114.3	112.8	110.2	114.7	113.8	112.5
East North Central								
Ohio	108.5	112.2	98.4	106.4	111.1	107.5	107.4	100.8
Indiana	89.2	91.5	84.4	88.4	87.1	83.2	83.0	77.6
Illinois	126.2	122.4	128.3	125.6	136.1	130.8	127.6	122.0
Michigan	108.1	115.9	99.1	107.7	112.8	105.6	102.1	98.2
Wisconsin	91.0	94.0	91.5	92.2	97.0	95.4	89.6	90.8
West North Central								
Minnesota	92.8	84.4	83.8	87.0	85.1	88.5	86.6	90.5
Iowa	100.5	80.1	77.1	85.9	82.1	81.2	75.2	73.6
Missouri	89.1	87.3	90.9	89.1	89.3	91.2	93.6	91.8
North Dakota	84.2	67.1	57.5	69.6	53.3	48.9	34.4	43.9
South Dakota	111.7	72.4	60.8	81.6	59.3	57.4	45.2	46.9
Nebraska	97.4	80.7	75.7	84.6	83.9	82.8	77.5	76.3
Kansas	95.9	89.3	83.3	89.5	76.1	75.0	75.4	66.8
South Atlantic								
Delaware	121.0	101.1	101.1	107.7	144.7	136.1	145.4	146.6
Maryland	107.0	111.6	111.2	110.0	110.5	115.2	121.0	127.4
D. C.	155.5	165.1	213.1	177.9	181.1	202.2	226.5	262.1
Virginia	66.3	62.7	62.8	63.9	61.9	61.5	69.6	70.3
West Virginia	72.6	84.0	76.4	77.7	65.7	65.9	67.7	64.3
North Carolina	59.8	52.1	49.7	53.9	47.5	47.0	46.9	46.6
South Carolina	63.5	48.5	41.0	51.0	38.4	38.6	38.6	39.2
Georgia	61.7	50.0	46.6	52.8	49.8	49.4	48.4	49.6
Florida	66.4	64.6	67.2	66.1	74.1	74.4	74.7	78.3
East South Central								
Kentucky	61.6	60.3	61.7	61.2	55.6	52.1	54.6	52.4
Tennessee	56.4	53.2	56.3	55.3	53.6	52.1	52.0	49.1
Alabama	52.3	45.6	45.4	47.8	46.1	42.6	42.0	40.2
Mississippi	53.4	38.2	37.6	43.1	40.5	32.5	32.9	31.4
West South Central								
Arkansas	57.3	47.4	45.7	50.2	43.4	35.7	39.5	38.6
Louisiana	67.1	63.4	64.2	64.9	59.0	57.4	60.1	59.6
Oklahoma	83.9	78.2	66.4	76.2	64.6	59.0	56.5	53.9
Texas	83.9	82.2	78.6	81.5	68.0	65.9	65.4	65.3
Mountain								
Montana	101.0	91.8	89.3	94.0	84.6	80.6	72.4	84.0
Idaho	99.8	87.2	83.1	90.0	71.6	79.6	69.9	67.3
Wyoming	140.7	130.5	135.9	135.7	96.3	93.6	90.0	93.3
Colorado	110.3	108.0	112.3	110.2	90.6	93.0	89.6	88.8
New Mexico	75.2	70.8	73.1	73.1	57.9	53.4	54.2	52.1
Arizona	112.2	109.7	91.5	104.4	84.1	82.4	80.2	78.6
Utah	87.5	83.7	81.8	84.3	79.5	80.9	71.5	77.1
Nevada	142.0	142.6	146.1	143.6	124.9	132.4	122.7	135.2
Pacific								
Washington	116.9	110.6	123.2	116.9	106.7	106.6	101.7	100.5
Oregon	117.6	108.2	112.2	112.6	97.2	99.4	97.0	95.8
California	136.6	149.4	163.0	149.7	141.5	142.5	141.0	143.1

(Continued on next page)

TABLE 4 (Continued)

STATE RELATIVES OF UNITED STATES PER CAPITA PERSONAL INCOME, 1919-1921 AND 1929-1954, BY YEAR

(A state relative is the state's per capita personal income expressed as a percentage of the United States' per capita personal income.)

State	1933	1934	1935	1936	1937	1938	1939	1940	1941
New England									
Maine	99.7	97.6	90.7	93.6	88.1	89.2	88.7	87.9	87.1
New Hampshire	111.7	112.8	104.9	100.4	98.6	101.3	100.5	97.3	98.3
Vermont	90.4	87.5	86.6	86.5	83.4	85.8	86.3	85.2	87.5
Massachusetts	152.0	145.6	136.9	134.5	128.3	128.5	130.8	131.8	125.4
Rhode Island	149.6	140.9	135.4	132.2	126.2	127.1	128.2	124.9	128.1
Connecticut	156.5	154.6	149.2	150.6	149.9	145.9	150.0	154.1	158.8
Middle Atlantic									
New York	169.1	161.7	153.2	151.7	146.4	150.3	148.4	146.2	138.4
New Jersey	141.1	136.6	133.0	133.5	130.9	132.8	135.1	138.2	133.5
Pennsylvania	112.3	114.0	109.5	112.2	110.6	106.6	107.7	108.9	107.2
East North Central									
Ohio	104.0	108.0	110.0	111.8	113.6	107.2	111.3	111.8	115.3
Indiana	79.2	84.4	88.8	89.9	95.1	89.9	93.4	92.9	101.0
Illinois	117.9	120.1	121.8	122.1	127.6	123.3	126.8	126.7	124.5
Michigan	93.1	106.9	111.9	115.4	119.0	108.5	112.2	114.1	115.0
Wisconsin	89.6	89.8	98.1	97.2	96.5	97.2	93.0	93.1	93.9
West North Central									
Minnesota	82.9	84.6	94.7	88.0	93.4	93.7	93.0	88.4	85.8
Iowa	67.7	63.4	88.4	72.5	88.7	86.3	84.4	84.2	84.4
Missouri	90.1	87.0	89.4	87.6	88.7	90.7	91.0	88.1	89.8
North Dakota	38.7	41.8	56.4	42.9	55.7	52.8	56.5	58.8	72.6
South Dakota	34.4	42.3	63.6	44.9	55.7	60.0	61.2	60.3	65.4
Nebraska	73.6	60.3	85.0	73.0	71.4	76.3	71.0	73.8	76.2
Kansas	66.9	67.4	75.6	71.4	73.5	72.5	68.4	71.6	76.8
South Atlantic									
Delaware	150.7	148.5	146.2	159.2	162.1	148.4	164.8	168.7	158.7
Maryland	124.0	123.2	115.5	115.5	115.9	120.1	118.9	119.7	121.4
D. C.	240.0	217.7	206.4	205.1	202.8	208.0	200.9	196.6	167.6
Virginia	75.5	74.2	73.1	72.3	72.8	73.4	75.9	78.3	80.8
West Virginia	69.3	73.5	71.4	72.8	72.6	70.4	69.6	68.4	68.8
North Carolina	55.2	57.9	57.0	55.2	56.0	56.2	56.8	55.1	59.2
South Carolina	46.4	48.5	47.9	47.4	46.6	47.2	49.1	51.6	54.5
Georgia	54.4	56.7	56.6	56.4	54.3	55.0	55.8	57.1	59.0
Florida	75.7	80.1	77.8	82.4	83.1	85.8	87.4	86.2	83.0
East South Central									
Kentucky	54.7	54.1	55.5	54.3	58.3	55.4	54.5	53.8	54.5
Tennessee	54.4	56.7	55.1	56.2	57.2	56.6	55.4	57.0	60.2
Alabama	44.0	48.5	45.6	46.4	45.7	46.1	45.0	47.4	52.2
Mississippi	34.9	39.0	37.1	41.6	38.4	38.0	36.9	36.6	43.5
West South Central									
Arkansas	41.3	41.8	42.6	44.8	43.1	42.9	43.5	43.0	47.0
Louisiana	60.3	61.5	60.6	60.9	60.7	65.6	64.2	61.0	62.4
Oklahoma	59.2	58.4	62.1	59.4	64.4	65.1	62.0	62.7	60.4
Texas	67.5	67.1	67.4	68.0	71.2	75.1	73.6	72.6	72.9
Mountain									
Montana	79.7	85.3	100.2	89.3	89.5	97.5	95.3	95.8	99.4
Idaho	60.8	89.4	83.3	86.3	73.0	79.9	78.1	78.0	82.6
Wyoming	97.3	95.3	103.6	101.5	104.9	104.9	105.2	102.2	108.9
Colorado	94.7	87.2	93.6	100.8	92.7	96.2	92.8	91.8	90.1
New Mexico	55.7	57.4	60.6	62.4	61.8	63.2	63.3	63.0	65.5
Arizona	80.0	83.4	86.0	85.0	85.9	88.8	85.8	83.5	87.3
Utah	80.0	74.2	83.0	87.1	78.5	85.4	83.1	81.8	83.9
Nevada	133.3	125.5	137.7	153.9	130.5	144.6	151.3	147.2	135.6
Pacific									
Washington	100.8	103.8	103.6	106.4	104.7	111.2	111.0	111.3	121.1
Oregon	96.8	103.8	98.3	103.8	98.4	103.2	104.7	104.7	116.6
California	144.3	140.0	137.9	142.3	137.2	145.0	139.4	141.2	140.3

(Continued on next page)

TABLE 4 (Continued)

STATE RELATIVES OF UNITED STATES PER CAPITA PERSONAL INCOME, 1919-1921 AND 1929-1954, BY YEAR

(A state relative is the state's per capita personal income expressed as a percentage of the United States' per capita personal income.)

State	1942	1943	1944	1945	1946	1947	1948	1949	1950
New England									
Maine	93.5	98.6	91.4	86.5	89.4	87.4	86.6	85.0	80.0
New Hampshire	93.4	87.8	87.8	89.6	91.7	91.8	89.4	90.0	88.7
Vermont	83.3	81.8	77.9	82.1	84.7	83.5	82.4	81.2	78.9
Massachusetts	118.2	114.4	108.9	109.5	111.9	109.0	106.6	107.8	111.3
Rhode Island	124.8	107.4	105.6	102.7	108.0	109.1	106.6	105.9	109.3
Connecticut	155.9	144.3	134.1	127.1	126.3	128.6	123.4	122.9	127.6
Middle Atlantic									
New York	128.6	125.1	128.6	133.2	135.4	130.3	126.6	127.1	126.0
New Jersey	128.7	130.0	130.9	128.9	122.4	119.3	116.2	117.4	120.5
Pennsylvania	103.6	102.8	103.8	102.8	101.9	102.4	101.8	102.9	105.0
East North Central									
Ohio	113.1	114.2	110.7	109.3	105.0	107.3	109.3	106.5	108.4
Indiana	100.4	102.7	100.3	101.1	95.5	99.0	101.4	98.7	102.1
Illinois	114.3	114.2	116.6	119.1	122.5	124.3	127.4	122.3	122.5
Michigan	115.2	122.2	116.2	106.9	105.5	110.5	108.6	108.8	112.9
Wisconsin	95.9	95.6	93.4	96.1	96.8	98.3	98.7	98.5	97.9
West North Central									
Minnesota	87.6	84.8	83.6	89.1	94.0	95.4	98.9	93.9	93.4
Iowa	90.8	90.3	82.4	86.6	96.6	90.4	108.9	95.5	96.7
Missouri	89.0	87.3	89.9	91.9	95.0	92.8	97.5	97.2	96.8
North Dakota	72.0	84.1	83.9	81.8	83.8	109.9	97.4	82.2	84.2
South Dakota	81.6	74.0	79.6	84.8	86.7	93.6	102.2	79.2	81.8
Nebraska	89.2	90.1	89.8	94.2	92.2	94.4	103.0	94.4	98.5
Kansas	93.4	93.8	97.5	93.9	89.4	97.9	89.9	90.1	92.4
South Atlantic									
Delaware	139.4	130.5	124.2	122.1	122.7	124.2	124.4	137.2	144.2
Maryland	123.2	117.2	111.5	106.8	105.1	102.6	102.7	105.1	106.6
D. C.	150.1	136.8	130.7	132.5	135.2	132.8	134.2	150.4	147.0
Virginia	86.0	76.1	75.2	76.7	79.3	76.1	78.3	79.7	81.5
West Virginia	67.4	67.0	68.8	72.1	73.7	78.2	80.7	76.8	73.6
North Carolina	63.3	62.7	64.1	66.5	68.7	67.9	66.5	66.5	67.8
South Carolina	59.4	58.0	60.6	60.2	61.1	59.2	61.9	60.6	58.8
Georgia	62.8	65.8	69.9	71.5	67.6	67.2	66.8	67.4	68.2
Florida	84.6	89.4	91.3	93.3	91.0	86.8	83.4	87.0	87.5
East South Central									
Kentucky	58.6	62.5	63.6	64.3	64.9	64.6	68.0	66.6	64.4
Tennessee	61.1	65.1	71.7	73.1	68.5	66.6	65.8	66.9	66.9
Alabama	56.7	59.1	61.6	63.2	59.6	60.3	60.3	58.6	58.2
Mississippi	48.4	47.9	52.5	50.8	48.4	50.3	53.0	48.3	48.9
West South Central									
Arkansas	51.8	49.1	56.3	58.5	58.4	54.6	59.6	56.4	53.8
Louisiana	65.2	71.1	73.6	72.3	66.4	67.0	70.6	76.6	73.0
Oklahoma	68.6	70.2	79.1	78.4	75.2	77.1	79.6	83.6	75.6
Texas	78.3	84.5	86.9	85.2	82.3	85.7	83.7	92.8	89.9
Mountain									
Montana	98.6	102.4	97.8	96.5	102.3	110.7	112.5	100.6	107.4
Idaho	99.4	91.1	90.4	90.3	93.6	95.1	90.2	89.6	85.5
Wyoming	103.8	103.6	102.9	101.9	107.3	113.1	109.4	114.9	108.8
Colorado	98.0	93.5	89.0	95.9	95.7	101.7	98.2	100.2	97.2
New Mexico	69.1	68.8	72.8	75.0	72.5	75.1	75.8	80.5	78.1
Arizona	98.8	89.5	86.8	89.7	86.7	87.3	85.6	90.1	86.8
Utah	97.9	102.7	88.6	91.4	87.6	89.5	85.8	88.6	85.9
Nevada	170.2	135.5	123.7	128.4	137.5	131.6	123.2	127.2	130.0
Pacific									
Washington	132.3	133.7	128.6	115.5	111.7	113.8	112.7	114.8	112.5
Oregon	125.4	127.1	118.5	111.9	111.8	115.4	113.3	113.0	107.8
California	140.9	139.8	132.5	128.0	132.4	127.5	123.2	124.8	124.1

(Continued on next page)

TABLE 4 (Continued)

STATE RELATIVES OF UNITED STATES PER CAPITA PERSONAL INCOME, 1919-1921 AND 1929-1954, BY YEAR

(A state relative is the state's per capita personal income expressed as a percentage of the United States' per capita personal income.)

State	1951	1952	1953	1954	Average 1929-1954
New England					
Maine	80.2	86.2	83.8	84.3	87.6
New Hampshire	90.4	88.9	87.2	90.7	93.2
Vermont	79.4	79.0	78.2	79.6	82.5
Massachusetts	111.3	109.5	107.7	108.6	117.0
Rhode Island	107.3	104.9	102.9	103.0	113.6
Connecticut	132.9	134.8	135.4	133.4	137.6
Middle Atlantic					
New York	121.6	120.6	120.1	122.2	134.2
New Jersey	121.4	122.3	125.1	125.4	126.8
Pennsylvania	105.9	106.5	105.8	100.8	105.6
East North Central					
Ohio	112.5	111.8	114.5	112.0	110.2
Indiana	103.2	102.6	108.2	103.6	98.2
Illinois	122.1	120.8	121.1	121.8	122.3
Michigan	112.8	112.6	118.7	114.0	111.8
Wisconsin	102.7	100.2	98.4	96.4	96.8
West North Central					
Minnesota	92.4	90.4	90.7	92.9	90.8
Iowa	94.0	92.5	86.0	94.2	89.3
Missouri	95.0	97.0	96.8	98.7	93.3
North Dakota	79.4	69.2	66.1	67.0	72.6
South Dakota	85.9	70.9	73.2	75.2	74.3
Nebraska	93.9	94.2	86.8	92.4	88.5
Kansas	91.9	99.8	92.4	95.4	87.9
South Atlantic					
Delaware	137.7	136.7	136.8	134.0	137.9
Maryland	107.5	109.6	110.6	109.6	111.3
D. C.	139.7	135.8	125.2	125.4	155.1
Virginia	83.3	83.9	82.3	83.6	78.1
West Virginia	74.0	73.9	71.8	69.6	72.0
North Carolina	67.8	66.4	66.0	67.2	62.9
South Carolina	63.4	64.3	62.7	60.1	56.7
Georgia	69.5	70.1	71.0	69.9	64.5
Florida	83.8	85.1	88.6	91.0	85.7
East South Central					
Kentucky	68.3	69.2	69.0	68.7	62.9
Tennessee	65.8	65.7	68.4	68.5	63.9
Alabama	60.3	62.5	62.6	61.6	56.4
Mississippi	48.1	49.0	49.0	49.3	46.2
West South Central					
Arkansas	54.9	55.0	54.8	55.3	51.8
Louisiana	71.4	72.0	72.8	73.6	68.5
Oklahoma	75.0	78.9	80.4	82.8	73.0
Texas	88.5	88.1	86.9	88.9	81.9
Mountain					
Montana	106.5	102.3	98.8	97.7	98.9
Idaho	87.2	89.9	82.4	81.0	85.6
Wyoming	114.4	106.2	103.0	100.5	105.0
Colorado	105.5	105.0	97.8	95.2	96.6
New Mexico	78.4	78.2	77.0	78.4	71.3
Arizona	94.3	95.1	89.2	89.4	88.3
Utah	88.1	86.2	84.0	83.8	86.3
Nevada	132.8	136.0	133.5	136.4	134.3
Pacific					
Washington	109.5	110.6	109.5	110.1	113.1
Oregon	106.1	105.3	100.2	99.3	108.1
California	124.6	124.1	122.6	122.2	131.1

Sources: 1919-1921, Maurice Leven, *Income in the Various States, Its Sources and Distribution, 1919, 1920, 1921* (New York, 1925); 1929-1954, table 1.

1954 average income relative and the percentage change between its relatives in 1929 and in 1953 and 1954 (table 5).[13] Thus per capita incomes of the lower-income states have tended to increase, while per capita incomes of the higher-income states have tended to decrease, relative to the national per capita income.

TABLE 5

STATE RELATIVES OF UNITED STATES PER CAPITA PERSONAL INCOME, AVERAGE 1929-1954 SIZE, AND PERCENTAGE CHANGES FROM 1929 TO 1953 AND 1954

State (arrayed by 1929-1954 average income)	Relatives of U. S. per capita income			State (arrayed by 1929-1954 average income)	Relatives of U. S. per capita income		
	Average size 1929-1954	Percentage change from 1929 to			Average size 1929-1954	Percentage change from 1929 to	
		1953	1954			1953	1954
Mississippi	46.2	21.0	21.7	Iowa	89.3	4.8	14.7
Arkansas	51.8	26.3	27.5	Minnesota	90.8	6.7	9.2
Alabama	56.4	35.9	33.7	New Hampshire	93.2	−11.2	− 7.6
South Carolina	56.7	63.2	56.4	Missouri	93.3	8.3	10.5
North Carolina	62.9	38.9	41.5	Colorado	96.6	7.9	5.1
Kentucky	62.9	24.0	23.5	Wisconsin	96.8	1.5	− .6
Tennessee	63.9	27.6	27.7	Indiana	98.2	24.2	19.0
Georgia	64.5	42.5	40.4	Montana	98.9	16.7	15.4
Louisiana	68.5	23.4	24.6	Wyoming	105.0	6.9	4.4
New Mexico	71.3	33.1	35.4	Pennsylvania	105.6	− 4.1	− 8.5
West Virginia	72.0	9.2	5.9	Oregon	108.1	3.2	2.2
North Dakota	72.6	23.9	25.6	Ohio	110.2	3.1	.8
Oklahoma	73.1	24.5	28.2	Maryland	111.3	.0	− .8
South Dakota	74.3	23.5	26.8	Michigan	111.8	5.2	1.0
Virginia	78.1	33.0	35.1	Washington	113.1	2.6	3.2
Texas	81.9	27.8	30.8	Rhode Island	113.6	−16.9	−16.9
Vermont	82.5	−12.3	−10.8	Massachusetts	117.0	−17.1	−16.4
Idaho	85.6	15.2	13.2	Illinois	122.3	−11.0	−10.6
Florida	85.7	19.5	22.7	New Jersey	126.8	− 5.6	− 5.3
Utah	86.3	5.6	5.4	California	131.1	−13.4	−13.7
Maine	87.6	− 1.9	− 1.4	New York	134.2	−27.1	−25.9
Kansas	87.9	21.4	25.4	Nevada	134.3	6.9	9.2
Arizona	88.3	6.1	6.3	Connecticut	137.6	− 7.5	− 8.9
Nebraska	88.5	3.4	10.1	Delaware	137.9	− 5.5	− 7.4

Source: table 1.

Since the state differentials are constantly shifting, the use of any single year as representative of a state's income level would introduce a random element into these computations. To avoid this random element, the average for the entire 1929-1954 period has been used to represent a state's income level.

Basing the percentage change in the state relatives on two single years is also likely to introduce some random or transitory elements. That 1929 was a cyclical peak has been well established, and it seemed

[13] The coefficient of determination between the state 1929-1954 average income relative and the 1953 state relatives expressed as percentages of the 1929 state relatives is —.60 for the 1954 relatives as percentages of the 1929 relatives, —.63.

desirable to include that year for this reason (as well as because it provides the maximum span of years over which to take a measurement). Whether 1953 or 1954 is the more comparable, cyclically, is a matter of conjecture. Averages of three years centered on a cyclical peak might provide a better basis for the above relation, but data for 1928 are not available. Consequently, it is not possible to treat 1929 and 1953 as peak years and to compare the 1928-1930 average incomes with those for 1952-1954. Rather, the relationship has been computed for two recent years. The differences between them are not large. Income level explains about 5 percent more of the state differences in the percentage changes in state income relatives when 1929 is compared with 1954 than when 1929 is compared with 1953.

If the 1919-1921 and the 1952-1954 periods are taken as occupying roughly comparable positions on the business cycle, and the percentage changes in income relatives are related to average 1929-1954 state income relatives, the same inverse relationship is found.[14] That the relationship is smaller than that between either 1929 and 1953 or 1929 and 1954 is due largely to the changes in state relatives between 1919-1921 and 1929. Whether these changes stem from statistical and conceptual noncomparabilities in the two series or reflect significant changes in the state differentials is not known.

Although there is a strong tendency, as average income increases, for per capita incomes in states with low incomes to increase more than in those with high incomes, the pattern of change is neither exact nor uniform. Something of the diversity of patterns may be seen in chart 2, in which states have been gathered into seven groups or panels according to the patterns of changes over the period. The states within a panel thus have approximately the same pattern of change, though with minor variations, and the arrangement of the states within panels was made by inspection. Consequently, reference should be made to table 4 for data on the percentage increases from one year to another, the income level of each of the states, and other classificatory detail.

Panel A presents the state relatives in graphic form for 16 states whose income relatives increased during the period with moderate fluctuations from year to year. Typically, they are low income states, although Arizona, Indiana, and Kansas have state incomes among the central rather than the lower third. The pattern of changes is one of decreasing relatives from 1929 to 1932-1933 and of increasing relatives to a peak late in the war, with the highest relative occurring in the 1948-1952 period. There

[14] The coefficient of determination is —.20, which is significant at the .01 level.

CHART 2

State Relatives of United States Per Capita Personal Income, 1929-1954

Panel A

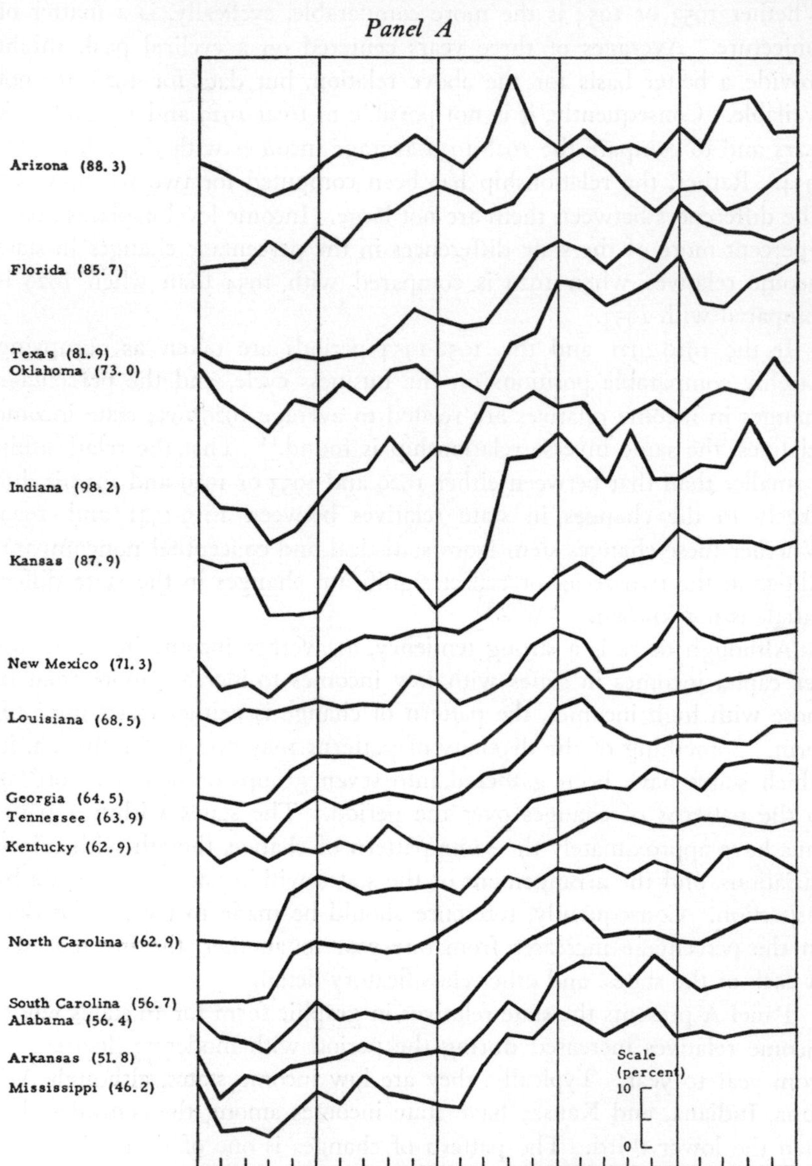

Note: The average 1929-1954 relative is in parenthesis following the state name.
Source: Table 4.

CHART 2 (Continued)

State Relatives of United States Per Capita Personal Income, 1929-1954

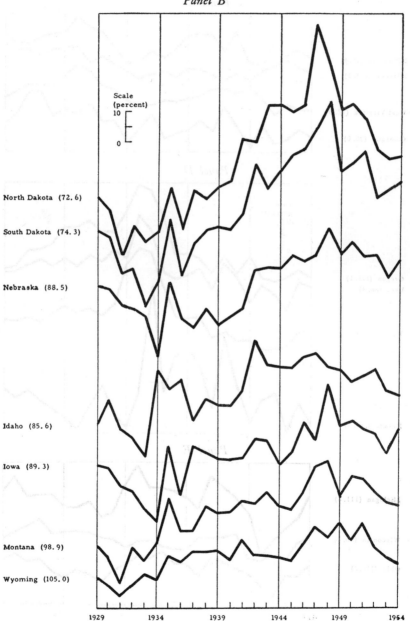

Panel B

Scale (percent)
10
0

North Dakota (72.6)
South Dakota (74.3)
Nebraska (88.5)
Idaho (85.6)
Iowa (89.3)
Montana (98.9)
Wyoming (105.0)

1929 1934 1939 1944 1949 1954

CHART 2 (Continued)

State Relatives of United States Per Capita Personal Income, 1929-1954

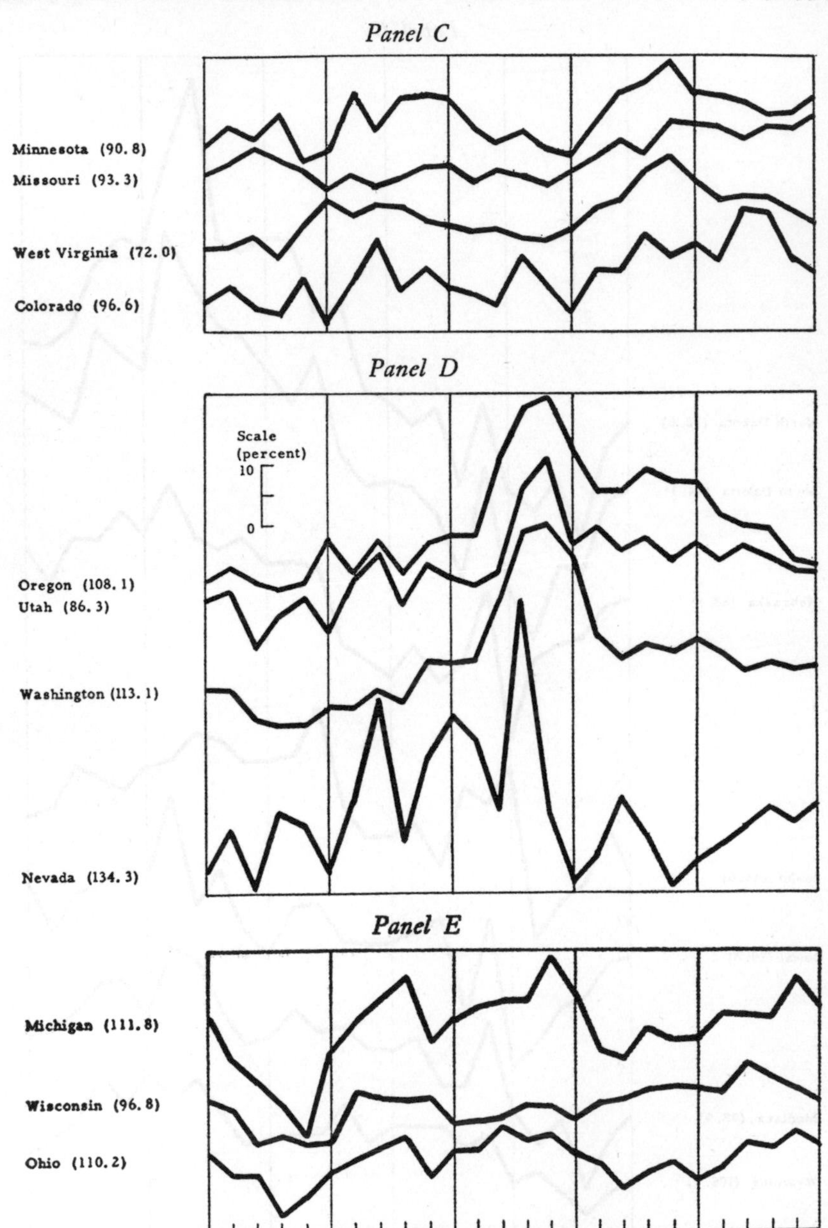

CHART 2 (Continued)

STATE RELATIVES OF UNITED STATES PER CAPITA PERSONAL INCOME, 1929-1954

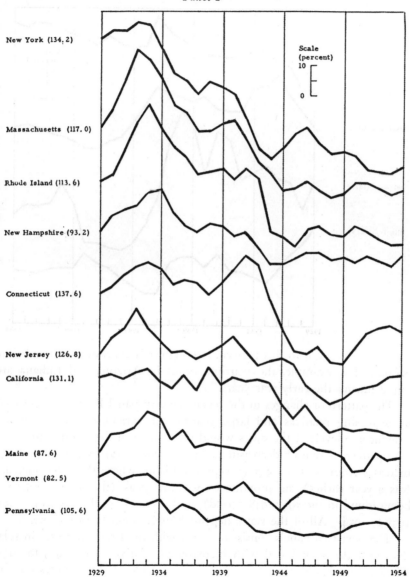

Panel F

CHART 2 (Continued)

STATE RELATIVES OF UNITED STATES PER CAPITA PERSONAL INCOME, 1929-1954

Panel G

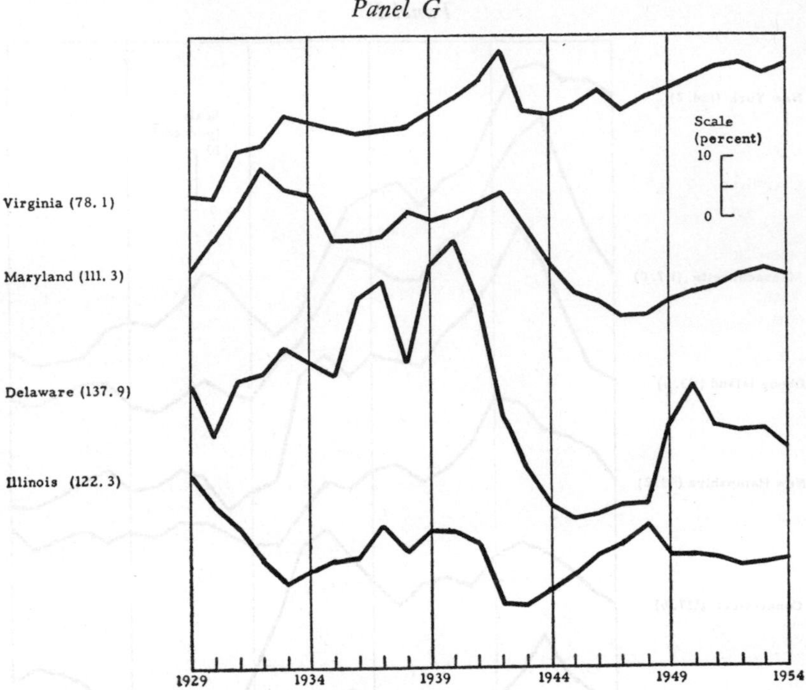

are exceptions even to this pattern, although it is expressed in broad time periods. For example, the wartime peaks in Arizona and Indiana are found during the early war years.

The pattern of changes in the seven states in panel B are characterized by increasing relatives and large year-to-year variation in the relatives. The income levels of the states would place them in the middle quartiles. The pattern is one of decreasing relatives from 1929 to 1931-1934, large increases from 1934 to 1935 (except for Idaho, where the large increase was a year earlier), no pronounced wartime peak (the highest relatives being found in the 1947-1948 period), and decreasing relatives from 1950-1951 to 1954. All of the states depend heavily upon farm income.

The next two panels consist of states with moderate increases in relatives over the period and with increases in relatives from 1929 to 1930. They are further distinguished by the amplitude of the changes and by their behavior during later years. The amplitude of changes in panel C is small compared to those in panel D. Of the four states in panel

C, only Colorado has a marked wartime peak (1942). The other states reach a peak in 1948. With the exception of West Virginia, which has a low income, the income levels of the other states are very close to the middle of the distribution. The four states in panel D have marked wartime peaks in 1942-1943, and their relatives tend to decrease after the war. With the exception of Utah, the states tend to have higher than average incomes.

Panel E consists of three states in which there is no marked change in relatives and the amplitude of year-to-year changes is very small. Each of these states, which have higher than average income levels, shows a moderate decrease in relatives from 1929 to 1933-1934.

The 10 states in panel F have decreasing relatives over the 1929-1954 period. Many of these states are among those with the highest income levels, although three New England states—New Hampshire, Maine, and Vermont—have incomes which place them in the central quartiles. These states, except for Connecticut, show an increase in relatives after 1929 and reach a peak during 1933-1934, when the average income level was lowest. Wartime peaks, if they exist, are not noticeable except in Connecticut (1941) and Maine (1943).

In a final panel have been gathered four states which do not seem to fit any of the above patterns. Virginia, which because of its income level seems to have characteristics in common with the states in panel A, is differentiated by large increases in relatives from 1930 to 1934, by an earlier wartime peak (1942), and by a secondary peak in 1952. Apparently Virginia's most significant changes occurred as the District of Columbia residential area expanded across the Potomac; since then, the income characteristics of the District significantly affect the pattern of change in Virginia.

While Maryland, another state significantly affected by the expansion of the District of Columbia, shows no significant change in the level of relatives from 1929 to 1953-1954 and has an income level similar to that of the states in panel E, the changes in its relatives are almost always opposite to those found in panel E.

Two states, Delaware and Illinois, which on the basis of their income levels might be expected to show decreases in their relatives and thus to be grouped with the states in panel F, actually show little or no net movement over the 1929-1954 period. On the latter basis they seem to be more nearly like the states in panel E. However, the year-to-year changes are much larger than those of the states in panel E, and only in an initial decline following 1929 do they show a similarity of pattern. The relatives for Delaware, whose average per capita income over the 1929-1954 period is higher than that of any other state, decrease from 1929 to 1930, increase by spurts to a peak in 1940, then steadily decrease from a relative of 169 in 1940 to one of 122 in 1945, increase to about the 1929 level by 1950, and decrease thereafter. The outstanding characteristic of the Illinois relatives is their decrease from 136 in 1929 to 118 in 1933, and except for the war years of 1942-1944, when they were in the neighborhood of 114-117, they have fluctuated in the range of 119-127.

The behavior of these relatives gives some clue as to why the coefficients of variation tend to move in a direction opposite from average per capita income. First, it may be recalled that it is the states with lower (higher) incomes whose relatives have tended to show an increase (decrease) over the entire period of 1929 to 1954, a period which tends to be dominated by rising income. An examination of the 1929-1933 depression period reveals that there is an opposite tendency. As average per capita income decreases, relatives of the lower (higher) income states tend to decrease (increase), thus increasing the relative dispersion measured by the coefficients of variation. The behavior of the individual states shows many departures from the timing of the group averages, however, and this effect is not so apparent in the recessions of 1937-1938, 1948-1949, and 1953-1954. Often the increase in the coefficient of variation is a year later than the decrease in income.

Regression

The state relatives examined in the previous section provide for direct comparisons of the changes in the per capita income of a state relative to the changes in that of the nation. If the per capita income of a state increases more between two years than does that of the nation, the state relative increases. Movements in the state relatives thus reflect changes in a state which are not proportional to the changes in the national average of the states. Such comparisons are valuable in that they reveal which states increased more, which less, than the average of all states. Unless each of the states were a representative cross-section of the forces which determine the level of income, there would be no reason to expect the state incomes to change proportionally. As a consequence, the changes in the national level cannot be used as a set of expected values against which to gauge the change in a particular state.

Both the coefficients of variation and the behavior of the state relatives indicate that with a rising income level the interstate per capita income differentials tend to become smaller; that is, with rising income the state per capita incomes tend to regress toward the mean. This fact provides a clue as to how the responses of individual states to changes in the income level may be gauged. Since there is evidence of regression, would a fitted regression line provide a statement of the amount of regression to be expected? If so, then the position of a state with respect to the regression line will provide a basis for gauging whether the observed change in a state's income is more or less than could be expected from the pattern of responses of all of the states. The remainder of this chapter will be devoted to this question.

Regression lines have been fitted only to the state per capita personal incomes of two pairs of years: 1929 and 1953, 1929 and 1954 (chart 3).

CHART 3

REGRESSION OF 1953 AND 1954 ON 1929 STATE PER CAPITA PERSONAL INCOME

Panel A

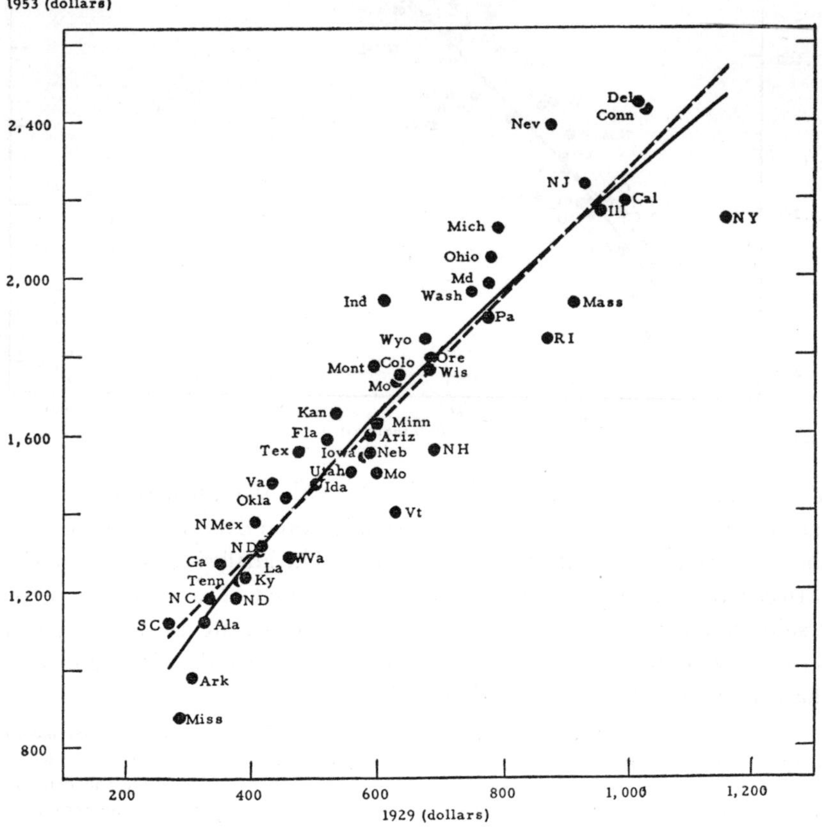

CHART 3 (Continued)

REGRESSION OF 1953 AND 1954 ON 1929 STATE PER CAPITA PERSONAL INCOME

Panel B

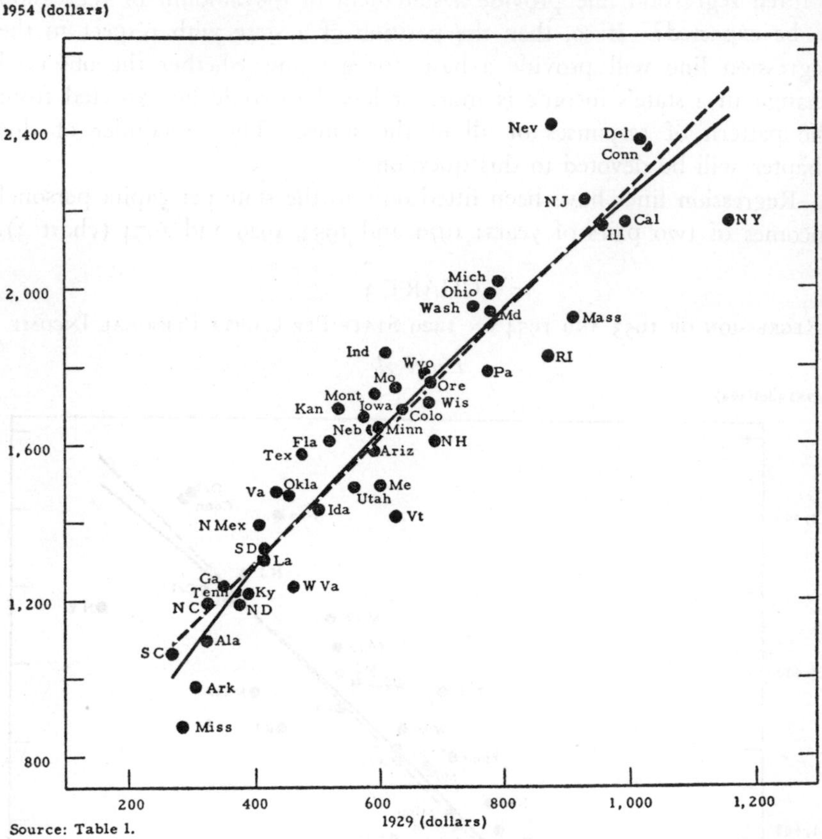

Source: Table 1.

These panels provide results for periods with the greatest number of intervening years for which state personal income data are available, and should be sufficient to illustrate the method. The analysis of the regression between these two pairs of years is supplemented by a summary of the results of an extensive analysis of the 1929-1949 state income payment series and of the Leven series for 1919-1921. The detailed results for the earlier period are provided in appendix A.[15]

[15] The size of the differences between the state income payments and personal income series, and the inconclusiveness of the 1929-1949 results, combine to make it appear worthwhile to rely on the results from the earlier series rather than to undertake the extensive computations required to incorporate the revisions in the state personal income series.

In fitting regression lines to the state per capita income data in chart 3, unweighted data were used. The differential changes in the population of the several states mean that only approximate population weights are available. Either an average of the 1929 and 1953 populations or the midyear population of some central year such as 1941 could have been used, but such a procedure is no more realistic than treating a state as a single observation. Weighting the states is tantamount to treating each person in the state as having the income characteristic of the state's average, and then entering the state's average in the regression as many times as there are people, although none of the possible weighting systems would produce interstate averages which equaled the national per capita income for a single year. Use of unweighted data in computing the regressions is based on the deviations of the states from the unweighted mean state income.

Two regression lines have been fitted to the data for 1929 and 1953 and for 1929 and 1954. One (shown as a dotted straight line) is fitted to the dollar per capita incomes. Such a line depicts the average change in the state incomes in terms of the dollar deviation from the mean state income. The percentage change in states more remote from the mean differs from that in states near the mean. When income is increasing, as it was from 1929 to 1953-1954, and the regression is positive, as it is here, the greater percentage increases are found below the mean, the smaller percentage increases above the mean.[16] For example, the percentage increase from 1929 to 1953 at South Carolina's 1929 level ($270) is 302 percent, while it is only 119 percent at New York's 1929 level ($1,159).

The other regression line (shown as a solid curved line) is fitted to the logarithms of the state per capita incomes.[17] This line depicts the average change in state incomes in terms of percentage (rather than dollar) deviations from the (geometric) mean state income. Although the 1953 logarithmic line provides a significantly better fit than does the linear line, that for 1954 does not.[18] Both logarithmic lines follow the

[16] The regression line is of the type $Y = a + bX$, where Y denotes the income of the latter year estimated from the former, X denotes the income in the earlier year, and a and b are constants. For 1953 and 1929, the value of a, the Y intercept, is $645, and b, the slope of the regression line, is 1.63. For 1954 and 1929, a is $657 and b is 1.59.

[17] It would appear as a straight line were the state per capita incomes plotted on logarithmic paper. It is of the type $\log Y = \log a + b \log X$, or $Y = aX^b$, with these symbols defined as they are in the previous footnote. The value of the constants are:

	log a	*b*
1929 and 1953	1.51042	.61397
1929 and 1954	1.52100	.60881

[18] In using analysis of variance to test the significance of the difference between the two regressions, the logarithmic line was assumed to be a curved line against a natural

linear lines quite closely. Within the range of the data the maximum difference between the two lines for 1929 and 1953 is found at the lower end of the distribution and amounts to $78. Like the linear regression, the logarithmic regression shows a percentage increase greater (273 percent) at South Carolina's than at New York's income level (113 percent). Unlike the linear regression, in which the regression toward the mean is proportional to dollar deviation from the mean state income, the logarithmic regression is greater at the upper than at the lower end of the distribution.

Although ample evidence has been developed (from the coefficients of variation and state income relatives) that regression does exist, it may be asked whether this phenomenon is to be expected on a priori grounds or whether it is a peculiarity of the particular data. One common-sense reason why we might expect to find regression in the relationship of the income of two years has almost general application. The extreme states—the states with lowest and the highest per capita incomes—in the absence of regression would become more extreme. The poor states would become relatively poorer and the rich still richer—a possibility, of course. But the extent to which historical accidents, unusual combinations of circumstances, or transient forces, rather than economic considerations, have produced the extreme income characteristics makes it unlikely that this extremeness will persist or grow more extreme. Phenomena of this type have been observed repeatedly.[19]

Are there specific reasons, however, why state per capita incomes might be expected to regress toward the mean? A brief examination of a few of the changes that accompany the increases in level of national income may provide an answer to this question.

First, consider the level of employment. Might not the larger gains in employment (whether measured by the reduction of the number totally unemployed or by the fuller employment of those partially employed) be expected to occur in those states where manpower resources are less fully employed? Certainly these states have room for expanded employment, and states with high employment would experience greater difficulty in increasing employment still further. Presumably there is a limit—full employment of their entire labor force—beyond which the high-employment states cannot go. The closer they are to that limit, the more difficult

scale and to have one fewer degrees of freedom. The 1953 logarithmic line was barely a significant improvement over the linear line at the .05 significance level.

[19] Harold E. Hotelling, "Review of Horace Secrist's *The Triumph of Mediocrity in Business*," *Journal of the American Statistical Association*, 28 (1933), 463-465. Cf. Secrist, "Reply" and Hotelling, "Rejoinder," *ibid.*, 29 (1934), 196-200.

it is likely to be for them to progress further. The per capita incomes resulting from the increase in employment will lie closer to the mean at both extremes.

Furthermore, as full employment is approached and even temporary and local labor shortages are experienced, changes in the wage and occupation structure are likely to reinforce the income effects of increased employment. Opportunities for employment in the more highly paid occupations will be filled first by those with known qualifications for the jobs from among those either unemployed or working in less remunerative occupations. If such opportunities persist, they are likely to be filled by promotion, perhaps even by promoting persons who have many, but not all, of the qualifications required for the job and paying them the higher rates while they acquire the remaining qualifications. Such shifts, in turn, leave openings in the next lower stratum of occupations. Somewhere in the occupational hierarchy, upgrading particular jobs may be necessary to keep them filled and may set into motion a train of wage adjustments. The adjustments are likely to be larger at the lower end of the scale, since it is here that additional inducements may be more effective in tapping a qualified labor supply. The wages required to keep filled some low productivity jobs, such as domestic service, may become so high that many prospective openings are priced out of the market. One result of such a series of shifts would be a narrowing of the differentials between occupations.[20] To some extent we might also expect some narrowing of the differentials between states, not so much because there is perfect mobility of labor as because the states with low per capita incomes tend to be states with low-paying industries, which are compelled to raise wages relatively more.[21]

Many other adjustments to a rising level of employment and economic activity operate with much the same effect. Agricultural prices, the source of much of the state income at the lower end of the income scale, fluctuate more than do the prices of manufactured products.[22] New plants, one method of expanding existing production, are likely to be

[20] F. Meyers, "Notes on Changes in the Distribution of Manufacturing Wage Earners by Straight-time Hourly Earnings, 1941-48," *Review of Economics and Statistics,* 32 (1950), 352-355, gives the results for the United States. Cf. P. W. Bell, "Cyclical Variations and Trend in Occupational Wage Differentials in American Industry since 1914," *ibid.,* 33 (1951), 329-337, and the literature there cited. See also Edwin Mansfield, "Wage Differentials in the Cotton Textile Industry, 1933-52," *ibid.,* 37 (1955), 77-82, and Herman P. Miller, *Income of the American People,* New York, 1955, chapter 5.

[21] See below, chapters 5 and 6.

[22] Clement Winston and Mabel A. Smith, "Income Sensitivity of Consumption Expenditures," *Survey of Current Business,* January 1950, p. 17.

located where labor, power, water, materials, etc., are available—that is, where existing resources are underemployed.[23] There is increased migration from the farms to urbanized places, and often this also means migration from lower-income to higher-income states.[24] The list can be extended.[25]

From these and similar considerations it may be expected that the per capita incomes of states near the bottom of the distribution will increase more than proportionally and those near the top of the distribution will increase less than proportionally; that is, there will be some regression toward the mean during periods of rising economic activity and a movement away from the mean during periods of decreasing economic activity.

Although there seems to be ample basis for concluding that regression is to be expected, the question still remains as to whether either of the regression lines fitted to the 1929 and 1953 or 1929 and 1954 data adequately describes the regression. For example, might not a curvilinear line better describe the expected changes among the states? If so, what kind of a curve might best fit the data?

If we confine our attention to chart 3, there is little to suggest that a better description of the data would be provided by some line that had more curve than the logarithmic linear regression line. If, for example, more curve was introduced at the upper end of the line, so that it would be closer to the point for New York, such a line would provide a poorer fit for Delaware and Connecticut. Similarly, more curve at the lower end of the line would provide a better fit for Arkansas and Mississippi, but a poorer fit for South Carolina. Experiments with fitting second degree parabolas did not prove helpful. Among the mathematically fitted curves, the logarithmic curve appears to provide the best description of these data. The use of the logarithmic curve, which curves downward at both extremes, rather than linear regression based on the dollar amounts, may be easily rationalized. States with extremely low incomes, such as the Southern states, while they have many partially used resources, may require much time-consuming capital expansion before they are able to respond to a given stimulus. At the other end of the distribution further expansion may prove uneconomical. The states near the mean, how-

[23] Cf. E. M. Hoover, *The Location of Economic Activity,* New York, 1948.

[24] The percent of the total population on farms decreased from 25 percent in 1930 to 23 percent in 1940 and to 16 percent in 1950. *Statistical Abstract of the United States, 1951,* pp. 14 and 912.

[25] Many additional adjustments have been treated in recent studies of two regions, C. B. Hoover and B. U. Ratchford, *Economic Resources and Policies of the South,* New York, 1951; New England Council, *The New England Economy,* Washington, 1951; and Seymour Harris, *The Economics of New England,* Cambridge, 1952.

ever, may be able economically to respond to a given stimulus more rapidly, in percentage terms, than those at either extremity of the distribution.

When the regressions for all of the possible pairs of years are computed, as they have been for 1929-1949 state income payments (appendix A), the weight of the evidence seems to suggest that a curvilinear line which starts somewhat below the linear one, rises somewhat faster to somewhere within the third quartile, and then curves downward to about or slightly below the linear regression at the upper end of the distribution might describe the changes in the state per capita incomes adequately. For the reasons given in appendix A, the exact position of such a line cannot be ascertained. It seems reasonably clear that it would lie fairly close to the linear regression throughout the distribution. It is also clear that for pairs of years when there is marked positive regression (that is, when the Y-intercept is $100 or more) such a line approximates much more closely the linear regression line than it does the line of proportional change (that is, a straight line through the origin and the mean state incomes).

Although some error is involved in using the logarithmic regression line as a statement of expectations, this error is less than would be involved in hypothecating changes in the states which are proportional to the changes in the simple average of all the states (that is, in the mean state incomes). If the logarithmic regression line is accepted as a statement of expectations, it then can be concluded that the states below this line have not experienced as much increase in income as would be expected from the pattern of behavior of all of the states. Such a statement treats the change from one period to another as a function not only of the change in average income, but also as a function of the state's income in the earlier of the years compared.[26]

Except for a few states in the central quartiles of the distribution, the states below the 1929 and 1953 logarithmic regression line (panel A, chart 3) are the same ones that are below the 1929 and 1954 logarithmic regression line (panel B). Some interest attaches to the states which are below the line in one year and above it in another. The states which

[26] Although regression is here used only to describe the differential behavior of the various states during the 1929-1954 period, this functional aspect of using the regression line as a set of expectations is worth emphasis. The position of the line for any initial-year income level is determined by the behavior of all the states; the only degrees of freedom sacrificed are those associated with the number of constants in the regression equation. It is not an estimate, in some sampling context, of the mean position of a large number of states all of which had the same initial-year income. Cf. Edward F. Denison, "Comment," in *Studies in Income and Wealth,* 21 (Princeton, 1956), 161-179.

change position with respect to the logarithmic regression line include Iowa, Nebraska, and Minnesota, all Midwest farming states. In addition, South Dakota and Illinois were definitely on one side or the other of the 1929 and 1953 regression line but were on or very close to that for 1929 and 1954. The behavior of these states indicates that the irregular and transitory factors affecting a state's income during a particular year can be quite large. This fact makes it hazardous to rely on generalizations about the behavior of individual states, based on the regression between a single pair of years.

While the mean state income of both 1953 and 1954 is well above that of 1929, there was a slight decrease from 1953 to 1954. The 1954 per capita incomes of 17 of the states were equal to or greater than those of 1953. That the two panels of the chart show so much similarity is due partially to the very large increase between 1929 and 1953, and partially to the smallness of the decrease from 1953 to 1954.

Chapter 3

CYCLICAL BEHAVIOR OF DIFFERENTIALS

As WITH most economic time series, state per capita personal incomes result from a mixture of cyclical, secular, and irregular elements. Before any of these sets of elements can be analyzed, they have to be separated from the other elements. When the series covers a sufficiently long period, a trend may be so pronounced that conclusions concerning it are little affected by ignoring the presence of cyclical forces. For example, it is generally accepted that over the past fifty years automobile manufacture has become a major industry and buggy manufacture has all but disappeared. During certain periods, such as the great depression of the early thirties, cyclical forces may become so pronounced that trends are almost completely overwhelmed. For relatively short periods, the problem of separating and measuring the sets of forces making for differential growth among the states is increased by the presence of forces making for differential cyclical variation among the states. Similarly, the existence of differential growth among the states increases the problem of isolating and measuring the response of individual states to business cycles.

It was suggested in the last chapter that because cyclical forces were ignored the behavior of the state relatives provides a doubtful clue as to differential state growth. This chapter accords primary emphasis to state cyclical patterns, though some attention is, as it must be, accorded secular forces. The investigation of the state responses to cyclical and secular forces is directed more toward understanding the behavior of the state income differentials during the period of 1929-1954 than it is toward making an incontrovertible separation and measurement of these two sets of forces for a particular state.

It is now well known that the cylical responses of individual industries or commodities vary greatly as to timing, magnitude, and the degree of price adjustments.[1] The onset of recession (or revival) in some

[1] Geoffrey Moore, *Statistical Indicators of Cyclical Revivals and Recessions*, National

industries precedes, while it follows in others, the average pattern of all industries. In some industries production is curtailed with the onset of recession, in an effort to equate supply and demand at going prices. In other industries prices are reduced in an attempt to clear the market of a stable supply of products. State incomes are affected by the differential cyclical behavior of industries and commodities. The income of a state like Michigan, for example, which tends to concentrate on the production of cyclically sensitive durable commodities, is likely to be more affected by a change in the business pace than is a state like Rhode Island, which tends to concentrate more on the less sensitive nondurables. Although personal income, which is based on income received rather than income produced, is not the most appropriate measure, it is not unreasonable to view the cyclical behavior of a state's income as the weighted average of the cyclical behavior of the commodities and services it produces.

It would be difficult to conceive of a period in which state income differentials are not affected by cyclical influences. The effect of these influences must be taken into account before it is possible to speak with confidence about differential state growth. Similarly, differential growth must be taken into account before cyclical influences may be measured with confidence. This chapter starts with a discussion of several of the methods that have been proposed for dealing with these ubiquitous sets of forces.

The Problem of Measurement

One method that has been used to measure trend seeks to avoid the effects of cyclical factors in much the same way that the use of annual data avoids the effects of seasonal variation. It involves the selection of widely separated years that occupy about the same position with respect to the business cycle and that are free from major distorting elements. It is then assumed that in each period the relationships of industries to one another are not dissimilar in any important respect. Thus, an appropriate choice of the periods to be compared can, it is hoped, eliminate cyclically based differentials. This method is appealing because of its simplicity.[2]

Bureau of Economic Research Occasional Paper No. 31, New York, 1950. See also J. M. Clark, *Strategic Factors in Business Cycles*, New York, 1934, and Gardiner C. Means, *Industrial Prices and Their Relative Inflexibility*, Senate Document 13, 74th Congress, 1st Session (1935).

[2] Charles F. Schwartz, "Regional Trends in Income Payments," *Survey of Current Business* (September 1948). These results are extended in Schwartz and Robert E.

This method depends upon the availability of data for two widely separated periods about which the judgment may be made that each is at approximately the same stage of the business cycle. For a single industry the selection of such a pair of years ordinarily does not present insurmountable problems. The average lead or lag of a single industry with respect to the turning points of a business cycle often can be determined with reasonable accuracy, although variations in timing are to be noted from one cycle to another for specific industries.[3] For an individual industry available data often make it possible to determine exact turning points, the amplitude of the recession and recovery periods, and other pertinent information. When many industries are being considered simultaneously, the selection of appropriate years is more difficult since each of the industries must be at about the same cyclical position in each of the years selected. Since the industrial composition of the states differs, the offsetting of one industry leading, another lagging, is of little help. The problem thus reduces to one of finding two sets of years during the 1929-1954 period when each of the states will occupy a comparable cyclical position.

The peak of the boom preceding the great depression occurred in 1929, the earliest year for which data are available. Since then, there have been three turning points introducing mild or limited recessions: 1937, 1948, and 1953. After these short-lived slow-downs, national income has again shown several years of steady increase. Whether any of these turning points might be comparable with 1929 is doubtful. Some light on this question may be gained by determining whether all of the states followed the change in the national per capita income. When national per capita income decreased, it is found that 1930 income was below that of 1929 in all 48 states; that 2 states had higher income in 1938 than in 1937; that 10 had higher incomes in 1949 than in 1948; and that 17 had higher incomes in 1954 than in 1953. Similar, though not such marked, differences are found as income turned upward from the cyclical troughs. Per capita incomes are found to be lower in one state in 1934 than in 1933, in two states in 1939 than in 1938, and in one state in 1950 than in 1949. This differential behavior could result from marked trends in some of the states, but if this were the case it would tend to be the same states which deviated at each of the peaks or troughs. The data hardly support this case. While five of the ten states in which 1929 income was greater than

Graham, Jr., "State Income Payments, 1948," *ibid.* (August 1949), and "State Income Payments, 1949," *ibid.* (August 1950).

[3] Moore, *op. cit.*

that of 1948 also had 1954 income greater than that of 1953, only one of them had greater income in 1938 than in 1937. One state, Nebraska, had smaller income in both 1934 and 1939 than in the previous years.

The percentage decreases following 1929 are quite large (chapter 2, table 2), totaling some 47 percent by 1933. Compared with these decreases, extending over a period of four years, the recessions since then have been mild. Only the 1937-1938 decrease of 8 percent is as large as that of any one of the years between 1929 and 1933. It seems doubtful that the cyclical position of each of the industries was the same in the later years as it was during any year of the great depression.

If the effects of cyclical forces cannot be avoided so that trend may be measured directly, it becomes necessary to take explicit account of these forces. There are three general approaches to this problem, each of which has its own peculiar data requirements, and the results provided emphasize various aspects of the problem. These approaches will be considered in turn.

The first approach is based on the assumption that the cyclical pattern of each particular industry is nation-wide. Such an assumption holds that the response of a specific industry to a change in the business climate is the same whether the industry is located in Maine or California, Washington or Georgia. If industrial classification is sufficiently detailed so that this assumption is acceptable, then it is possible to ascertain whether a particular industry has grown relatively more in one state than in another. Since the same cyclical pattern is assumed present in every state, it is necessary only to express the activity in each state as percentages of the national total for the industry for each year to obtain direct evidence on relative growth by state. Index number techniques provide a way of aggregating this information and of ascertaining the growth of each state relative to that of the nation. Since each industry provides its own base and the states are taken relative to that base, presumably it would matter little whether the measurements are made when the industry is booming or is depressed. The influence of the points on the business cycle chosen for measurement becomes important, however, in choosing the weights with which to combine the results for several industries. Ideally, such weights should include periods of both rising and falling income and be of sufficient length to dampen the effects of random influences.

Since it is based on data classified industrially, this method is applicable only where there is no significant difference between the location of the activity giving rise to income and the location of the recipient. Except for a few areas in which workers commute across state lines, the method is adequate to deal with wage and salary and proprietors' income. For property income and probably for transfer payments, the locational differences are too great. This limitation alone is sufficient to make the method unavailable for dealing with all of personal income. Moreover, only for the manufacturing sector, and then only for census years, are wage and salary data available in sufficient industrial detail.

It may be worth noting that, while the effects of cyclical variation are fully taken into account, this method provides no direct information on the differential response of the states to cyclical influences. However, when adequate information is available on the trends of each of the states, the deviations from these trends provide the information necessary for computing cyclical behavior.

The second approach is similar to the first but involves the aggregation of industries with similar cyclical patterns. Thus, in addition to assuming that the cyclical pattern of each industry is nation-wide, it also assumes that industries may be classified according to their cyclical patterns, so that only the differences between relatively few classes need be recognized.[4] This additional assumption introduces a degree of approximation that is difficult to measure. It should be noted, however, that in grouping industries explicit account is taken of variations in cyclical patterns; the major groups provided in the standard classification system often are based on other criteria.

In addition to being subject to all of the limitations of the individual industry approach, the second approach is crude enough that little reliance can be placed on more than a rank order of the states by trend—that is, that one state increased more or decreased less than another state. Even this type of conclusion may be shaky for two states having much the same trends.

The third approach, and the one used here, uses multiple regression to separate and measure directly the cyclical characteristics of the states. Forces making for a trend are noted only when they are marked. Even then they are treated as residuals unexplained by cyclical variations. The measures provided for these residuals cannot always be interpreted as

[4] The question of selecting criteria suitable for grouping industries according to cyclical pattern is left open. Presumably there is more than one way that this could be done while holding the amount of within-class variance within acceptable limits. In my *Wisconsin during the Depression,* Madison, 1936, industries were grouped according to a classification of their principal products, with the categories based on those of John M. Clark, *Strategic Factors in Business Cycles,* New York, 1934. This classification appeared to be highly correlated with the cyclical pattern of each industry. Such a classification could be applied only to the manufacturing sector.

measures of trend alone, and often must be taken only as indicative that trends do exist.

The measure adopted, called a sensitivity index, is designed to reflect the average percentage change in a state's per capita income which is associated with a unitary percentage change in national per capita income (table 6). The sensitivity index for Maine, for example, indicates that a 1.00 percent change in national per capita income is associated with a change in Maine's per capita income of 0.93 percent *in the same direction*. Thus, Maine's per capita income changes relatively less than that of the nation and may be said to be relatively insensitive. On the other hand, Michigan's sensitivity index of 1.05 shows that a 1.00 percent change in national per capita income is associated with a change in Michigan's per capita income of 1.05 percent, again in the same direction. Thus, Michigan may be said to be relatively sensitive to cyclical fluctuations.

Sensitivity Indexes

The sensitivity indexes were computed by ordinary regression methods for each state for the period 1929-1954.[5] Before the simple regression coefficient between state and national per capita incomes was accepted as the state's sensitivity index, however, it was tested to see whether there was any significant time-order in the differences between the state per capita incomes computed from the simple regression equation containing the sensitivity index and the National Income Division estimates from which the regression was computed.[6] When there was a significant time-order in the differences, the net coefficient computed from the multiple regression was accepted in lieu of the simple coefficient. Otherwise, the simple coefficient was accepted as the sensitivity index. When time proved a significant variable, the net regression coefficient of time was saved for further analysis and is called the time-factor index.

The time-factor index shows the rate by which income changed annually over and above the change accounted for by the sensitivity index.

[5] If for a particular state we let X_1 represent the state per capita personal income and X_2 represent the national per capita personal income for each of the 26 years from 1929 to 1954, and to the logarithms of X_1 and X_2 we fit a least-squares regression line of the type: $\log X_{12} = \log a + b_{12} \log X_2$, where X_{12} represents state per capita personal income estimated from X_2, the coefficient b is the crude sensitivity index.

[6] This was done by introducing a second independent variable, X_3, time (year minus 1941), and computing the multiple regression: $\log X_{1.23} = \log a' + b_{12.3} \log X_2 + X_3 \log b_{13.2}$. Analysis of variance was then used to test whether the additional variance accounted for by the introduction of X_3 was significant at the .05 level of probability. This test is equivalent to fitting a trend line to the differences between the computed and the National Income Division estimates ordered by year and testing to see if the trend line departed significantly from zero.

TABLE 6

PERSONAL INCOME SENSITIVITY AND TIME-FACTOR INDEXES, BY STATE

State	Sensitivity index	Time-factor index	Average error (percent)
New England			
Maine	.93	...	3.2
New Hampshire	.86	...	2.2
Vermont	.98	–.4	1.5
Massachusetts	.78	...	3.1
Rhode Island	.78	...	2.6
Connecticut	.87	...	3.5
Middle Atlantic			
New York	.94	–1.1	2.3
New Jersey	.90	...	2.6
Pennsylvania	.94	...	2.0
East North Central			
Ohio	1.02	...	2.5
Indiana	1.06	.7	3.3
Illinois	1.06	–.5	2.6
Michigan	1.05	...	4.3
Wisconsin	1.05	...	2.0
West North Central			
Minnesota	1.03	...	3.6
Iowa	1.17	...	6.1
Missouri	1.05	...	2.3
North Dakota	1.47	...	14.1
South Dakota	1.44	...	11.2
Nebraska	1.21	...	5.4
Kansas	1.25	...	3.9
South Atlantic			
Delaware	.75	1.0	5.5
Maryland	.90	...	3.1
D. C.	.58	...	5.3
Virginia	.85	1.9	2.3
West Virginia	1.05	...	3.9
North Carolina	.96	1.8	4.2
South Carolina	.96	2.4	5.1
Georgia	1.04	1.3	3.6
Florida	.96	1.0	3.2
East South Central			
Kentucky	1.18	...	2.4
Tennessee	1.19	...	3.9
Alabama	1.27	...	4.4
Mississippi	1.28	...	6.0
West South Central			
Arkansas	1.14	.9	5.0
Louisiana	1.05	.7	2.9
Oklahoma	1.24	...	3.8
Texas	1.10	.9	2.6
Mountain			
Montana	.98	1.3	5.0
Idaho	1.14	...	7.1
Wyoming	.96	.8	3.5
Colorado	1.06	...	3.2
New Mexico	1.08	1.3	2.7
Arizona	1.07	...	3.0
Utah	1.08	...	4.6
Nevada	.97	...	5.4
Pacific			
Washington	1.07	...	5.0
Oregon	1.07	...	5.6
California	.94	–.4	2.0

Source: table 1. For method of computation, see text.

Significant time-factor indexes were found for only 17 states. The index for Indiana, for example, shows that, in addition to a change of 1.06 percent being associated with a 1.00 percent change in national per capita income, the per capita income of Indiana has been growing at a rate of 0.7 percent per year. This figure represents a cumulative growth in Indiana per capita income of 18.2 percent over the 1929-1954 period and is not explained by the association of the state and national changes.

The sensitivity and time-factor indexes, together with a knowledge of the national per capita income level, would provide the same estimate of state per capita income as that provided by the National Income Division if the state differentials were the results of only regular and persistent forces. The fact that the cyclical patterns of some industries vary from one cycle to another, the presence of specific and transitory forces (such as floods, droughts, strikes, fires, and governmental action such as soldiers' bonuses), and the differential and ever-changing trends experienced by various commodities and industries, combine to make for differences between the two sets of estimates. These differences have been treated as estimating errors, and their average magnitude is shown in the final column of table 6.[7] Only in the Dakotas do these average errors exceed 8 percent. The Dakotas, where income depends largely on highly volatile agricultural sources, have the highest sensitivity indexes of all the states. The size of the errors attaching to them is a warning that indexes for these states are not very reliable. Thirty-one of the remaining states have average errors of less than 4 percent.

Limitations

Before the sensitivity and time-factor indexes are analyzed further, their limitations should be made explicit.

As with most time series there is the inevitable conflict between the advantages gained by way of additional degrees of freedom, as the time period and number of observations are increased, and the possibility that the ubiquitous small changes will cumulate to the point that they affect the relationships in a fundamental way. The period covered consists of the 26 years from 1929 through 1954.

This periods includes the great depression, World War II, the postwar reconversion period, and the Korean affair. Can any of these times be considered "normal" in the sense that economic forces determine the distribution of economic activity among the states? Certainly if electric refrigerators were the subject of study, the data relating to the war and early postwar period would have to be omitted, since during these years the supply of refrigerators was limited by governmental (rather than

[7] The percentage errors shown are the average of the 26 absolute differences, $(X_1 - X_{12})$ or $(X_1 - X_{1.23})$ expressed as a percentage of the computed figure, e.g., $100 \Sigma (X_1 - X_{12}) / X_{12} / 26$, where the sum is taken over the 26 years. The averages are used in lieu of the customary standard error of estimate as a measure of the dispersion of points about the regression line, because the latter would be given in logarithms and would require additional computations to appraise.

economic) action. Must some years be omitted from an analysis of personal income? I think not.[8]

The comprehensiveness of personal income as a measure of economic activity would seem to make the omission of troubled years unnecessary. It is true, of course, that many of the governmental decisions taken during the war were not based on economic considerations alone. Camps were located, roads were built, production of certain items curtailed or prohibited, materials allocated, and families uprooted and moved from their customary homes. Such decisions affect the distribution of income among the states. Even the removal of persons from one area to another, whether accomplished by economic inducements or by the exercise of eminent domain proceedings, often resulted in lifting the per capita income of both the area from which they departed and the area to which they moved. The pace of the economic activity during the war was such that labor scarcities developed in many places, and the government was continuously faced with problems of allocating scarce resources. Basically, economic inducements rather than patriotic appeal were used in solving these problems. The conditions under which these economic inducements could be realized were often distasteful but did not prevent the achievement of a high level of economic activity. Another reason for including the war years is the great interest in how the states responded to the economic stimuli provided by mobilization for defense.

This is not to say that the period of war mobilization and reconversion did not engender many temporary and irregular forces affecting state income. It is necessary only to recall the uneven geographic distribution of war-associated construction and of the bonuses paid veterans by some states to know that irregular elements were present and of significant magnitude. The contention is only that when a comprehensive measure such as personal income is the basis of the analysis, the reasons for excluding the years in which these irregular events can be positively identified are not as compelling as when the subject of analysis is distinctly limited. The reason for this contention may be summarized by saying that the direct alternatives, as well as their secondary and more remote effects, are also included in the measure. Were there trade barriers among the states, then the altering of these barriers might be sufficient reason for omitting years during which the alterations were effective. But even in the case of state soldier bonuses, some of their effects are

[8] Cf. Schwartz, *op. cit.*, p. 11, ". . . the war may be viewed as one big random element."

likely to cross state lines. Moreover, many of the products and services purchased by the government in increased quantities during a war are also purchased in other years. Public works, for example, are likely to be an irregular source of income whenever and wherever they are undertaken. If their number and amount are small, they are likely to have a greater differential effect among the states than when they are large and their location widespread. Nor is the construction activity undertaken by government much different from similar activity undertaken in response to private decisions. The construction of a hotel in Nevada or of a large chemical plant in South Carolina can give a short-run lift to the per capita income of the state.

Random or irregular elements, whenever they occur, affect the relationship of some state incomes to national per capita income. It is conceivable that the pattern of these irregular influences might be such that they affect the size of the sensitivity indexes, but this result is not to be expected. If the pattern of such elements is truly a random one, their influence will be confined to the error component. Thus, a small state like Nevada might be expected to have a larger error component than a large state like New York, simply on the score that a single irregular influence might be large enough to become apparent in Nevada while many of them would have to be cumulative in one direction even to be noticeable in a densely populated state. Similarly, states deriving large portions of their income from farming, which is particularly susceptible to irregular influences of weather and market conditions, might be expected to have higher errors than the more industrialized states.

The methods used for deriving the sensitivity and time-factor indexes work best when the periods of increasing and of decreasing income are equally frequent and when their amplitudes are approximately the same. Were all changes in the same direction, say toward increasing income, the method could not be used. The "sensitivity index" which could be computed from such data would reflect only the average percentage by which a state's income increased for each one-percent increase in national income. Such an index would not be reversible. It would include both trend and cyclical forces.[9] The period for which data are available does not meet these conditions completely. Only 7 of the 25 year-to-year

[9] For an extreme example see Edward F. Denison, "Comment" on my "Analysis of Interstate Income Differentials: Theory and Procedure," in *Studies in Income and Wealth*, vol. 21, Princeton, 1957. Louis J. Paradiso and Clement Winston, "Consumer Expenditure-Income Patterns," *Survey of Current Business* (September 1955), pp. 23-32, had difficulty with this fact in dealing with 1947-1954 consumers' expenditures.

changes were decreases (chapter 2, table 2).[10] The average size of the percentage change from the previous year is approximately 10 percent for years of both increase and decrease. Although fewer than a third of the years show a contraction of income, apparently such years are numerous enough to permit the derivation of a reversible sensitivity index.[11]

Although there are enough periods of contraction during 1929-1954 to provide a reversible sensitivity index that reflects cyclical forces chiefly, it is possible that some element of trend is also contained. Significant time-factor indexes were found for only 17 of the states. If the sensitivity indexes did not reflect some elements of trend, would not more of the states have significant time-factor indexes? A definitive answer to such a question is not possible. There are both technical and substantive reasons why many states do not show significant time-factor indexes. First, the test for significance is fairly rigorous. Too, the manner in which the time-factor index is computed is equivalent to computing a simple logarithmic regression between residuals from the least-squares logarithmic regression of state and national per capita incomes.[12] Consequently, even though a real trend existed but departed widely from the logarithmic linear form, the logarithmic linear time-factor index might be nonsignificant.

When a least-squares linear trend line is fitted to the logarithms of the national per capita personal income (chart 4), the line intersects the curve about two-thirds of the way from the 1929 peak to the 1933 trough, about one-half of the way from the 1938 trough to the 1948 peak, and at about one-third of the way from the 1953 peak to the 1954 trough. The curve is S-shaped around the linear trend. Much the same type of fit is found for the states.[13] The slope of the trend lines, in logarithmic form, is .02722 for the nation and varies from .02070 in New York to .04046 in North Dakota. Whether a state has a significant time-factor index depends not only on the state having a logarithmic linear trend which differs from the one for the nation, but also on the departures from the state and national linear trends. If the departures differ in direction,

[10] The reference cycles of the National Bureau of Economic Research for the 1929-1950 period show 77 months of contraction and 187 months of expansion. Daniel Creamer, *Personal Income during Business Cycles,* Princeton, 1956, table A.

[11] If the indexes were not reversible, larger errors could be expected during years of contraction. The average size of the errors during periods of contraction is not markedly different from their size during periods of expansion. See below.

[12] Ragnar Frisch and F. V. Waugh, "Partial Time Regressions as Compared with Individual Trends," *Econometrica,* 1 (1933), 387.

[13] These relatively poorly fitting logarithmic linear trends assure that the sensitivity indexes will be significant by any formal test.

then the more highly they are correlated the more likely there is to be a significant time-factor index. Departures in the same directions are more likely to produce a significant time factor when the correlation is not too high. Basically, the existence of a significant time-factor index is dependent upon the time-order of the departures from the logarithmic linear trends.

CHART 4

PER CAPITA PERSONAL INCOME, UNITED STATES, 1929-1954, SHOWING LEAST-SQUARES LOGARITHMIC LINEAR TREND

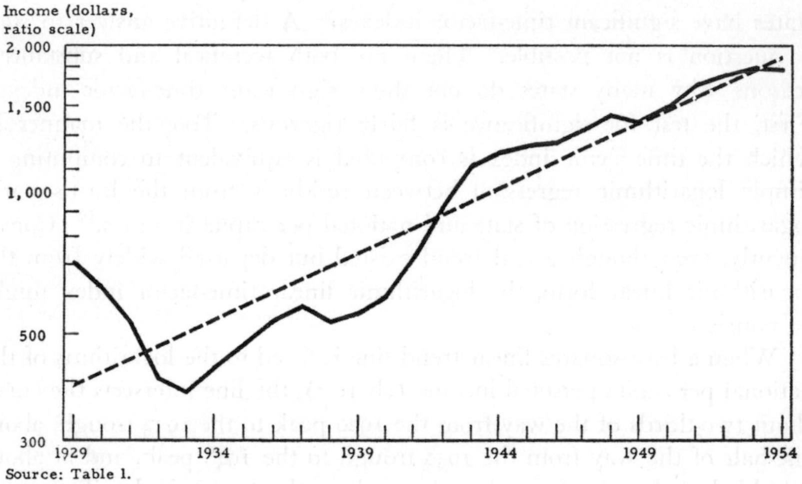

Source: Table 1.

It would be desirable to be able to take more explicit account of changes in industrial composition, particularly since the sensitivity indexes are supposed to reflect the differences between a state's and the nation's industrial composition, at least with respect to the differential cyclical response of each industry. Since year-to-year changes in a state's industrial composition are not included in its sensitivity indexes, the sensitivity index must be interpreted as reflecting only the average industrial composition of the state over the period 1929-1954. The sensitivity index provides a measure of the average change in the per capita income of a state relative to a change in the national per capita income. Differential changes in income-determining factors among the states are more likely to show up in the time-factor index (if they have been present for some time) or as errors. Some of these differential changes, such as inflation, may be cyclical phenomena, so that it is desirable to include their effects in the sensitivity index. But the differential changes during 1929-1954, which are based on the development or expansion of new industrial plants and the abandonment of existing plants, are likely to persist. Such changes fit the commonly accepted notions of secular trend and should be included in the time-factor index. The techniques used are inadequate for making precise classificatory distinctions between cyclical and secular forces on economic grounds.[14]

Presumably a curvilinear trend, which would better take into account the changes in the state composition of industry, could be fitted to the state and national per capita personal incomes. Deviations from such trends would afford a superior basis for computing sensitivity indexes. The latter then could be expected to be more nearly free of elements which properly should be included in the time-factor indexes. That such curvilinear trends were not fitted is due primarily to the fact that only highly subjective free-hand methods were available for this purpose. Moreover, the linear relation is fairly strong, and while there is a danger that some trend elements may be caught up in the sensitivity index, this danger is present whenever the trend adjustment does not accurately reflect the true situation.

But these technical difficulties, serious as they may be, do not tell the whole story. The industries which comprise the states' economies differ widely in their sensitivity, and until this fact is taken into account, it is not possible to discern whether a trend exists or not. If one goes back to chart 2 (in chapter 2) and compares the state relatives for Texas and Oklahoma, it may be seen that they trace approximately the same course. Yet there is a significant time-factor index for Texas, but none for Oklahoma. Since Oklahoma has been losing population steadily since 1930, presumably as an adjustment to low incomes, an upward trend in its

[14] One bit of evidence that appears to give support to the contention that during a period of rising income like 1929-1954 the sensitivity indexes will pick up and reflect many of the forces which more properly should be classified as secular is found in a comparison of the indexes for states which had a significant time-factor index on the basis of 1929-1950 income payments data but not on the basis of 1929-1954 personal income data. There are 11 such states, of which 7 had positive time-factor indexes, ranging from 0.6 to 1.7, and 4 had negative time-factor indexes, ranging from —0.4 to —0.9. The sensitivity indexes based on personal income are larger than those based on income payments for the seven states having positive time-factor indexes based on income payments, but insignificant ones based on personal income. The change was in the opposite direction for the four states with negative time-factor indexes based on income payments, but none for 1929-1954 personal income. An examination of the income relatives for these states does not reveal clearly why the time-factor indexes should be significant for 1929-1950 but not for 1929-1954. In most cases the state relatives have moved in an opposite direction after about 1948 or have remained at approximately the same level from 1945-1948 to 1953-1954, but this is true for some of the states in which the time-factor index is significant for both periods or for neither one.

income might be expected. Yet the sensitivity index shows that its economy is more sensitive than that of Texas. Can this be interpreted to mean that for Oklahoma the sensitivity index has picked up some of the trend, while the same procedures have for Texas adequately distinguished between cyclical and secular forces? Such a hypothesis does not seem reasonable. More likely the answer is to be found in Oklahoma's greater dependence on crude oil production, farming, and government.

The above discussion seems to point to the conclusion that the presence of a significant time-factor index is strong evidence of the existence and direction of a secular trend, whether the latter stems from the differential growth of the state's industries, over and above the apparent growth associated with cyclical changes, or from a changing industrial composition. It also seems reasonable to conclude that the absence of a significant time-factor index is not sufficient proof that the forces making for a secular trend (other than a level one) do not exist. Rather, it suggests that the trend, if any, is small relative to the cyclical pattern of responses and to irregular and transitory elements in the state's income. Whether or not a significant time-factor index is found, the sensitivity indexes in table 6 have enough of a range to cast doubt on the use of the percentage changes from 1929 to 1953 or 1954 in table 5 as measures of trend.

At best the time-factor indexes can be used as indicators of "growth," that is, the cumulative changes in per capita income which are not accounted for by the sensitivity indexes. The time-factor indexes, although cast in logarithmic linear form, indicate nothing about the shape of the trend and, like most trend lines, cannot be extrapolated to later years.

Differential sensitivity indexes

The states with higher per capita incomes tend to be less sensitive to cyclical change than do the lower-income states (table 7). If the states are divided into quartiles by the average size of their 1929-1954 per capita incomes, the states in the highest income quartile tend to have sensitivity indexes of less than unity, those in the next quartile indexes which approximate unity, and those in the two lowest quartiles indexes which are above unity.[15] Except for the extreme errors for the Dakotas, there are no significant differences among the quartiles with regard to size of the average error. Time-factor indexes tend to be positive, larger, and more frequent in the lowest quartile; three of the four negative time-factor indexes are found in the highest quartile. One positive time-factor index,

[15] The average size of the sensitivity indexes is .92 in the top quartile, 1.02 in the second quartile, 1.10 in the third quartile, and 1.14 in the lowest quartile.

that for Delaware, the state with the highest average income and the lowest sensitivity index for the 1929-1954 period, is also found in the top quartile.

TABLE 7

PERSONAL INCOME SENSITIVITY AND TIME-FACTOR INDEXES, ARRAYED BY SIZE OF STATE 1929-1954 AVERAGE PER CAPITA PERSONAL INCOME

State	1929-1954 average per capita personal income	Sensitivity index	Time-factor index	Average error (percent)	State	1929-1954 average per capita personal income	Sensitivity index	Time-factor index	Average error (percent)
D. C.	$1,508	.58	...	5.3	Nebraska	$860	1.21	...	5.4
Delaware	1,340	.75	1.0	5.5	Arizona	858	1.07	...	3.0
Connecticut	1,337	.87	...	3.5	Kansas	854	1.25	...	3.9
Nevada	1,305	.97	...	5.4	Maine	851	.93	...	3.2
New York	1,304	.94	−1.1	2.3	Utah	830	1.08	...	1.6
California	1,274	.94	−.4	2.0	Florida	833	.96	1.0	3.2
New Jersey	1,233	.90	...	2.6	Idaho	832	1.14	...	7.1
Illinois	1,189	1.06	−.5	2.6	Vermont	802	.98	−.4	1.5
Massachusetts	1,137	.78	...	3.1	Texas	796	1.10	.9	2.6
Rhode Island	1,104	.78	...	2.6	Virginia	759	.85	1.9	2.3
Washington	1,099	1.07	...	5.0	South Dakota	722	1.44	...	11.2
Michigan	1,087	1.05	...	4.3	Oklahoma	710	1.24	...	3.8
Maryland	1,082	.90	...	3.1	North Dakota	706	1.47	...	14.1
Ohio	1,071	1.02	...	2.5	West Virginia	700	1.05	...	3.9
Oregon	1,051	1.07	...	5.6	New Mexico	693	1.08	1.3	2.7
Pennsylvania	1,026	.94	...	2.0	Louisiana	666	1.05	.7	2.9
Wyoming	1,021	.96	.8	3.5	Georgia	627	1.04	1.3	3.6
Montana	961	.98	1.3	5.0	Tennessee	621	1.19	...	3.9
Indiana	954	1.06	.7	3.3	Kentucky	611	1.18	...	2.4
Wisconsin	941	1.05	...	2.0	North Carolina	611	.96	1.8	4.2
Colorado	939	1.06	...	3.2	South Carolina	551	.96	2.4	5.1
Missouri	907	1.05	...	2.3	Alabama	548	1.27	...	4.4
New Hampshire	906	.86	...	2.2	Arkansas	503	1.14	.9	5.0
Minnesota	883	1.03	...	3.6	Mississippi	449	1.28	...	6.0
Iowa	868	1.17	...	6.1					

Source: tables 1 and 6.

The correlation between income and the sensitivity indexes is not high, but it is sufficient to explain the tendency (noted in chapter 2) for the interstate coefficients of variation to change inversely with the level of income.[16] A state with a high income level and a low sensitivity will, as national income increases, tend to increase more slowly than average. Its income will be above the mean in both the beginning and later periods, but its income will lie closer to the mean after the increase. Similarly, a state with a low income level and a high sensitivity will, with an increase in the national level, experience a larger than average increase, resulting in its income also lying closer to the mean. Thus with an increase in income it can be expected that the states will tend to lie

[16] The coefficient of determination between average 1929-1954 per capita personal income and the sensitivity index is —.33.

relatively closer to the mean, and the interstate coefficients of variation will decrease. Conversely, with a decrease in national income, the states with high income and low sensitivity will tend to decrease less, while those with low income and high sensitivity will decrease more than proportionally. The result is some spreading of the relative interstate differences. This inverse relationship between income and relative dispersion is known as the accordion effect.[17]

The accordion effect

A state's per capita personal income may be estimated from its sensitivity index and the nation's per capita personal income. An estimate thus obtained reflects chiefly the influences of changes in the level of personal income and the state's pattern of responses to such changes. Such estimates are largely free of the influences of random or irregular elements; if the state has a time-factor index, the estimates are net of this influence also. When such estimates are made for all states, it is then possible to compute an interstate coefficient of variation which reflects the influence of cyclical responses (table 8, column 4). Such a set of interstate coefficients describes the accordion effect of cyclical changes in its least disturbed form.

Compared with the coefficients of variation computed from the National Income Division estimates, the coefficients based solely on the sensitivity indexes move inversely with every change in the level of personal income (chart 5). Since the level of these coefficients is adjusted to those of the National Income Division at the center of the period, 1940-1941, they start somewhat lower in 1929, rise somewhat faster to 1932, and then continue to rise slightly to a peak in 1933. They then decrease somewhat more slowly than those for the National Income Division estimates. The interstate coefficients based on the sensitivity index, which are geared entirely to changes in the level of personal income, change much more smoothly and regularly than those based on the National Income Division estimates. The latter, while showing an inverse relation to personal income level, show increases with increasing income in 1936, 1939, 1940, 1946, 1950, 1952, and 1953, and show decreases with decreasing income in 1933, 1938, and 1954. Most of these discrepancies occur near the turning points of the cycle, and typically are not of any magnitude.

[17] John L. Fulmer, "Factors Influencing State Per Capita Income Differentials," *Southern Economic Journal,* 16 (1950), 273; and Edgar M. Hoover and Joseph L. Fisher, "Research in Regional Economic Growth," in *Problems in the Study of Economic Growth,* New York, 1949, pp. 201 ff.

TABLE 8

INTERSTATE COEFFICIENTS OF VARIATION FOR STATE PER CAPITA PERSONAL INCOME, ESTIMATED BY THE NATIONAL INCOME DIVISION AND COMPUTED FROM THE SENSITIVITY AND TIME-FACTOR INDEXES, 1929-1954

Year (1)	United States per capita personal income (2)	Coefficients of variation (percent) based on state per capita personal incomes				
		Estimated by National Income Division (3)	Computed from: Sensitivity index: Alone (4)	Computed from: Sensitivity index: And time index (5)	Computed from: Time index alone (6)
1929	$ 703	35.8	31.1	34.6	32.8
1930	621	37.7	32.3	35.4	32.4
1931	526	39.7	34.0	36.7	32.1
1932	398	41.1	37.1	39.2	31.8
1933	373	40.1	37.9	39.7	31.4
1934	421	37.4	36.5	38.1	31.1
1935	470	33.7	35.3	36.7	30.8
1936	531	36.1	33.9	35.2	30.5
1937	570	34.1	33.2	34.2	30.2
1938	524	33.5	34.1	34.9	30.0
1939	553	34.8	33.5	34.1	29.7
1940	592	34.9	32.8	33.1	29.4
1941	716	32.1	30.8	31.0	29.2
1942	906	29.2	28.6	28.5	28.9
1943	1,099	26.5	26.9	26.5	28.6
1944	1,192	23.4	26.3	25.6	28.5
1945	1,231	21.8	26.0	25.1	28.2
1946	1,247	22.8	25.9	24.7	28.0
1947	1,313	22.5	25.5	24.0	27.8
1948	1,417	21.1	25.0	23.2	27.7
1949	1,378	21.9	25.2	23.2	27.5
1950	1,487	23.2	24.7	22.4	27.3
1951	1,646	22.8	24.1	21.5	27.2
1952	1,720	22.9	23.8	21.0	27.0
1953	1,788	23.3	23.6	20.5	26.9
1954	1,768	22.9	23.7	20.4	26.8
Memoranda:					
1919	613	26.5	32.5	39.3	36.4
1920	660	31.7	31.7	38.3	36.0
1921	549	35.1	33.6	39.6	35.6

Col. 2: table 3.
Col. 3: table 1. In computing these coefficients neither the standard deviation nor the mean state income were weighted by population.
Cols. 4-6: Based on table 6. For method of computation see text.

Similar estimates of expected income may be made by using both the sensitivity and the time-factor indexes. The interstate coefficient of variation computed from these estimates will reflect all but the irregular or random elements in the National Income Division series (table 8, column 5). This series of coefficients starts somewhat higher, rises to a higher peak in 1933, and then decreases somewhat faster to a level some 3.3 percentage points below those based solely on the sensitivity indexes. For the terminal years, 1952-1954, the sensitivity and time-factor estimates

CHART 5

INTERSTATE COEFFICIENTS OF VARIATION FOR PER CAPITA PERSONAL INCOME AS ESTIMATED BY THE NATIONAL INCOME DIVISION AND AS COMPUTED FROM THE SENSITIVITY AND TIME-FACTOR INDEXES, 1929-1954

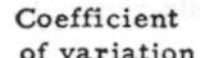

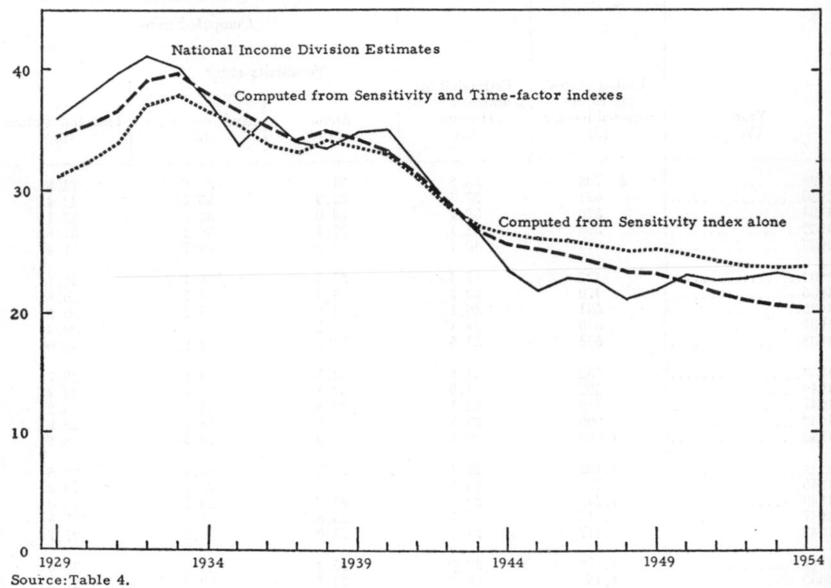

Source: Table 4.

have the lowest interstate coefficients of variations of any of the three series, largely as a consequence of the series having been centered on 1940-1941; had it been centered on 1949, for example, this would not have been the case. As it is, the interstate coefficients computed from estimates based on both indexes follow those computed from the National Income Division estimates more closely than those based on sensitivity estimates alone.

The interstate coefficients of variation based on series computed from the indexes provide an opportunity to measure roughly how much of the observed decrease in the coefficients based on the National Income Division estimates may be due to cyclical changes, and how much to the regular but more persistent forces reflected by the time-factor indexes. Although irregular elements presumably have been eliminated by the use of sensitivity and time-factor indexes, we shall use three-year averages centered on the peaks and troughs to dampen the effects of any irregular elements remaining in the figures. Thus treated, the coefficients for the

National Income Division series decrease by 45 percent, from a peak in 1930-1932 to a trough in 1947-1949. The coefficients based on estimates from the two indexes decreased by 47 percent, from a peak in 1932-1934 to a trough in the terminal years, 1952-1954. Using the coefficients in columns 4 and 6 of table 8 to obtain similar estimates of the decreases for the sensitivity and for the time-factor indexes taken separately, we find a decrease of 36 percent in the series based on sensitivity indexes alone and a decrease of 14 percent in the series based on the time-factor index alone. From these figures we can say that roughly two-thirds of the observed decrease in the coefficients of variation is due to cyclical influences and about one-third to those persistent elements caught up in the time-factor index.

These calculations tend to indicate that the accordion effect was powerful, but incapable of explaining the entire narrowing of interstate differentials observed for the 1929-1954 period. To some extent differential trend factors also have been at work during the period, although these are difficult to identify and harder to measure for individual states. It should be emphasized that these calculations are intended only as a description of the behavior of the interstate coefficients during the period under study. They cannot be extrapolated; the logarithmic linear form of time-factor indexes on which they are based is more a matter of statistical convenience than of an attempt to delineate the shape of the forces which are at work.[18] The behavior of the interstate coefficients during recent years is sufficient to raise doubts about their probable future behavior. Are the extremely low coefficients for 1945-1949 due to transient elements associated with the aftermath of the war? Are the slightly higher coefficients for 1950-1954 due to the disturbing influences of the Korean affair and its aftermath? Have the forces making for a downward trend in these coefficients become exhausted to the point that forces operating in the other direction are in the ascendancy? It seems clear that most of the decrease in these coefficients occurred during the war years, 1941-

[18] This point may be underlined by reference to the findings based on a similar analysis of 1929-1950 state income payments, and published in "Cyclical and Secular Changes in State Per Capita Incomes, 1929-1950," *Review of Economics and Statistics,* 36 (1954), 320-330. In this study, about one-half of the observed decrease in the interstate coefficients was attributed to each component. The interstate coefficients of variation for the income payments and personal income series differ by as much as 2.8 percentage points in 1936, and by more than 1.0 percentage points in seven out of eight years between 1933 and 1940. For the most part, however, the differences are about of the magnitude that results from the periodic revisions of a single series. Consequently, most of the difference in the portions attributed to sensitivity and to time-factor index elements is due to the inclusion of the years since 1950 in the analysis.

1945, and that since that time they have fluctuated within the range of 21.1–23.3 percent.

Estimating errors

The sensitivity and time-factor indexes are valuable in that they permit separating, though crudely, cyclical and secular forces and, somewhat more precisely, separating the combination of these two sets of elements from those that are irregular, temporary, or random. A crude measure of the latter is provided by the differences between the estimates based on the indexes and those prepared by the National Income Division. These differences have been labeled, in tables 6 and 7, average errors of estimate. They implicitly assume that the National Income Division's estimates are "true" and that those prepared from the indexes are approximations of them. One reason for the differences between them is that the indexes presumably contain none of the effects of irregular elements. These estimating errors are worth examining to see if they contain any patterns which may throw further light on the income differentials during the 1929-1954 period.

An error is found for each state for each year.[19] Thus, there are 1,248 estimating errors for the 48 states over the 26 years. When these are pooled into a single distribution, it is found that they range from − 32 to + 42 percent, with a mean of 0.3 percent (table 9). The distribution is both too peaked near the mean and has too many extreme frequencies to be normally distributed. Almost 80 percent of the errors are less than 6 percent, and some 63 percent of the errors are less than 4 percent, of the figure estimated from the indexes.

TABLE 9

FREQUENCY DISTRIBUTION OF PERSONAL-INCOME ESTIMATING ERRORS

Size of error (percent)[a]	Number[b]	Size of error (percent)[a]	Number[b]
Negative errors		*Positive errors*	
20.0 and larger	6	0.0- 1.9	214
15.0-19.9	8	2.0- 3.9	162
10.0-14.9	19	4.0- 5.9	105
8.0- 9.9	23	6.0- 7.9	52
6.0- 7.9	56	8.0- 9.9	30
4.0- 5.9	99	10.0-14.9	42
2.0- 3.9	178	15.0-19.9	12
0.0- 1.9	235	20.0 and larger	7
		Sum	1,248

[a]The difference between state per capita personal income as estimated by National Income Division and as estimated from the sensitivity and significant time-factor indexes (table 6) expressed as a percentage of the latter. A minus sign indicates that the estimate based on the indexes exceeds the National Income Division estimate.

[b]A percentage error was computed for each of the 48 states for each of 26 years.

[19] See above, note 7.

The inclusion of time as a variable in computing and testing the sensitivity and time-factor indexes is a precaution against the possibility of the estimating errors of each particular state having any time-pattern.[20] This precaution, however, would not prevent the errors for most of the states from being predominantly in one direction or larger than usual during a particular year. Except for one depression year, 1931, and three war years, 1942-1944, the average size of the errors among the states is less than 5 per cent (table 10). They are smallest (2.4 percent) in 1950.

TABLE 10

PERSONAL-INCOME ESTIMATING ERRORS, 1929-1954, BY YEAR

Year	Estimating errors[a] (percentages)			Number of states with estimating errors less than	
		Range			
	Average size[b]	Lowest	Highest	3 percent	5 percent
1929	3.2	−11.1	10.8	26	39
1930	3.5	−17.1	5.7	29	38
1931	5.2	−31.8	6.4	18	30
1932	3.8	− 9.7	7.1	22	30
1933	4.6	−24.6	6.2	17	32
1934	4.6	−16.7	18.9	26	33
1935	4.5	− 4.7	25.5	21	36
1936	3.6	−15.8	12.6	32	37
1937	3.4	− 7.3	11.2	23	40
1938	3.3	− 5.8	12.9	21	38
1939	2.9	− 7.3	12.6	32	40
1940	2.9	− 5.2	11.1	29	40
1941	4.3	− 7.9	24.3	20	32
1942	6.9	− 8.2	26.3	16	22
1943	5.6	− 8.5	18.9	17	23
1944	5.4	− 8.9	13.3	13	25
1945	4.3	− 8.1	12.3	21	32
1946	3.6	− 8.3	11.9	26	36
1947	4.2	− 6.9	41.8	29	37
1948	4.6	− 7.5	24.5	23	34
1949	2.7	− 7.5	8.9	32	40
1950	2.4	− 6.6	8.3	35	45
1951	2.7	− 7.8	6.8	27	38
1952	3.5	−21.3	6.0	29	39
1953	4.6	−26.2	5.4	24	31
1954	4.5	−24.7	4.5	19	34

[a]The difference between state per capita personal income as estimated by National Income Division and as estimated from the sensitivity and time-factor indexes (table 6), expressed as a percentage of the latter. A minus sign indicates that the estimate based on the indexes exceeds the National Income Division estimate.

[b]The mean absolute size of the errors for the 48 states.

That the average size of these errors is not due entirely to one or two extreme items is evidenced by the frequency with which states had errors of less than 3, less than 4, and less than 5 percent. During the war years nearly half of the states had errors larger than 5 percent. The average

[20] Also, the errors for each of the states were charted and the charts reviewed to make sure that the errors for some states did not have a residual time trend.

size of the errors has been, however, affected by a few extreme items in about half of the years. These extremely large errors are found primarily for a few agricultural states; the Dakotas, Nebraska, Idaho, and Mississippi account for most of them. The large difference between the National Income Division's estimate for Nevada in 1942 and the sensitivity estimate was due largely to war construction, a temporary phenomenon.

With an increase in personal income from $716 in 1941 to $1,231 in 1945, an increase of 72 percent in four years, it may be expected that the impact on the several states would be uneven. During such a period procedures which are dependent upon regular and repetitive relationships are likely to yield estimates that are wide of the mark. The larger errors are those in which the sensitivity and time-factor indexes underestimated the income as reported by the National Income Division. During the four years from 1942 to 1945, the income of some 17 states was underestimated by 10 percent or more during at least one of the years. In 1942 the income of some 13 states was underestimated by the indexes; for the following years the number of states was 5 in 1943, 6 in 1944, and 4 in 1945. Apparently the rapid rise in agricultural prices during these years was responsible for the extremely rapid increase in per capita personal income in six states, and was a contributing factor in several others. Construction for war purposes also apparently contributed to the rapid and extreme increases in some states.

There were several other years in which five or more states had estimating errors which exceeded 10 percent: 1931, 1934, 1935, 1936, 1948, 1953, and 1954. With the exception of 1931 and 1936, these were years close to a turning point in the business cycle. Because of their industrial composition some of the states had different turning points from that of the nation, and this fact could contribute to the extreme errors in these years. The sensitivity index, particularly, is too crude a tool to provide for the lead or lag of a state with regard to the national turning point in a cycle.

Of the 94 instances in which the sensitivity estimates differed from those of the National Income Division for a specific year by 10 percent or more, 48 are accounted for by five agricultural states—North Dakota (15), South Dakota (15), Idaho (7), Mississippi (6), and Iowa (5). The average errors for these five states, 6-14 percent, are larger than those for any other state. The errors for specific years for North Dakota range as high as 42 percent in 1947, and there are six other years in which they exceed 20 percent; in South Dakota the highest error is 26 percent in 1935, and there are four other years in which the errors exceed 20 percent. The maximum error in the other three of these states ranges from 17 to 19 percent. The only other states with errors exceeding 15 percent in any one year are: Nebraska in 1934, Oregon and Washington in 1942 and 1943, Nevada in 1942, and Utah in 1942 and 1943.

If it is concluded that these five agricultural states should be excluded since their per capita personal incomes fluctuate too irregularly to be reflected adequately by sensitivity indexes (none have significant time-factor indexes), the average size and range of errors presented in table 10 are changed substantially (table 11). The prevalence of the remaining large estimating errors is even more markedly connected with the war years or with the turning points of the cycle—periods in which the state distributions are likely to be disturbed most.

The extremely large and frequent errors in a few of the agricultural states plus an occasional large error in states with large but less dominant

TABLE 11

PERSONAL-INCOME ESTIMATING ERRORS FOR 43 STATES, 1929-1954, BY YEAR[a]

Year	Estimating errors[b] (percentages)			Number of states with estimating errors less than	
		Range			
	Average size[c]	Lowest	Highest	3 percent	5 percent
1929	3.0	− 8.5	10.8	23	36
1930	3.2	−13.6	5.7	26	35
1931	4.1	−13.5	6.4	18	29
1932	3.7	− 9.2	7.1	19	27
1933	3.7	−12.3	6.2	16	31
1934	3.6	−16.7	12.0	26	33
1935	3.4	− 4.7	14.9	20	35
1936	2.6	− 3.7	12.6	32	37
1937	3.2	− 7.3	9.8	21	38
1938	2.9	− 5.8	7.2	20	35
1939	2.5	− 7.3	10.7	30	38
1940	2.5	− 5.2	11.1	28	38
1941	3.8	− 7.9	11.0	18	30
1942	6.1	− 8.2	26.3	16	22
1943	5.5	− 8.5	18.9	15	20
1944	5.1	− 8.1	12.8	13	23
1945	4.0	− 8.1	12.3	21	30
1946	3.1	− 8.3	11.0	25	35
1947	2.9	− 6.9	10.3	28	35
1948	3.5	− 7.5	10.9	22	33
1949	2.8	− 7.5	8.9	29	35
1950	2.4	− 6.6	8.3	31	40
1951	2.6	− 6.4	6.8	25	35
1952	2.7	− 5.8	6.0	28	37
1953	3.4	−11.1	5.4	24	31
1954	3.6	−11.4	4.5	18	33

[a]The states excluded are North Dakota, South Dakota, Idaho, Mississippi, and Iowa. Otherwise this table is similar to table 10.

[b]The difference between state per capita personal income as estimated by National Income Division and as estimated from the sensitivity and time-factor indexes (table 6), expressed as a percentage of the latter. A minus sign indicates that the estimate based on the indexes exceeds the National Income Division estimate.

[c]The mean absolute size of the errors for the 43 states.

agricultural sources of income suggest that the agricultural and nonagricultural sources of income should be investigated separately.

Sensitivity of Farm and Nonfarm Income

In the previous section it was noted that the per capita personal income of a few states which derive large proportions of their income from farming—the Dakotas, Iowa, Idaho, and Mississippi—did not appear to be adequately represented by the sensitivity and time-factor indexes for personal income. In this section the sensitivity of farm and of nonfarm income will be analyzed separately.

Farm income consists of the net income of farm proprietors plus farm wages; wages exclude employee contributions under the social security programs but include payments in kind. Farm proprietors' income consists of the sum of "(1) cash receipts from farm marketings of crops and livestock, (2) payments to farmers under the Government's soil conservation and related programs, (3) the value of food and fuel produced and consumed on farms, (4) the gross rental value of farm dwellings, and (5) the value (positive or negative) of the changes in inventories of crops and livestock," minus the expenses of production, flowing to individual proprietors, partners, and producers' co-operatives.[21] Similar flows to farm corporations, which would reach individuals in the form of dividends, interest, or labor income, are excluded. Also excluded is the interest on loans made for agricultural purposes. All income not treated as farm income is treated as nonfarm income, so that the sum of farm and nonfarm income is personal income.

The value of changes in farm inventories deserves particular attention since it is subject to large year-to-year fluctuations. Its inclusion makes farm proprietors' income a measure of net income from current production rather than the net receipts of farm operators during the year. Additions to farm inventories are valued at the midyear selling prices, so that the profit or loss on inventory changes is assigned as of the time when the goods are produced rather than as of the time when the goods are sold.[22] While the other items composing farm income must always be positive, farm inventories must either cumulate continuously or be reduced during some years. The value of the inventory reduction is an offset against farm marketings, so that a measure of net profit or loss from current-year production is obtained.

In a few instances, farm proprietors' losses have exceeded farm wages

[21] *Survey of Current Business* (September 1955), p. 13.

[22] This treatment differs from that of nonfarm inventories, which are valued at cost prices.

so that the farm income for a state is negative (appendix C, table 61).[23] The negative farm incomes are subtracted from nonfarm incomes in arriving at state personal income. While this procedure is proper from the standpoint of measuring income flows to the residents of a state from current production, it does open the door to large and erratic changes in personal income.

The farm-income share of personal income varies from about 1 percent in Rhode Island and Massachusetts to 25 percent or more in seven states—Arkansas, Idaho, Mississippi, Nebraska, Iowa, and the Dakotas (table 12). The farm-income share, on a national basis, has varied from about 5 percent of personal income in 1932 and 1953-1954 to more than 9 percent in 1935, 1942, 1946, and 1948. Similar variations are to be noted in each of the states. In some states the variations have been extreme. In the Dakotas, for example, the farm share of personal income has varied from less than zero, when farm income was negative, to more than 40 percent during the war years. In every state the range of the farm-income shares during 1929-1954 has been half as large as the average size of the 1929-1954 farm shares, and in 20 states the range exceeds the average share.

In making these comparisons state per capita farm and nonfarm incomes have been used. The per capita adjustment eliminates, though roughly, differences in state populations. When an inclusive concept such as personal income is used, there appears to be no objection to the use of the entire population in making such an adjustment. The question may be asked, however, whether such a procedure is warranted when only a part of the income flowing to the residents of a state is the subject of the adjustment. Would it not be preferable to adjust for differences in the number of individuals (or families) who contribute to or are the recipients of the particular flow? Should not farm income be adjusted for the number of farmers, or the number of farm residents, rather than for the total population of a state? There would be much to argue for affirmative answers to these questions if the purpose of the investigation were confined to finding out, for example, how particular segments of the population fared during particular years. In terms of the farm-nonfarm shares of personal income, the transformation of both to a per capita basis is equivalent to computing the shares based on aggregate flows without the per capita adjustment. Comparisons between years are affected, however, since the use of the total population does not take

[23] The states and years for which farm incomes were negative are: North Dakota, 1931; South Dakota, 1933 and 1934; Nebraska, 1934; and Nevada, 1931, 1934, and 1937.

TABLE 12

FARM-INCOME SHARE OF PERSONAL INCOME, 1929-1954, BY STATE

State	Average 1929-1954	Range during period[a]: Lowest[b]	Highest	Relative[c]
New England				
Maine	8.3	3.4	11.7	100
New Hampshire	4.3	2.4	6.1	86
Vermont	12.3	6.6	16.7	82
Massachusetts	1.2	.9	1.6	58
Rhode Island	.9	.6	1.2	67
Connecticut	2.2	1.4	2.8	64
Middle Atlantic				
New York	1.6	.9	2.2	81
New Jersey	1.7	1.2	2.2	59
Pennsylvania	2.3	1.5	3.3	78
East North Central				
Ohio	4.7	3.1	7.7	98
Indiana	9.5	6.9	15.2	87
Illinois	5.4	2.8	8.2	100
Michigan	4.1	2.1	6.6	110
Wisconsin	11.6	7.0	15.5	73
West North Central				
Minnesota	15.5	6.0	22.4	106
Iowa	28.6	5.9	39.3	117
Missouri	10.4	5.3	14.5	88
North Dakota	38.8	− 7.0	58.9	170
South Dakota	36.3	−15.5	49.8	180
Nebraska	25.5	− 4.9	34.2	153
Kansas	19.3	6.6	31.8	131
South Atlantic				
Delaware	5.4	2.6	7.7	94
Maryland	3.3	1.9	5.1	97
Virginia	8.6	4.6	15.7	129
West Virginia	5.7	3.3	9.1	102
North Carolina	17.3	12.6	26.3	79
South Carolina	14.3	7.2	24.6	122
Georgia	12.0	6.2	20.5	119
Florida	8.4	6.3	10.6	51
East South Central				
Kentucky	15.4	10.1	24.3	92
Tennessee	12.2	6.2	19.6	110
Alabama	13.1	7.0	22.3	117
Mississippi	26.1	19.1	38.6	75
West South Central				
Arkansas	25.0	17.5	33.0	62
Louisiana	10.2	6.2	16.7	103
Oklahoma	13.9	7.5	21.0	97
Texas	12.8	7.6	19.4	92
Mountain				
Montana	23.9	4.8	35.4	128
Idaho	25.5	16.1	35.6	76
Wyoming	18.3	8.6	26.5	98
Colorado	12.0	4.1	15.7	97
New Mexico	15.3	8.3	28.5	132
Arizona	15.0	8.6	21.3	85
Utah	9.9	4.5	15.2	108
Nevada	8.2	− 1.1	14.3	188
Pacific				
Washington	9.0	6.3	12.8	72
Oregon	10.3	6.4	13.4	68
California	7.0	4.6	9.1	64
United States	7.6	5.2	9.7	59

Column heading: Farm income as a percentage of personal income.

[a]The years in which farm income was the smallest (or largest) percent of personal income need not be the same for every state.

[b]A minus sign indicates that farm proprietors' losses exceeded farm wages.

[c]The range is the difference between the highest and lowest percentages farm income is of personal income. The relative range is the range expressed as a percentage of the average percentage farm income is of personal income.

Source: tables 1 and 61.

into account the migration to and away from farms. Farm income per farm plus nonfarm income per nonfarm family, however, might not equal personal income per family and thus would require separate treatment throughout. Much of the presentation in terms of farm-income shares adequately reflects the nonfarm shares, since one is the complement of the other.

The direction of changes from the previous year in farm income has been the same as those found for personal income in all but four years (chart 6). The onset of recovery in farm income in 1933 preceded that in personal income by one year; there was a sharp but short-lived farm income recession in 1936; and farm income started decreasing in 1952 and has decreased continuously through 1954, thus anticipating by two years the decrease in personal income. The rates of change from the previous year are larger for farm than for nonfarm income, and since 1947 the two series have shown considerable divergence. In part, this divergence may reflect only a continuation of the long-term decline in the importance of agriculture, but in the presence of cyclical fluctuations which differ both as to timing and magnitude from those of nonfarm income it is difficult to verify.

CHART 6

PER CAPITA FARM, NONFARM, AND TOTAL PERSONAL INCOME, UNITED STATES, 1929-1954

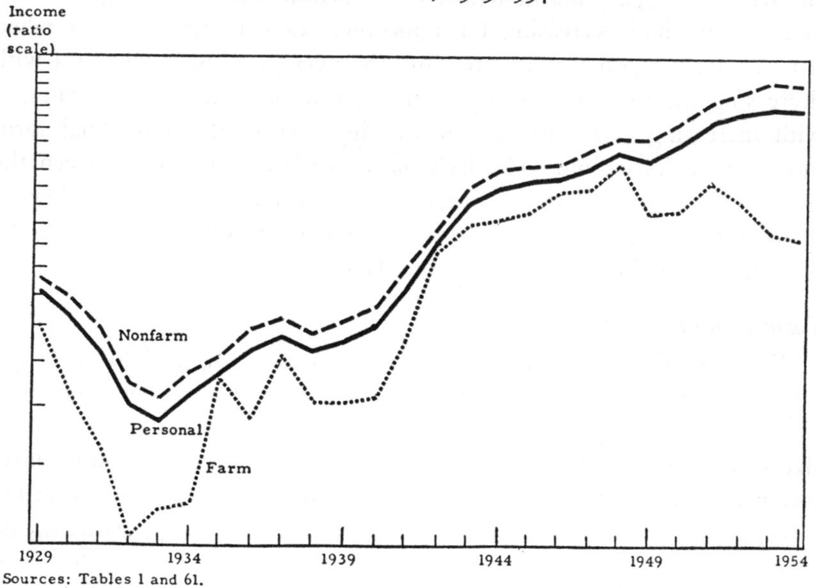

Sources: Tables 1 and 61.

TABLE 13

NUMBER OF STATES IN WHICH PER CAPITA FARM INCOME CHANGED FROM THE PREVIOUS YEAR IN A DIRECTION OPPOSITE FROM THAT OF THE NATION, 1930-1954, BY YEAR

Year	Direction of change from previous year, U. S. per capita farm income[a]	Number of states with changes in opposite direction	Year	Direction of change from previous year, U. S. per capita farm income[a]	Number of states with changes in opposite direction
1930..........	−	6	1945..........	+	13
1931..........	−	7	1946..........	+	10
1932..........	−	4	1947..........	+	24
1933..........	+	10	1948..........	+	16
1934..........	+	19	1949..........	−	8
1935..........	+	3	1950..........	+	25
1936..........	−	15	1951..........	+	6
1937..........	+	9	1952..........	−	8
1938..........	−	7	1953..........	−	8
1939..........	0	..[b]	1954..........	−	15
1940..........	+	18			
1941..........	+	2			
1942..........	+	0			
1943..........	+	8			
1944..........	+	22			

[a]A minus sign indicates that per capita farm income in the year shown was less than it was in the previous year; a plus sign that per capita farm income was greater; and a zero that it was the same in both years.

[b]Since the U. S. per capita farm income was $41 in both 1938 and 1939, any change could be counted as in an opposite direction. Per capita farm income increased in 22 states, decreased in 20 states, and remained the same in 6 states.

Source: appendix table 61.

While per capita farm and nonfarm income, on a national level, tend to change in the same direction most of the time, the changes in state per capita farm income often depart from the national pattern (table 13). In 1947 and 1950, years in which farm income was increasing, one-half of the states had decreasing farm income. During the 15 years when national farm income was increasing, the average number of states with decreasing income, 12, was larger than the average number of states, 9, with increasing farm income during the 9 years when national farm income was decreasing. The lack of concordance in signs between the direction of change in state and national farm income reflects an element of irregularity large enough to obscure, if not destroy, any state-national pattern that might be expected in the data.

Farm-income sensitivity

When sensitivity and time-factor indexes are computed for state per capita incomes, the indexes are found to be larger in states deriving larger shares of income from farming (table 14),[24] a fact which suggests that the size of the sensitivity indexes depends upon the size of per capita farm income. The states with the smaller farm-income shares tend to be the

[24] The coefficient of determination between the farm-income sensitivity indexes and the average farm share of 1929-1954 personal income is .34. Nebraska, Nevada, and the Dakotas, which had farm losses in some years, are excluded from this calculation.

more heavily populated states where per capita farm income tends to be small. However, in many of these states farm income *per farm* would compare more favorably with that of other states.

The sensitivity indexes also tend to have a pronounced geographic

TABLE 14

FARM-INCOME SENSITIVITY AND TIME-FACTOR INDEXES, BY STATE

State	Sensitivity index	Time-factor index	Average error (percent)
New England			
Maine	.91	...	17.0
New Hampshire	.64	...	10.9
Vermont	.90	−1.9	6.8
Massachusetts	.73	...	9.6
Rhode Island	.53	...	11.1
Connecticut	.65	...	8.6
Middle Atlantic			
New York	.93	−1.5	6.5
New Jersey	.67	1.2	8.7
Pennsylvania	.78	...	4.8
East North Central			
Ohio	.83	...	8.5
Indiana	1.04	...	8.8
Illinois	1.13	...	11.9
Michigan	.78	...	6.6
Wisconsin	1.09	...	7.0
West North Central			
Minnesota	1.28	...	12.7
Iowa	1.50	...	20.6
Missouri	1.14	...	8.8
North Dakota[a]	2.44	...	50.4
South Dakota[b]	2.01	...	25.7
Nebraska[c]	1.38	...	13.1
Kansas	1.63	−1.9	13.1
South Atlantic			
Delaware	.73	...	10.3
Maryland	.69	− .9	5.9
Virginia	.66	...	9.6
West Virginia	.63	...	7.5
North Carolina	.73	1.7	9.4
South Carolina	.84	...	11.2
Georgia	.80	...	8.8
Florida	.88	...	16.3
East South Central			
Kentucky	.98	...	8.3
Tennessee	.82	...	7.3
Alabama	.80	...	8.9
Mississippi	.98	...	13.6
West South Central			
Arkansas	.81	2.2	9.2
Louisiana	.81	...	9.0
Oklahoma	1.15	...	12.8
Texas	.91	...	8.8
Mountain			
Montana	1.19	3.6	26.0
Idaho	1.03	...	15.6
Wyoming	1.05	...	15.1
Colorado	1.27	...	17.5
New Mexico	.96	...	11.6
Arizona	.78	3.5	16.8
Utah	1.01	...	23.2
Nevada[d]	.80	...	21.6
Pacific			
Washington	.92	...	8.0
Oregon	.86	...	9.8
California	.83	...	9.1

[a]Excludes 1931.
[b]Excludes 1933 and 1934.
[c]Excludes 1934.
[d]Excludes 1931, 1934, and 1937.
Source: appendix table 61.

pattern. Along the Eastern seaboard, from New Hampshire southward to North Carolina, there is a band of states with sensitivity indexes of less than .75. Excluding these states, there is a band of states with indexes, between .75 and .99 which extends from Maine, Vermont, New York, and Michigan southward to Florida, and then follows the southern border to California, and the Pacific border northward to Washington. The remaining states have indexes exceeding 1.00, with the highest indexes (greater than 1.25) in the Plains states.

Unitary sensitivity indexes would be expected if agriculture were a homogeneous industry with a stable distribution among states and the diffierences in the farm share the only differences between states. The indexes show at least as much dispersion as did those for personal income. This fact alone would be sufficient to indicate the nonhomogeneity of farms as sources of income.

Coupled with the disperse indexes are exceedingly high estimating errors. The average estimating errors for farm income are higher than those for personal income in every state, and 34 of the states have farm-income estimating errors which exceed 15 percent for five or more years. In every year the estimating errors for five or more states exceed 15 percent. In the presence of errors of such magnitude it is not surprising that time-factor indexes were significant for only nine of the states.

Because of the exceedingly high estimating errors, the farm-income sensitivity indexes must be rejected as reliable indicators of the pattern of state responses to changes in the level of national farm income. Rather, the size of these errors is further evidence of the erratic behavior of state per capita farm income. Even if state per capita nonfarm income behaved in a regular and orderly pattern, the addition of per capita farm income to it, to obtain state per capita personal income, would be analogous to adding a random element to some stable function. Although the effect of an erratic element will be greater where it is a large share of the total, it will have some disturbing effects even when it is a relatively small share. Thus, farm income must be included among the random and irregular elements discussed in connection with the estimating errors attached to the sensitivity indexes based on personal income.

If farm income disturbs the relationship between the changes in a state's level of per capita personal income and in the national level, perhaps the removal of the disturbing element will further the analysis. The subtraction of farm income from personal income yields nonfarm income. An analysis of the behavior of nonfarm income should provide indexes which are partially free, at least, from the disturbing element of farm income. Nonfarm income, however, will not be wholly free of the effects of erratic changes in farm income. Farm and nonfarm incomes are interrelated by numerous transactions, and rapid changes in farm income will require adjustments in the nonfarm as well as the farm sectors of the economy. Moreover, the effects of urban-rural migration which accompany such changes are not taken into account.

Nonfarm-income sensitivity

The sensitivity indexes based on per capita nonfarm income are, for most states, about the same size as those computed from per capita personal income (table 15). The largest differences in the two sets of indexes are found for the states with large income shares derived from farm sources. Among the eight states which derive, on the average, 23 percent or more of their personal income from farms, the differences between the sensitivity indexes based on personal income and those based on nonfarm income amounted to .08 — .55. A difference of this magnitude is found in only three states outside this group—Indiana, Minnesota, and Nevada—and apparently the cause in these cases is the presence of a significant time-factor index for either personal income or nonfarm income but not for the other.[25] The shift from a personal to a nonfarm-income base left the indexes of five states unchanged and resulted in changes of .01 or .02 for another 20 states. The changes are about as frequent in one direction as another and about as frequent among those indexes below unity as among those above unity.

Only one state, North Carolina, had a sensitivity index based on personal income which was less than unity and one based on nonfarm income which was greater than unity. In four states, the Dakotas, Idaho, and Minnesota, the personal-income indexes are above unity, while the nonfarm indexes are below it. In these four states there are significant positive time-factor indexes for nonfarm income, but not for personal income.

There is only a weak association between the size of the sensitivity indexes and the percentage of personal income constituted by nonfarm

[25] For example, the time-factor index for Indiana personal income is .7 and significant; the farm-income index is also .7 and the nonfarm index .4, but neither is significant. For Indiana the difference between the gross sensitivity index (that is, when the influence of time is ignored) and the net index (that is, net of the influence of time) is larger for both nonfarm and personal income than is the difference between the nonfarm and personal-income gross sensitivity indexes or the net sensitivity indexes. The large difference shown for Indiana is thus the cumulation of the differences between these two sets of differences.

TABLE 15

NONFARM-INCOME SENSITIVITY AND TIME-FACTOR INDEXES, BY STATE

State	Sensitivity index	Time-factor index	Average error (percent)
New England			
Maine	.90	...	3.5
New Hampshire	.87	...	2.2
Vermont	.95	...	2.2
Massachusetts	.78	...	2.4
Rhode Island	.78	...	2.3
Connecticut	.87	...	3.6
Middle Atlantic			
New York	.95	−1.2	2.2
New Jersey	.90	...	2.4
Pennsylvania	.99	− .4	1.4
East North Central			
Ohio	1.03	...	2.6
Indiana	1.16	...	3.7
Illinois	1.07	− .7	2.5
Michigan	1.06	...	4.7
Wisconsin	1.04	...	2.1
West North Central			
Minnesota	.90	.7	3.6
Iowa	1.09	...	3.6
Missouri	1.04	...	2.3
North Dakota	.92	2.2	7.4
South Dakota	.91	2.0	4.2
Nebraska	1.11	...	3.4
Kansas	1.21	...	4.0
South Atlantic			
Delaware	.76	1.0	5.6
Maryland	.91	...	2.8
Virginia	.86	2.2	2.8
West Virginia	1.07	...	4.3
North Carolina	1.02	1.7	3.1
South Carolina	.97	2.8	5.0
Georgia	1.07	1.6	3.8
Florida	.95	1.0	3.9
East South Central			
Kentucky	1.13	.6	2.2
Tennessee	1.12	.9	3.6
Alabama	1.22	.9	4.5
Mississippi	1.36	...	5.9
West South Central			
Arkansas	1.30	...	4.6
Louisiana	1.07	.8	3.3
Oklahoma	1.26	...	3.4
Texas	1.12	1.0	2.5
Mountain			
Montana	.89	1.0	5.2
Idaho	.99	1.3	3.6
Wyoming	.95	1.0	2.6
Colorado	1.04	...	3.2
New Mexico	1.03	2.0	2.8
Arizona	1.03	...	3.3
Utah	1.09	...	3.8
Nevada	.81	1.1	4.5
Pacific			
Washington	1.07	...	5.8
Oregon	1.09	...	5.4
California	.90	...	2.2

Source: Based on the differences between tables 1 and 61.

(or farm) income.[26] In this sense, at least, the nonfarm sensitivity indexes can be said to be largely independent of the farm-nonfarm distribution of income within the states.

Nonfarm time-factor indexes are significant in 22 states, 5 more than had significant personal-income time-factor indexes. Thirteen states had

[26] The coefficient of determination is .11, which is significant at the .05, but not the .02 probability level.

significant time-factor indexes for both sets of data. The nonfarm time-factor indexes are not significant for four states, Arkansas, Vermont, Indiana, and California, which have significant personal-income time-factor indexes.[27] The nine states for which significant time-factor indexes are found only for the nonfarm component include four farm states, the Dakotas, Idaho, and Minnesota; three southern states, Kentucky, Alabama, and Tennessee; and two others, Nevada and Pennsylvania. The nonfarm time-factor indexes tend to be slightly larger than those based on personal income.

As was the case with personal income, there is a marked tendency for the nonfarm time-factor indexes to vary with the size of nonfarm income. Ten of the 19 positive time-factor indexes occur in states in the lowest quartile of 1929-1954 nonfarm income, and two of the three negative time-factor indexes occur in the uppermost quartile. Much the same distribution is found when the time-factor indexes are distributed by the 1929-1954 average size of personal income.

The finding of a significant time-factor index when the analysis is based on nonfarm income, for example, but none when the analysis is based on personal income, affects the relative size of the coefficients. When the time-factor coefficient is positive, the net regression coefficient is smaller than the gross coefficient between state and national income; a negative time-factor coefficient is accompanied by a net sensitivity index that is larger than the gross one. The net sensitivity indexes are accepted only when time is a significant factor in the analysis. Although a nonsignificant time-factor index is usually small, and the difference between the gross and net coefficients is also small, this small difference increases the observed difference in the size of the sensitivity coefficients based on nonfarm and personal incomes. For this reason, not all of the observed differences in the size of the nonfarm and personal-income coefficients can be attributed directly to the removal of the farm component from personal income in the 13 states for which significant time factors were found in one, but not both, income series. Some of the difference must be attributed to the indirect effects of farm income—that is, to the effects of farm income on the time-factor indexes.

The average nonfarm estimating errors for a few farm states are substantially lower than those found for personal income. For the remaining states the differences between the two income series are small, with

[27] Two of these states, Arkansas and Vermont, are among the states with significant farm time-factor indexes. Apparently, the farm component helped to make the personal-income indexes significant.

about one-half having larger nonfarm estimating errors and about one-half having larger personal-income errors.

Most of the nonfarm estimating errors that exceed 10 percent relate to the war years, 1941-1945. These are also the years with the largest average errors (table 16).[28] During these war years the extreme estimates obtained

TABLE 16
NONFARM ESTIMATING ERRORS, 1929-1954, BY YEAR

Year	Estimating errors[a] (percentages)			
	Average size[b]	Range		Number of states with estimating errors less than percent 3
		Lowest	Highest	
1929	3.6	−10.7	11.6	25
1930	2.9	−11.0	3.6	31
1931	3.2	− 8.6	7.1	27
1932	3.6	− 8.9	7.5	18
1933	3.3	−13.6	7.6	26
1934	3.1	− 5.5	10.2	29
1935	2.3	− 4.9	8.5	37
1936	2.6	− 4.5	11.6	32
1937	3.2	− 8.1	11.0	28
1938	3.0	− 5.6	7.7	23
1939	2.2	− 5.0	8.2	36
1940	3.0	− 6.1	11.6	26
1941	4.9	−11.5	12.1	20
1942	7.7	−19.0	31.2	13
1943	6.9	−15.5	19.2	5
1944	5.7	−14.0	14.4	14
1945	4.8	− 9.5	17.8	19
1946	3.0	− 7.9	8.8	25
1947	2.5	− 7.0	9.2	34
1948	3.1	− 7.6	12.7	30
1949	3.9	− 8.1	20.3	27
1950	2.7	− 6.2	11.2	34
1951	2.7	− 6.4	7.9	32
1952	2.4	− 8.0	7.8	31
1953	2.9	−10.8	4.2	29
1954	3.2	−10.9	5.1	27

[a] The difference between state per capita nonfarm income as estimated by the National Income Division and from the nonfarm sensitivity and time-factor indexes (table 15), expressed as a percentage of the latter. A minus sign indicates that the estimate based on the indexes exceeds the National Income Division estimate.
[b] The mean size of the errors (without regard to signs) for the 48 states.

from the nonfarm sensitivity and time-factor indexes differ from the National Income Division estimates by more than do the extreme estimates based on the personal-income indexes. For about two-thirds of the non-war years the estimating errors based on nonfarm income are less extreme than those based on personal income. The tendency for the extreme nonfarm estimating errors to be concentrated in the war period (when

[28] Of the 1,248 percentage errors for the 48 states and 26 years, 58 errors exceed 10 percent. Of those exceeding 10 percent, 41 relate to 1941-1945. By year, the numbers are: 1941, 5; 1942, 13; 1943, 8; 1944, 9; and 1945, 6. The largest number exceeding 10 percent in any other year is 3.

the rapid and uneven expansion of war-connected production was a large and transient force affecting state income differentially) suggests that for nonfarm income, at least, the inclusion of the war years does not invalidate the sensitivity and time-factor indexes. The frequency of extreme nonfarm estimating errors in North Dakota and Mississippi suggests that the exclusion of farm income is not a sufficient adjustment to make the farm states susceptible to description by devices such as the sensitivity and time-factor indexes, which depend upon regular and repetitive patterns of behavior. This suggestion is not supported, however, in the other farm states which have few errors, or none, which exceed 10 percent in the nonwar years.[29]

Conclusions

Several conclusions follow from the above discussion. First, the farm component of state per capita personal income behaves too erratically to be dealt with meaningfully in a simple regression framework. As has been seen, state per capita farm incomes simply do not follow the national farm-income pattern. Whether this is the consequence of using an industrial category as broad as agriculture, which includes small truck gardens and vast cattle ranches, hillside vineyards and sweeping wheat farms, each with its own geographic concentrations, or whether it is the consequence of interfarm dispersion within each limited type of farm category has not been investigated. Certainly farm income is more likely to be affected by floods, drought, heat waves, and late frosts—each a random element of the weather situation—than are other forms of economic activity. Because of the erratic behavior of farm income, the state farm sensitivity indexes cannot be relied upon.

Moreover, the inclusion of the farm component in state per capita personal income serves to disturb the personal-income sensitivity analysis, primarily by affecting the time-factor indexes and the average size of estimating errors. For the states with a large farm-income component, little confidence can be placed in the personal-income sensitivity indexes because of extreme estimating errors. For states with only moderate or small farm-income shares, the estimating errors arising from irregularities in farm income appear to affect the size of the sensitivity indexes less than the significance of the time-factor indexes is affected.

Conceptually, nonfarm per capita income is not as appropriate as per

[29] North Dakota has errors exceeding 10 percent in seven and Mississippi in five years. Other states with extreme errors in three or four years are Michigan, South Carolina, Alabama, Washington, and Oregon, none of which has extremely large farm-income shares.

capita personal income for describing the pattern of state responses to changes in the national income level. For all but two or three states, however, nonfarm income is relatively free from the disturbing influences of erratic changes in farm income, a fact which permits the use of sensitivity analysis, a technique designed to reflect regular and repetitive patterns of behavior. Consequently, more confidence can be placed in the statistical results, although they fail to reflect the total changes in income from all sources. Certainly, for states with large farm components, the indexes based on per capita personal income do not command confidence, and the indirect effects of farm-income variations often give rise to intolerably large and numerous nonfarm estimating errors. On the other hand, the similar magnitudes of the nonfarm and personal-income sensitivity indexes for the remaining states tend to increase the confidence with which these can be taken as indicative of the relative sensitivity of the economies in all but a few farm states.

A comparison of the time-factor indexes computed from the three series also suggests that statistically it is desirable to exclude farm income from the analysis. The indexes computed from the nonfarm series are more nearly in accord with popular notions about which of the states are experiencing relative gains or declines. The test of significance for the time-factor index is an exacting one, and it is possible that in some states with nonsignificant time-factor indexes there exist definite trends which cannot be described adequately by logarithmic regression lines. The failure of a time-factor index to pass a test of significance, however, is indicative of a pattern of irregular or cyclical deviations from the national pattern of income changes, deviations which make hazardous the use of selected years for ascertaining trends. An examination of the state income relatives (in chapter 2, table 4) for the states which have large percentage changes in the income relatives during 1929-1954, but do not have significant time-factor indexes, reveals either a marked cyclical pattern in the year-to-year changes or that the change in the level of income relatives occurred within the span of four or five years rather than as the result of persistent changes in one direction over most of the period. To rely entirely on selected years is to risk confusing a large but single change, such as a change in the relative price level of an important commodity or the construction of a defense plant, with the persistent and irreversible changes ordinarily associated with secular change.

Delaware is the only state with a significant time-factor index which differs in sign from the change in income relatives. The decrease in its income relatives is traceable to property income; the relatives for other types of income have increased. Property income is a much larger share of personal income in Delaware than in any other state, and its income relatives clearly reflect both the relative decrease in property income on the national level and the decrease in Delaware property income relative to that of the nation. Property income does not dominate the Delaware sensitivity and time-factor indexes, though it is probably responsible for the large estimating errors attached to them. The positive time-factor index found for Delaware apparently reflects the increase in importance of per capita labor income as a share of Delaware's personal income and its level relative to that of the nation. A decision as to whether Delaware's income is undergoing a secular change, whether the direction of this change is up or down, and whether the secular forces are likely to grow, diminish, or merely persist, involves not only a choice of statistical method, but also decisions as to whether the changes observed in particular industries and types of incomes have run their course.

That significant time-factor indexes are found for more states when farm income is excluded suggests that if other segments of personal income, either those with extremely stable shares (e.g., trade) or with unstable cyclical patterns (e.g., construction), were also excluded, additional states would have significant time-factor indexes for the remaining income. Two comments are in order: First, an understanding of the secular forces at work and some judgment as to whether these forces will persist can be best obtained by an examination of the detailed industries which comprise a state's economy. Moreover, there is no reason to expect that all industries in a state will move in the same direction. The problem here, however, is one of assaying the general course of a state's income from all industrial sources and from all types of payments. If the individual sources of income are separately investigated, some method will have to be found for weighting and combining the results so that some judgment can be formed regarding the aggregate of all industries in a state. Secondly, the exclusion of farm income does not wholly remove the effects of large and erratic changes in farm income, especially in states where it is an important income source. In a few states, such as the Dakotas, nonfarm income is so affected by the fluctuations in the excluded farm income that the regression technique breaks down and neither the sensitivity nor the time-factor indexes can be relied upon. Fortunately, there are but few such states. Unfortunately, these same irregular movements in farm income affect other types of measures.

In a few states the time-associated influences are so marked that almost any method is likely to reflect their direction and extremeness. There can be little doubt that in such states the observed changes in income relatives contain some element of trend. The downward trend in New York and the upward trend in South Carolina are cases in point. For most states, however, more evidence than the observed changes in income relatives is needed to establish even the direction of a trend. The time-factor indexes help in this regard.

Chapter 4

INCOME COMPONENTS

So FAR, our concern has been with the behavior of state per capita personal income from all sources. Even so, it was found desirable to separate farm from nonfarm income to gain a better understanding of the sources of the differential cyclical and secular behavior of the aggregate. Other components of personal income may also be distinguished and subjected to separate study. One of the more fruitful classifications of personal income is based on the type of service for which the income payment is made. Thus, personal income may be viewed as the sum of the flows of labor income, proprietors' income, property income, and transfer payments. An examination of the interstate differentials in these flows, plus some attention to the farm and nonfarm sources of proprietors' income, is the subject of this chapter.

Personal income measures these component flows as of the time when they are actually received by persons. Thus, they include factor returns from both past and present economic activity, and they exclude factor returns from current-year productive activity which are withheld, in the form of personal contributions for social insurance or business savings, for future payment. Consequently, the personal-income components cannot be used to judge whether there have been shifts in factor returns over a period.[1] They do show, however, the form in which income reaches the residents of the several states. Some of the year-to-year changes may reflect basic changes in the relative economic importance of the factors, such as the relative increases in the productivity of labor and capital;

[1] For recent discussion of changes in factor returns, see Jesse Burkhead, "Changes in the Functional Distribution of Income," *Journal of the American Statistical Association,* 48 (1953), 192; Edward F. Denison, "Distribution of National Income," *Survey of Current Business* (June 1952), p. 16, and "Income Types and the Size Distribution," *American Economic Review, Papers and Proceedings,* 44 (1954), 254; and George J. Schuller, "The Secular Trend in Income Distribution by Type, 1869-1948; A Preliminary Estimate," *Review of Economics and Statistics,* 35 (1953), 302.

others, however, may reflect only transitory phenomena, such as short-lived increase in corporate savings.

The interstate differentials in the component income flows provide one means of getting at the sources of some of the observed differences in the interstate behavior of personal income. Are there one or more per capita components which are nearly equal in every state? Do the large interstate differences in personal income arise from one or two of the components, while the contribution of the other components is negligible or offsetting? Is the tendency for interstate differentials to increase as the income level decreases, and to decrease as the income level increases, also found to be typical of the behavior of individual components and of some combinations of several components?

Knowledge of the interstate distribution of the individual components is also of some importance. Has the decline of interest as a share of personal income been accompanied by a changing distribution among the states? Has the increase in labor income been shared in by all states? Have transfer payments become more important only in the states where labor income is a relatively large share, or are they as important in states relatively more dependent upon farming?

Average Components

The relative flow of labor income can be expected to be larger in the highly industrialized states than in the sparsely populated and farm-oriented states. Among the latter, the flow of proprietors' income will be relatively large. Recipients of property income may choose their place of residence, at least to some extent, without regard to the location of the property or business activity producing the income. Some transfer payments, such as unemployment insurance or workmen's compensation, are distributed under rules which require a close proximity of the recipients' residence and his usual industrial activity. Other transfer payments, such as old-age pensions and veterans' benefits, may be distributed under rules which do not include residence requirements; these rules, however, may make qualifying for the transfer payment more attractive in some localities than in others.[2]

When state per capita personal income and its components are averaged over the entire period of 1929-1954, so that the effects of changes during

[2] For detailed studies of the state distribution of transfer payments in relation to income, see Howard G. Schaller, "Veterans Transfer Payments and State Per Capita Incomes, 1929, 1939, and 1949," *Review of Economics and Statistics*, 35 (1953), 325; and "Social Security Transfer Payments and Differences in State Per Capita Incomes, 1929, 1939, and 1949," *ibid.*, 37 (1955), 83.

the period are minimized, these expectations are found to be fulfilled (table 17). It should be noted that, just as personal income is the sum of the components, per capita personal income is the sum of the per

TABLE 17

AVERAGE 1929-1954 PER CAPITA INCOME COMPONENTS, BY STATE
(Dollars per capita)

State	Personal income	Labor income	Proprietors' income			Property income	Transfer payments
			Total	Farm	Nonfarm		
New England							
Maine	851	538	136	51	85	133	44
New Hampshire	906	599	113	25	88	146	47
Vermont	802	501	142	65	77	118	40
Massachusetts	1137	775	101	9	92	202	60
Rhode Island	1104	770	89	7	83	187	57
Connecticut	1337	925	122	18	104	245	45
Middle Atlantic							
New York	1304	863	145	15	130	240	56
New Jersey	1233	881	130	14	115	178	44
Pennsylvania	1026	717	109	18	90	151	50
East North Central							
Ohio	1071	749	144	43	100	134	44
Indiana	954	652	169	80	88	95	39
Illinois	1189	815	170	56	114	158	46
Michigan	1087	786	136	38	98	122	42
Wisconsin	941	594	190	93	97	118	38
West North Central							
Minnesota	883	518	216	119	97	104	44
Iowa	868	412	321	223	98	97	38
Missouri	907	565	182	83	99	116	44
North Dakota	706	320	293	221	72	59	34
South Dakota	722	320	306	228	78	62	34
Nebraska	860	435	292	194	97	99	35
Kansas	854	471	250	145	105	95	37
South Atlantic							
Delaware	1340	817	149	55	94	339	36
Maryland	1082	744	129	24	105	170	40
D. C.	1508	1038	123	...	123	260	86
Virginia	759	537	116	54	62	77	28
West Virginia	700	507	89	35	55	67	36
North Carolina	611	373	158	96	61	53	27
South Carolina	551	362	116	68	48	45	27
Georgia	627	401	133	65	68	62	31
Florida	833	510	151	50	100	129	43
East South Central							
Kentucky	611	371	144	85	59	62	34
Tennessee	621	387	139	70	69	61	35
Alabama	548	350	119	65	54	48	31
Mississippi	449	230	155	104	50	34	29
West South Central							
Arkansas	503	263	162	107	55	43	35
Louisiana	666	423	130	56	74	74	40
Oklahoma	710	410	173	85	87	81	46
Texas	796	485	179	80	99	96	35
Mountain							
Montana	961	532	286	185	101	98	45
Idaho	832	454	272	170	102	68	38
Wyoming	1021	635	243	133	110	104	38
Colorado	939	557	197	88	109	126	58
New Mexico	693	421	166	83	83	71	36
Arizona	858	537	189	92	97	88	44
Utah	839	552	159	66	93	84	44
Nevada	1305	862	224	61	162	176	43
Pacific							
Washington	1099	724	199	75	123	119	57
Oregon	1051	653	237	82	156	111	49
California	1274	814	214	61	153	186	59
United States	972	636	160	61	98	132	44

Source: appendix C, tables 62-67.

capita components. Thus the adjustment for differences in state populations does not affect the relationship of the components to the total.

Per capita labor and property incomes and transfer payments tend to be larger in states with the larger per capita personal incomes. However, there is no relation between the size of a state's per capita proprietors' income and its per capita personal income. This absence of relationship is a result of a marked tendency for per capita nonfarm proprietors' income to be larger in states with the larger per capita personal incomes, and of a weaker, though significant, tendency for per capita farm proprietors' income to be larger in the states with smaller per capita personal incomes.[3] Thus, the size of a state's per capita personal income is large or small not just because one component tends to be large or small, but because all the components except farm proprietors' income tend to be larger or smaller than average. Farm proprietors' income, on the other hand, tends to be largest where the sum of the other per capita components is smallest.

The differences in the average size of the components, ranging as they do from the $44 per capita transfer payment to the $636 per capita labor-income component, make it difficult to tell by inspection which of the components varies most by state. That there is considerable variation among states in each of the components is obvious from an inspection of table 17. When the interstate coefficient of variation for each of the components and combinations of components is computed, it can be seen that with the single exception of transfer payments each of the components has a larger relative interstate dispersion than does per capita personal income (table 18). The most disperse of the per capita components is property income, followed by labor income, proprietors' income, and transfer payments. With all but the smallest of components showing more relative interstate dispersion than personal income, and with all of the components except proprietors' income correlated with personal income, it may be asked how combinations of these components can have less relative interstate dispersion than the separate components. This question will now be examined.

For purpose of illustration, the combination of labor and proprietors' income will be examined first. The use of a particular combination per-

[3] The coefficients of determination between the average 1929-1954 state per capita personal income and the per capita components and subcomponents are: labor income, .95; property income, .87; transfer payments, .68; proprietors' income, .00; nonfarm proprietors' income, .74; and farm proprietors' income, —.26. In computing these coefficients the averages of the 1930, 1940, and 1950 midyear populations in each state were used as weights.

TABLE 18

INTERSTATE COEFFICIENTS OF VARIATION FOR AVERAGE 1929-1954 PER CAPITA INCOME COMPONENTS AND COMBINATIONS OF COMPONENTS

Component or combination of components	Coefficient of variation (percent)
Single components	
Labor income	30.0
Proprietors' income	29.2
Farm proprietors' income[a]	72.9
Nonfarm proprietors' income[a]	26.7
Property income	45.1
Transfer payments	21.5
Combinations of two components	
Labor and proprietors' income	23.4
Labor and property income	32.0
Labor income and transfer payments	29.1
Proprietors' and property income	23.9
Proprietors' income and transfer payments	23.2
Property income and transfer payments	38.4
Combinations of three components	
Labor, proprietors' and property income	25.9
Labor and proprietors' income and transfer payments	23.0
Labor and property income and transfer payments	31.1
Proprietors' and property income and transfer payments	22.8
Combination of all four components	
Per capita personal income	25.5

[a] Subcomponents of proprietors' income.
Source: computed from table 17. The coefficient of variation is the standard deviation expressed as a percentage of the mean. Per capita figures are used throughout. The averages of the midyear 1930, 1940, and 1950 state populations were used to weight both the means and standard deviations.

mits phrasing the question in more specific terms. If the sum of labor and proprietors' income is obtained for each state, so that a new state series is generated, would the new series have more or less dispersion than either labor income or proprietors' income? The answer to this question will depend upon the two coefficients of variation, for the labor and proprietors' income components, and upon the correlation between their state distributions.[4] If both labor income and proprietors' income in a

[4] This may be seen by an examination of the formulas used to compute the coefficient of variation for the combined series. The standard deviation for the combined series, s_{1+2}, may be obtained from:

$$s^2_{1+2} = s^2_1 + s^2_2 + 2r_{12}s_1s_2,$$

where the subscripts 1 and 2 denote the individual components and r_{12} is the coefficient of correlation between the two components. The coefficient of variation for the combined series is $s_{1+2}/\overline{X}_{1+2}$, where $\overline{X}_{1+2}$ is the mean of the combined distributions and is equal to the sum of the means of the individual components. The value of s_{1+2}, the standard deviation of the combined distributions, is smallest when $r_{12} = -1.00$, making $s_{1+2} = s_1 - s_2$; is largest when $r_{12} = +1.00$, making $s_{1+2} = s_1 + s_2$; and is intermediate when $r_{12} = 0$, making $s_{1+2} = (s^2_1 + s^2_2)^{\frac{1}{2}}$. It will be recognized that the last formula, $s_{1+2} = (s^2_1 + s^2_2)^{\frac{1}{2}}$, is the well-known one of the relationship of the hypotenuse of a triangle

state are larger than average, then their sum also is larger than the average of the combination.[5] Under such circumstances the coefficient of variation would be larger than that for either labor or proprietors' income. On the other hand, if the states with larger than average values of one of the components tend to have smaller than average values for the other component—that is, if the state distributions of the two components are negatively correlated, then (unless the negative correlation is perfect) no precise inference can be made about the size of the coefficient of variation of the combination relative to the sizes of the coefficients for the individual components. The negative correlation operates in the direction of reducing the coefficient for the combination, but there is no guarantee that it will make the coefficient for the combination less than either of the individual component coefficients.

Table 18 shows that the interstate coefficient of variation for labor and proprietors' income combined is less than the coefficient for either labor or proprietors' income. The implication is that in states where proprietors' income is particularly strong, labor income tends to be relatively weak.[6] This might be expected from the general consideration that obtaining a proprietors' income, especially from farming, typically precludes a person from working for a wage or salary, at least on more than a part-time basis.

The only other combination of per capita components which has a smaller coefficient of variation than either of the components taken separately is that for proprietors' and property income. Perhaps this is due to some interstate difference in the degree to which small businesses are incorporated. The coefficient for the labor- and property-income combination is less than that for property alone, but larger than that for labor alone. The combinations with transfer payments result in coefficients for the combination which are larger than the coefficient for transfer payments but smaller than those for the other income included in the combination.

If data were available, each of the components could, of course, be further subdivided. Labor income might be subdivided along industrial lines; property income might be separated into corporate-dividend income and other property income; and so on. Thus, each of the components

to the sides which form a right angle. Since the hypotenuse is always greater than either of the sides forming the right angle, r_{12} must be less than zero for s_{1+2} to be smaller than either s_1 or s_2; how much less than zero will depend upon the size of both s_1 and s_2.

[5] The extreme case would be one in which the rank order of the states was the same with respect to each component.

[6] The coefficient of correlation between the average 1929-1954 state per capita labor and proprietors' components is —.21.

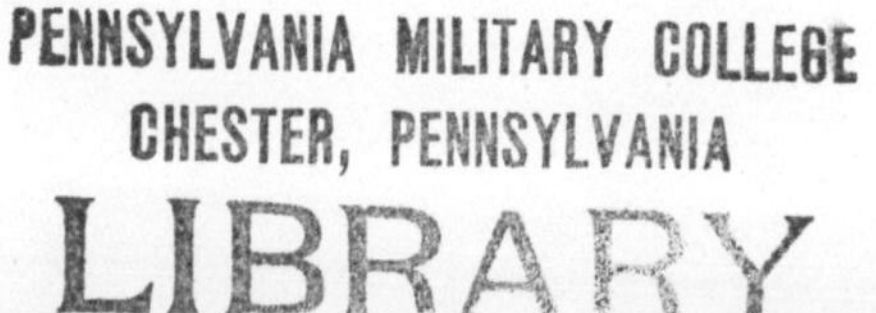

could be viewed as a combination of two or more subcomponents. Data are available for the farm and nonfarm subcomponents of proprietors' income.

The state distribution of average 1929-1954 per capita farm proprietors' income is very disperse, having an interstate standard deviation almost three-fourths the average size of the subcomponent. On the other hand, nonfarm proprietors' income has less relative interstate dispersion than any of the components except transfer payments. The state distributions of these two subcomponents are inversely correlated, farm proprietors' income tending to be larger in states in which per capita nonfarm proprietors' income is smaller.[7] One consequence is that the interstate coefficient of variation for proprietors' income is much smaller than the coefficient for the farm proprietors' subcomponent and only moderately larger than the coefficient for the nonfarm proprietors' subcomponent.

The combinations of three components may be interpreted in much the same way. There are, however, several ways of looking at these combinations of three components. The combination of labor, property, and proprietors' income, for example, may be obtained by combining labor with the combination of property and proprietors' income, or by combining property with the combination of labor and proprietors' income, or by combining proprietors' income with the combination of labor and property income. The interstate coefficient of variation for this combination of three components is smaller than the coefficient for either of the three components taken separately or for the combination of labor and property incomes, but larger than the coefficient for labor and proprietors' or property and proprietors' income.

When transfer payments or proprietors' income is combined with the combination of labor and property incomes, the three-component combination has less relative interstate dispersion than the combination of labor and property incomes. The relative interstate dispersion for the combination of three components which omits either transfer payments or proprietors' income is larger than that for personal income. Thus, excluding either proprietors' income or transfer payments from personal income leaves a three-component combination—either of labor, property, and transfers or of labor, property, and proprietors' income—which has more relative interstate dispersion than does per capita personal income. The size and interstate distribution of proprietors' income and transfer payments are such that when either is combined with another component or

[7] The coefficient of correlation between the average 1929-1954 state per capita farm and nonfarm proprietors' income subcomponents is —.23.

combination of components, the resulting combination has less relative interstate dispersion. The property- and labor-income components tend to act in an opposite direction, though not as consistently.

For the 1929-1954 period as a whole, each of the individual components except transfer payments has more relative interstate dispersion than does per capita personal income. This is also the case for combinations of two components with the exception of the combination of labor and property incomes and of each of these with transfer payments. Thus, while transfer payments tend to be complementary to labor and property income—that is, to be larger where these items are smaller, the size of transfer payments is not large enough to narrow greatly the relative interstate dispersion. The two combinations of three components which have more interstate dispersion than personal income are those which omit proprietors' income or transfer payments.

Composition of Personal Incomes, 1929-1954

The interstate differences in per capita personal income make it difficult to ascertain, by inspection at least, whether, for example, an $862 per capita labor income is a larger component of Nevada's per capita personal income than a $565 one is of Missouri's per capita personal income. By expressing each of the state average 1929-1954 components as a percentage of the average personal income for the same period, this difficulty can be overcome (table 19). The percentage components are identical whether they are computed from aggregates or per capita figures; that is, they are independent of population differences among the states. They are not, however, entirely independent of the size of personal income since the sum of the percentage components must equal 100; an unduly large per capita component, property income, for example, may serve to depress the percentages for the other components.

Except for proprietors' income and its farm subcomponent, there is less relative interstate dispersion in the percentage than in the per capita components of state per capita personal income for the 1929-1954 period taken as a whole.[8] The labor and nonfarm proprietors' percentage components are less disperse than transfer payments, which on a per capita basis was the least disperse of the components. Even property income, which per capita varied from $34 in Mississippi to $339 in Delaware, on a percentage basis varied in the same states from only 7.6 to 25.3 percent.

[8] The unweighted interstate coefficients of variation for the percentage components in table 19 are: labor income, 11 percent; nonfarm proprietors' income, 15 percent; transfer payments, 18 percent; property income, 28 percent; proprietors' income, 40 percent; and farm proprietors' income, 74 percent.

TABLE 19

AVERAGE 1929-1954 COMPOSITION OF PERSONAL INCOME, BY STATE
(Percentages of personal income)

State	Labor income	Proprietors' income			Property income	Transfer payments
		Total	Farm	Nonfarm		
New England						
Maine	63.2	16.0	6.0	10.0	15.6	5.2
New Hampshire	66.1	12.5	2.8	9.7	16.1	5.2
Vermont	62.5	17.7	8.1	9.6	14.7	5.0
Massachusetts	68.2	8.9	.8	8.1	17.8	5.3
Rhode Island	69.7	8.1	.6	7.5	16.9	5.2
Connecticut	69.2	9.1	1.3	7.8	18.3	3.4
Middle Atlantic						
New York	66.2	11.1	1.1	10.0	18.4	4.3
New Jersey	71.5	10.5	1.1	9.3	14.4	3.6
Pennsylvania	69.9	10.6	1.8	8.8	14.7	4.9
East North Central						
Ohio	69.9	13.4	4.0	9.3	12.5	4.1
Indiana	68.3	17.7	8.4	9.2	10.0	4.1
Illinois	68.5	14.3	4.7	9.6	13.3	3.9
Michigan	72.3	12.5	3.5	9.0	11.2	3.9
Wisconsin	63.1	20.2	9.9	10.3	12.5	4.0
West North Central						
Minnesota	58.7	24.5	13.5	11.0	11.8	5.0
Iowa	47.5	37.0	25.7	11.3	11.2	4.4
Missouri	62.3	20.1	9.2	10.9	12.8	4.9
North Dakota	45.3	41.5	31.3	10.2	8.4	4.8
South Dakota	44.3	42.4	31.6	10.8	8.6	4.7
Nebraska	50.6	34.0	22.6	11.3	11.5	4.1
Kansas	55.2	29.3	17.0	12.3	11.1	4.3
South Atlantic						
Delaware	61.0	11.1	4.1	7.0	25.3	2.7
Maryland	68.8	11.9	2.2	9.7	15.7	3.7
D. C.	68.8	8.2	....	8.2	17.2	5.7
Virginia	70.8	15.3	7.1	8.2	10.1	3.7
West Virginia	72.4	12.7	5.0	7.9	9.6	5.1
North Carolina	61.0	25.9	15.7	10.0	8.7	4.4
South Carolina	65.7	21.1	12.3	8.7	8.2	4.9
Georgia	64.0	21.2	10.4	10.8	9.9	4.9
Florida	61.2	18.1	6.0	12.0	15.5	5.2
East South Central						
Kentucky	60.7	23.6	13.9	9.7	10.1	5.6
Tennessee	62.3	22.4	11.3	11.1	9.8	5.6
Alabama	63.8	21.7	11.9	9.9	8.8	5.7
Mississippi	51.2	34.5	23.2	11.1	7.6	6.5
West South Central						
Arkansas	52.3	32.2	21.3	10.9	8.5	7.0
Louisiana	63.5	19.5	8.4	11.1	11.1	6.0
Oklahoma	57.7	24.4	12.0	12.2	11.4	6.5
Texas	60.9	22.5	10.0	12.4	12.1	4.4
Mountain						
Montana	55.4	29.8	19.2	10.5	10.2	4.7
Idaho	54.6	32.7	20.4	12.3	8.2	4.6
Wyoming	62.2	23.8	13.0	10.8	10.2	3.7
Colorado	59.3	21.0	9.4	11.6	13.4	6.2
New Mexico	60.8	24.0	12.0	12.0	10.2	5.2
Arizona	62.6	22.0	10.7	11.3	10.3	5.1
Utah	65.8	19.0	7.9	11.1	10.0	5.2
Nevada	66.1	17.2	4.7	12.4	13.5	3.3
Pacific						
Washington	65.9	18.1	6.8	11.2	10.8	5.2
Oregon	62.1	22.5	7.8	14.8	10.6	4.7
California	63.9	16.8	4.8	12.0	14.6	4.6
United States	65.4	16.5	6.3	10.1	13.6	4.5

Source: table 17.

Labor and property incomes tend to be larger percentages, and proprietors' (principally farm proprietors') income and transfer payments tend to be smaller percentages, of personal income in the states with higher per capita personal incomes.[9] This tendency for the percentage proprietors'-income component is largely a reflection of farm proprietors' income; the small interstate differences in what percentage nonfarm proprietors' income is of personal income do not appear to be associated with the size of personal income.

Marked geographic concentrations are found only for the percentage property and farm components. Nine states, all located along the Eastern seaboard, received 15 percent or more of their personal income in the form of property incomes. Farm proprietors' income was more than 15 percent of personal income in 10 states, of which 3 were in the South and the remainder in the West North Cental and Mountain states. When a large percentage of personal income in a state was received either as property or farm proprietors' income, the percentage received as labor income was somewhat smaller than average.

When labor and farm proprietors' income are combined, they account for about 72 percent of personal income, and there is very little relative interstate dispersion.[10] The combination varies only from 65 percent in Delaware (where the percentage property-income component is largest) to 78 percent in South Carolina (where the percentage property-income component is among the three smallest). There is a weak inverse association between what percentage this combination is of personal income and the size of personal income.[11]

During the 1929-1954 period labor and transfer payments became an increasing, and property incomes a decreasing, percentage of personal income (table 20). In seven of the eight years from 1929 to 1936, labor income accounted for less than 62 percent of personal income; during 1937-1940 it was 62-63 percent; and since 1941 it has been more than 64 percent of personal income. Transfer payments have increased from less than 2 percent in 1929-1930 to about 5 percent in 1946-1954. Property income, on the other hand, which was more than 20 percent of personal income in 1929-1933, decreased in importance steadily during 1934-1941, and has varied within the narrow range of 10-12 percent of personal in-

[9] The coefficients of determination between state per capita personal incomes and the state percentage components are: for labor income, .19; for proprietors' income, —.34; for property incomes, .53; and for transfer payments, —.44. Similar coefficients for the subcomponents of proprietors' income are: farm, —.36; nonfarm, —.04. All of the coefficients except the one for nonfarm proprietors' income are significant at the .01 probability level.

[10] The coefficient of variation for the labor and farm proprietors' percentage share of personal income is 4.1 percent.

[11] The coefficient of determination between state percentage shares of personal income accounted for by labor and farm proprietors' income and state per capita personal income is —.29.

TABLE 20

Composition of United States Personal Income, 1929-1954, by Year
(Percentages of personal income)

Year	Labor income	Proprietors' income: Total	Proprietors' income: Nonfarm[a]	Proprietors' income: Farm[a]	Property income	Transfer payments
1929	59.2	17.2	10.2	7.0	21.9	1.7
1930	60.6	15.1	9.6	5.4	22.4	1.9
1931	60.1	13.2	8.5	4.7	22.5	4.2
1932	61.6	10.5	6.7	3.7	23.7	4.2
1933	61.9	11.7	6.7	5.1	21.9	4.5
1934	63.6	13.0	8.5	4.5	19.4	4.0
1935	61.2	17.4	8.9	8.5	17.4	4.0
1936	61.8	15.4	9.6	5.8	17.8	5.1
1937	62.3	17.3	9.6	7.7	17.1	3.3
1938	62.8	16.1	9.9	6.3	16.9	4.2
1939	63.0	16.0	10.1	5.9	16.9	4.1
1940	63.2	16.6	10.8	5.9	16.1	4.0
1941	64.3	18.2	11.4	6.8	14.3	3.2
1942	66.0	19.5	11.3	8.1	12.0	2.5
1943	68.7	19.0	11.3	7.6	10.3	2.0
1944	69.2	18.5	11.3	7.2	10.1	2.2
1945	67.0	18.8	11.6	7.2	10.4	3.7
1946	62.4	20.1	12.2	7.9	11.1	6.4
1947	64.3	18.2	10.6	7.7	11.2	6.2
1948	64.8	18.5	10.4	8.1	11.3	5.4
1949	65.1	16.6	10.4	6.2	12.2	6.0
1950	64.8	16.0	10.1	5.9	12.5	6.6
1951	67.2	16.1	9.8	6.3	11.8	4.9
1952	68.7	14.8	9.5	5.3	11.6	4.9
1953	69.8	13.4	9.1	4.3	11.8	5.0
1954	68.8	13.2	9.0	4.2	12.4	5.6

[a]Subcomponents of proprietors' income.
Sources: appendix C, tables 62-67.

come during 1942-1954. Proprietors' income and its farm and nonfarm components, while volatile, have shown no pronounced trends.

The Leven estimates for 1919-1921 combine such transfer payments as were made during those years with labor income, so that it is necessary to deal with their combination rather than with the two components separately. The share of total income represented by labor income and transfer payments in 1920-1921 is about the same as that found in the National Income Division estimates for a decade later. The Leven estimates for 1919, of the share represented by this combination, however, is smaller than it was at any time during the 1929-1954 period; and although the share of labor income and transfer payments has increased over the latter period, the large jump in 1919-1920 makes it doubtful whether this single reading is evidence of a longer trend. Proprietors' income was a larger share in 1919-1921 than at any time during the later period. Property income, on the other hand, which decreased from 1929 to 1954, was a smaller share in 1919-1921 than in 1929-1954. The behavior of

TABLE 21

INTERSTATE COEFFICIENTS OF VARIATION OF PER CAPITA INCOME COMPONENTS AND COMBINATIONS OF COMPONENTS, 1919-1954, BY YEAR

Year	Per capita personal income[a]	Per capita individual components						
		Labor	Proprietors'			Property	Transfers
			Total	Farm[b]	Nonfarm[b]		
1919	27.6	n.a.	28.0	n.a.	n.a.	54.1	n.a.
1920	33.1	n.a.	23.6	n.a.	n.a.	54.9	n.a.
1921	37.3	n.a.	29.9	n.a.	n.a.	59.3	n.a.
1929	36.9	40.6	24.2	66.1	36.7	60.8	29.7
1930	38.9	39.9	27.4	66.7	35.1	61.1	30.0
1931	39.5	40.3	22.5	56.3	35.5	62.4	21.9
1932	41.0	39.8	21.1	53.5	35.8	66.2	28.0
1933	39.4	38.5	24.8	60.6	38.1	68.8	34.3
1934	36.9	36.9	27.3	80.5	32.9	66.2	36.8
1935	33.7	37.3	29.2	62.9	33.4	63.6	40.9
1936	34.4	36.9	23.8	59.1	33.0	60.8	27.4
1937	32.6	37.0	26.4	63.1	32.1	59.3	36.6
1938	32.9	36.1	24.3	62.0	32.4	56.4	40.0
1939	33.1	36.5	24.2	63.6	32.4	55.6	38.6
1940	33.1	36.4	25.7	67.7	33.0	54.6	40.6
1941	30.6	35.5	29.1	72.1	30.7	52.0	35.8
1942	26.9	32.9	34.4	78.5	29.8	45.6	32.4
1943	25.8	30.8	33.7	78.3	30.1	42.4	30.7
1944	23.6	28.4	30.4	75.0	30.0	40.3	26.9
1945	22.7	26.9	29.5	73.5	29.4	39.6	21.4
1946	23.6	30.2	32.1	74.9	28.7	38.1	18.9
1947	22.6	29.6	38.5	87.9	26.9	37.5	18.2
1948	21.4	27.7	41.5	92.5	24.5	35.5	22.1
1949	21.2	26.5	30.0	72.9	23.7	33.9	21.0
1950	21.8	27.1	34.3	86.5	24.0	35.3	21.5
1951	21.3	26.6	32.4	77.5	23.0	34.4	20.6
1952	20.9	25.3	30.5	80.0	20.3	34.0	20.6
1953	21.2	25.5	25.6	75.6	19.8	33.5	19.0
1954	20.8	24.4	30.2	89.5	19.0	32.8	18.1

(Continued on next page)

these two items, considered in the light of the data for the later period, makes it doubtful whether the same classification of property and proprietors' income was made in the two sets of estimates. Because of these doubts little reliance can be placed on the trends these figures indicate.

If we may judge by preliminary data for 1939-1951, there was little year-to-year change in the interstate coefficients of variation for the percentage components, except for property incomes. The interstate coefficients for the percentage property-income component decreased from 39 percent in 1939 to 22-23 percent during 1946-1951.[12]

[12] See my earlier article, "State Per Capita Income Components, 1919-1951," *Review of Economics and Statistics*, 38 (1956), 449, where the analysis is based on the components of state income payments as published in the *Survey of Current Business*. The 1939-1941 data are from the August 1945 issue; those for 1942-1947 from the August 1950 issue; those for 1948-1949 from the August 1952 issue; and those for 1950 and 1951 from the

TABLE 21 (Continued)

INTERSTATE COEFFICIENTS OF VARIATION OF PER CAPITA INCOME COMPONENTS AND COMBINATIONS OF COMPONENTS, 1919-1954, BY YEAR

Year	Combinations of two per capita components						Combinations of three per capita components			
	Labor and			Proprietors' and			All components except			
	Property	Proprie- tors'	Trans- fers	Property	Trans- fers	Property and transfers	Labor	Proprie- tors'	Property	Trans- fers
1919	n.a.	n.a.	37.7	25.9	n.a.	n.a.	n.a.	40.2	23.7	n.a.
1920	n.a.	n.a.	39.3	30.5	n.a.	n.a.	n.a.	41.7	30.2	n.a.
1921	n.a.	n.a.	38.4	40.8	n.a.	n.a.	n.a.	42.8	33.6	n.a.
1929	45.3	31.6	40.2	35.6	22.9	58.2	35.2	44.9	31.5	37.4
1930	45.0	33.4	39.4	40.0	26.0	58.1	39.5	44.5	33.3	39.2
1931	45.7	34.4	38.9	42.0	20.5	55.6	39.6	44.5	33.7	40.3
1932	46.3	34.8	38.8	47.2	19.3	59.8	44.7	45.3	34.4	41.8
1933	45.4	32.6	38.1	45.4	20.2	62.0	43.3	44.6	32.4	39.8
1934	42.5	31.2	36.7	41.6	22.5	60.3	40.4	42.1	31.3	37.1
1935	42.0	28.0	37.3	31.2	24.0	58.2	31.3	41.7	28.9	33.7
1936	41.1	30.2	35.9	35.0	20.7	52.5	33.5	40.1	29.8	34.9
1937	40.5	28.0	36.6	28.9	22.8	54.6	29.9	40.1	28.6	32.7
1938	39.5	28.9	36.0	30.3	21.2	52.0	30.5	39.3	29.2	32.8
1939	39.6	29.4	36.3	30.2	21.9	51.2	30.3	39.4	29.6	33.3
1940	39.2	29.3	36.2	30.4	24.4	50.5	30.8	39.3	29.8	33.0
1941	37.7	27.8	35.1	27.8	26.8	47.9	28.0	37.3	27.8	30.6
1942	34.2	25.0	32.6	25.7	31.3	42.3	25.6	33.9	25.1	26.9
1943	31.7	24.5	30.6	25.9	31.5	39.6	25.6	31.5	24.7	25.8
1944	29.3	22.2	28.1	23.1	27.8	37.1	22.9	29.1	22.3	23.6
1945	28.2	21.2	26.4	23.4	25.2	34.2	22.3	27.8	21.1	22.8
1946	31.0	23.0	28.6	24.4	24.2	29.5	21.4	29.6	22.2	24.4
1947	30.3	22.0	28.0	25.7	28.6	29.0	22.2	28.9	21.2	23.3
1948	28.3	20.5	26.7	27.0	31.6	29.9	23.8	27.5	20.1	22.0
1949	27.1	20.4	25.1	21.8	22.5	27.4	19.6	26.0	19.7	21.8
1950	27.9	21.1	25.6	23.8	24.3	27.8	20.8	26.5	20.3	22.6
1951	27.2	20.5	25.5	22.4	24.8	28.7	20.3	26.3	20.0	21.8
1952	26.0	19.7	24.4	20.9	22.7	28.3	20.0	25.2	19.7	21.4
1953	26.0	20.3	24.5	18.6	18.7	27.9	18.4	25.2	20.1	21.7
1954	25.2	19.7	23.5	20.3	20.3	27.0	19.2	24.4	19.6	21.3

[a]Per capita personal income is, of course, the sum of all four components.
[b]Subcomponents of proprietors' income.
Sources: 1919-1921: Leven, *op. cit.*; 1929-1954: appendix C, tables 62-67. The state per capita personal incomes were weighted by the state's midyear populations. The coefficient of variation is the standard deviation expressed as a percentage of the mean.

PER CAPITA COMPONENTS BY YEAR, 1919-1954

The relative interstate dispersion of per capita proprietors' income tended to increase over the 1929-1954 period; that of the other per capita personal income components to decrease (table 21). Per capita property income, like per capita personal income, tended to become relatively more disperse as income decreased following 1929, and then to show successively less relative interstate dispersion thereafter. None of the other com-

August 1953 issue. Although these income payment components differ slightly from the personal income components, the differences for this purpose appear to be minor. Because of the year-to-year stability in the interstate coefficients of variations, it was not believed worthwhile to recompute these measures on the basis of the personal income components.

ponents displayed this precise pattern. The relative interstate dispersion of labor income was higher in 1929-1932 than in any of the years thereafter; that of transfer payments, which, unlike the other components, increased in absolute amounts during the 1929-1932 period, was somewhat erratic, decreasing in 1931 and then increasing thereafter to a peak in 1935; that of proprietors' income increased in 1930 only to decrease to its lowest point in 1932.

The year-to-year changes in the relative interstate dispersion of proprietors' income are larger than for any other component. When the farm and nonfarm subcomponents are examined, it is found that the farm subcomponent is largely, though not entirely, responsible for the unique behavior of proprietors' income (chart 7). For every year the

CHART 7

INTERSTATE COEFFICIENTS OF VARIATION FOR FARM, NONFARM, AND ALL PROPRIETORS' INCOME, 1929-1954

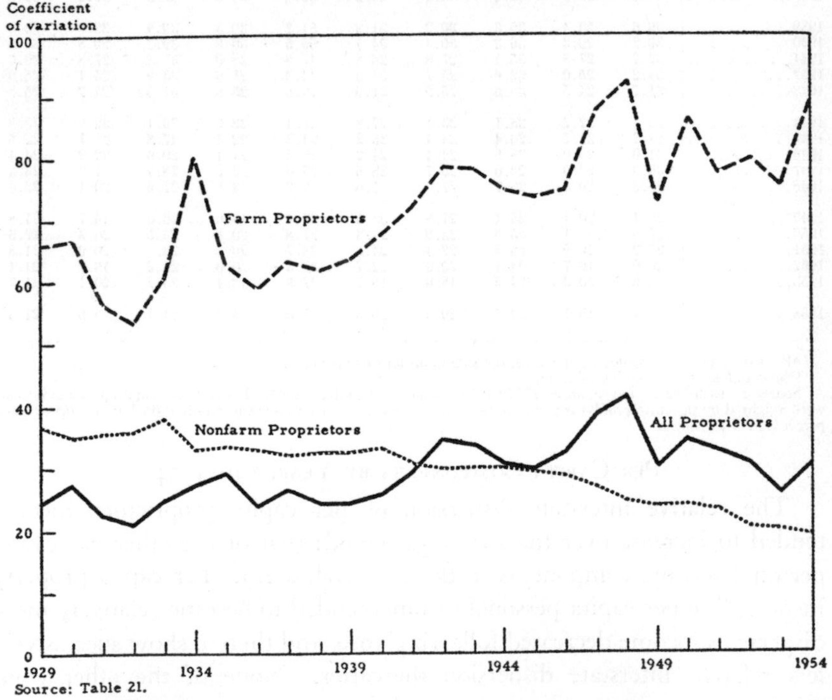

Source: Table 21.

interstate distribution of farm proprietors' income is relatively more disperse than any other component, subcomponent, or combination of components for which there are data. Too, the year-to-year changes on two occasions were as large as the 1954 coefficient for nonfarm proprietors' income. Nonfarm proprietors' income became relatively less disperse following 1929, but increased in 1932-1933, so that it was more disperse in 1933 than in any other year. Since 1933 the relative interstate dispersion of nonfarm proprietors' income has steadily decreased, with the only halting steps occurring in 1935, 1940, 1943, and 1950. While proprietors' income will be used extensively in the succeeding analysis, the fact that it is greatly influenced by, and has many of the characteristics of, farm proprietors' income will color the role it plays in combining with other components to determine the interstate distribution of personal income.

Among the combinations of two per capita components, only the combinations of proprietors' with labor and with property income are difficult to summarize. For the other combinations the decrease over the period in relative interstate dispersion is the only fact that need be added to the summary measures provided by the 1929-1954 averages. In view of the increasing relative interstate dispersion for proprietors' income, the decreasing dispersion for the combination of proprietors' income and transfer payments indicates that transfer payments became an increasingly effective offset in states in which proprietors' income decreased relatively. Most of the decrease in the relative interstate dispersion for this combination occurred after 1945.

When 1929-1954 averages are used, the combinations of proprietors' and property incomes and of proprietors' and labor incomes have approximately the same relative interstate dispersion. With increasing dispersion in proprietors' income and decreasing dispersion in property and labor incomes, these long-period averages ignore significant differences in trend. The relative interstate dispersion of both combinations decreased over the period, with the larger decrease in the proprietors' and property income combination (chart 8). Except for the 1935 combination of proprietors' and labor income, the relative interstate dispersion of each combination was larger than that of proprietors' income before 1941 and smaller thereafter.

The combination of three per capita components may be viewed, as has been mentioned before, as a combination of a single component with a combination of two components. Such a viewpoint yields three comparisons for each combination of three components. For example, the combination of labor, property, and proprietors' incomes yields comparisons between labor and the combination of property and proprietors' incomes, between property and the combination of labor and proprietors'

CHART 8

INTERSTATE COEFFICIENTS OF VARIATION FOR LABOR, PROPERTY, AND PROPRIETORS' INCOME, AND THEIR COMBINATIONS, 1929-1954

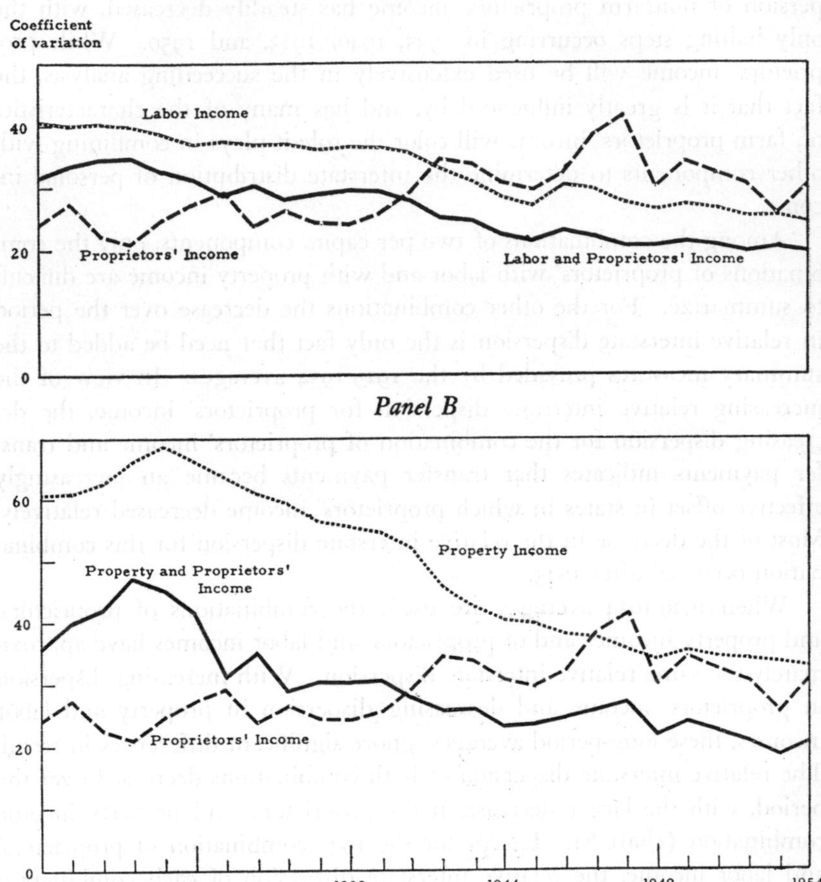

Source: Table 21.

incomes, and between proprietors' and the combination of labor and property incomes. To avoid the cumbersomeness of such multiple comparisons, each of four combinations of three components is compared only with per capita personal income—that is, with the combination of all four components. The difference between per capita personal income and the combination of the per capita proprietors', property, and labor incomes, for example, yields the difference which can be attributed to the effect of excluding transfer payments from personal income.

All of the combinations of three components show decreasing relative interstate dispersion over the period. The exclusion of transfer payments from per capita personal income has the smallest effect, changing the interstate coefficients of variation by .8 percentage points or less in any year. In five of the years, 1935 and 1941 to 1944, the exclusion of transfer payments left the relative interstate dispersion unchanged. In 1938 and 1940, the relative interstate dispersion of per capita personal income was slightly greater than that for the combination which excluded transfer payments, indicating that in these years the interstate distribution of transfer payments tended to accentuate the interstate differences in the other components.

The exclusion of per capita labor income from personal income results in lower relative interstate dispersion in every year except 1930 to 1934 and 1948. During the 1930-1934 period, the interstate dispersion of property income was particularly high, while property income was greater than proprietors' income and was little affected by the small amounts of transfer payments. In 1948 both transfer payments and proprietors' income had more relative interstate dispersion than in the years immediately before and after 1948, and apparently some of the increased dispersion was due to increased amounts of these items in states with the higher property incomes. Typically, labor income is higher in states with the higher property, nonfarm proprietors', and transfer payments.

The interstate distribution of per capita personal income is relatively more disperse when proprietors' income is excluded, and relatively less disperse when property income is excluded. The relative interstate dispersion of per capita income excluding property income, while smaller than that for per capita personal income, shows less downward trend than any of the three-component combinations. Thus, the downward trends in the relative size and interstate dispersion of property incomes play a leading role in the downward trend of the relative interstate dispersion of per capita personal income.

The relative interstate variation of the 1919-1921 per capita components (estimated by Leven), while somewhat more consistent than are the percentage components with the 1929-1954 coefficients, has behavioral characteristics that are difficult to reconcile with those of the latter period. The year-to-year variations within the 1919-1921 period tend to be as large as those found during 1929-1954 for the combinations that include proprietors' income. The labor income and transfer payments combination is of approximately the same level and has approximately the same amplitude of year-to-year change as is found in the latter period. When these two are combined with property income, the level is lower than would be expected on the basis of the data for the later years, presumably because of the smaller relative interstate variation in property incomes coupled with its smaller share of the total (above, table 20). Proprietors' income is volatile in the data for both periods, and it would be difficult to say whether its relative interstate variation in 1919-1921 was more or less than would be expected on the basis of the 1929-1954 data. When proprietors' income is combined with property income, the year-to-year changes in relative interstate dispersion tend to be cumulative, rather than compensating as they are in the 1929-1954 period.

Accordion Effect

In chapter 2 it is shown that the relative interstate dispersion of per capita personal income tends to decrease as the national level of personal income increases, and vice versa. One clue as to how this accordion effect operates on relative interstate dispersion is provided by the inverse association between state income level and the size of the state's sensitivity index (chapter 3). It is also found that the decrease in the relative interstate dispersion of per capita personal income over the 1929-1954 period is greater than can be explained by the accordion effect. Do all, or only some, of the components and combinations of components show the same accordion effect? Is there also some trend in the changes in the relative interstate dispersion of the components and their combinations, not accounted for by the accordion effect? If so, what is the direction of this trend? This section will be devoted to an examination of these questions.

With the exception of proprietors' income, its farm subcomponent, and its combination with transfer payments, the accordion effect is found in all of the components and their combinations (table 22). For example, as the national level of labor income increases, the relative interstate dispersion of labor income decreases, and vice versa. On the other hand, there is a direct association between the national level of per capita farm proprietors' income and its relative interstate dispersion—that is, they tend to change together and in the same direction. The accordion effect is most marked for labor income and the combinations of components in which it is included. It is least marked for transfer payments and nonfarm proprietors' income.

When time is introduced as an independent variable and a multiple correlation computed, time is a significant variable for all of the individual components except labor income. Except for the single com-

TABLE 22

RELATIONSHIP OF CHANGES IN INTERSTATE COEFFICIENTS OF VARIATION TO CHANGES IN INCOME LEVEL AND TIME, 1929-1954, BY COMPONENT AND COMBINATION OF COMPONENTS

Per capita component or combination of components	Coefficients of determination[a] between interstate coefficient of variation and			
	Level of specified income			Time, net of level of specified income (partial)
	Simple	And time (multiple)	Net of time (partial)	
Single components				
Labor income	−.90	*	−.34	*
Proprietors' income	.58	.82	.30	.57
Farm proprietors' income[b]	.60	.73	.16	.31
Nonfarm proprietors' income[b]	−.67	.77	*	.32
Property income	−.70	.75	−.45	−.17
Transfer payments	−.67	.93	−.52	.79
Combination of two components				
Labor and proprietors' income	−.91	*	−.46	*
Labor and property income	−.91	*	−.55	*
Labor income and transfer payments	−.92	*	−.40	*
Proprietors' and property income	−.76	*	*	*
Proprietors' income and transfer payments	*	.88	.31	.86
Property income and transfer payments	−.84	.86	−.57	−.16
Combination of three components				
Labor, proprietors' and property income	−.91	*	−.50	*
Labor and proprietors' income and transfer payments	−.93	*	−.51	*
Labor and property income and transfer payments	−.93	*	−.60	*
Proprietors' and property income and transfer payments	−.86	*	−.34	*
Combination of all four components				
Per capita personal income	−.92	.97	−.56	−.59

*Coefficient not significant at .05 probability level.
[a]The sign has been retained to show the direction of the relationship. The logarithms of the interstate coefficient of variation and of the income components were used in obtaining these coefficients of determination.
[b]Subcomponents of proprietors' income.
Sources: Coefficients of variation, table 21; income level, table 2, and appendix C, tables 62-67.

ponents, however, time is significant only for two combinations of two components and for per capita personal income.

One of the weaknesses of working with the gross relationship between the interstate coefficients of variation and the national income level for a period such as 1929-1954 is that there is a pronounced upward drift in income levels and a pronounced downward drift in the coefficients for most of the components. While income levels probably decreased in enough years to provide a reversible relationship,[13] the intensity of these drifts often is enough to insure significant coefficients of determination. Thus, time, as reflected in the income level, may be largely responsible

[13] The relationship is between the logarithms of the variables, so that the regression coefficient would, if it were calculated, describe the percentage change in the coefficient of variation associated with a one percent change in the level of income. When the sign of the regression coefficient is negative, the changes are in opposite directions; when the sign is positive, the changes are in the same direction.

for the size of the coefficients of determination. The coefficients of partial determination provide an adequate separation of the two sets of interrelated forces, the changes in level and in time.

After the influence of time is taken into account, the relationship between changes in income level and the coefficients of variation has the same sign in all but two cases. The apparent relation between relative interstate dispersion of nonfarm proprietors' income and changes in its level is due to the fact that both variables are related to time. The apparent relationship for the combination of proprietors' and property incomes is traced to the combined effects of changes in level and time, neither of which is significant after account is taken of the effects of the other.

Only property income, taken alone and in combination with transfer payments, shows a tendency to become less disperse over the period than can be accounted for by changes in its level. Changes in the relative interstate dispersion of labor income are adequately accounted for by changes in its level, and time is not significant as an independent variable. The relative interstate dispersion of proprietors' income and transfer payments, on the other hand, tends to increase. The marked tendency toward decreasing relative interstate dispersion observed for per capita personal income thus apparently stems largely from the behavior of per capita property income. Property income tends to be a larger share of personal income in states with higher per capita personal incomes; it has been a decreasing share of personal income over the 1929-1954 period; and, on a per capita basis, it is becoming more nearly equally distributed among the states. These three facets of its behavior have combined to exert a powerful influence on the relative interstate dispersion of per capita personal income.

Chapter 5

OCCUPATIONAL EARNINGS

One of the sources of variation in state per capita incomes is in the varying occupational structure of the states. Both the wage and salary earnings for different occupations and the numbers in each occupation vary from state to state. The *Census of Population, 1950* provides data for 1949 which permit a rough, though fairly acceptable, analysis of state earning differentials in these terms. Wages and salaries were almost two-thirds of personal income in 1949.

Occupational Earnings Distribution

The average annual earnings of those persons in the experienced labor force who received wages and salaries in 1949 varied by occupation from a low of $488 among private household laundresses, living out, to a high of $7,335 among airplane pilots and navigators (table 23). When male and female wage and salary workers are considered separately, the range of occupational averages is narrowed slightly for males, from $551 for newsboys to $7,412 for airplane pilots and navigators, and drastically for females, from $250 among apprentices in the building trades, not elsewhere classified, to $4,118 among lawyers and judges. The differences in the distribution of occupational averages for male and female wage and salary workers is based largely on the almost universal tendency for the females in a particular occupational category to have lower average earnings than the males.[1] One consequence of the male-female differ-

[1] Thirteen of the 14 occupations in which female earnings are higher than those of male workers are predominantly male occupations: "athletes"; "telegraph messengers"; "newsboys"; "members of the armed forces" (i.e., not employed since leaving the armed forces); "apprentice bricklayers and masons, carpenters, and electricians"; "bootblacks"; "marshals and constables"; "lumbermen, draftsmen, and woodchoppers"; "laborers in saw-mills, planing mills, and millwork"; "laborers in ship and boat building and repairing"; and personal service workers in "nonmanufacturing industries." "Library attendants" is a predominantly female occupation.

TABLE 23

FREQUENCY DISTRIBUTION OF 1949 AVERAGE ANNUAL OCCUPATIONAL EARNINGS
(Number of occupations)

Average Annual Earnings	Males	Females	All Earners
Under 1,000	5	27	10
1,000-1,249	5	27	8
1,250-1,499	5	53	14
1,500-1,749	12	70	23
1,750-1,999	33	81	41
2,000-2,249	44	58	49
2,250-2,499	52	30	55
2,500-2,749	61	26	52
2,750-2,999	44	18	30
3,000-3,249	26	16	25
3,250-3,499	34	10	27
3,500-3,749	17	2	17
3,750-3,999	17	2	11
4,000-4,249	9	1	8
4,250-4,499	7		15
4,500-4,749	11		8
4,750-4,999	11		11
5,000-5,249	8		6
5,250-5,499	8		2
5,500-5,749	4		3
5,750-5,999	2		2
6,000 and over	6		5
All occupations	421	421	422

Source: computed from an unpublished tabulation, identified as D-6, of a 3.3 percent sample of 1950 census of population returns. Aggregate wages were computed by multiplying the midpoint of each wage and salary class by the number in the class and summing over all classes. The midpoint of the $10,000-and-over class was assumed to be $17,500, a figure obtained by rounding averages of earnings reported in *Statistics of Income*, part I, for several years. In computing the averages, only class 1 and 2 workers ("private wage and salary workers" and "government workers") who reported wage income were included. Occupational categories chiefly for the self-employed (farmers; self-employed managers, proprietors, etc.; unpaid farm laborers; and self-employed farm service laborers) have been omitted.

entials is that the average annual earnings of all workers in an occupational category will tend to be between the corresponding averages for males and females, considered separately.

The average earnings for a particular occupation are based on the reported 1949 wage and salary earnings of a 3.3 percent sample of all persons who were classified (1) as either "private wage and salary workers" or "government workers," (2) as attached to the occupation, and (3) as having wage or salary income in 1949.[2] The income of workers who were self-employed or were unpaid family workers during the census week (ordinarily a week in April 1950) does not enter these computations. Occupational classification is on the basis of the job held during the census week or, for those unemployed at that time, on the basis of the last job held. Persons having no wage and salary income in 1949 are excluded.

Although certain occupational categories are clearly designed for the

[2] For definitions of these and subsequent terms used in this section, see "Introduction," vol. 2, *U. S. Census of Population, 1950*.

self-employed (e.g., "Managers, officials, and proprietors (n. e. c.)—self-employed"), a few persons in these categories may have had 1949 wage and salary income, either from employment which differed from that during the census week or as supplementary to their self-employment income. Some 24 occupational categories[3] clearly designed for the self-employed are omitted from this analysis. For a number of occupations, such as those of professional workers, in which there are both self-employed and wage earners, the number of private wage workers and government employees with 1949 wage or salary income is large enough to make it possible to compute acceptable average wage and salary earnings.

The most detailed census classification of occupations is still fairly broad. Within a single category there is room for a wide variety of operations and a still wider range of skills with which the operations are performed. Simply to mention that persons of differing ages, training, and experience can be classified in the same occupation on the basis of the job held during a particular week is enough to make this point. Too, while the basis of the classification is the job held during a given week, the earnings refer to the previous entire calendar year. Thus, there is room for considerable variation to arise from differences in occupations during the income year, in the length of the work year, and in the length of the work weeks during the year. For only one characteristic, sex, do the data make a direct distinction.

The use of the occupational averages implicitly assumes that the earning differences between occupations are significantly greater than the variation within the occupational categories. Although this assumption has not been tested explicitly, the relatively large number of cases in each occupation and the wide range of occupational averages (table 23) would lead to the conclusion that the occupational classification as a whole is significant, even though the differences between a pair of occupational categories may not be so. Of more importance for present purposes is the assumed existence of a hierarchy of occupations, so that within a given setting, for example, carpenters will have a unit pay scale always somewhat higher than construction laborers and lower than engineers. There are some data which show that this assumption is not too unreasonable.[4]

[3] These are farmers, unpaid family workers, self-employed farm service laborers, and 21 categories of managers, officials, and proprietors—self-employed.

[4] Herman P. Miller, in *Income of the American People,* New York, 1955, pp. 55-58 and 108-109, on the basis of a study of 1939 and 1949 census data for those intermediate occupations for which comparable data are available, shows that there is a strong tendency for

State Variation in Earnings

The population census also provides the data necessary to estimate by state the 1949 average annual wage and salary earnings of persons in the experienced labor force who reported 1949 wage or salary income (table 24, column 2). By state these earnings varied from $1,408 in Mississippi to $2,974 in Michigan and $3,000 in the District of Columbia.

The average annual earnings per wage and salary worker reported by the census for 1949 were $2,556; when the National Income Division estimate is made comparable insofar as possible, it is about 13.4 percent higher. There are many facets of census techniques which contribute to some understatement of income on census returns.[5] In common with many enumerative surveys, the census reports rely heavily on the knowledge and memory of the person (typically the housewife) whom the enumerator is able to interview. Although wage and salary income is somewhat better reported than income from other sources, it still appears to be underreported. In part, this may be due to failure to recall, and thus to report, wages and salaries from temporary and secondary jobs or from overtime, bonuses, and other sources of nonrepetitive payments. In part, it may reflect the respondent's lack of information, particularly when asked to report for workers dependent on piece-work rates or tips.

If every person's earnings were underreported to the same extent, or if the extent to which reported earnings deviated from true earnings were uncorrelated with any of the characteristics which vary significantly by state, then the underreporting in the census figures might affect the earnings level but not the relative position of the states.

There is some evidence, however, that wage and salary income is underreported to a greater relative extent at higher than at lower earning levels. Whether there is also greater underreporting in the higher than in the lower earnings of states can be examined by comparing the average earnings reported by the census and those estimated by the National Income Division, after the latter are adjusted to make them as conceptually comparable as possible with census definitions (chart 9). Among the states with the lowest earnings, the adjusted National Income Di-

the occupations to maintain their same relative position over the 1939-1949 period. This tendency is accompanied by a tendency for the earning rates of the lower-ranking occupations to increase relative to the higher-ranking occupations, and for the relative dispersion within the occupations to decrease. There are only 158 intermediate occupations for males and 67 for females. Were information on earnings rates for each detailed occupation available by state for even a single year, an examination of whether every state had the same occupational hierarchy would test this assumed relationship much more adequately.

[5] Herman P. Miller, "An Appraisal of the 1950 Census Income Data," *Journal of the American Statistical Association*, 48 (1953), 28-43.

TABLE 24

Reported and Rate-Constant 1949 Average Annual Occupational Earnings, by State, for All Wage and Salary Workers

State (1)	Average annual earnings: Reported (2)	Average annual earnings: Rate-constant (3)	Differences between state and national: Reported earnings (4)	Differences between state and national: Rate-constant earnings (5)	Difference between state reported and rate-constant earnings (6)	Percentage differences; attributable to occupational: Composition (national weights) (7)	Percentage differences; attributable to occupational: Earning rates (state weights) (8)
New England							
Maine	$2,065	$2,346	$−491	$−171	$−281	−6.8	−13.6
New Hampshire	2,193	2,392	−363	−125	−199	−5.0	−9.1
Vermont	1,997	2,363	−559	−154	−366	−6.1	−18.3
Massachusetts	2,610	2,570	54	53	40	2.1	1.5
Rhode Island	2,359	2,508	−197	−9	−149	−.4	−6.3
Connecticut	2,795	2,636	239	119	159	4.7	5.7
Middle Atlantic							
New York	2,921	2,588	365	71	333	2.8	11.4
New Jersey	2,959	2,646	403	129	313	5.1	10.6
Pennsylvania	2,630	2,542	74	25	88	1.0	3.3
East North Central							
Ohio	2,797	2,644	241	127	153	5.0	5.5
Indiana	2,652	2,586	96	69	66	2.7	2.5
Illinois	2,936	2,629	380	112	307	4.4	10.5
Michigan	2,974	2,660	418	143	314	5.7	10.6
Wisconsin	2,586	2,562	30	45	24	1.8	.9
West North Central							
Minnesota	2,472	2,546	−84	29	−74	1.2	−3.0
Iowa	2,312	2,482	−244	−35	−170	−1.4	−7.4
Missouri	2,422	2,512	−134	−5	−90	−.2	−3.7
North Dakota	2,007	2,400	−549	−117	−393	−4.6	−19.6
South Dakota	2,028	2,397	−528	−120	−369	−4.8	−18.2
Nebraska	2,262	2,490	−294	−27	−228	−1.1	−10.1
Kansas	2,372	2,564	−184	47	−192	1.9	−8.1
South Atlantic							
Delaware	2,752	2,554	196	37	198	1.5	7.1
Maryland	2,652	2,552	96	35	100	1.4	3.8
D. C.	3,000	2,499	444	−18	501	−.7	16.7
Virginia	2,277	2,401	−279	−116	−124	−4.6	−5.4
West Virginia	2,412	2,490	−144	−27	−78	−1.1	−3.2
North Carolina	1,841	2,235	−715	−282	−394	−11.2	−21.4
South Carolina	1,740	2,169	−816	−348	−429	−13.8	−24.7
Georgia	1,801	2,241	−755	−276	−440	−11.0	−24.4
Florida	2,064	2,303	−492	−214	−239	−8.5	−11.6
South Central							
Kentucky	2,024	2,399	−532	−118	−375	−4.7	−18.5
Tennessee	1,956	2,369	−600	−148	−413	−5.9	−21.1
Alabama	1,832	2,292	−724	−225	−460	−8.9	−25.1
Mississippi	1,408	2,180	−1,148	−337	−772	−13.4	−54.8
Arkansas	1,594	2,244	−962	−273	−650	−10.8	−40.8
Louisiana	2,114	2,383	−442	−134	−269	−5.3	−12.7
Oklahoma	2,238	2,527	−318	10	−289	.4	−12.9
Texas	2,277	2,445	−279	−72	−168	−2.9	−7.4
Mountain							
Montana	2,461	2,443	−95	−74	18	−2.9	.7
Idaho	2,300	2,397	−256	−120	−97	−4.8	−4.2
Wyoming	2,557	2,498	1	−19	59	−.8	2.3
Colorado	2,412	2,526	−144	9	−114	.4	−4.7
New Mexico	2,364	2,422	−192	−95	−58	−3.8	−2.5
Arizona	2,397	2,382	−159	−135	15	−5.4	.6
Utah	2,610	2,594	54	77	16	3.1	.6
Nevada	2,839	2,420	283	−97	419	−3.9	14.8
Pacific							
Washington	2,774	2,526	218	9	248	.4	8.9
Oregon	2,668	2,430	112	−87	238	−3.5	8.9
California	2,870	2,551	314	34	319	1.4	11.1

Col. 2—Computed from table 94, *Census of Population, 1950*, for each state. The averages relate to wage and salary workers with 1949 earnings. The midpoint of the $10,000-and-over class was assumed to be $17,500 (see table 23).

Col. 3—Estimated from the occupational averages underlying table 23 and the state's experienced labor force in each occupation (table 73, *Census of Population, 1950*, for each state). These computations were made by the Bureau of the Census as a special tabulation.

Col. 4—The difference, column 2 minus $2,556, the weighted average of column 2.

Col. 5—The difference, column 3 minus $2,517, the weighted average of column 3. The numbers in the experienced labor force were used as weights. The result is the difference between state and national occupational composition weighted by national average annual occupational earnings.

Col. 6—The difference, column 2 minus column 3. The result is the difference between state and national average annual occupational earnings weighted by the number in each occupation in the particular state. These differences are affected by the $39 discrepancy between the weighted averages of columns 2 and 3.

Col. 7—Column 5 expressed as a percentage of the weighted average of column 3 ($2,517).

Col. 8—Column 6 expressed as a percentage of column 2.

CHART 9

NATIONAL INCOME DIVISION AND CENSUS ESTIMATES OF STATE AVERAGE ANNUAL EARNINGS OF WAGE AND SALARY WORKERS, 1949

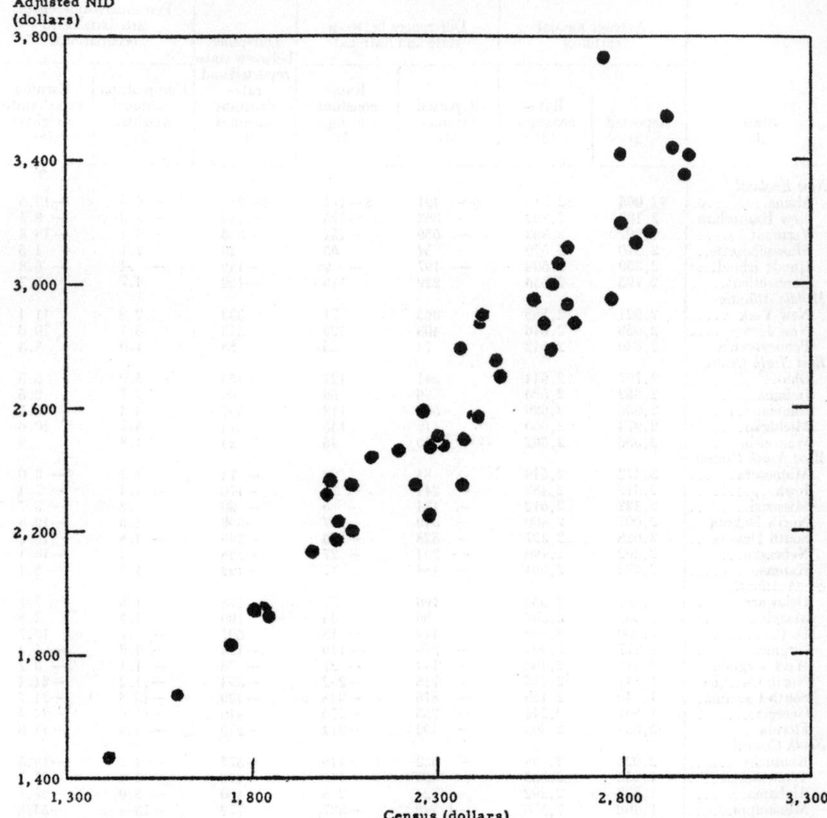

Sources: The National Income Division estimates of state wage and salary income were adjusted to conform roughly with Census definitions, by subtracting from them the sum of military wages and salaries and farm wages paid in kind, and dividing the remainder by the number of wage and salary income recipients shown in the *Census of Population, 1950*. Nonfarm wages paid in kind should also have been subtracted from the National Income Division state wage and salary income figures, but state estimates of nonfarm wages paid in kind were not available. The Census data are from table 4, column 2.

vision estimates are only about 3 percent higher than those of the census. At the other end of the distribution, the differences are in the neighborhood of 14-16 percent, somewhat higher than average.[6] The inability

[6] The least-squares regression line fitted to these data is $X_{12} = -505 + 1.332X_2$ (where X_{12} is the adjusted National Income Division state annual earning per worker estimated from X_2, the state average annual earnings of wage and salary workers reported in the population census). Such a line indicates that, on the average, census earnings are about 3 percent below the adjusted National Income Division estimates at the level of the state with the

to remove nonfarm wages paid in kind from the National Income Division estimates could account for some part of these interstate differentials in the two series only if in-kind payments tended to be relatively larger in the areas showing higher earnings, a condition which seems highly unlikely.

Thus, the census wage and salary income estimates clearly seem to be biased in the direction of greater relative underreporting as state earnings per worker increase.

One consequence of this bias is that the census distribution of state earnings per worker is more closely grouped around the mean—that is, the census earnings are less disperse than the adjusted National Income Division estimates. The tendency toward a more compact grouping of the states by size of average earnings would not be of great importance for the present analyses if the rank order of the states were the same in both distributions. Although there is a strong tendency in this direction, such is not the case.[7] The states which have a higher rank on the basis of the National Income Division estimates than on the basis of census data do not appear to have any important characteristic which differentiates them significantly from the states which have lower ranks on the same basis. Farm and highly industrialized states, sparsely and densely populated states, and high- and low-income states all are represented in both groups. There is some tendency for states west of the Mississippi to have lower ranks and those east of the Mississippi to have higher ranks on the basis of National Income Division estimates.[8] Except for the slight differences based on the broad geographic distinction provided by the Mississippi River, the differences in rank order appear to be random.

The effects of the state biases in the enumerative census data are difficult to appraise. When there are alternative methods of analysis, a method may be chosen which tends to dampen these effects on the final results; but such a choice is rarely available, nor has any method been found for adjusting the basic census data for these biases. The census data must be used as they are without adjustment, if at all. An appraisal of the significance of the analytical results, however, must take some

---

lowest census earnings, and 16 percent below at the level of the state with the highest census earnings. This regression line differs significantly from a line of proportional change, $X'_{12} = 1.134X_2$, which passes through the origin and the weighted means of the two earnings series.

[7] The coefficient of rank correlation between the two distributions is .96.

[8] West of the Mississippi River, 14 states have lower and 7 states higher ranks on the basis of adjusted National Income Division estimates than on the basis of census earnings. East of the Mississippi, 8 states have lower and 13 higher ranks on the same basis.

account of the interstate differentials between the enumerative census data and the estimates prepared by the National Income Division largely on the basis of establishment data.

State Rate-Constant Earnings

Some part of the differences between the state and national reported average annual earnings of wage and salary workers (table 24, column 4) may be due to varying state occupational compositions. A state with a relatively larger proportion of its labor force attached to the lower-paying occupations might be expected to have a lower average annual wage and salary earning than a state with a relatively smaller proportion in these categories. The effects of these compositional differences may be appraised by computing, for each state, an average earning that reflects only differences in occupational composition. This may be done by weighting the national average annual earning in an occupation by the number in the experienced labor force in the state attached to the occupation, and summing the results for all occupations to obtain an estimated average earning figure for the state (table 24, column 3). Since the same national occupational earnings are used in each state (only occupational composition is allowed to vary), these figures may be said to be rate-constant.

Although the state rate-constant earnings are expressed in dollars, their similarity to constant-weight index numbers is readily apparent. Rate-constant earnings provide one method of valuing the occupational composition of each of the states. The average annual earning of all wage and salary workers in the nation in a particular occupation is used as the weight for the (relative) numbers in a particular occupation. If the state rate-constant earnings were divided by their average (the rate-constant earning for the nation), the quotient, expressed to base 100, would provide an index number showing the relative value of a state's occupational composition (with the national occupational composition equal to 100). While the conversion of the rate-constant earnings to index-number form might help to avoid some misinterpretation, the dollar form has been retained for expository purposes.[9]

Attention should be called to several circumstances which make the

[9] The similarity of rate-constant figures to physical-volume index numbers, coupled with the fact that index numbers are constructed under a set of formal rules, should help to avoid attempts to interpret the rate-constant figures in a causal framework. Actually changing the occupational earning rates in each state to the point that the rates were the same throughout the nation would, of course, start (or be part of) a chain of interactions which would also change the state occupational structure. The use in these computations of the same occupational earning rate in each state is intended only as a statistical device for valuing the occupations and combining their values into a series of figures comparable

results only approximations: First, the occupational averages (distributed in table 23) were computed from a 3.3 percent sample and are subject to some sampling error; however, for most occupations the sample is large enough to keep the error small. Moreover, the data were collected by class interval, and the uppermost open-end class ($10,000 and over) has a fairly low limit for many professional and managerial occupations. Too, the tabulation from which these occupational averages were computed included only the earnings of those whose wage and salary income exceeded their self-employment income. Secondly, the average reported earnings by state were computed from tables relating to wage and salary income reported by persons in the experienced labor force. Thus, these data included persons primarily self-employed but with some 1949 wage and salary earnings, and excluded wage earners who reported no wage and salary earnings for 1949. Thirdly, the only state data by detailed occupation suitable for computing a state rate-constant earning relate to the total numbers of persons in the experienced labor force. These numbers include both the self-employed and persons without 1949 wage and salary income. The only corrective measure which appeared feasible was to omit from the analysis the occupational categories designed chiefly for the self-employed. It was not possible to accord separate treatment to those persons in the other categories with only self-employed income, with only wages and salaries, and with both wages and salaries and self-employment income.

Despite the statistical and conceptual differences among the three bodies of data used, only moderate differences appear at the national level. The national average reported earning, $2,556 per worker, probably is the firmest of the available figures. The weighted average of occupational earnings (derived from the data underlying table 23) is about 1.1 percent lower, $2,528; and the weighted average of the state rate-constant earnings, $2,517 (table 24, column 3), is about 1.5 percent lower. Smaller differences are found for males and larger differences for females.[10] A number of factors affect these comparisons. A larger proportion of the females in the experienced labor force were without wage and salary

between states. The technical aspects of constructing and interpreting these rate-constant earnings are discussed in appendix B.

[10] The national average earnings for males and females computed from these bodies of data are:

	Males	*Females*
Reported earnings	$2,910	$1,667
Occupational earnings (3.3 percent sample data)	2,905	1,648
Rate-constant earnings	2,908	1,616

For males, occupational and rate-constant earnings differ from reported earnings by 0.1 to 0.2 percent; for females, by 1.1 to 3.1 percent.

earnings in 1949, and of all persons without earnings the females tended to be attached to the lower-paying occupations.[11] The number of females included in the 3.3 percent sample tabulation is a larger proportion of females in the experienced labor force and matches more closely the number of females with wage and salary income than do the corresponding figures for males.[12] Too, there is some evidence that a larger proportion of males than of females in the occupational classifications primarily for the self-employed (and thus excluded) have some wage and salary income.[13]

Even at the national level, where their size can be measured, these factors are difficult to evaluate. The biases that they introduce in the rate-constant figures for particular states are unknown. Unless their differential effects among states are large, the differences between the state and national rate-constant earnings may be accepted as indicative of the differences in state occupational composition (table 24, columns 5 and 7). In most states the effect of holding rates constant is to reduce the difference between the state and national earnings: in only three of the states—Utah, Wisconsin, and Wyoming—are the differences increased.[14] Thus some but not all of the differences in state earnings may be

[11] This tendency is confirmed by an examination of the D-6 tabulation underlying table 23, in which the number of wage and salary workers without earnings is shown. Approximately 9.8 percent of the male and 15.1 percent of the female wage and salary workers were without 1949 earnings. When the occupations are classified as having earnings above or below the average of the major occupational group in which they are located, and wage and salary workers without earnings are distributed by these categories, it is found that 80 percent of the females and 55 percent of the males are in occupations with earnings below the major-group average.

[12] The number of female wage and salary workers and government employees represented by the 3.3 percent sample (i.e., 30 times the number of returns) is 94.6 percent of the females in the experienced labor force in the categories included in this analysis; the corresponding percentage for males is 91.4 percent. The 3.3 percent sample represents 98.3 percent of the females reporting wage and salary income; the corresponding percentage for males is 91.3.

[13] When the number of self-employed workers without wage and salary income, as shown in the 3.3 percent sample tabulation, is compared with the numbers in the self-employment classifications excluded from this analysis, the following results are obtained:

	Males	*Females*
(1) Thousands of self-employed workers without wage or salary income	2,349	714
(2) Thousands of persons in the experienced labor force in occupational categories chiefly for self-employed persons	6,981	774
(3) Line (1) as a percent of line (2)	33.6	92.2

These comparisons could be affected by sampling error and should be taken only as indicative.

[14] For the sake of clarity it should be noted that the above statement is based on the absolute size of the differences in columns 4 and 5. In a state like Pennsylvania the deviations of reported and rate-constant earnings are in different directions from their national averages, but the rate-constant earning deviation is the smaller.

attributable to differences in occupational composition among the states.

Some notion of how much the state occupational compositions vary from the national composition is afforded by column 7. In this column, the rate-constant earnings (column 3) are looked upon as the occupational composition of a state weighted by average occupational earnings, and the difference for the state from the national average occupational composition is expressed as a percentage of the national average. Thus, it can be said that Maine's occupational composition is 6.8 percent less remunerative than that of the nation as a whole; since it is less remunerative, it can be called an "unfavorable" composition.[15] The interstate range is from South Carolina's unfavorable (13.8 percent below average) to Michigan's favorable (5.7 percent above average) occupational composition. Most of the 19 states with favorable occupational compositions include a large metropolitan center or are located, like Connecticut, in a heavily populated and industrialized area. The most unfavorable occupational compositions are found in the South. Five states—Arkansas, Georgia, North Carolina, Mississippi, and South Carolina—have occupational compositions which depart from the national average by more than 10 percent.

The differences between state reported and rate-constant earnings can be used to obtain some indication of the magnitude of the state differences in rates for similar occupations (table 24, columns 6 and 8). Since data on the average earnings of persons within a particular occupation are not available by state, it is not possible to compute a state composition-constant earning using national occupational composition as weights.[16] Consequently, the weights used in computing these columns vary from one state to another. This fact seriously limits the interstate comparableness of these data. Although the state-weighted earning-rate differences contribute little toward an understanding of interstate differentials, they

[15] Although the terms "favorable" and "unfavorable" will be used throughout the remainder of this book without quotation marks, they are put in quotation marks here to call attention to the technical sense in which they are used as adjectives to modify the noun "composition." A favorable (unfavorable) composition means only that the state's rate-constant earning is larger (smaller) than the national average earning.

[16] As shown in appendix B, the figures in column 6 can be expressed as:

$$\Sigma p_1 q_1 - \Sigma p_o q_1 = \Sigma q_1 (p_1 - p_o),$$

where p is an occupational rate, q the relative number in an occupation, the subscript 1 is for state and o for national, and the summation is taken over all occupations. This formula is the expression for the differences in state and national rates weighted by state occupational composition. Data for p_1 are not available, and without them it is not possible to compute $\Sigma p_1 q_o$, and

$$\Sigma p_1 q_o - \Sigma p_o q_o = \Sigma q_o (p_1 - p_o),$$

that is, the difference in state and national rates weighted by national occupational compositions.

have been included for their value in describing the economy of a particular state, when the state is considered separately.

The differences in state and national rates (weighted in each state by its own occupational composition) tend to have the same sign and to be somewhat larger than the differences attributed to compositional differences. The similarity of signs indicates only that states with unfavorable compositions also tend to have occupational rates below those of the nation. The fact that the state-weighted differences in rates are larger than the differences in composition (when their signs are the same) means only that a state rate tends to deviate from national rates predominantly in one direction. The very notion of an occupational hierarchy would lead to the expectation that this would be the case. The comparative size of columns 5 and 6 is not appropriate for use as a measure of the relative importance of composition and rates in explaining the differences in reported earnings.[17]

The percentage differences attributed to occupational earning rates (table 24, column 8) provide a measure for each particular state, considered separately, of the relative extent to which its occupational earnings depart from the national average. For example, the entry for Maine indicates that Maine occupations, on the average, are 13.6 percent less remunerative than are Maine's particular occupations in the nation. The Maine figure is not, however, strictly comparable with the one for Rhode Island. First, Maine and Rhode Island have differing occupational compositions (as evidenced by columns 5 and 7), so that the percentages are computed on different bases. Consequently, the magnitude of the entry in column 8 is determined both by the state's occupational composition and by the deviations of the state's occupational rates from the national rates. An unfavorable occupational composition thus will help to increase the size of an unfavorable rate structure by contributing to a smaller base. On the other hand, a favorable composition will contribute to a larger base and thus reduce the percentage deviation of rates. Since both rates and composition tend to deviate in the same direction, the negative rate deviations tend to be larger, and the positive deviations smaller, than they would be if they were weighted by the national occupational composition.

Occupational earnings of males

The state differences in male occupational earnings follow closely those found for all wage and salary workers (table 25).[18] The occupa-

[17] See appendix B. The measurement of the portion of variation in state reported earnings explained by rate-constant earnings is discussed later in this chapter.

[18] The dollar differences shown as columns 4-6 in table 24 were included only to facili-

TABLE 25

REPORTED AND RATE-CONSTANT 1949 AVERAGE ANNUAL OCCUPATIONAL EARNINGS, BY STATE, MALE WAGE AND SALARY WORKERS

State (1)	Average annual earnings: Reported (2)	Average annual earnings: Rate-constant (3)	Percentage differences attributable to occupational: Composition (national weights) (4)	Percentage differences attributable to occupational: Earning rates (state weights) (5)
New England				
Maine	$2,347	$2,672	− 8.1	−13.8
New Hampshire	2,533	2,766	− 4.9	− 9.2
Vermont	2,279	2,690	− 7.5	−18.0
Massachusetts	3,059	3,005	3.3	1.8
Rhode Island	2,727	2,921	.4	− 7.1
Connecticut	3,252	3,060	5.2	5.9
Middle Atlantic				
New York	3,359	3,051	4.9	9.2
New Jersey	3,420	3,089	6.2	9.7
Pennsylvania	3,012	2,915	.2	3.2
East North Central				
Ohio	3,204	3,031	4.2	5.4
Indiana	3,020	2,949	1.4	2.4
Illinois	3,374	3,032	4.3	10.1
Michigan	3,347	3,012	3.6	10.0
Wisconsin	2,958	2,920	.4	1.3
West North Central				
Minnesota	2,840	2,938	1.0	− 3.5
Iowa	2,657	2,841	− 2.3	− 6.9
Missouri	2,769	2,915	.2	− 5.3
North Dakota	2,234	2,719	− 6.5	−21.7
South Dakota	2,279	2,713	− 6.7	−19.0
Nebraska	2,586	2,858	− 1.7	−10.5
Kansas	2,689	2,943	1.2	− 9.4
South Atlantic				
Delaware	3,202	2,970	2.1	7.2
Maryland	3,033	2,971	2.2	2.0
D. C.	3,397	3,037	4.4	10.6
Virginia	2,546	2,765	− 4.9	− 8.6
West Virginia	2,652	2,749	− 5.5	− 3.7
North Carolina	2,081	2,630	− 9.6	−26.4
South Carolina	1,998	2,570	−11.6	−28.6
Georgia	2,081	2,666	− 8.3	−28.1
Florida	2,398	2,732	− 6.1	−13.9
South Central				
Kentucky	2,223	2,703	− 7.0	−21.6
Tennessee	2,213	2,750	− 5.4	−24.3
Alabama	2,089	2,675	− 8.0	−28.1
Mississippi	1,584	2,566	−11.8	−62.0
Arkansas	1,760	2,544	−12.5	−44.5
Louisiana	2,402	2,769	− 4.8	−15.3
Oklahoma	2,493	2,906	− .1	−16.6
Texas	2,560	2,816	− 3.2	−10.0
Mountain				
Montana	2,731	2,735	− 5.9	− .1
Idaho	2,571	2,688	− 7.6	− 4.6
Wyoming	2,815	2,788	− 4.1	1.0
Colorado	2,722	2,897	− .4	− 6.4
New Mexico	2,571	2,720	− 6.5	− 5.8
Arizona	2,641	2,700	− 7.2	− 2.2
Utah	2,937	2,937	1.0	.0
Nevada	3,146	2,742	− 5.7	12.8
Pacific				
Washington	3,080	2,860	− 1.7	7.1
Oregon	3,016	2,733	− 6.0	9.4
California	3,242	2,941	1.1	9.3

Col. 2—Computed from table 94, *Census of Population, 1950*, for each state. The averages relate to wage and salary workers with 1949 earnings. The midpoint of the $10,000-and-over class was assumed to be $17,500 (see table 23).

Col. 3—Estimated from the occupational averages underlying table 23 and the state's experienced labor force in each occupation (table 73, *Census of Population, 1950*, for each state). These computations were made by the Bureau of the Census as a special tabulation.

Col. 4—The difference, column 3 minus $2,908 (the weighted average of column 3) expressed as a percentage of $2,908. The numbers in the experienced labor force were used as weights in obtaining the mean of column 3. The result is the difference between the state and national occupational compositions weighted by national average annual occupational earnings, expressed as a percentage of the latter.

Col. 5—The difference, column 2 minus column 3, expressed as a percentage of column 2. This is the difference between state and national average annual occupational earnings weighted by the number in each occupation in the particular state, expressed as a percentage of the state average. These percentages are affected by a $2 discrepancy between the weighted averages of columns 2 and 3.

tional composition of male wage and salary workers in 18 of the states is somewhat more favorable than that for all workers, and is less favorable in the remainder. Those with the more favorable compositions tend to be concentrated along the Atlantic seaboard; Missouri is the only such state west of the Mississippi River. The differences in the states' occupational compositions for males and for all workers tend to be small (averaging about 1.5 percentage points), with the largest differences found in the District of Columbia, West Virginia, Montana, and Wyoming.

Although the state-weighted earning-rate differences are not comparable among states, there seems to be no reason why those for males and for all workers in the same state cannot be compared.[19] The differences between the male occupational earning-rate differentials and those of all workers tend to be small, averaging only 1.8 percentage points per state. In 10 of the Southern states, the District of Columbia, and New Mexico, these differences exceed 3 percentage points; in 23 states they are less than 1 percentage point. The occupational earning-rate differentials tend to be slightly larger for male than for all wage and salary workers; in only 16 states and the District of Columbia are the male earning differentials smaller.

Occupational earnings of females

The 1949 average annual earnings reported for females with wage or salary income was $1,667, about 57 percent of that for males. The level of earnings for females wage and salary workers is lower than that for males in every state (tables 25 and 26). As a percentage of the average annual earnings of male wage and salary workers, the earnings of females ranged from a low of 51 percent in Delaware to 64 percent in North Carolina and 72 percent in the District of Columbia. Only in the District of Columbia did the earnings of females average as much as $2,000.

The absolute size of the state differences in occupational composition tends to be larger for female than for male wage and salary workers. The state occupational compositions for females range from an unfavorable 16.2 percent in Mississippi to a favorable 6.7 percent in Connecticut. In most of the states the occupational composition for females is more favorable (that is, the percentage difference due to composition has a lower negative or higher positive value) than that for males; in two states—Vermont and South Dakota—it is more favorable by as much as

tate exposition. They have been omitted from table 25 and similar tables, although they may be computed from the data given.

[19] Such a comparison is analogous to comparing the price index for all commodities with that for one of its segments, such as the foods price index.

TABLE 26

REPORTED AND RATE-CONSTANT 1949 AVERAGE ANNUAL OCCUPATIONAL EARNINGS, BY STATE, FEMALE WAGE AND SALARY WORKERS

State (1)	Average annual earnings: Reported (2)	Average annual earnings: Rate-constant (3)	Percentage differences a tributable to occupationa: Composition (national weights) (4)	Percentage differences a tributable to occupationa: Earning rates (state weights) (5)
New England				
Maine	$1,375	$1,579	− 2.3	−14.8
New Hampshire	1,463	1,627	.7	−11.2
Vermont	1,304	1,604	− .7	−23.0
Massachusetts	1,704	1,700	5.2	.2
Rhode Island	1,622	1,685	4.3	− 3.9
Connecticut	1,834	1,724	6.7	6.0
Middle Atlantic				
New York	1,985	1,694	4.8	14.7
New Jersey	1,888	1,686	4.3	10.7
Pennsylvania	1,625	1,624	.5	.1
East North Central				
Ohio	1,697	1,649	2.0	2.8
Indiana	1,640	1,634	1.1	.4
Illinois	1,883	1,695	4.9	10.0
Michigan	1,867	1,680	4.0	10.0
Wisconsin	1,589	1,643	1.7	− 3.4
West North Central				
Minnesota	1,571	1,646	1.9	− 4.8
Iowa	1,425	1,622	.4	−13.8
Missouri	1,595	1,622	.4	− 1.7
North Dakota	1,336	1,597	− 1.2	−19.5
South Dakota	1,351	1,623	.4	−20.1
Nebraska	1,442	1,634	1.1	−13.3
Kansas	1,445	1,621	.3	−12.2
South Atlantic				
Delaware	1,644	1,588	− 1.7	3.4
Maryland	1,691	1,595	− 1.3	5.7
D. C.	2,451	1,719	6.4	29.9
Virginia	1,537	1,561	− 3.4	− 1.6
West Virginia	1,491	1,593	− 1.4	− 6.8
North Carolina	1,327	1,488	− 7.9	−12.1
South Carolina	1,213	1,426	−11.8	−17.6
Georgia	1,210	1,421	−12.1	−17.4
Florida	1,292	1,400	−13.4	− 8.4
South Central				
Kentucky	1,389	1,560	− 3.5	−12.3
Tennessee	1,329	1,525	− 5.6	−14.7
Alabama	1,174	1,421	−12.1	−21.0
Mississippi	952	1,354	−16.2	−42.2
Arkansas	1,069	1,449	−10.3	−35.5
Louisiana	1,304	1,439	−11.0	−10.4
Oklahoma	1,478	1,600	− 1.0	− 8.3
Texas	1,444	1,525	− 5.6	− 5.6
Mountain				
Montana	1,521	1,602	− .9	− 5.3
Idaho	1,355	1,573	− 2.7	−16.1
Wyoming	1,551	1,604	− .7	− 3.4
Colorado	1,580	1,645	1.8	− 4.1
New Mexico	1,582	1,582	− 2.1	.0
Arizona	1,610	1,558	− 3.6	3.2
Utah	1,531	1,662	2.8	− 8.6
Nevada	1,871	1,565	− 3.2	16.4
Pacific				
Washington	1,825	1,630	.9	10.7
Oregon	1,666	1,598	− 1.1	4.1
California	1,936	1,648	2.0	14.9

Col. 2—Computed from table 94, *Census of Population, 1950*, for each state. The averages relate to wage and salary workers with 1949 earnings. The midpoint of the $10,000-and-over class was assumed to be $17,500 (see table 23).

Col. 3—Estimated from the occupational averages underlying table 23 and the state's experienced labor force in each occupation (table 73, *Census of Population, 1950*, for each state). These computations were made by the Bureau of the Census as a special tabulation.

Col. 4—The difference, Column 3 minus $1,616 (the weighted average of column 3), expressed as a percentage of $1,616. The numbers in the experienced labor force were used as weights in obtaining the average of column 3. The result is the difference between the state and national occupational compositions weighted by national average annual occupational earnings, expressed as a percentage of the latter.

Col. 6—The difference, column 2 minus column 3 expressed as a percentage of column 2. This is the difference between state and national average annual occupational earnings weighted by the number in each occupation in the particular state, expressed as a percentage of the state average. These percentages are affected by a $57 discrepancy between the weighted means of columns 2 and 3.

6 percentage points, and in eight more states—Maine, New Hampshire, West Virginia, North Dakota, Montana, Idaho, New Mexico, and Oregon—it is more favorable by 4-5 percentage points. Most of the 16 states in which the occupational composition for female wage and salary workers is less favorable than for males are located in the South; those outside the South are New York, New Jersey, Ohio, Indiana, and Kansas.

Rate deviations tend to have the same signs as composition deviations (table 26, columns 4 and 5) for female wage and salary workers. In 11 states unfavorable rates are coupled with a favorable composition, although the percentage differences due to occupational composition in 9 of these states are less than 2 percent. In five states—Delaware, Maryland, Arizona, Nevada, and Oregon—above-average rates are coupled with unfavorable occupational compositions. This concordance between the signs of the percentage differences attributable to composition and to rates has been noted also for male and for all wage and salary workers.

Relation of male and female occupational earnings

The reported average annual earnings of male and female wage and salary workers in the several states are much more closely related than are the state rate-constant earnings.[20] A scatter diagram of the state male and female rate-constant earnings (chart 10) displays the problem.

A regression line passing through points at about $1,525 on the left hand border (where male earnings are $2,500) and $1,710 on the right border (where male earnings are $3,100) provides a reasonably good linear fit for the states outside of the three Southern divisions. It is impossible, by inspection, to find a line that adequately expresses the relationship for the Southern states. If we treat West Virginia and Kentucky as a part of the non-South (and these two states seem to be represented adequately by a regression line fitted to the non-South), then a line parallel to the line for the non-South but about $100 lower appears to be about as good as any. For this or any other line, the remaining dispersion is great. If the association between male and female earnings in the non-South is taken as the criterion, such a line would mean that the occupational composition of females in the South is about $100 per year lower than would be indicated by the occupational composition of the males.

The two major occupational groups with the lowest earnings, farm laborers and domestic household workers, are particularly large in the South. Although farm laborers have the lowest average earnings of any major group, there are about six times as many men as women in this

[20] The coefficients of determination between state male and female reported earnings is .91; between state male and female rate-constant earnings, .62.

CHART 10

MALE AND FEMALE RATE-CONSTANT OCCUPATIONAL EARNINGS, BY STATE, 1949

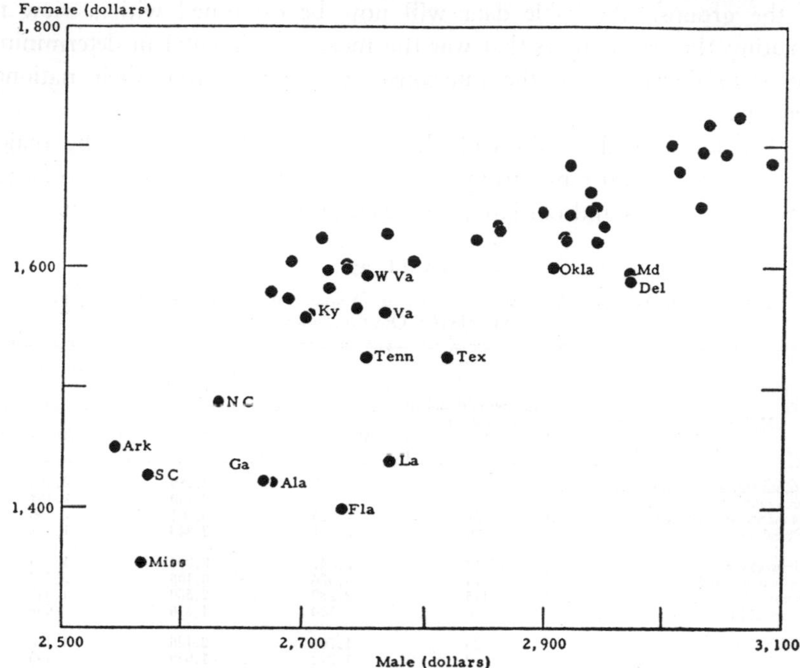

Note: Earnings are average annual earnings per worker.
Source: Tables 25 and 26.

category; consequently, the relatively large numbers of farm laborers in the South would be expected to affect the levels of both males and females. There are, however, about 22 females for every male in household work, the other low-wage industry. With the exception of West Virginia and Kentucky, all of the states in the Southern divisions have larger than average percentages of their labor force in private household work. The percentage of women engaged in relatively better-paid occupations, such as clerical work, is smaller in the Southern states. In part this may be a reflection of the large numbers of Negroes in the South; but in part it must be attributed to the interaction of such circumstances as a large rural population, low female participation in the labor force, and a lack of employment opportunities for females in the better-paid occupations.

Composition within Major Groups

The deviation of a state's rate-constant earning from the national average is the consequence of (1) compositional deviations within the major occupational groups, (2) concentrations of workers within certain major groups, and (3) differences between the average annual earnings of the groups. Available data will now be examined with a view to isolating the set of forces that was the most instrumental in determining the state deviations of the rate-constant earnings from their national average.

Average annual earnings of all wage and salary workers by major occupational group range from $730 among household workers to $4,915 among managers and officials (table 27). One of the major groups con-

TABLE 27

REPORTED AVERAGE ANNUAL EARNINGS OF WAGE AND SALARY WORKERS, 1949, BY SEX AND MAJOR OCCUPATIONAL GROUP

Major occupational group	Number of detailed occupations[a]	Average annual earnings[b] (dollars)		
		All workers	Males	Females
Professional and technical	56	3,467	4,289	2,328
Farm managers	1	2,722	2,739	2,152
Managers and officials	37	4,915	5,301	2,488
Clerical workers	20	2,361	2,948	1,991
Salesworkers	12	2,641	3,304	1,319
Craftsmen and foremen	73	3,076	3,108	2,002
Operatives	115	2,289	2,560	1,549
Household workers	6	730	1,316	699
Service workers	26	1,700	2,126	1,158
Farm laborers and foremen	2	1,042	1,089	499
Laborers	73	1,910	1,926	1,451
All groups[c]	422	2,517	2,910	1,667

[a]Occupational categories designed primarily for self-employed persons are omitted.
[b]Computed from an unpublished tabulation, identified as D-6, of a 3.3 percent sample of 1950 census of population returns, by the methods described in the source note to table 23.
[c]This average includes "occupations not reported."

sists of a single category, farm managers.[21] Obviously, for this group the average occupational earning will be the same for both detailed and major occupation. But the other major groups consist of from 2 to 115 detailed occupations, each with its own average earning. Since there are only two detailed occupations for the farm-laborer group, it may be used for illustrating the meaning of a favorable (or unfavorable) group composition. The national average annual earning of farm foremen is $2,381 and of farm laborers $1,027. When these averages are weighted by the numbers in the experienced labor force (17,143 foremen and 1,569,106 laborers), a group average of $1,042 is obtained. States with higher proportions of foremen will have higher group rate-constant earnings and thus may be

[21] Farmers are chiefly self-employed and are thus omitted. The "occupations not reported" group also is omitted from table 27.

TABLE 28

OCCUPATIONAL COMPOSITION WITHIN MAJOR OCCUPATIONAL GROUPS, ALL WAGE AND SALARY WORKERS, 1949, BY STATE

State (arrayed by rate-constant earning[a])	Rate constant earning[a] (dollars)	Major occupational group[b] (sign of state minus national rate-constant average annual earning)									
		Profession-al and technical	Man-agers and officials	Clerical workers	Sales-workers	Crafts-men and foremen	Opera-tives	House-hold workers	Service workers	Farm labor-ers and foremen	Labor-ers
South Carolina	2,169	−	−	−	−	−	−	−	−	−	−
Mississippi	2,180	−	−	+	−	−	−	−	−	−	−
North Carolina	2,235	−	−	−	−	−	−	−	−	−	−
Georgia	2,241	−	−	+	−	−	−	−	−	−	−
Arkansas	2,244	−	−	+	−	−	−	−	−	−	−
Alabama	2,292	−	−	+	−	−	−	−	−	−	−
Florida	2,303	−	−	−	−	−	−	−	−	+	−
Maine	2,346	−	−	+	−	−	−	+	−	−	−
Vermont	2,363	−	−	+	−	−	−	+	−	−	−
Tennessee	2,369	−	−	+	−	−	−	−	−	−	−
Arizona	2,382	−	−	−	−	−	+	0	−	+	−
Louisiana	2,383	−	−	−	−	−	+	−	−	+	−
New Hampshire	2,392		−	+	−	−	−	+	−	+	−
South Dakota	2,397	−	−	+	−	−	+	+	−	−	−
Idaho	2,397	−	−	+	−	−	+	−	−	−	−
Kentucky	2,399	−	−	+	−	−	−	−	−	−	−
North Dakota	2,400	−	−	+	−	−	+	+	−	−	−
Virginia	2,401	+	−	+	−	−	−	−	−	−	−
Nevada	2,420	−	−	−	−	−	+	+	−	+	−
New Mexico	2,422	−	−	−	−	−	+	−	−	+	−
Oregon	2,430	−	−	−	−	−	−	+	−	−	−
Montana	2,443	−	−	+	−	−	+	−	−	+	+
Texas	2,445	−	−	−	−	−	+	−	−	+	−
Iowa	2,482	−	−	−	−	−	+	+	−	−	−
Nebraska	2,490	−	−	+	−	−	+	+	−	−	−
West Virginia	2,490	−	−	+	−	+	+	+	−	−	+
Wyoming	2,498	−	−	+	−	+	+	−	−	+	+
D. C.	2,499	+	−	−	−	−	−	−	−	+	−
Rhode Island	2,508	−	+	−	−	−	−	+	+	+	−
Missouri	2,512	−	+	+	+	−	−	−	−	−	−
Colorado	2,526	−	−	−	−	−	+	+	−	+	−
Washington	2,526	+	−	+	−	−	−	+	−	+	−
Oklahoma	2,527	−	−	−	−	−	+	−	−	−	−
Pennsylvania	2,542	−	−	−	+	−	+	−	−	+	−
Minnesota	2,546	−	+	+	+	−	+	+	−	−	−
California	2,551	+	−	−	+	−	−	+	−	+	−
Maryland	2,552	+	+	−	−	−	−	−	+	−	+
Delaware	2,554	+	+	−	−	+	+	+	+	−	+
Wisconsin	2,562	−	+	+	−	+	+	+	+	−	+
Kansas	2,564	−	+	+	−	−	+	−	−	−	−
Massachusetts	2,570	−	+	−	+	+	−	+	+	+	+
Indiana	2,586	−	+	+	−	+	+	−	+	−	+
New York	2,588	+	+	−	+	+	−	+	+	−	+
Utah	2,594	−	−	−	−	−	+	−	−	−	+
Illinois	2,629	+	+	+	+	+	+	+	+	−	+
Connecticut	2,636	+	+	−	+	+	+	+	+	+	+
Ohio	2,644	+	+	+	−	+	+	+	+	−	+
New Jersey	2,646	+	+	−	+	+	−	+	+	+	+
Michigan	2,660	+	+	+	−	+	+	+	+	−	+

[a]Based on all detailed occupations (table 24).

[b]"Farm managers," a single detailed occupation as well as a major group, is excluded. The categories for the self-employed in the "managers and officials" group are also excluded; see table 27.

Source: The rate-constant earning for a state within a major group was computed by multiplying the number of persons in the state's experienced labor force attached to a detailed occupation, by the national average annual earning of the occupation, summing these products over all detailed industries in the major group, and dividing by the number of persons in the experienced labor force in the group. A state whose rate-constant earning exceeds the national rate-constant earning for the major group (table 27) has a "favorable" occupational composition within the major group, indicated by a plus (+) sign in the table. Similarly, when the national exceeds the state rate-constant earning for a group, the state has an "unfavorable" composition within the major group, indicated by a minus (−) sign.

said to have a favorable group occupational composition; those with smaller proportions of foremen will have an unfavorable group occupational composition.

Only in the two Carolinas is the occupational composition unfavorable for every group (table 28). For these states, at least, there is clear evidence that their unfavorable occupational composition is not entirely the product of the concentration of workers in a few low-wage occupations or major occupational groups, although such concentrations may exist and contribute to the low level of the rate-constant earnings. Among the 12 states with the lowest rate-constant earnings, none have favorable group compositions in more than two groups (table 29). These favor-

TABLE 29

NUMBER OF STATES WITH MAJOR OCCUPATIONAL GROUP COMPOSITIONS DIFFERING IN SIGN FROM THE COMPOSITION OF ALL DETAILED OCCUPATIONS, 1949, BY MAJOR OCCUPATIONAL GROUP, RATE-CONSTANT EARNING QUARTILE, AND SEX
(Number of states)

Quartile (based on state rate-constant earnings[a])	Major occupational group									
	Professional and technical	Managers and officials	Clerical workers	Salesworkers	Craftsmen and foremen	Operatives	Household workers	Service workers	Farm laborers and foremen	Laborers
All wage and salary workers										
Lowest	—	—	7	—	—	2	2	—	3	—
Second	1	—	7	—	—	8	6	—	5	1
Third	4	7	9	5	9	6	6	7	5	8
Highest	5	1	6	7	2	3	3	2	9	1
Male wage and salary workers										
Lowest	—	—	11	—	—	—	3	1	3	—
Second	1	—	12	—	2	3	6	4	7	2
Third	8	1	8	3	3	6	6	3	8	3
Highest	2	3	6	5	3	1	4	4	8	2
Female wage and salary workers										
Lowest	9	1	—	4	1	2	—	1	3	—
Second	4	3	4	1	3	3	5	3	8	4
Third	10	6	9	8	8	8	3	7	2	5
Highest	9	3	6	6	5	5	1	3	2	3

[a]The state rate-constant earnings are given in tables 24-26. The quartiles are based on the 48 states; the District of Columbia is excluded from this table.

Source: The top panel, relating to all wage and salary workers, is based on a count of the states in table 8 with signs which differ from those for rate-constant earning. The other two panels were prepared similarly, although tables similar to table 8 are not shown.

able group compositions are most frequent (for seven states) in the clerical group, which includes baggagemen, dispatchers, railway mail clerks, mail carriers, telegraph operators, and railway ticket agents, whose wage or salary rates tend to be determined on a nation-wide basis. Favorable group compositions are also found in the operatives, household-worker, farm-laborer and farm-foremen groups. In the next quartile (states with rate-constant earnings between $2,392 and $2,482), 5 of the 12 states have favorable compositions in three or four groups; favorable compositions are found most frequently in the operatives, clerical, and household-worker groups.

In the third quartile, five of the states have rate-constant earnings below, and seven states above, the national average. Of those below the national average, all have favorable compositions in three to five groups. Above the national average, all of the states have unfavorable compositions in half or more of the groups. This would indicate that the favorable state compositions are the result of a heavy concentration in a few occupations or major groups which offer high earnings. Oklahoma is an extreme case of such a concentration. With unfavorable group compositions in all but the operatives group, the number of operatives in the experienced labor force attached to the petroleum-refining industry, with its average annual earning of $3,843, is large enough not only to make the operatives group composition favorable, but also to make the occupational composition of the entire state favorable.

Among the 12 states with the highest rate-constant earnings, all except Kansas and Utah have favorable group compositions in all but one to four of the groups. In this extreme quartile there is again evidence that their favorable composition tends to persist in each of the major groups.

Much the same picture emerges when male and female wage and salary workers are considered separately. The tendency for the occupational composition within the major groups to be predominantly in one direction is strongest in the lowest quartile, is present but weaker in the highest quartile, and is almost nonexistent in the central quartiles. Too, the tendency appears to be slightly stronger for all wage and salary workers than for the workers of either sex, considered separately. In the case of male wage and salary workers, North Carolina is the only state with an unfavorable occupational composition within every major group; every other state has major groups with both favorable and unfavorable compositions. In the case of female workers, New Jersey is the only state with a favorable composition for every group.

Regional Concentrations of Occupations

Additional light may be thrown on this question by examining the regional concentration of the detailed occupations. There are some 67 occupations in which 50 percent or more of the workers are located in one of the four census regions (table 30). For the most part, the occupational concentration is a reflection of industrial concentration. For example,

TABLE 30

NUMBER OF DETAILED OCCUPATIONS HAVING 50 PERCENT OR MORE OF EMPLOYEES IN ONE CENSUS REGION, BY MAJOR GROUP, 1950[a]

Major occupational group	Number of occupations in group	Number of occupations with 50 percent or more of employees in one census region[b]				
		All regions	Northeast	North Central	South	West
Professional and technical	56	1	1			
Farm Managers	1					
Managers and officials	37					
Clerical Workers	20					
Salesworkers	12					
Craftsmen and foremen	73	10	3	6	1	
Operatives	115	26	14	5	6	1
Household workers	6	2			2	
Service workers	26	1			1	
Farm laborers and foremen	2					
Laborers	73	27	13	6	8	
All groups[c]	421	67	31	17	18	1

[a]Employees assumed equal to the number in the experienced labor force attached to the occupation.
[b]The census regions consist of two or more census divisions. For the states included in each region, see *U. S. Census of Population, 1950*, Vol. II.
[c]"Occupation not reported" is omitted.
Source: *U. S. Census of Population, 1950*, Vol. II, Pt. 1, U. S. Summary, table 158.

both the operatives and the laborers in the apparel and accessories industry are concentrated in the Northeast. Earnings in these occupations are below their group averages and may contribute importantly to the unfavorable operatives group composition in New York.

The 67 occupations which have 50 percent or more of the workers in one census region tend to have fewer workers than average. While the 67 occupations are 15.9 percent of the 421 occupations, only 11.9 percent of the experienced labor force is attached to them. The occupations concentrated in the South account for 8.8 percent, in the Northeast, 7.0 percent, in the North Central, 5.5 percent, and in the West, about 0.2 percent, of the total experienced labor force. To the extent that these regional concentrations are the consequence of within-region concentrations in two or three states, the rate-constant figures could be affected more importantly than would be indicated by these percentages. The effect of such concentrations on the rate-constant earning of a state depends upon the average earning of the concentrated occupations relative to the average for all occupations in the particular state and in the United States.[22]

[22] How this operates may be seen by examining a hypothetical example. Suppose that an "operatives" category of 1,000 workers with a national earning of $3,000 was subdivided into two categories, A and B. Suppose further that subcategory A had 100 workers with an average earning of $1,500 and B some 900 workers with an average earning of $3,167, and that one low-income state, say Georgia, had 80 percent of A and 1 percent of B. Before the subdivision, the occupation would have contributed $267 thousand (89 x 3,000)

There seems to be no easy way to gauge the effects of these observed concentrations on the state rate-constant earnings. Obviously, some assumptions would have to be made about the similarity of the skills and training required by various occupations before a framework could be constructed which would permit such a test. A start could be made by assuming that the concentrated occupations are essentially similar to some other occupation, combining the two occupations, and computing the net effect on rate-constant earnings. Such a procedure amounts to the construction of a new classificatory system, using the existing structure as building blocks. Little that is worthwhile could come from such a test. It would not tell us, for example, whether the skill and training components in two or more occupations are essentially the same. It would only provide a measure of the effects of telescoping further the existing classificatory system.

Two conclusions emerge from this discussion. Onc is that the measures provided depend in large part on the classificatory system that gives rise to various state and national averages. Were a different system used, different results would be obtained. Consequently, the results can be interpreted only in terms of the occupational classes provided by the census. The second conclusion is that to the extent that the existing occupational classes incorporate distinctions based more on location than on differences in skills, training, age, and other personal attributes of the workers, the state rate-constant figures will be affected. Since there are marked interstate rate differentials and the introduction of locational criteria tends to incorporate these rate differentials in the rate-constant figure, we may expect such rate-constant figures to tend to deviate more from the national average.

Occupational Composition and Interstate Earning Differentials

The question may now be raised as to how much of the observed interstate earning differential is explained by interstate differences in occupational composition.[23] In the discussion of table 24 above, it was mentioned

to Georgia's rate-constant earning aggregate. After the subdivision, the two subcategories would contribute only $149 thousand (80 x 1,500 plus 9 x 3,167), thus resulting in a lower average annual rate-constant earning for Georgia. The effect of the subdivision is to allow Georgia's lower pay scale to affect greatly the national level of earnings in subcategory A. Georgia's heavy concentration in this category would tend to make the Georgia composition unfavorable, with smaller differences between its rates and the national rates. On the other hand, if the national earnings of the two subcategories were approximately the same, or if the average subcategory earnings deviated from the average of all industries in the same direction, the effects would be minimized.

[23] This question is touched upon in my "Analysis of Interstate Income Differentials: Theory and Practice," in *Studies in Income and Wealth,* 21 (Princeton, 1957), 113-166.

that the relative sizes of the rate-constant (column 5) and state-weighted composition-constant (column 6) adjustments were not suitable for this purpose. The basis for this objection must now be made explicit, but first it should be made clear just what it is that is to be measured.

Average annual earnings for 1949 are different for all but four pairs of the 48 states (table 24, column 2).[24] The state earnings varied from $1,408 in Mississippi to $2,974 in Michigan. The question that is being raised is one of the extent to which these interstate differentials may be explained by interstate differentials in occupational composition. Such a question relates to the simultaneous treatment of all the interstate differentials, not just to the comparison of a single pair of states nor to the comparison of a single state with the nation. It is thus concerned with the interstate *distribution* of occupational earnings. Moreover, it is concerned with the interstate distribution of occupational composition. Unless one is willing to assume that the interstate distribution of occupational compositions and the occupational rate structures are, in some real sense, independent (that is, that a change in the observed rates for a state would not be accompanied by a change in the state's occupational composition), the relationships between state rates and compositions must be taken into account.

A comparison of the difference between state and national rate-constant earnings with the differences between reported and rate-constant earnings does not meet these requirements. The state percentage differences attributable to composition have a common base, the weighted mean of the several states, and thus are comparable. A weighted average of these percentages implicitly treats composition as wholly independent of all other factors.[25] The state-weighted percentage differences attributed to occupational earning rates consist of both the nationally weighted differences in rates and the net effect of their interactions with compositional differences.[26] The weighted average of these percentage differences due to rates, plus the interaction with compositions, are also implicitly treated as independent of all other factors. Unless the case can be made for treating rates and composition as truly independent, their interrelationships must be included in the analysis. These interrelationships include not

[24] Texas and Virginia each had reported earnings of $2,277; other pairs are Colorado and West Virginia, $2,412; Massachusetts and Utah, $2,610; and Maryland and Indiana, $2,652.

[25] Since the rate-constant earnings have been expressed as percentages of their weighted mean, a weighted arithmetic average of them would be zero. Thus, it would be necessary to take their weighted absolute deviation from zero, or their weighted quadratic mean—that is, their standard deviation—as a measure of dispersion.

[26] See appendix B.

only the net effects of the interaction between rates and composition within each of the states, but also their interactions among states.[27] There appears to be no satisfactory way of partitioning these joint effects among the rate- and composition-constant particles.

The rate-constant earnings were computed to obtain figures which could be compared among states without the distorting effects of interstate rate differences. In making these computations, only the net effects of composition differences are taken into account.[28] If our concern is with the importance of these differences relative to the differences in rates, it would seem more reasonable to count all occupational differences rather than just those not offset by changes in an opposite direction; that is, the two entire *distributions* of occupational composition should be compared. Similar treatment should be accorded rates. Some disposition of the joint particle (similarly computed) would have to be made, and since satisfactory methods for doing this are not available, the presence of the particle would have to be recognized and its magnitude used as an indication of the extent of approximation in the rate- and composition-constant particles.

These difficulties appear sufficient to discourage the use of the relative importance of the two sets of nationally weighted differences as explanatory variables even when all the necessary data are available. In the present case, the lack of data necessary to compute a nationally weighted composition-constant earning further compounds these difficulties.

One alternative measure, the coefficient of determination between state reported earnings and state rate-constant earnings, is worth investigation. The coefficient of determination provides a direct measure of the proportion of the variation in a dependent variable (state reported earnings) which is explained by the variation in an independent variable (state rate-constant earnings). For the 1949 state occupational earnings, the coefficient of determination for all wage and salary workers (table 24, columns 2 and 3) is .87; for male wage and salary workers (table 25, columns 2 and 3) it is .88; and for female wage and salary workers (table 26, columns 2 and 3) it is .77.

[27] Using the symbols in note 16 above, the difference between two states, designated by subscripts 1 and 2, can be written:

$$\Sigma p_1 q_1 - \Sigma p_2 q_2 = \Sigma p_o(q_1 - q_2) + \Sigma q_o(p_1 - p_2) + \Sigma(p_1 - p_2)(q_2 - q_o) + \Sigma(p_1 - p_o)(q_1 - q_2)$$

For simultaneous comparisons for 48 states, there would be 1,128 pairs of terms included in these joint particles. In economic terms, this is a question of the effects of differentials among states, in both composition and rates, on the levels in each state.

[28] See appendix B. It is shown there that if $(q_1 - q_o)$ is positive for some occupations, it must be negative for others. The rate-constant particle, $\Sigma p_o (q_1 - q_o)$, is the algebraic sum of these positive and negative figures.

The coefficient for all wage and salary workers thus indicates that interstate variation in occupational composition accounts for about 87 percent of the interstate variation in reported earnings. Such a measure is wholly statistical in the sense that it contains no implication concerning the existence or nonexistence of any causal relationship between the two series. It reflects not only the independent effects of compositional differences, which are reflected by the interstate differences within the rate-constant series, but also any secondary, tertiary, or other effects to the extent that these are correlated with the independent effects.[29] These correlated effects, which are five to eight times the magnitude of the independent effects, may include some of the interstate variation in occupational earning rates. A strong tendency for the interstate drift of occupational composition and earning rates to be in the same direction has been noted. While occupational earning rates are not explicitly treated in this formulation, they are included to the extent that the two series are correlated.[30] This is as it should be since the joint effects, which contain the covariation between rate and composition differentials, are available to reinforce the independent effects of either variable.

The state-specific occupational earning rates, which are the statewide averages of all wage and salary workers attached to an occupation, are a composite of many influences. In addition to reflecting the occupational hierarchy in the rate structure, which may be assumed to be fairly stable from state to state, the state-specific earning rates may also be affected by interstate differences in the composition by age, education, experience, color, and sex, in the length of the work week and work year, and in the ratio of the self-employed to the wage and salary workers in some occupations. The correlated effects included in the coefficient of determination thus may include more than the level of the occupational rate structure and the relationship of this level to occupational composition. There also may be found some influence of the many forces which give rise to varia-

[29] A percentage distribution of the total variation explained statistically by the independent and correlated factors follows:

	Wage and Salary Workers		
	All	*Male*	*Female*
		(percentages)	
Explained by independent effects of composition	10	10	12
Explained by correlated effects	77	78	65
Total explained (coefficient of determination)	87	88	77
Unexplained	13	12	23
Total interstate variation in reported earnings	100	100	100

The method and rationale for this breakdown are given in appendix B.

[30] The coefficient of determination between the percentage differences attributable to composition and to (state-weighted) earning rates is .77.

tion in earning rates within an occupation both at the state and national levels. While the data necessary to isolate and separately measure these influences are not available, it is important to recognize that the interstate difference in occupational earning rates may stem from something other than mere locational differences in earning levels for essentially the same degree of skill in the performance of essentially the same functions.

The independent effects of interstate compositional differences alone show that occupational composition can account for a significant proportion of the interstate variation in reported earnings.[31] When both the independent and correlated effects of occupational composition are taken into account, interstate compositional differences are capable of statistically accounting for about six-sevenths of the interstate variation in reported earnings. Although these measures are only approximations due to deficiencies in the data—the differential underreporting of income and the use of employment during a single week more than three months removed from the end of the income period as the basis for the classification by occupation, the results nevertheless are impressive.

[31] Based on the ratio of the variance explained by the independent effects of occupational composition to the residual variance, the independent effects are highly significant.

Chapter 6

INDUSTRIAL EARNINGS

A FURTHER OPPORTUNITY to examine the interstate earning differentials is provided by several bodies of industrial data. The official estimates of state personal income provide an industrial distribution of wages and salaries, the only income item so distributed by state.[1] Detailed data are available from the *Census of Manufactures, 1947* on manufacturing production workers, from the *Census of Business, 1948* on wholesale-trade employees, and from a variety of sources on government employees and payrolls in 1929, 1939, and 1952; the *Census of Population, 1950* provides pertinent data on the 1949 wage and salary income of individuals, classified by their industrial attachments in April 1950.

The occupational classification used in the preceding chapter was presumed to reflect the basic level of skill used by each person in the experienced labor force in order to obtain a wage and salary income. It was found, however, that there was considerable dispersion within each occupational category and that part of this dispersion was associated with geographic location (state). In contrast, the industrial data have some dispersion built into the series. Each industry, however narrowly defined, has varying proportions of differing skills among its complement of workers. The occupational composition of workers within an industry often will vary among plants of differing size, between plants with integrated and those with specialized operations, and among plants of similar size and kind within the same company or within the same city. Since an industry is not homogeneous with regard to the skills employed in it, the industry averages analyzed in this chapter cannot be

[1] Some may also consider proprietors' income to be distributed by industry since it is shown separately for farm and nonfarm proprietors. For 1954 data see Charles F. Schwartz and Robert E. Graham, Jr., "Personal Income by States, 1929-54," *Survey of Current Business* (September 1955), table 4.

expected to reflect as basic a determinant of interstate differences as do occupational averages.

The industrial distribution of wage and salary income in the various states is, nevertheless, of great interest. Since it is industrial activity which provides varying employment opportunities, a state's industrial structure and its occupational structure are interrelated. A state with an industrial composition heavily weighted in the direction of capital-intensive, high value-added industries can be expected to provide relatively more employment opportunities for persons with highly developed skills than can a state with a composition of industry heavily weighted in other directions. Moreover, the connection of the use of resources to industrial composition is more familiar than is its connection to occupational composition.

Industrial Composition of Wages[2]

Some perspective on the industrial sources of differential wage and salary income is afforded by the National Income Division's distribution of wage and salary payments among 11 broad industrial groups.[3] On a national level, manufacturing is the largest of the particular categories for which separate estimates are available for the 1939-1951 period (table 31). Trade, which accounts for about one-sixth of all wages and salaries, is the next largest and is followed by the government, service, and transportation industries. Each remaining industry accounts for less than 5 percent of all wages and salaries.

Since 1929, the national industrial composition of wages and salaries has been relatively stable.[4] The most marked changes were the wartime increases in manufacturing and government and the postwar increase in

[2] The substance of this section appeared in my "State Per Capita Income Components, 1919-1951," *Review of Economics and Statistics*, 38 (1956), 449-464.

[3] The wage and salary data used in this section were supplied by the National Income Division in 1953. The classification used does not follow exactly that used in the personal income series, Schwartz and Graham, *op. cit.*, table 4, for 1954. The principal difference in classification is that the data used here show separate estimates for power and communication industries but combine the estimates for government into a single category. Too, these data contain a "miscellaneous" category, which since 1942 has included 2-3 percent of wage and salary income, all not specifically allocated to other industries. It is, therefore, a statistical decrepancy in the industrial distribution of wages and salaries. In the revised industrial distribution published for 1954, this "discrepancy" is eliminated. At the time the data for this section were supplied, industrial distributions were available only for 1929, 1933, and 1939-1951. Revised distributions covering each year from 1929 to 1955 are now shown in *Personal Income by States since 1929*, Washington, 1956. As in the revised series, the wages and salaries on which this section is based are gross of employee contributions for social insurance.

[4] *National Income Supplement to the Survey of Current Business, 1954*, Washington, 1954, table 15. This statement is strictly true only for the broad industrial groups considered here.

TABLE 31

AVERAGE 1939-1951 INDUSTRIAL COMPOSITION OF LABOR INCOME, BY STATE
(Percentages of total labor income)

State	Agriculture	Mining	Manufacturing	Construction	Transportation	Power
New England						
Maine	2.8	.2	42.7	3.3	6.0	1.1
New Hampshire	2.2	.1	47.2	3.5	4.9	1.4
Vermont	7.0	1.1	38.4	2.5	7.7	1.3
Massachusetts	.8	.2	42.4	3.6	5.7	1.0
Rhode Island	.5	.1	48.7	5.0	3.7	1.3
Connecticut	.9	.1	55.5	3.8	3.6	.9
Middle Atlantic						
New York	.8	.3	33.8	3.6	6.7	1.0
New Jersey	.8	.3	48.4	4.1	7.5	1.1
Pennsylvania	.8	6.3	42.8	3.9	7.6	1.3
North Central						
Ohio	.8	1.1	49.7	4.1	7.2	1.0
Indiana	1.4	1.3	51.2	4.3	6.7	1.0
Illinois	.8	1.9	40.4	4.2	8.0	1.1
Michigan	.7	.8	56.3	3.3	4.1	1.2
Wisconsin	2.9	.3	47.2	4.3	5.5	1.2
Minnesota	3.2	2.2	28.3	4.9	10.4	1.2
Iowa	5.5	.6	28.3	4.2	10.3	1.3
Missouri	1.7	1.0	31.7	4.1	10.6	1.2
North Dakota	19.4	1.0	4.8	4.5	10.8	1.3
South Dakota	10.8	2.2	9.6	4.8	7.9	1.2
Nebraska	5.3	.2	17.3	5.3	11.8	.6
Kansas	3.9	3.7	23.7	5.7	13.4	1.6
South Atlantic						
Delaware	2.2	.0	47.5	5.9	10.2	.7
Maryland	1.5	.6	35.0	6.0	8.5	1.2
D. C.	....	....	3.6	3.8	3.4	.9
Virginia	2.2	2.6	23.3	5.7	7.9	.8
West Virginia	.7	30.3	27.2	3.3	7.1	1.5
North Carolina	2.7	.3	39.9	4.4	5.2	.9
South Carolina	5.7	.2	36.8	4.1	4.7	.9
Georgia	3.1	.6	29.8	4.0	7.9	1.0
Florida	3.6	.8	13.8	6.9	8.4	.9
South Central						
Kentucky	2.4	12.3	23.9	4.2	10.2	1.1
Tennessee	1.7	1.9	32.8	7.0	7.9	.3
Alabama	2.1	5.2	33.8	4.0	8.6	1.2
Mississippi	4.3	1.1	23.4	5.6	8.5	1.2
Arkansas	7.4	3.5	19.9	6.6	9.6	1.5
Louisiana	3.2	4.7	22.8	6.5	10.5	1.7
Oklahoma	3.5	9.6	16.6	5.0	9.3	1.6
Texas	3.7	6.6	19.1	6.1	9.4	1.3
Mountain						
Montana	9.6	10.1	12.3	5.6	11.8	1.7
Idaho	11.6	4.7	14.8	7.2	9.5	1.3
Wyoming	10.8	12.8	8.2	7.3	13.7	1.0
Colorado	6.3	4.1	17.1	5.4	9.1	1.3
New Mexico	5.9	9.1	6.7	9.3	9.7	1.4
Arizona	6.3	8.3	9.7	7.7	8.0	1.5
Utah	2.2	9.6	13.8	7.4	10.3	1.1
Nevada	3.3	7.3	7.4	12.3	12.4	.7
Pacific						
Washington	3.7	.6	29.8	6.1	8.0	.8
Oregon	4.1	.3	35.2	5.4	9.9	1.2
California	3.9	1.3	25.9	6.1	6.2	1.0
United States	2.1	2.3	35.8	4.6	7.3	1.1

(Continued on next page)

construction as sources of wages and salaries. There are few indications of a trend, and it is possible that even these few contain large elements of cyclical response.

The 1939-1951 average industrial composition varied widely among the states. For example, manufacturing, which accounted for less than 5

TABLE 31 (Continued)

AVERAGE 1939-1951 INDUSTRIAL COMPOSITION OF LABOR INCOME, BY STATE
(Percentages of total labor income)

State	Communication	Trade	Finance	Government	Service	Miscellaneous
New England						
Maine	1.2	14.1	2.2	15.5	7.0	4.0
New Hampshire	1.4	12.9	2.7	11.4	10.0	2.3
Vermont	1.4	13.6	4.1	11.4	9.0	2.4
Massachusetts	1.3	17.0	4.1	12.6	9.1	2.1
Rhode Island	1.1	13.7	3.1	13.9	7.5	1.4
Connecticut	1.1	13.1	4.7	7.0	7.7	1.4
Middle Atlantic						
New York	1.8	19.7	6.4	11.5	11.3	3.2
New Jersey	1.3	12.6	3.4	10.5	7.5	2.4
Pennsylvania	1.0	14.3	3.2	9.9	7.3	1.7
North Central						
Ohio	.9	14.9	2.5	9.0	6.7	2.1
Indiana	1.0	12.9	2.3	9.2	6.1	2.7
Illinois	1.5	18.0	4.0	9.8	8.0	2.2
Michigan	1.0	13.6	2.2	8.7	6.5	1.6
Wisconsin	1.1	15.5	2.8	9.9	6.8	2.3
Minnesota	1.2	20.2	4.2	12.4	9.4	2.5
Iowa	1.4	20.7	3.6	12.0	7.4	3.0
Missouri	1.5	20.0	4.0	11.6	8.8	2.7
North Dakota	1.3	22.8	3.5	18.3	8.5	3.9
South Dakota	1.4	21.2	2.8	23.4	8.6	6.3
Nebraska	1.8	20.9	5.0	18.8	9.1	3.9
Kansas	1.3	15.9	2.7	17.1	6.8	4.3
South Atlantic						
Delaware	.7	12.2	3.1	8.5	7.1	1.7
Maryland	1.1	14.0	3.2	17.8	8.1	3.1
D. C.	1.6	15.2	3.4	55.0	11.0	2.1
Virginia	1.0	13.9	2.8	29.5	7.9	2.4
West Virginia	.8	11.2	1.6	8.4	5.7	2.1
North Carolina	.8	14.7	3.3	17.2	8.3	2.2
South Carolina	.7	12.5	2.0	22.4	8.0	2.0
Georgia	1.6	17.2	3.1	19.9	9.5	2.3
Florida	1.3	20.3	3.4	25.0	12.2	3.4
South Central						
Kentucky	1.0	14.7	2.6	16.4	8.6	2.7
Tennessee	1.2	16.7	3.4	15.2	9.3	2.7
Alabama	.9	13.6	2.4	18.0	7.9	2.4
Mississippi	1.3	12.3	2.3	26.7	10.3	2.9
Arkansas	1.2	17.1	2.6	18.4	9.1	3.0
Louisiana	1.2	16.4	2.7	17.8	9.7	2.9
Oklahoma	1.6	17.9	3.0	20.5	7.6	3.9
Texas	1.3	18.5	3.3	18.6	8.0	4.0
Mountain						
Montana	1.1	18.5	2.4	17.1	6.8	2.9
Idaho	1.3	19.3	2.1	17.9	6.8	3.5
Wyoming	1.0	13.8	2.0	19.9	6.9	2.6
Colorado	2.0	19.6	3.0	20.7	8.7	2.8
New Mexico	.9	15.5	2.2	28.4	7.6	3.3
Arizona	1.2	18.2	2.5	24.7	8.6	3.3
Utah	1.4	17.5	2.6	24.6	6.6	2.9
Nevada	1.4	16.9	1.3	21.3	13.7	1.9
Pacific						
Washington	1.3	16.5	3.7	20.2	6.7	2.8
Oregon	1.4	18.2	2.7	12.2	7.1	2.4
California	1.5	18.8	3.7	17.6	11.5	2.5
United States	1.3	16.6	3.7	14.1	8.6	2.6

Source: Unpublished estimates supplied by the National Income Division.

percent in North Dakota and the District of Columbia, accounted for more than 50 percent of all wages and salaries in Connecticut, Indiana, and Michigan. Agricultural wages and salaries, which for the United States accounted for 2.1 percent of all wages and salaries, accounted for less than 1.0 percent in 10 states and for more than 10.0 percent in 4 states.

The interstate range of the shares of all wages and salaries accounted for by the trade and service industries, on the other hand, is confined within moderate limits.

When the relative interstate variation of the wages and salaries of each industry, expressed as a percentage of all wages and salaries, is measured by the coefficient of variation, mining, which depends in large part on the spotty distribution of mineral resources, is clearly the most geographically disperse of the industries treated here (table 32). Agriculture, with coefficients ranging from 67 to 109 percent, clearly ranks next. The interstate coefficients for manufacturing are all in the range of 47 to 53 percent. The year-to-year variation of construction wages and salaries ranges from 24 to 71 percent after 1939, and in 1933 the dispersion was as large as the mean. The next group of industries, with coefficients predominantly in the range of 30 to 40 percent, includes the government, finance, transportation, and miscellaneous industries. The remaining industries—service, trade, communication, and power—have coefficients in the range of 16 to 30 percent.

The interstate coefficients of variation for wages and salaries tend to decrease over the period being studied.[5] To what extent do the decreasing coefficients of variation indicate that the industrial composition of the states is becoming more alike also? If each state had the same percentage industrial distribution of wages, every coefficient of variation in table 32 would be zero. A reduction in the coefficients over the years would indicate a tendency in this direction.[6] An examination of table 32 shows that there has been some tendency toward less relative interstate dispersion in manufacturing, transportation, and communication. An upward trend is to be noted for the power industry and miscellaneous industries. Most industries show no pronounced trend. Their fluctuations apparently are attributable to the shifting importance of industries occasioned by the war effort. Agriculture, construction, trade, finance, and government displayed more relative interstate dispersion during 1942-1944, the peak of war production, with mining and service lagging one and two years.[7]

[5] See also chapter 4. The coefficients of variation shown in table 32, being unweighted, differ slightly from the weighted coefficients shown in table 21. In table 32, which deals with the percentage shares of the various industries, all wages and salaries are treated as a 100-percent share.

[6] Wage and salary payments are the product of man-hours spent in an industry and the hourly rates. It would, of course, be possible for all the states to have the same percentage distribution of man-hours, for instance, but to have some dispersion arise from differences in wage rates.

[7] The shifts in relative importance among the detailed industries within the major industry groups treated here could give rise to the interstate dispersion.

TABLE 32

Coefficients of Variation for Industrial Shares of State Labor Income, Specified Years, 1929-1951[a]

Year	All labor income[b]	Industry											
		Agriculture	Mining	Manufacturing	Construction	Transportation	Power	Communication	Trade	Finance	Government	Service	Miscellaneous
Average 1939-1951	31.3	90.2	145.6	48.2	33.0	28.4	24.5	22.[illegible]	17.8	29.7	34.6	19.3	31.4
1951	29.4	85.1	148.5	47.0	26.5	28.4	29.3	21.4	17.8	26.4	33.5	27.0	34.3
1950	29.6	83.6	145.6	47.8	29.8	27.6	27.2	21.1	16.9	26.3	32.0	24.3	35.4
1949	28.1	83.3	141.7	47.8	29.7	27.5	25.3	21.2	16.5	27.4	29.7	23.8	35.0
1948	29.0	95.8	148.1	48.3	30.1	28.4	26.2	21.5	18.1	28.3	30.7	24.2	33.9
1947	30.9	95.9	150.5	48.3	32.8	28.9	25.4	22.4	18.5	28.8	32.1	23.2	33.5
1946	31.5	90.4	150.9	49.7	35.3	28.2	25.3	21.3	18.2	29.2	33.6	18.9	33.3
1945	28.6	99.9	156.4	48.0	55.4	30.3	25.7	22.6	18.8	33.4	41.8	17.4	31.7
1944	31.1	105.9	159.7	48.6	59.4	31.2	26.6	24.2	20.8	36.8	46.7	19.2	32.4
1943	34.3	108.6	153.7	50.0	66.1	31.7	30.8	27.0	21.9	39.3	46.6	20.1	33.1
1942	38.2	103.2	145.2	51.7	71.3	32.1	27.9	27.2	20.2	38.5	42.3	21.2	30.4
1941	39.0	88.5	134.1	52.8	38.2	32.0	24.2	28.0	18.8	34.7	31.8	21.1	30.6
1940	39.3	73.4	130.8	50.9	34.1	30.5	22.2	27.6	16.9	35.0	26.5	21.3	28.6
1939	38.3	66.9	131.4	50.1	24.4	29.8	17.8	28.6	15.9	36.8	25.2	21.6	27.2
1933	39.7	67.0	136.4	49.8	100.1	28.5	28.1	28.1	15.7	38.1	27.5	26.5	22.5
1929	41.2	79.3	134.2	47.4	34.8	33.3	33.9	24.1	18.5	35.5	27.5	25.7	23.3

[a] The industrial shares are expressed as percentages of labor income in each state. The coefficients of variation are based on unweighted data—i.e., the observation for each state is treated on a par with the observation for each other state.

[b] All industries combined.

Source: Unpublished estimates supplied by the National Income Division.

Apparently the reduction in relative interstate dispersion in per capita wage and salary payments does not come from an increasing similarity in the industrial composition of the states. Rather, the reduction appears to stem from selective wage-equalizing shifts within industries, which operate to equalize state per capita wage and salary income. While it is still possible that results obtained from the analysis of a single year's detailed data for a broad industrial segment, such as manufacturing, are wholly the product of the special circumstances peculiar to the specific year, this finding should increase the confidence with which such results can be treated as indicative of the persistent element operating within the segment.

Of the three industrial segments for which detailed data are available—manufacturing, wholesale trade, and government—only manufacturing both provides a large percentage of all wage and salary income and is relatively disperse among the states. The government industries occupy an intermediate position with respect to both criteria. To the extent that wholesale and retail trade display similar characteristics, the interstate dispersion of wholesale trade may be expected to be small. Moreover, its aggregate wage and salary income is smaller than that of the other two segments.

Manufacturing Production-Worker Earnings[8]

For the analysis of regional differentials, the production-worker earning data in the *Census of Manufactures, 1947* are superior, in many respects, to those for any other industrial segment or for manufacturing for any earlier year. Since the census data are based on establishment reports, the more important of which are prepared by accountants with access to adequate records, they are not subject, as is the individual reporting in the population censuses, to the variation in the ability of respondents to recall pertinent information. Although the production-worker concept was newly introduced in the 1947 manufactures census, it was designed to clear up some of the ambiguities in the wage-earner concept used in a number of previous censuses, and there is little reason to think that differences among firms in its interpretation affected the reports in any important respect.

For present purposes, probably the most important innovation in the 1947 census was the extension of the inquiry on production-worker man-

[8] Much of the material in this section appears in my "Contribution of Manufacturing Wages to Regional Differences in Per Capita Income," *Review of Economics and Statistics*, 33 (1951), 18-28.

hours to all industries.[9] As a unit for reporting the physical volume of labor input that closely corresponds to the dollar amounts shown on specific payrolls, the production-worker man-hour is relatively free of ambiguity. It is not, for example, subject to random elements such as turnover, unpaid vacations, and temporary layoffs due to material shortages, which may affect the number of persons on a specific payroll.[10]

The manufactures census, since it is based on establishment reports, reflects the location of the establishment rather than the residence of the production workers. When geographic units as large as states are used, differences in establishment location and production-workers' residences are likely to arise only in reference to the relatively few plants near state borders.

Within the manufacturing segment of the nation's economy there are wide variations in the average hourly earnings of production workers. In part, at least, these variations are associated with the industrial characteristics of the plants in which the workers are engaged. The average hourly earnings of production workers in the 430 industries for which man-hour data are published vary from $0.65 in the raw cane sugar industry to $2.32 in the photo-engraving industry (table 33).[11] A state's manufacturing

TABLE 33
AVERAGE HOURLY EARNINGS OF PRODUCTION WORKERS, 430 MANUFACTURING INDUSTRIES, 1947

Average hourly earnings (cents)	Number of Industries	Average hourly earnings (cents)	Number of Industries
60- 69	3	130-139	68
70- 79	5	140-149	39
80- 89	23	150-159	15
90- 99	55	160-169	5
100-109	52	170-179	2
110-119	82	180 and over	3
120-129	78		

Source: *Census of Manufactures, 1947.*

earnings will therefore be affected by the kinds of manufacturing industries which are located in the state, as well as by a number of other factors, such as occupational wage rates.

By weighting the man-hours spent in each industry in a state by the

[9] The *Census of Manufactures, 1939* provided man-hour data for 171 industries. Earlier censuses had provided this information for even fewer industries.

[10] The average number of production workers reported in the *Census of Manufactures, 1947* is derived from the number of production workers on the payrolls during the pay periods ending nearest the middle of each month.

[11] The *Census of Manufactures, 1947* classifies plants into 458 industries, but man-hour data are published by industry for only 430. However, man-hour data have been shown by states for all major industry groups for which other data are published.

national average hourly earning in that industry, it is possible to compute for a state a weighted average hourly earning which will differ from the national average hourly earning only to the extent that state and national industrial compositions differ (table 34, column 4).[12] Since industrial earning rates have been held constant in this computation, the resulting figure has been designated the rate-constant earning.

By comparing a state's rate-constant hourly earning with that of the nation ($1.24 in 1947), a measure can be obtained of the extent to which industrial compositions differ among the states (table 34, column 5). Since the same set of weights (national average hourly earnings for each industry) has been used in computing the state rate-constant hourly earnings, they are comparable among states.

Michigan has the most favorable industrial composition, producing average hourly earnings 12.1 percent above the national average. At the other extreme, the composition of North Carolina industry is the most unfavorable, 19.1 percent below the national average. Many of the more highly industrialized and more populous states have a favorable composition, but there are some 32 states with unfavorable compositions, 10 of them 10 percent or more below the national average.

The only divisions that have a favorable composition are the East North Central and Middle Atlantic divisions. Manufactures composition is most unfavorable in the three Southern divisions.

Since the average hourly earning in each specific industry is used in computing a state's rate-constant hourly earning, the differences among states in the hourly earnings of workers within an industry have been ignored. By comparing the reported and rate-constant hourly earnings, the effect of the differences in national and state earnings can be measured (table 34, column 6). State weights (state composition of industry measured in man-hours) are used to calculate both the reported and the rate-constant earnings, and the differences between them provide a comparison only between each state, taken separately, and the nation. The weights differ from one state to another so that these differences cannot be used to compare earning rates in one state with those in another.[13]

[12] The methods are the same as those used in computing rate-constant occupational earnings. See chapter 5 and appendix B.

[13] To be comparable among states, as well as on a state-national basis, a composition-constant earning would be needed. By weighting state-specific industrial hourly earnings by the national man-hours, a composition-constant series, in which only earning rates differed, could be obtained. Such a series could be closely approximated for manufactures, but the requisite data are not available for any other industrial segment. Because of the limited usefulness of the composition-constant figures, they were not computed. See appendix B.

TABLE 34

Reported and Rate-Constant Manufacturing Production-Worker Hourly Earnings, 1947, by State

State (1)	Reported man-hours (millions) (2)	Average hourly earnings (dollars)		Percentage differences attributable to	
		Reported (3)	Rate-constant (4)	Industrial composition (national weights) (5)	Industry earning rates (state weights) (6)
New England					
Maine	190	1.05	1.12	−10.0	− 6.5
New Hampshire	136	1.07	1.13	− 8.8	− 5.9
Vermont	65	1.02	1.15	− 7.4	−11.4
Massachusetts	1,229	1.19	1.21	− 2.8	− 1.5
Rhode Island	261	1.14	1.18	− 4.9	− 3.8
Connecticut	693	1.27	1.29	3.5	− 1.1
Middle Atlantic					
New York	2,867	1.33	1.25	.5	6.4
New Jersey	1,237	1.33	1.26	1.7	5.0
Pennsylvania	2,458	1.24	1.27	2.0	− 2.1
East North Central					
Ohio	1,992	1.37	1.34	7.7	2.2
Indiana	936	1.32	1.31	5.6	.5
Illinois	1,972	1.33	1.29	3.5	3.5
Michigan	1,652	1.48	1.39	12.1	5.9
Wisconsin	726	1.25	1.28	2.5	− 2.1
West North Central					
Minnesota	306	1.17	1.23	− 1.5	− 4.2
Iowa	238	1.16	1.23	− 1.0	− 6.2
Missouri	542	1.12	1.21	− 2.4	− 7.6
North Dakota	8	1.00	1.15	− 7.7	−12.8
South Dakota	18	1.08	1.16	− 7.0	− 6.3
Nebraska	84	1.04	1.18	− 4.9	−12.3
Kansas	129	1.17	1.28	2.7	− 8.5
South Atlantic					
Delaware	60	1.17	1.20	− 3.2	− 2.9
Maryland	386	1.19	1.27	2.2	− 6.5
D. C.	21	1.30	1.30	4.1	.5
Virginia	387	.99	1.12	−10.2	−11.0
West Virginia	216	1.24	1.26	1.4	− 1.3
North Carolina	696	.92	1.01	−19.1	− 8.3
South Carolina	355	.93	1.03	−17.3	− 9.6
Georgia	456	.88	1.03	−17.2	−14.8
Florida	140	.92	1.07	−14.1	−14.2
East South Central					
Kentucky	227	1.04	1.17	− 6.2	−11.0
Tennessee	391	.95	1.13	− 9.3	−16.2
Alabama	380	.98	1.15	− 7.5	−14.8
Mississippi	148	.78	1.03	−17.6	−24.0
West South Central					
Arkansas	125	.82	1.02	−17.9	−20.0
Louisiana	231	.99	1.16	− 6.6	−14.6
Oklahoma	95	1.11	1.28	2.8	−13.1
Texas	512	1.09	1.24	− .5	−11.9
Mountain					
Montana	28	1.28	1.19	− 4.5	7.6
Idaho	31	1.21	1.06	−14.5	13.7
Wyoming	9	1.38	1.33	6.7	4.2
Colorado	93	1.18	1.25	.2	− 5.0
New Mexico	13	1.09	1.16	− 7.1	− 5.7
Arizona	24	1.22	1.17	− 5.7	4.3
Utah	41	1.17	1.24	− .5	− 5.1
Nevada	5	1.38	1.23	− 1.3	12.1
Pacific					
Washington	243	1.46	1.18	− 4.8	23.3
Oregon	182	1.46	1.08	−12.9	34.7
California	1,070	1.42	1.26	1.5	12.5

Cols. 2 and 3: from *Census of Manufactures, 1947.*

Col. 4: Computed by summing over all industries in a state the product of the number of man-hours reported by a particular industry in the state times the national average hourly earning of the industry, and dividing the sum by the total number of man-hours reported for the state. The basic computations were made by the Bureau of the Census as a special tabulation from detailed industry data for all 4-digit industries, although the results were made available only in the form of group totals which can be published without disclosing data concerning individual firms.

Col. 5: The difference, column 4 minus $1.24 (the national average hourly earning of all manufacturing production workers), expressed as a percentage of $1.24. The percentages were computed before the earnings were rounded.

Col. 6: The difference, column 3 minus column 4, expressed as a percentage of column 3. The percentages were computed before the earnings were rounded.

The entry for Maine, for example—6.5 percent—can be interpreted as indicating that on the average, Maine hourly earnings are 6.5 percent below those of the nation *for the manufacturing industries found in Maine in 1947*. A similar interpretation can be applied to the entry for New Hampshire; on the average New Hampshire hourly earnings are 5.9 percent below those of the nation for the manufacturing industries found in New Hampshire in 1947. But since Maine and New Hampshire may have differing compositions of manufacturing industries, we cannot conclude from the relative size of their deviations from the national average that Maine's hourly earnings are 10 percent lower than those in New Hampshire.[14] About all that can be concluded is that, given the differences in the industrial composition of the two states, Maine's hourly earning rates deviate more from the national average than do New Hampshire's.

Although the percentage differences in table 34, column 6, are not comparable among states, the entry for each state provides a state-national comparison which is free of the disturbing influence of compositional differences. In this respect the state-weighted percentage difference is superior to a comparison of the gross differences between the reported earnings and their national average, since such a comparison includes the effects of both compositional and rate differences.

Rate-constant earnings enter into the differences both in state industrial composition and in state-national earning-rate comparisons. Consequently, the rate-constant concept in a manufacturing context warrants closer examination.

The assumption that an industry, as distinguished by the Bureau of the Census,[15] is homogeneous with respect to the forces which are responsible for the industry's average hourly wage, is necessarily implied in the computation of each state's rate-constant hourly earning. Differences in the amount and type of capital, in the type and degree of skill required from the workers, in the manner in which the final product is priced and marketed, in the extent to which the workers are organized in-

[14] This figure is the difference between the entries for Maine and New Hampshire expressed as a percentage of the entry for New Hampshire. A comparison of this kind is analogous to comparing two price indexes based on differing commodities and differing weights.

[15] The Bureau of the Census closely follows the standard industrial classification prepared by the Technical Committee on Industrial Classification, Division of Statistical Standards, Bureau of the Budget, for use by all government agencies. See *Standard Industrial Classification Manual,* vol. 1, Manufacturing Industries, Washington, 1945. The Bureau of the Census has described the departures from the standard industrial classification in the *Census of Manufactures, 1947*.

to unions, in the degree to which the product is subject to seasonal factors, and in many other forces[16] will make for variation in the hourly earnings of production workers. Undoubtedly some of these forces are responsible for differences in the average hourly earnings in plants within a single industry. It is, for example, unlikely that plants with only a few employees will require the same range of occupations that will be found in large plants in the same industry. While heterogeneousness will give rise to some error and impair the usefulness of industry averages, it will not vitiate their use unless the errors are large or the intra-industry differences are associated with a region.

For most industries there is little evidence of heterogeneousness. A pulp mill in the South is probably more closely related to a pulp mill in the North than to the paper mill next door. The differences among industries found in the *Census of Manufactures, 1947* appear to be significant. Most of the differences in average hourly earnings have persisted from one census to another.[17] Although not conclusive, this fact indicates that the forces which determine the industry average are associated with some stable industrial characteristic and are not the result of random or chance factors which could be expected to rearrange the array of industrial earnings from one census to another.[18] Exceptions, of course, can be found. The sawmill industry, for example, appears to differ markedly from one region to another with respect to organization, degree of mechanization, degree of unionization, and type of lumber cut.[19]

[16] Cf. Sumner H. Slichter, "Notes on the Structure of Wages," *Review of Economics and Statistics,* 32 (1950), 80-91; Jacob Perlman, "Extent and Causes of Differences in Hourly Earnings," *Journal of the American Statistical Association,* 35 (1940), 1-12; and D. E. Cullen, "The Interindustry Wage Structure, 1899-1950," *American Economic Review,* 46 (1956), 353-369.

[17] The coefficient of determination between the average hourly earnings in 1939 and 1947 for the 95 industries for which man-hour data were collected in 1939, and for which the industrial classifications are comparable, is .85.

[18] The stability of the industrial structure alone would tend to increase the confidence with which results for a single census year can be interpreted. This stability, coupled with the inherent difficulties of "moving" industries from one state to another, probably means that the state earning differentials found in one census will persist over several years. Later censuses will afford an opportunity to test this more completely. The 1954 average hourly earnings of manufacturing workers estimated for each state by the Bureau of Labor Statistics, as shown in the *Statistical Abstract of the United States, 1955,* p. 216, are highly correlated with the census figures for 1947 (table 34, column 3); the coefficient of determination between the two series is .88. Herman P. Miller, in "Changes in the Industrial Distribution of Wages in the United States: 1939-1949," in *Studies in Income and Wealth,* 23 (Princeton, 1957), 355-420, also finds considerable stability in the population-census industrial earnings over the 1939-1949 decade.

[19] Man-hour data are published only for sawmills producing a million board-feet or more. For this group of mills the average hourly earnings range from $0.65 in the East South Central division to $1.59 in the Pacific division. If the industrial classification distinguished

Another source of difficulty in the use of national averages to separate industrial from regional differences in earnings is the tendency for particular industries to be concentrated in a particular state or region. For example, 79 percent of cigarette manufacture, measured by production-worker man-hours, is in the South Atlantic division. Cigarette manufacture, with its average earnings of $1.12 per hour, lowers the rate-constant earnings of the South Atlantic states, increasing the unfavorableness of their position. This raises the question of whether the relatively low earnings are a result of industrial characteristics which would cause a relatively low wage wherever cigarette plants are located, or whether the low industry average is chiefly the result of the industry's location in a low-earning area.

The examples just discussed, while not easy to appraise, appear consistent with the generally held belief that industrial characteristics are more powerful than location in determining an industry's wage structure.[20]

The large number of census classifications operates both to limit the number of industries containing two groups of plants which have marked structural differences, and to increase the number which are highly concentrated geographically.[21]

The tendency to be noted in table 34 for most of the states in a census division to have industrial compositions which depart from the national average in a similar direction does not appear to persist within the 20 major industrial groups. A rate-constant average hourly earning for each major industrial group within each of the census regions has been computed and compared with the national average for the corresponding

---

the types of operation associated with portable and fixed sawmills, one would expect the average hourly earnings in the Pacific Northwest, where the fixed mill is common, to be the higher. The effect of combining the two types is to overstate the rate-constant earnings for the South and understate those of the Pacific Northwest. In addition to the description of the industry in the *Census of Manufactures, 1947,* see Vernon H. Jensen, *Lumber and Labor,* New York, 1945, pp. 15-18.

[20] This conclusion implies that the variance of the average hourly earnings among the 458 industries within the 48 states is significantly larger than their variance among the 48 states within the 458 industries. A table of average hourly production-worker earnings for each of the 458 industries in each of the 48 states is needed to test this hypothesis, and although most of the required data are available, such a test has not been made. For reasons given in chapter 5 and appendix B, the data given in table 34, columns 5 and 6, cannot be used to estimate the relative size of the two variances.

[21] There are 108 industries for which there is clear evidence that 50 percent or more of the man-hours were expended in one geographic division. For another 65 industries, the evidence is not so clear, since data are available only by area (two or three divisions combined). It is possible that some of these industries, also, are concentrated in a single division.

major group. When the detailed industries in a major group for a particular region tend to be heavily weighted toward the lower-earning industries within the major group, the region will have an unfavorable composition for the major group. If the unfavorable (favorable) compositions found for states within a region were due solely to the lower (higher) skills available in the region, then we might expect the compositions within the major groups to be unfavorable (favorable). Such is not the case. There is no significant tendency for the favorable and unfavorable within-group compositions to be distributed among regions in a systematic manner.[22] The distributions of the within-group compositions among regions appear to be random, and they do not follow the regional pattern found in table 34. From this finding we may conclude that differences among the major groups account for the chief contribution to regional differences in industrial composition and that the within-major-group contribution to these differences is small.

On the other hand, if a census division as a whole has hourly earnings smaller (larger) than the national average for the industries found in the region, there is a strong tendency for the hourly earnings of the major group to deviate from the national average in the same direction.

When reported average hourly earnings are larger (smaller) than rate-constant earnings for a census division, reported earnings tend to be larger (smaller) in each of the major industry groups. Since the industry weights differ from region to region, each region must be analyzed separately. In the two South Central regions rate-constant earnings exceed reported earnings in every major group, and in the South Atlantic and West North Central regions there is only one major group (tobacco products) in which this is not the case. In the New England region, rate-constant earnings exceed reported earnings for all but three major groups (tobacco products, textile mill products, and leather and leather products). In the Pacific region, reported earnings exceed rate-constant earnings in all but the petroleum and coal products major group. In the Middle Atlantic region there are four major groups (paper and allied products, fabricated metal products, nonelectrical machinery, and transportation equipment), and in the East North Central region there are five major groups (textile mill products, apparel and related products,

[22] Based on a rank-order test. See Milton Friedman, "The Use of Ranks to Avoid the Assumption of Normality Implicit in the Analysis of Variance," *Journal of the American Statistical Association*, 32 (1937), 675-701. The probability that the ranks would differ by chance alone as much as they did is approximately .10. A table showing the within-group compositions by census regions is given in my "Contribution of Manufacturing Wages to Regional Differences in Per Capita Income," *loc. cit.* The analysis there followed a somewhat more detailed method which led to essentially the same conclusion.

leather and leather products, electrical machinery, and instruments and related products) in which reported earnings do not exceed rate-constant hourly earnings. In the Mountain states, where reported earnings exceed rate-constant hourly earnings by only 0.1 percent, there are only six major groups in which this pattern persists.[23] The persistence of the area patterns within the major industry groups would increase the confidence with which the regional patterns could be used to rank the areas by earning levels despite the differences in industry weights. If this is done, the three Southern and the West North Central regions are low-earning areas, the Pacific region is a high-earning area, and the four remaining regions are average-earning areas.

Since the discussion of manufacturing earnings will gain from comparisons with the earnings of other industrial segments, the discussion of manufacturing earnings will be resumed after the data available for other segments have been introduced. Attention is now turned to wholesale-trade earnings.

Wholesale-Trade Earnings[24]

A similar, though somewhat less precise, analysis of the average annual earnings of the 2.2 million wholesale-trade employees of merchant wholesalers, manufacturers' sales branches with stocks, petroleum bulk stations and terminals, and assemblers of farm products can be made on the basis of data from the *Census of Business, 1948.*[25] These employees are classified by 244 kinds of business.

The average annual earning of paid wholesale-trade employees in 1948 was $3,357. When classified by kind of business, wholesale-trade earnings are slightly more disperse than the hourly earnings of manufacturing production workers (table 35).[26] The average annual earnings

[23] The differences, reported minus rate-constant hourly earnings, expressed as a percentage of the latter, by regions, for all manufacturing industries are:

New England	—2.4	South Atlantic	— 9.0
Middle Atlantic	+2.9	East South Central	—15.5
East North Central	+2.8	West South Central	—13.5
West North Central	—7.0	Mountain	+ .1
		Pacific	+16.5

Detailed figures by region and major industrial group have been shown in *ibid.*, table 4.

[24] The substance of this section appeared in my "State Wholesale Trade Earnings, 1948," *Southern Economic Journal,* 22 (1955), 212-220.

[25] This study excludes manufacturers' sales offices without stocks, and agents and brokers, which the census includes in wholesale trade. Neither group is engaged to any appreciable degree in the physical handling of the goods that they sell, nor do they normally maintain stocks. The two omitted groups reported 192,000 employees as of November 15, 1948.

[26] The average annual earnings of employees of each kind of business are computed by dividing the payroll for the entire year by the average number of paid employees. The

in the central two-thirds of the kinds-of-business classification range from \$2,900 to \$4,200, a range of about \$1,300. Manufacturing production-worker earnings within this range, assuming a 2,000-hour year, would include about six-sevenths of the manufacturing industries. Whether this difference in dispersion is due to statistical differences in the annual and hourly units used or whether it is traceable to the more substantial differences in seasonality, the greater prevalence of part-time employment in some industries, and a greater range of skills, is not known.

TABLE 35

Average Annual Earnings of Wholesale-Trade Employees, 244 Kinds of Business, 1948

Average annual earnings	Kinds-of-business (number)	Average annual earnings	Kinds-of-business (number)
Less than \$2,300	8	3,700-3,899	28
2,300-2,499	8	3,900-4,099	14
2,500-2,699	8	4,100-4,299	15
2,700-2,899	10	4,300-4,499	10
2,900-3,099	20	4,500-4,699	7
3,100-3,299	30	4,700-4,899	5
3,300-3,499	32	4,900-5,099	10
3,500-3,699	29	5,100-and more	10

Source: *Census of Business, 1948*, Wholesale Trade, U. S. Summary, table 1E. The above tabulation excludes agents and brokers and manufacturers' sales offices without stocks.

Two limitations to the use of these average annual earnings for computing state rate-constant earnings need early attention. The first is that classification by kind of business limits, but does not eliminate, the dispersion in the composition of skills and occupations within the kind-of-business classification. Each establishment is likely to have its own unique composition of skills, and any classificatory device not based directly on skills will contain some dispersion within it. The extent of the approximation is determined partially by the number and characteristics of the kind-of-business categories employed. The 244 categories employed in the 1948 census of wholesale trade appear sufficiently numerous to eliminate much of the diversity among establishments. More categories would lead to a definition of "kind of business" so narrow that only a handful of establishments in each category could be clearly classified. The remainder would be borderline cases fitting one category about as well as another.[27]

average number of paid employees is obtained by summing the numbers reported for the work weeks which ended nearest the 15th of March, of July, and of November 1948, and dividing by 3.

[27] If carried to an extreme, enough categories could be created to accommodate practically every establishment in some one narrowly defined kind-of-business classification. For most purposes such categories would be meaningless. Too, such a large number of cate-

The second limitation relates to the approximate character of average annual earnings. The payroll figure reported by each establishment presumably is based on accounting records and is highly reliable. The number of employees, however, is based on only three payroll periods and is subject to a number of transient influences. Seasonal peaks, varying rates of turnover, varying lengths of work weeks, and many other similar factors can affect the differences in average annual earnings between establishments and between kinds of businesses. Although the error thus induced is likely to be small, it is present nevertheless.

With these limitations of the kinds-of-business classifications in mind, it is possible to use the kinds-of-business average earnings to compute for each state a rate-constant earning which reflects only differences in kind-of-business composition (table 36). The most favorable kind-of-business composition is found in New York (12.2 percent above the national average); the most unfavorable composition is in Idaho (19.2 percent below the national average). Of the 11 states with favorable compositions, 7 are along the Eastern seaboard. Missouri is the only state west of the Mississippi River with a favorable composition. Although wholesale trade is generally associated with large metropolitan centers, all of the states that have such centers do not have favorable compositions, while Rhode Island and Tennessee do.

Some insight as to the source of the differences in kind-of-business composition can be obtained by carrying out a similar analysis for each of the major kind-of-business groups. This has been done for the 15 groups including more than two kinds of businesses. The nine census divisions are used as the basis for a geographic distribution, providing a table which shows the percentage differences for each of the nine geographic divisions in the kind-of-business composition within each of 15 kind-of-business groups. In this table the United States composition for the kind-of-business group, rather than for all wholesale trade, is used as the base. By ranking the percentage differences for a group from the largest negative difference to the largest positive difference, it is possible to test whether the within-group differences are associated with geographic division.[28] Such a test indicates that differences at the di-

gories would result in a high geographical concentration of the establishments in a particular category, and thus would prevent a decision as to whether the observed differences in earnings were attributable to differences in the skills required or to geographical differences in pay for similar skills. A real test of the kinds-of-business classifications used would depend upon knowledge of the variance within each category. Such information is not available.

[28] Friedman, *op. cit.*

TABLE 36

Reported and Rate-Constant Wholesale-Trade Employee Annual Earnings, 1948, by State

State (1)	Average number of employees (thousands) (2)	Average annual earnings (dollars)		Percentage differences attributable to kind-of-business	
		Reported (3)	Rate-constant (4)	Composition (national weights) (5)	Earning Rates (state weights) (6)
New England					
Maine	10	2,770	3,184	− 5.1	−13.0
New Hampshire	4	2,818	3,197	− 4.7	−11.9
Vermont	3	2,948	3,212	− 4.2	− 8.2
Massachusetts	75	3,519	3,475	3.6	1.3
Rhode Island	11	3,179	3,476	3.6	− 8.5
Connecticut	25	3,374	3,342	− .4	1.0
Middle Atlantic					
New York	338	4,076	3,764	12.2	8.3
New Jersey	56	3,485	3,426	2.1	1.7
Pennsylvania	141	3,224	3,409	1.6	− 5.4
East North Central					
Ohio	111	3,471	3,382	.8	2.6
Indiana	42	3,269	3,229	− 3.7	1.2
Illinois	164	3,651	3,399	1.3	7.4
Michigan	77	3,574	3,314	− 1.2	7.8
Wisconsin	39	3,310	3,277	− 2.3	1.0
West North Central					
Minnesota	49	3,133	3,249	− 3.1	− 3.6
Iowa	31	2,913	3,042	− 9.3	− 4.2
Missouri	80	3,205	3,379	.7	− 5.2
North Dakota	8	2,896	2,972	−11.4	− 2.6
South Dakota	7	2,778	2,975	−11.3	− 6.6
Nebraska	21	2,907	3,148	− 6.2	− 7.6
Kansas	22	2,736	3,066	− 8.6	−10.8
South Atlantic					
Delaware	5	3,599	3,625	8.1	− .7
Maryland	31	3,017	3,256	− 2.9	− 7.4
D. C.	16	3,568	3,476	3.6	2.6
Virginia	33	2,776	3,003	−10.5	− 7.6
West Virginia	17	3,218	3,295	− 1.8	− 2.3
North Carolina	34	2,793	3,170	− 5.5	−11.9
South Carolina	13	2,743	3,191	− 4.9	−14.0
Georgia	40	2,973	3,279	− 2.3	− 9.3
Florida	44	2,715	2,972	−11.4	− 8.6
East South Central					
Kentucky	23	2,908	3,253	− 3.0	−10.6
Tennessee	36	2,965	3,370	.5	−12.0
Alabama	25	2,762	3,247	− 3.2	−14.9
Mississippi	13	2,456	3,160	− 5.8	−22.3
West South Central					
Arkansas	13	2,602	3,118	− 7.0	−16.6
Louisiana	34	2,923	3,327	− .8	−12.1
Oklahoma	23	2,972	3,236	− 3.5	− 8.2
Texas	107	2,928	3,233	− 3.6	− 9.4
Mountain					
Montana	7	2,998	3,141	− 6.4	− 4.5
Idaho	7	2,750	2,711	−19.2	1.5
Wyoming	2	2,946	3,156	− 5.9	− 6.7
Colorado	23	2,975	3,267	− 2.6	− 8.9
New Mexico	4	2,801	3,240	− 3.4	−13.5
Arizona	8	3,055	3,072	− 8.4	− .6
Utah	11	3,123	3,328	− .8	− 6.2
Nevada	1	3,517	3,236	− 3.5	8.7
Pacific					
Washington	41	3,380	3,196	− 4.7	5.8
Oregon	26	3,442	3,209	− 4.4	7.3
California	200	3,400	3,192	− 4.8	6.5

Cols. 2 and 3: *Census of Business, 1948.* Only the wholesale-trade employees of merchant wholesalers, manufacturers' sales branches with stocks, petroleum bulk stations and terminals, and assemblers of farm products are included. Excluded are manufacturers' sales offices without stocks and agents and brokers.

Col. 4: Computed by summing over all kinds of business in a state the products of the number of employees reported for a particular kind of business in a state times the national average annual earning for that kind of business, and dividing the sum by the total number of employees reported for the state. Since it was not possible for the Bureau of the Census to publish data by detailed kind of business for every state, the actual computations of this column were made by the Bureau of the Census as a special tabulation. While all 244 kinds of business were used in making these computations, the results were made available only in the form of group totals which can be published without disclosing data concerning the operations of individual establishments.

Col. 5: The difference, column 4 minus $3,357 (the national average annual earning of all wholesale trade employees), expressed as a percentage of $3,357. The percentages were computed before rounding.

Col. 6: The difference, column 3 minus column 4, expressed as a percentage of column 4. The percentages were omputed before rounding.

visional geographic level within the major kind-of-business groups contribute significantly to the regional differences in kind-of-business composition. The observed differences in composition, thus, are not entirely the product of differences in the geographic distribution of the major groups; these between-group differences are supplemented and reinforced by differences within the groups by detailed kind of business. This is a somewhat different situation from that found for manufactures, where intragroup composition apparently contributed but little to rate-constant earnings.

A comparison of the reported and rate-constant earnings for each state provides a measure of state-national earning differences for each state's kinds of businesses.

Nevada, which pays 8.7 percent more than the average based on its kind-of-business composition, is closely followed by New York, which for its kinds of business pays 8.3 percent above average. At the other end of the scale, Mississippi pays 22.3 percent less than average for the kinds of business found there. Of the 15 states paying more than average compensation for their kinds of business, 10 are located in the Middle Atlantic, East North Central, and Pacific divisions.

When the differences between the reported payrolls and those computed from the kind-of-business composition for each of the nine geographic divisions are examined, the differences are found to persist for each major kind-of-business group. The sign of the difference in each of the 20 major kind-of-business groups is the same as the sign for the geographic division as a whole in four divisions, is the same in 19 out of the 20 groups in three more divisions, is the same in 16 out of the 20 groups in the Pacific division, and is the same in 13 out of the 20 groups in the New England division.

Earnings of Government Employees[29]

The interest in state earning differentials of government employees stems from the disproportionate increase after 1940 in the number of employees of the federal government[30] and from curiosity as to whether the numerous federal policies affecting the distribution of income among persons also are designed to affect state differentials, more than from the absolute size of their effects on the state earning differentials of all em-

[29] This section is based largely upon unpublished material developed by Howard G. Schaller while he was with the Study of Differences in State Per Capita Incomes.

[30] The number of federal employees increased from .9 million in 1939 to 2.4 million in 1952, an increase of 161 percent. During this period the employees of state and local governments increased from 3.1 to 3.8 million, an increase of about 22 percent.

ployees.[31] The federal government could manage its activities in several ways that would affect the state earning differentials of its employees.

Perhaps the most obvious method would be through the location of governmental activities in areas where other income is low. Presumably, in these areas federal government pay rates would exceed those provided by alternative employment. There is, however, no evidence that this method has been used effectively.[32]

Federal pay rates offer another avenue for affecting state earning differentials. The policy written into the Classification and Postal Pay Acts, of paying the same rate for similar work wherever it is performed, is calculated to operate in the direction of leveling state differentials. The policy of having rates fixed by a local wage board in accordance with those prevailing in the community where the work is to be performed is designed to be neutral with regard to its direct effects on state earning rates, though it may indirectly affect them by increasing the demand for the relevant skills.[33] The data necessary to weight the effectiveness of each of these policies individually, and to distinguish their direct from their secondary effects, are not available. With the data at hand, about the best that can be done is to use methods similar to those used for manufacturing and wholesale trade and then to try to relate the results to these problems.

The interstate relative range of government employees' average annual earnings in 1952 was about three-fifths of what it was in 1939 (table 37).[34] This reduction in the relative range is the result of a tendency for the percentage increase in earnings from 1939 to 1952 to be higher in states with the lower 1939 earnings.[35] There is a tendency for the earnings of

[31] Government employees were approximately 8.8 percent of the employed labor force in 1939 and 10.0 percent in 1952. *Statistical Abstract of the United States, 1953*, p. 186.

[32] Federal government employees, as a percentage of the population, tended to be more numerous in high-income states in 1939; there was no relationship in 1952. The coefficient of determination between the number of federal employees and income, both taken per capita, was .23 in 1939; in 1952 it was .07, a figure that does not differ significantly from 0.

[33] In June 1952 the pay rates of 45 percent of federal employees were fixed in accordance with the Classification Act, 36 percent by Wage Board decisions, 15 percent in accordance with the Postal Pay Act, and 4 percent by miscellaneous methods. Civil Service Commission, *Pay Structure of the Federal Civil Service, June 30, 1952* (1953).

[34] The District of Columbia is excluded from these calculations. The relative range is the range divided by the mean. The range in 1939 was from a low of $787 in Mississippi to a high of $1,855 in New York State. In 1952 it was from a low of $2,540 in Arkansas to a high of $4,044 in Washington. The national average of all government employees increased from $1,445 in 1939 to $3,512 in 1952, or by 143 percent.

[35] The coefficient of determination between the percentage increase from 1939 to 1952 and the 1939 level of government employees' earnings is —.70.

TABLE 37

Reported and Rate-Constant Earnings of Government Employees, 1939 and 1952, by State

State	Number of employees (thousands)		Average annual earnings (dollars)				Percentage differences attributable to			
			Reported		Rate-constant		Composition of governments (national weights)		Governments earning rates (state weights)	
(1)	1939 (2)	1952 (3)	1939 (4)	1952 (5)	1939 (6)	1952 (7)	1939 (8)	1952 (9)	1939 (10)	1952 (11)
New England										
Maine	30.3	39.5	940	3,071	1,456	3,544	.8	.9	−35.4	−13.3
New Hampshire	20.3	16.4	1,353	3,246	1,413	3,359	− 2.2	−4.4	− 4.2	− 3.4
Vermont	10.4	12.4	1,315	2,981	1,450	3,465	.3	−1.3	− 9.3	−14.0
Massachusetts	160.3	209.5	1,566	3,499	1,439	3,454	− .4	−1.7	8.8	1.3
Rhode Island	23.2	31.9	1,548	3,241	1,480	3,523	2.4	.3	4.6	− 8.0
Connecticut	52.5	61.5	1,428	3,581	1,405	3,379	− 2.8	−3.8	1.6	6.0
Middle Atlantic										
New York	459.5	667.2	1,855	3,865	1,440	3,437	− .3	−2.1	28.8	12.5
New Jersey	124.6	170.9	1,728	3,770	1,414	3,464	− 2.1	−1.4	22.2	8.8
Pennsylvania	288.9	352.9	1,458	3,511	1,433	3,540	− .8	.8	1.7	− .8
East North Central										
Ohio	201.0	284.7	1,467	3,525	1,418	3,500	− 1.9	− .3	3.5	.7
Indiana	93.6	131.7	1,290	3,399	1,411	3,472	− 2.4	−1.1	− 8.6	− 2.1
Illinois	216.3	312.3	1,771	3,706	1,448	3,492	.2	− .6	22.3	6.1
Michigan	146.1	207.8	1,590	3,934	1,408	3,405	− 2.6	−3.0	12.9	15.5
Wisconsin	100.7	105.6	1,386	3,558	1,410	3,393	− 2.4	−3.4	− 1.7	4.9
West North Central										
Minnesota	98.7	104.0	1,218	3,450	1,411	3,425	− 2.4	−2.5	−13.7	.7
Iowa	73.9	85.1	1,133	3,081	1,414	3,402	− 2.1	−3.1	−19.9	− 9.4
Missouri	104.3	138.9	1,328	3,000	1,444	3,512	− .1	.0	− 8.0	−14.6
North Dakota	20.6	22.2	893	3,216	1,436	3,460	− .6	−1.5	−37.8	− 7.1
South Dakota	27.2	26.5	830	3,034	1,427	3,515	− 1.2	.1	−41.8	−13.7
Nebraska	49.0	59.7	1,049	3,046	1,429	3,491	− 1.1	− .6	−26.6	−12.7
Kansas	61.0	72.9	1,044	3,141	1,417	3,475	− 1.9	−1.1	−26.3	− 9.6
South Atlantic										
Delaware	8.4	11.5	1,406	3,323	1,420	3,398	− 1.7	−3.2	− 1.0	− 2.2
Maryland	71.0	154.0	1,724	3,930	1,547	3,675	7.1	4.6	11.4	6.9
D. C.	106.5	171.9	2,044	4,097	1,704	3,836	17.9	9.2	20.0	6.8
Virginia	100.5	204.6	1,434	3,646	1,521	3,679	5.3	4.8	− 5.7	− .9
West Virginia	40.8	53.6	1,102	2,958	1,414	3,424	− 2.1	−2.5	−22.1	−13.6
North Carolina	70.0	115.3	1,073	2,878	1,419	3,432	− 1.8	−2.3	−24.4	−16.1
South Carolina	41.7	71.9	1,013	2,698	1,447	3,504	.1	− .2	−30.0	−23.0
Georgia	66.4	135.9	998	2,970	1,434	3,559	− .8	1.3	−30.4	−16.5
Florida	58.5	128.8	1,171	3,120	1,425	3,460	− 1.4	−1.5	−17.8	− 9.8
East South Central										
Kentucky	61.5	86.1	1,140	2,976	1,429	3,534	− 1.1	.6	−20.2	−15.8
Tennessee	66.5	111.8	1,178	3,052	1,464	3,517	1.3	.1	−19.5	−13.2
Alabama	61.1	115.3	982	2,996	1,448	3,570	.2	1.7	−32.2	−16.1
Mississippi	49.5	60.0	787	2,577	1,450	3,445	.3	−1.9	−45.7	−25.2
West South Central										
Arkansas	41.6	51.5	935	2,540	1,451	3,499	.4	− .4	−35.6	−27.4
Louisiana	65.6	95.8	1,157	2,978	1,429	3,449	− 1.1	−1.8	−19.0	−13.7
Oklahoma	63.4	103.4	1,104	2,996	1,427	3,574	− 1.2	1.8	−22.6	−16.2
Texas	148.5	299.1	1,281	3,220	1,435	3,536	− .7	.7	−10.7	− 8.9
Mountain										
Montana	24.9	24.9	1,270	3,597	1,499	3,477	3.7	−1.0	−15.3	3.5
Idaho	18.5	21.5	1,168	3,356	1,440	3,481	− .3	− .9	−18.9	− 3.6
Wyoming	10.9	14.5	1,168	3,314	1,475	3,534	2.1	.6	−20.8	− 6.2
Colorado	41.2	74.8	1,358	3,434	1,447	3,580	.1	1.9	− 6.2	− 4.1
New Mexico	19.8	34.4	1,177	3,319	1,494	3,581	3.4	2.0	−21.2	− 7.3
Arizona	18.7	36.1	1,400	3,725	1,513	3,526	4.7	.4	− 7.5	5.6
Utah	20.6	53.2	1,210	3,393	1,435	3,685	− .7	4.9	−15.7	− 7.9
Nevada	6.4	11.3	1,603	3,713	1,511	3,560	4.6	1.4	6.1	4.3
Pacific										
Washington	69.2	136.1	1,544	4,044	1,459	3,577	1.0	1.9	5.8	13.1
Oregon	41.8	61.1	1,399	3,915	1,448	3,456	.2	−1.6	− 3.4	13.3
California	250.7	603.8	1,647	3,962	1,436	3,540	− .6	.8	14.7	11.9
United States	4,006.6	6,156.0	1,445	3,512	1,445	3,512	.....	....	.....	.....

Col. 2: The number of federal government employees engaged in the executive branch, the Government Printing Office, and the Government Accounting Office in each state was estimated by averaging the numbers at the beginning and end of 1939 as shown in the *Annual Report of the Civil Service Commission, 1940*. Since federal government employees

government employees to be higher in states which have high incomes from other sources in both years, though this tendency is more marked in 1939 than in 1952.[36]

Available data make it possible to distinguish clearly only three categories of government employment, analogous to the industrial and kind-of-business categories used for manufacturing and wholesale trade. These are federal government, state and local education, and other state and local government. In part, this difficulty is conceptual; for example, there is wide variation among the states as to what is a local government function. Chiefly, however, the difficulty reflects the failure of government to provide regular and consistent statistical information on its own activities.[37] These three categories provide a meager base for computing a meaningful rate-constant earning for the government employees in the various states. One consequence of the small number of categories is that the ranges of the rate-constant earnings are but 13 to 20 percent of the ranges of reported earnings.[38] Despite these serious shortcomings of the

[36] The coefficients of determination between the state average annual earnings of all government employees and state per capita incomes are .86 for 1939 and .66 for 1952.

[37] For example, the most recent census of governments is for 1942. See table 68, below.

[38] The difficulty may be seen more clearly by an examination of the national averages for the annual earnings in the three categories. These averages and their 1939-1952 percentage increases are:

Government category	Average earnings 1939	Average earnings 1952	Percentage increase 1939–1952
Federal	$1,760	$3,913	122
State and local education	1,355	3,413	152
Other state and local	1,349	3,160	134

In 1939 the state and local government averages differed by only $6, so that the rate-

in the District of Columbia were reported as a unit, they were distributed by residency among Maryland, Virginia, and the District of Columbia on the basis of *Census of Population, 1940* data. The average number of state and local government employees is shown in Bureau of Labor Statistics, *Employment and Payrolls of State and Local Governments, 1929-1939* (1946). The estimates include part-time as well as full-time employees.

Col. 3: The average number of federal employees in the executive branch, the Government Printing Office, and the Government Accounting Office was computed from monthly data in Civil Service Commission, *Monthly Reports of Employment, Executive Branch of the Federal Government*, and these averages were distributed by state in proportion to the average of the numbers in each state on December 31, 1951, June 30 and December 31, 1952, as shown in the *Annual Report of the Civil Service Commission, 1952*, and in tables supplied by the Commission. Employees working in the District of Columbia were distributed by state of residence on the basis of *Census of Population, 1950* data. Average monthly employment by state and local governments was calculated from the data in *State Distribution of Public Employment, 1952*, and then distributed by state in accordance with the October 1952 state distribution given in Allen D. Manvel, "Regional Differences in the Scale of State and Local Government," *National Tax Journal*, 7 (1954), 112-113.

Col. 4: The averages shown are the sum of federal, state, and local government payrolls for the year, divided by the number of employees shown in column 2. The estimated aggregate federal payrolls and their distribution among states were supplied by the National Income Division. State and local government payrolls, by state, were estimated by multiplying by 12 the 1939 average monthly payroll for each state shown in Bureau of Labor Statistics, *Employment and Payrolls of State and Local Governments, 1929-1939* (1946).

Col. 5: The averages shown are the sum of federal, state, and local government payrolls for 1952, divided by the number of employees in column 3. The estimates were supplied by the National Income Division.

Col. 6: The sum of the products of the 1939 number of employees in a "type of government" times the 1939 national average earning of employees in that "type of government," divided by the total number of employees (column 2), where the three "types of government" are federal; state and local education; and state and local noneducation.

Col. 7: Same as column 6, except that 1952 data are used.

Col. 8: The difference, the rate-constant earning in column 6 minus the weighted average of column 6 ($1,445), expressed as a percentage of the latter.

Col. 9: The difference, the rate-constant earning in column 7 minus the weighted average of column 7 ($3,512), expressed as a percentage of the latter.

Col. 10: The difference, column 4 minus column 6, expressed as a percentage of column 6.

Col. 11: The difference, column 5 minus column 7, expressed as a percentage of column 7.

basic data, the rate-constant earnings appear to provide for many states the correct sign, if not magnitude, of the state's deviation from the national composition. For other states, however, particularly those whose rate-constant earnings do not differ greatly from the national average, it is doubtful whether table 37 provides even a reliable sign.

Of the 29 states with unfavorable compositions of government employees in 1939, all but 8 still had unfavorable compositions in 1952. Of the remaining 19 states and the District of Columbia, which had favorable compositions in 1939, all but 7 states still had favorable compositions in 1952. There does not appear to be any characteristic in common to the states changing from a favorable to an unfavorable composition between 1939 and 1952, or vice versa.[39] Each of the census regions except the West North Central had states with both favorable and unfavorable compositions. Many of the states with large metropolitan centers had unfavorable compositions in both years, and the most notable exception, Maryland, probably reflects chiefly the fact that many federal employees working in the District of Columbia live in Maryland. To the extent that large cities are associated with high income, the unfavorable compositions found in such areas would suggest that the federal government had tended to avoid them in locating its centers of activity.[40]

The percentage difference between the reported and rate-constant earnings is affected by the extent to which the rate-constant figures reflect

constant earnings basically reflect only the differences in the proportions of federal employees in the states. The differences between categories are somewhat wider in 1952, but the 1939-1952 increases in government employment were larger in the categories with the smaller percentage increases in earnings. The 1939-1952 percentage increases in number of employees are: federal government, 161 percent; state and local education, 16 percent; and other state and local government, 26 percent. The larger increases are the consequence of disproportionate expansions in the direction of force-account construction and manufacturing activities—that is, a change in the distribution of governmental functions. See Solomon Fabricant, *The Trend of Government Activities in the United States Since 1900*, New York, 1952. If the categories were sufficient to accord separate treatment to these force-account workers, presumably the range of rate-constant earnings would be increased; at least, the rate-constant earnings would reflect state differences due to changes in earning levels and those due to internal changes in the composition of employees.

[39] The states with favorable 1939 and unfavorable 1952 compositions are Vermont, Illinois, South Carolina, Mississippi, Arkansas, Montana, and Oregon. Those with unfavorable 1939 and favorable 1952 compositions are Pennsylvania, South Dakota, Georgia, Kentucky, Oklahoma, Texas, Utah, and California. It may be noted that both high- and low-income states and all census regions are represented.

[40] That the unfavorable composition in these states is not due entirely to a tendency for the number of state and local (i.e., lower-paid) employees per capita to increase with city size is evidenced by the fact that the number of federal employees per capita is below the national average in New York, New Jersey, Pennsylvania, Illinois, Michigan, Ohio, and Missouri.

compositional differences. Since there is reason to believe that the three categories for which data are available are too broad to reflect many of the differences in function, the figures denoting the size of the earning differentials after composition is taken into account must be used with caution. Moreover, the fact that the compositions vary from one state to another limits their usefulness for comparisons among states. Consequently, only comparison between 1939 and 1952 will be made.

In all except seven states, the signs of the earning differentials are the same for both years.[41] In another six states the 1952 percentage differences were larger than those for 1939. For the remaining 35 states and the District of Columbia, the signs of the percentage differences were the same in both years, but the size of the percentage differences was smaller in 1952. This would indicate that the dispersion in the state earnings of government employees had decreased between 1939 and 1952, even after changes in composition had been taken into account. It would be extremely difficult, however, to maintain successfully that this effect was the result of a federal policy or combination of policies aimed at reducing interstate differentials. The fact that the average earnings of state and local government employees have increased more than those of federal government employees, and that this differential increase has contributed to the observed decrease in interstate dispersion, would argue against such an interpretation. Nor is it clear whether the tendency often noted for the earnings of lower-paid skills to increase more, or the diluting of the composition of federal government-employee skills by the greater expansion in force-account undertakings, has contributed more to the smaller percentage increase in federal government-employee earnings. Moreover, there is slightly less tendency in 1952 than in 1939 for the earnings of state and local employees to be higher in states with higher per capita incomes; for federal government employees this tendency is less marked and did not change significantly from 1939 to 1952.[42]

[41] Except for the small change in Pennsylvania, which apparently is due to the change from an unfavorable to a favorable composition, these changes are reflected in the observed earnings. In Rhode Island, the observed earnings of both federal and noneducational state and local government employees in 1939 were above and in 1952 were below the national averages. The observed earnings of state and local educational employees in Minnesota, Montana, Arizona, and Oregon in 1939 were below and in 1952 were above the national averages. Similar changes in the observed earnings of federal employees are also to be found in Montana, and of noneducational state and local government employees in Wisconsin and Oregon.

[42] The coefficients of determination between state per capita incomes and the average annual earnings of state and local government education employees are .79 in 1939 and .59 in 1952; of noneducational state and local government employees are .81 in 1939 and .66 in 1952; and of federal government employees are .15 in 1939 and .18 in 1952. The difference between the latter pair of coefficients is not significant.

Population-Census Industries, 1949

The information on 1949 wage and salary income collected from a 20 percent sample of persons in the *Census of Population, 1950,* when classified by the industrial attachments of the recipients in April 1950, provides another opportunity to examine the relationship of industrial structure to interstate earning differentials. The population census covers the entire range of industrial activity, although it provides only 146 industrial classifications; thus it is the only body of primary data covering more than a few industrial segments. The data on earnings were obtained by personal interview with the recipients and are unlikely to be as reliable as data supplied by establishments, from the standpoint either of industrial classification or of the amount of earnings.[43] However, these data provide the only opportunity that we have to obtain some notion of the direction of the contributions of industrial segments not covered by the detailed censuses of establishments. For the manufacturing, wholesale-trade, and government segments, the population census provides some limited data for an additional year. As part of a comprehensive body of data, they provide some perspective for the findings for the individual industrial segments and the relationships among them.

The interstate range of rate-constant average annual industrial earnings of wage and salary workers is about one-third that of the reported earnings (table 38). The state reported average annual wage and salary earnings were derived from the same body of data and are identical with those used in the analysis of occupational income (chapter 5, table 24). The state rate-constant industrial earnings, however, were derived for each state by weighting the average annual wage and salary income for each of 146 industries by the numbers in the experienced labor force attached to the industry.[44] In addition to the difficulties inherent in enumerative data and in the fact that place of residence and industrial attachment typically relate to a week in April 1950, while income relates to the calendar year 1949, difficulties which were discussed in connection with the occupational data (chapter 5), there are several aspects of these data that are unique when dealt with in an industrial framework.

The experienced labor force, the only magnitude available by state for

[43] The census industrial earnings data are the same as those used for the analysis of occupational earnings. For a discussion of their limitations, particularly the association of the underreporting of income with the level of state earnings, see chapter 5.

[44] The list of industries and the average annual income for each are shown in appendix C, table 68. The method of computing these averages is there described. The industry averages range from $792 in private household domestic service to $4,128 in security and commodity brokerage and investment companies. Approximately two-thirds of the industries have average earnings between $2,100 and $3,300.

TABLE 38

REPORTED AND RATE-CONSTANT INDUSTRIAL EARNINGS OF ALL WAGE AND SALARY WORKERS, 1949, BY STATE

State (1)	Number in the experienced labor force (thousands) (2)	Average annual earnings (dollars)		Percentage differences attributable to	
		Reported (3)	Rate-constant (4)	Industrial composition (national weights) (5)	Industry earning rates (state weights) (6)
New England					
Maine	311	2,065	2,350	− 6.2	−12.1
New Hampshire	203	2,193	2,367	− 5.5	− 7.4
Vermont	126	1,997	2,353	− 6.0	−15.1
Massachusetts	1,874	2,610	2,520	.6	3.6
Rhode Island	316	2,359	2,501	− .1	− 5.7
Connecticut	835	2,795	2,608	4.2	7.2
Middle Atlantic					
New York	6,011	2,921	2,534	1.2	15.3
New Jersey	1,982	2,959	2,603	4.0	13.7
Pennsylvania	3,916	2,630	2,569	2.6	2.4
East North Central					
Ohio	2,943	2,797	2,638	5.4	6.0
Indiana	1,378	2,652	2,616	4.5	1.4
Illinois	3,401	2,936	2,605	4.0	12.7
Michigan	2,329	2,974	2,690	7.7	10.3
Wisconsin	1,154	2,586	2,529	1.0	2.3
West North Central					
Minnesota	934	2,472	2,502	− .1	− 1.2
Iowa	753	2,312	2,457	− 1.9	− 5.9
Missouri	1,290	2,422	2,500	− .2	− 3.1
North Dakota	141	2,007	2,355	− 6.0	−14.8
South Dakota	159	2,028	2,352	− 6.1	−13.8
Nebraska	375	2,262	2,461	− 1.7	− 8.1
Kansas	561	2,372	2,554	2.0	− 7.1
South Atlantic					
Delaware	120	2,752	2,540	1.4	8.3
Maryland	879	2,652	2,534	1.2	4.7
D. C.	379	3,000	2,584	3.2	16.1
Virginia	1,045	2,277	2,412	− 3.7	− 5.6
West Virginia	590	2,412	2,508	.2	− 3.8
North Carolina	1,171	1,841	2,246	−10.3	−18.0
South Carolina	605	1,740	2,195	−12.3	−20.7
Georgia	1,054	1,801	2,264	− 9.6	−20.5
Florida	972	2,064	2,275	− 9.1	− 9.3
East South Central					
Kentucky	754	2,024	2,414	− 3.6	−16.2
Tennessee	936	1,956	2,381	− 4.9	−17.8
Alabama	837	1,832	2,329	− 7.0	−21.3
Mississippi	459	1,408	2,183	−12.8	−35.5
West South Central					
Arkansas	450	1,594	2,264	− 9.6	−29.6
Louisiana	779	2,114	2,411	− 3.7	−12.3
Oklahoma	626	2,238	2,538	1.4	−11.8
Texas	2,488	2,277	2,463	− 1.6	− 7.6
Mountain					
Montana	183	2,461	2,424	− 3.2	1.5
Idaho	169	2,300	2,364	− 5.6	− 2.7
Wyoming	95	2,557	2,511	.3	1.8
Colorado	431	2,412	2,474	− 1.2	− 2.5
New Mexico	182	2,364	2,442	− 2.5	− 3.2
Arizona	231	2,397	2,363	− 5.6	1.4
Utah	213	2,610	2,579	3.0	1.2
Nevada	62	2,839	2,401	− 4.1	18.2
Pacific					
Washington	819	2,774	2,469	− 1.4	12.4
Oregon	553	2,668	2,354	− 6.0	13.3
California	3,991	2,870	2,497	− .3	14.9
United States	52,067	2,556	2,504	......	2.1

Col. 2: The numbers shown in the *Census of Population, 1950*, state tables No. 79, have been adjusted to exclude the farm self-employed and unpaid family workers and those in the "industry not reported" group. The adjustment for the farm group was made by substituting the number of farm laborers, foremen, and managers for the number attached to agriculture.

Col. 3: Calculated from *Census of Population, 1950*, state tables 94. These earnings are identical with those shown in table 24 (chapter 5).

Col. 4: Computed by multiplying the average annual earnings in an industry (appendix table 68) by the number in the experienced labor force in the industry, summing over all industries, and dividing the sum by the total number in the experienced labor force (column 2).

Col. 5: The difference, column 4 minus $2,504 (the weighted average of column 4), expressed as a percentage of $2,504.

Col. 6: The difference, column 3 minus column 4, expressed as a percentage of column 4.

weighting industrial average earnings, includes wage and salary workers, unpaid family workers, and the self-employed.[45] A number of industries, and agriculture in particular, include all classes of workers in the experienced labor force. With the few exceptions when government is specified as the employer, none of the industrial classifications were constructed for one particular class of worker. Consequently, the industries in which the self-employed are prevalent are likely to be overrepresented. An adjustment seems feasible only for agriculture. Here the number of farm laborers, foremen, and managers, taken from the occupational data, can be substituted for the number in the experienced labor force attached to agriculture.[46] Because of the seasonal nature of agriculture and the fact that April is an off-season month in many areas, this adjustment may result in some underestimation of agricultural income. The data necessary to make a more precise adjustment are not at hand, and the underrepresentation stemming from seasonality is slight compared with the overrepresentation which would result from the inclusion of the self-employed and unpaid family workers.[47]

The weighted average of the state rate-constant earnings of all workers is 2 percent less than the national reported earnings.[48] By comparing the

[45] Class 1 and 2 workers (wage and salary workers for private employers or government) are the only ones included in the unpublished tabulation from which the industrial average earnings were computed. For definitions of each group, see the introduction to *Census of Population, 1950*, vol. 2.

[46] If the 3.3-percent sample counts of wage and salary workers on the unpublished D-9 tabulation, which is the basis for the industry average earnings (see appendix table 68), are compared with the complete counts of the experienced labor force, it is found that 74 percent of those attached to agriculture are self-employed or unpaid family workers. Similar comparisons for other major industry groups show that 20 to 29 percent of persons attached to the trade and business and repair service groups, 10 to 19 percent of those in the construction, finance, insurance and real estate, and the three other service groups, and less than 10 percent of the remaining groups are in the self-employed and unpaid family-worker categories.

[47] The industry average annual earning for agriculture, $1,149, was retained in computing the rate-constant industry earnings. Since it is more than the average found for farm laborers, $1,027, some over-estimation of agricultural earnings may come from this source.

[48] The weighted mean earnings computed in various ways follow:

Reported earnings (of all wage and salary income recipients, from *Census of Population, 1950*, vol. 2, table 144)	$2,556
Industry earnings (average earnings in each of 146 industries weighted by the number of wage and salary workers in each industry, from the unpublished tabulation of 3.3 percent of census returns)	2,528
State rate-constant earnings (weighted by the number in the experienced labor force, adjusted to exclude the farm self-employed and unpaid family workers and the "industry-not-reported" group)	2,504

The difference between the mean reported earning of all recipients of wage income and the mean of the industry earnings computed from the sample tabulation is the algebraic sum of (1) sampling errors, (2) minor amounts of wages or salaries received by those

state rate-constant with its weighted average, $2,504, rather than with the national reported average annual earning, the effect of this discrepancy on the measurement of the direction and magnitude of state compositional differentials is minimized. The full effects of the discrepancy are present in comparisons of state reported and rate-constant earnings. While the average magnitude of the discrepancy (2.0 percent) is indicated by a comparison of the national figures, the magnitude for any one state, which can deviate in either direction from the national average, is unknown. This fact must be taken into account in using such comparisons to indicate the size and direction of the state-weighted earning-rate differentials.[49]

The number of detailed industries used in computing the rate-constant earnings can also affect the size and dispersion of the state rate-constant earnings (table 39). The population census provides only 59 industrial categories for the manufacturing segment, as compared with the 458 available from the manufacturing census. One result is that state deviations may be affected. For manufacturing it has been found that major-group differences are more important than within-group composition in determining the rate-constant earnings. Consequently, the range of average annual earnings for manufacturing employees does not differ greatly in the two censuses. The difference between Michigan and North Carolina in the rate-constant hourly earnings computed from the manufacturing census is about $0.38 per hour, or $680-760 for an 1,800-2,000-hour year, while the difference between the rate-constant annual earnings computed from the population-census data for these two states is $787. Both within-group and between-group differences contribute to the state rate-constant earning of wholesale-trade employees, so that the differences in classificatory detail are more marked. The business census lists 244 kinds-of-business categories for wholesale trade, while the population census has only 10 such categories. If the difference between New York, which has the most favorable composition, and Idaho, which has a very unfavorable composition, is used to indicate the range in the rate-constant earnings, it is $1,053 when based on the business-census data and $210 when based on the population-census data. Much the same effect is obtained by com-

whose primary classification is that of self-employed, and (3) differences between the actual and assumed midpoints of the wage and salary classes on the sample tabulation. In addition, the difference between the weighted mean of the state rate-constant and the mean industry earning is affected by the difference between the number in the experienced labor force and the number of wage and salary workers.

[49] Presumably the adjustment for the farm self-employed would minimize the contribution of this major group to the discrepancy. The discrepancy would probably be larger than average in states with relatively more of their labor force in industry groups in which the self-employed are relatively numerous—that is, in trade, business and repair services, and construction.

paring the ranges of state rate-constant average annual earnings computed from the 146 detailed population-census industries and the 12 major groups into which they typically are combined. For the detailed industries, the interstate range is $513; for the major groups, $299. Although it is relatively easy to pick examples to illustrate cases of either more or less interstate dispersion, the mechanism depends upon three sets of factors, and it is difficult to assay their relative weights on a priori grounds.

The interstate dispersion in rate-constant earnings depends upon the earning differences between major groups, the dispersion within major groups, and the concentration of the experienced labor force in particular industries.

The range in earnings between major groups is great, but is accounted for largely by the $1,020 difference between the earnings of farm and personal service workers and those of the next higher earning groups, professional service, trade, and entertainment and recreation workers. The range among the manufacturing, mining, and construction groups is only $239, and their earnings differ from those of the highest earning group by another $154. The lower-earning farm, trade, and service groups include some 44 percent of all workers, and a relative decrease in their number in favor of higher-paid groups can have an important effect on a state's rate-constant income, whether such a figure is based on detailed industry or major-group averages.

The differences in earnings within major groups are also substantial. In all but the public administration group, the range of average earnings among detailed industries exceeds $1,000, and in three groups the within-group range exceeds the difference between the highest and lowest group averages.

The tendency toward concentration of the labor force in specific groups is shown in the last two columns of table 39, and the concentration in specific industries within the groups is reflected through the effects on income, in the column in which the range in rate-constant group earnings is expressed as a percent of the maximum possible range—i.e., the range of detailed industry earnings within the group. The tendency toward concentration in specific detailed industries is coupled with large within-group earning differences in the mining and manufacturing groups, and to a somewhat lesser extent in the public administration and personal service groups.

The evidence of the approximate character of the population-census data on industry earnings is convincing; nevertheless, the evidence so far does not point to outright rejection. Attention is now turned to an exam-

TABLE 39

INTERINDUSTRY AND INTERSTATE DISPERSION OF EARNINGS, BY MAJOR INDUSTRY GROUP, 1949

Major industrial group (1)	Number of detailed industries (2)	Reported earnings				State rate-constant earnings				Percent of experienced labor force		
			By detailed industry					Range				
		Average (3)	Lowest (4)	Highest (5)	Range (6)	Lowest (7)	Highest (8)	Amount (9)	% of industry (10)	U. S. average (11)	Lowest state (12)	Highest state (13)
01 Agriculture, forestry, and fisheries	3	1,225	1,149	2,277	1,128	2,183	2,696	513	45	3.4	.8	10.7
02 Mining	4	2,861	2,496	3,672	1,176	2,529	3,612	1,083	92	1.9	.1	23.4
03 Construction	1	2,637	.....	.....	.....	.....	.....	.....	..	7.2	5.5	13.7
Manufacturing	59	2,776	1,799	4,104	2,305	2,284	3,285	1,001	43	29.1	4.8	45.5
04 Durable goods	27	2.876	1,799	3,425	1,626	2,098	3,104	1,006	62	15.5	1.1	36.5
05 Nondurable goods[a]	32	2,648	1,900	4,104	2,204	2,280	3,555	1,275	58	13.6	2.9	29.5
07 Transportation, communication, and other public utilities	16	2,996	2,021	3,786	1,765	2,930	3,096	166	9	8.7	5.0	15.1
08 Wholesale and retail trade	30	2,328	1,354	3,719	2,365	2,139	2,375	236	10	21.0	16.4	28.9
Wholesale trade	10	3,154	2,729	3,719	990	3,030	3,262	232	23	3.9	2.2	5.9
Retail trade	20	2,138	1,354	3,116	1,762	2,008	2,185	177	10	17.1	14.2	23.0
09 Finance, insurance, and real estate	4	2,911	2,339	4,128	1,789	2,793	3,031	238	13	3.7	1.7	5.8
Services	24	2,017	792	4,071	3,279	1,718	2,166	448	14	20.0	15.5	29.1
10 Business and repair	5	2,683	2,442	3,907	1,465	2,512	2,861	349	24	2.8	1.9	4.7
11 Personal	6	1,292	792	1,888	1,096	1,087	1,491	404	37	7.0	4.7	13.2
12 Entertainment and recreation	4	2,484	1,180	4,071	2,891	2,220	2,634	414	14	1.1	.7	7.1
13 Professional and related	9	2,312	1,911	3,873	1,962	2,263	2,455	192	10	9.1	7.6	13.5
14 Public administration	4	3,030	2,793	3,202	409	2,957	3,129	172	42	4.9	3.0	10.4

[a] Includes miscellaneous goods.

Cols. 1-6: Based on appendix C, table 68.

Cols. 7-8: The rate-constant earning in each state and major industry was computed by multiplying the national average annual earning in an industry (appendix C, table 68) by the numbers in the experienced labor force in the industry, summing over all industries in the group, and dividing the sum by the total number in the experienced labor force. The calculations were made by the Bureau of the Census as a special tabulation. The number in the experienced labor force in agriculture was adjusted to exclude the farm self-employed and unpaid family workers; see table 38, column 2.

Col. 10: Column 9 expressed as a percentage of column 6.

Cols. 11-13: Based on table 43.

ination of whether those data may be used to extend the analyses of the data for manufacturing, wholesale trade, and governments to an additional year.

Consistency of Results

Detailed data relating to the manufacturing and wholesale-trade segments are available only for single years, and those relating to government for only 1939 and 1952. The population-census industry data, although less detailed, appear to provide an opportunity to see whether the findings based on detailed data tend to persist. Two related questions are of interest: First, do the results based on the broader categories in the population-census data provide results which are consistent with the more detailed establishment censuses? Secondly, do the classifications of states with regard to their favorable or unfavorable industrial composition tend to persist over a period of time so that results for a single year have more than transitory significance? Unfortunately, a negative answer to either of these questions precludes a satisfactory answer to the other from the data at hand. Unless the enumerative and establishment data furnish consistent results, their comparison cannot tell us whether differences between the two sets of data are due to changing compositions or to the lack of statistical comparableness of the two sets of data. Similarly, unless the state industrial compositions are stable over a period of time, it would be difficult to test the consistency of the two bodies of data since they relate to different years.

Manufactures

The population and detailed establishment censuses for manufactures suggest that the compositional patterns of the states are fairly stable over the 1947-1949 period. The deviations from the national average composition tend to be slightly smaller in the 1949 than in the 1947 data, although some 20 states had more pronounced deviations from the national average in 1949. Despite the differing numbers of industrial categories in the two sets of data, the percentage differences attributed to composition for 1949 (table 40), differed from those for 1947 (table 34) by less than 5 percentage points in some 35 states.[50] However, in eight states with un-

[50] A frequency distribution of the differences between the percentage differences attributed to composition in the two bodies of data follows:

Difference (percentage points)	*States* (number)
0.0- 2.4	26
2.5- 4.9	9
5.0- 7.4	11
7.5- 9.9	1
10.0-12.4	2

TABLE 40

RATE-CONSTANT AVERAGE ANNUAL EARNINGS OF WAGE AND SALARY WORKERS ATTACHED TO MANUFACTURING, 1949, BY STATE

State (1)	Number in the experienced labor force (thousands) (2)	Rate-constant earnings (dollars) (3)	Percentage differences from national average (4)
New England			
Maine	118	2,376	−14.4
New Hampshire	87	2,407	−13.3
Vermont	36	2,585	− 6.9
Massachusetts	719	2,658	− 4.3
Rhode Island	144	2,583	− 7.0
Connecticut	368	2,852	2.7
Middle Atlantic			
New York	1,875	2,698	− 2.8
New Jersey	770	2,820	1.6
Pennsylvania	1,452	2,782	.2
East North Central			
Ohio	1,155	2,962	6.7
Indiana	537	2,954	6.4
Illinois	1,171	2,894	4.3
Michigan	1,030	3,071	10.6
Wisconsin	423	2,837	2.2
West North Central			
Minnesota	193	2,797	.8
Iowa	154	2,868	3.3
Missouri	339	2,728	− 1.7
North Dakota	7	2,898	4.4
South Dakota	12	2,787	.4
Nebraska	48	2,840	2.3
Kansas	91	3,022	8.9
South Atlantic			
Delaware	42	2,944	6.1
Maryland	232	2,838	2.2
D. C.	28	3,034	9.3
Virginia	243	2,520	− 9.2
West Virginia	122	2,808	1.2
North Carolina	423	2,284	−17.7
South Carolina	217	2,307	−16.9
Georgia	296	2,380	−14.3
Florida	113	2,509	− 9.6
East South Central			
Kentucky	155	2,679	− 3.5
Tennessee	247	2,574	− 7.3
Alabama	234	2,541	− 8.5
Mississippi	94	2,325	−16.2
West South Central			
Arkansas	89	2,430	−12.5
Louisiana	138	2,774	− .1
Oklahoma	76	3,033	9.3
Texas	383	2,965	6.8
Mountain			
Montana	20	2,717	− 2.1
Idaho	21	2,407	−13.3
Wyoming	7	3,285	18.3
Colorado	60	2,884	3.9
New Mexico	13	2,742	− 1.2
Arizona	22	2,741	− 1.3
Utah	29	2,901	4.5
Nevada	3	2,776	.0
Pacific			
Washington	190	2,606	− 6.1
Oregon	140	2,256	−18.7
California	825	2,849	2.6
United States	15,192	2,776	.....

Col. 2: *Census of Population, 1950*, state tables no. 79.

Col. 3: Computed by multiplying the 1949 national average annual earning in a manufacturing industry (appendix C, table 68) by the number in the experienced labor force attached to the industry in 1950, summing over all manufacturing industries, and dividing the sum by the total number in the experienced labor force in the manufacturing industries (column 2). These calculations were made by the Bureau of the Census as a special tabulation.

Col. 4: The difference, column 3 minus $2,776, the weighted average of column 3, expressed as a percentage of $2,776. These percentage differences provide a measure of the interstate differences in the industrial composition of manufacturing industries.

favorable compositions on the basis of the 1947 detailed data, these differences were large enough for the same states to have favorable compositions on the basis of the 1949 data; New York was shifted in an opposite direction, from favorable in 1947 to unfavorable in 1949.[51] The question immediately arises of whether these apparent differences reflect real changes in the distribution of employees or man-hours among the state's industries or whether they are only statistical differences in the two bodies of data. The data at hand afford considerable evidence that the latter is possible; however, detailed data from another census of manufactures are required to provide a reliable answer.

Among the states with compositions that are favorable in one period and unfavorable in another, there are six whose percentage deviations, based on the detailed 1947 data, are less than 2 percent. For these states relatively minor shifts in either the industry average earnings which are used as weights, or the relative numbers of employees in the various industries, could easily change the direction of the percentage deviation from the national average. Texas is among these states, and the change in sign of the Texas deviation can perhaps be accounted for by comparing it with its neighboring state, Oklahoma, where petroleum refining is an important industry also. In Oklahoma petroleum refining was important enough in 1947 to account for the state's favorable composition. When population data are used, Oklahoma's composition is even more favorable, probably because of the relative increase in petroleum-refining earning rates, 1947-1949.[52] Differential changes in earning rates, particularly in the chemical industries, might easily account for the shift in Delaware's position, though such changes are difficult to isolate among the 41 chemical industries listed in the manufactures census and the 4 listed in the

[51] The states with unfavorable 1947 and favorable 1949 compositions are: Delaware, Minnesota, Iowa, North Dakota, South Dakota, Nebraska, Texas, Utah, and Nevada. The 1949 composition of Nevada was equivalent to that of the nation.

[52] Petroleum refining is a single industrial category in both bodies of data. The average annual earning of petroleum-refinery production workers was $3,480 in 1947 (total wages of production workers divided by the average number of production workers as reported in the *Census of Manufactures, 1947*) and $4,180 in 1949 (population-census data), a difference of 19 percent. Based on the same sources, the average annual earning of all manufacturing workers was $2,520 in 1947 and $2,776 in 1949, a difference of 10 percent. Since 1947 and 1949 petroleum-refinery earnings differed more than the average of all industries, a state with the same relative number of workers in petroleum refining would have a more favorable composition in 1949 than in 1947. Although the above figures were taken from the two bodies of data with which we have been working, it is worth noting that the Bureau of Labor Statistics' average hourly earnings of petroleum-refining production workers for 1949, when compared with the census figures for 1947, do not bear out the differential increase in earnings for this industry. *Statistical Abstract of the United States, 1951*, p. 200.

population census. Differential shifts in the relative number of workers, although small by ordinary standards, might easily account for the compositional differences in the five states in this group which have fewer than 50,000 manufacturing employees.

Two observations emerge from the above discussion: First, during periods of rapidly changing prices and earning rates, the measurement of industrial composition is affected by the leads and lags of individual industries in respect to rate adjustment. This factor may be looked upon as irregular or transitory, but it is powerful enough to disturb conclusions drawn from the statistics for a single year. Secondly, when year-to-year changes are of importance, it is necessary to have data which are strictly comparable with regard to both the classifications and the measures used. Even then, small deviations from the national average can hardly be relied upon to establish firmly the favorable or unfavorable industrial composition of a state.

Wholesale trade

The telescoping of the industrial classification in the wholesale-trade area—from 244 kinds of business in the 1948 business census to 10 industries in the 1950 population census—is even more drastic than that for manufacturing. One result is that there is very little variation in the rate-constant earnings based on the population-census data: from 3.9 percent below the national average in Florida to 3.4 percent above it in New York (table 41). In contrast, the range based on the business-census data is from 19.2 percent below the national average in Idaho to 12.2 percent above it in New York. An examination of the average annual earnings for each of the 10 wholesale-trade industries shows that only two—food and related products, and farm products, raw materials—are below the average of all wholesale trade (see appendix C, table 68). An unfavorable composition of wholesale trade within a state means only that the state has relatively more employees in these two broad industries. Fewer states had unfavorable compositions based on the 1949 population-census data; this is a result of the shifting of nine states from an unfavorable classification on the basis of the 1948 business-census data to a favorable classification on the basis of the population-census data for 1949, and a shifting of five states in the opposite direction.[53] It seems reasonably clear, however, that this apparent shifting in classifications could result solely from the telescoping of the industries into fewer and broader cate-

[53] The states with unfavorable compositions in 1948 and favorable ones in 1949 are Connecticut, Louisiana, Oklahoma, Montana, Wyoming, New Mexico, Nevada, Washington, and Oregon. Those with favorable compositions in 1948 and unfavorable ones in 1949 are

TABLE 41

Rate-Constant Average Annual Earnings of Wage and Salary Workers Attached to Wholesale Trade, 1949, by State

State (1)	Number in the experienced labor force (thousands) (2)	Rate-constant earnings (dollars) (3)	Percentage differences from national average (4)
New England			
Maine	10	3,059	−3.0
New Hampshire	5	3,101	−1.7
Vermont	4	3,100	−1.7
Massachusetts	69	3,146	− .3
Rhode Island	9	3,174	.6
Connecticut	24	3,165	.3
Middle Atlantic			
New York	300	3,262	3.4
New Jersey	68	3,172	.6
Pennsylvania	117	3,151	− .1
East North Central			
Ohio	98	3,157	.1
Indiana	45	3,137	− .5
Illinois	137	3,156	.1
Michigan	68	3,153	− .0
Wisconsin	40	3,140	− .4
West North Central			
Minnesota	51	3,127	− .9
Iowa	40	3,084	−2.2
Missouri	63	3,176	.7
North Dakota	8	3,064	−2.9
South Dakota	8	3,092	−2.0
Nebraska	20	3,071	−2.6
Kansas	26	3,098	−1.8
South Atlantic			
Delaware	3	3,117	−1.2
Maryland	30	3,149	− .2
D. C.	8	3,145	− .3
Virginia	33	3,115	−1.2
West Virginia	15	3,141	− .4
North Carolina	33	3,126	− .9
South Carolina	15	3,130	− .8
Georgia	37	3,125	− .9
Florida	50	3,030	−3.9
East South Central			
Kentucky	26	3,125	− .9
Tennessee	36	3,149	− .2
Alabama	25	3,123	−1.0
Mississippi	14	3,107	−1.5
West South Central			
Arkansas	16	3,095	−1.9
Louisiana	33	3,162	.3
Oklahoma	26	3,156	.1
Texas	114	3,145	− .3
Mountain			
Montana	6	3,161	.2
Idaho	8	3,052	−3.2
Wyoming	2	3,170	.5
Colorado	20	3,144	− .3
New Mexico	6	3,175	.7
Arizona	9	3,047	−3.4
Utah	10	3,151	− .1
Nevada	2	3,187	1.0
Pacific			
Washington	34	3,166	.4
Oregon	25	3,175	.7
California	197	3,113	−1.3
United States	2,041	3,154	....

Col. 2: *Census of Population, 1950*, state tables no. 79.

Col. 3: Computed by multiplying the 1949 national average annual earning in a wholesale-trade industry (appendix C, table 68) by the number in the experienced labor force attached to the industry in 1950, summing over all wholesale trade industries, and dividing the sum by the total number in the experienced labor force in the wholesale trade industries (column 2). These calculations were made by the Bureau of the Census as a special tabulation.

Col. 4: The difference, column 3 minus $3,154, the weighted average of column 3, expressed as a percentage of $3,154. These percentage differences provide a measure of the interstate differences in the industrial composition of wholesale trade industries.

gories, unaccompanied by any change in the relative numbers of employees in each kind of business listed under wholesale trade.

As a partial test of this hypothesis, the 1948 kinds-of-business categories were telescoped into 10 categories, averages computed for them, and new 1948 state rate-constant figures computed which reflect only the compositional differences among these broad categories.[54] The range of average annual earnings in these 10 categories is $2,088, more than twice the $990 range shown by the population-census categories. Even for groups, such as petroleum bulk plants, which have names similar to those in the population census, there appears to be little comparableness, in part, perhaps, because of the inclusion of the self-employed as well as employees in the population-census data. These rate-constant earnings show mild versions of many of the same characteristics as those based on the population-census data. They have a limited interstate range, from $2,856 in Idaho to $3,549 in New York.[55] More states have favorable industrial compositions in terms of these 10 larger groups than in terms of the 244 detailed industries, as a consequence of a shift of four states, from unfavorable compositions on the basis of detailed industries to favorable

---

Massachusetts, Pennsylvania, the District of Columbia, Tennessee, and Delaware. The 14 states affected had about 20 percent of wholesale-trade employees in 1948.

[54] The 10 categories were obtained by telescoping the 20 major groups in the *Census of Business, 1948*. The major groups included in each category and average annual earnings for the category are:

Major groups included	*Average annual earning*
(1) Grocery, confectionery, meat wholesalers; (2) Farm products (edible) distributors; (3) Beer, wine, distilled spirits wholesalers; and (5) Tobacco distributors;	$3,116
(4) Drugs, chemicals, and allied products wholesalers;	3,364
(6) Dry goods, apparel wholesalers;	4,464
(9) Farm products (raw materials) merchants; and (20) Assemblers of farm products;	2,376
(10) Automotive wholesalers;	3,166
(11) Electrical, electronic, appliance distributors; (12) Hardware, plumbing-heating goods wholesalers; and (13) Lumber, construction materials distributors;	3,594
(14) Machinery, equipment, supplies distributors;	3,587
(19) Petroleum bulk plants, terminals and LP gas facilities;	3,096
(7) Furniture, home furnishings wholesalers; (8) Paper, allied products wholesalers; and (15) Metal, metalwork (except scrap) distributors;	3,896
(16) Scrap, waste materials dealers; (17) Other merchant wholesalers; and (18) Manufacturers' sales branches, sales offices.	3,466

[55] The interstate range for the 244 wholesale-trade industries is $1,053; for the 10-category condensation considered here, $693; and for the population-census categories, $232.

TABLE 42

Signs of Within-Major-Group Industrial Composition, 1949, by State

State (arrayed by rate-constant earning)	Rate-constant earning[a] (dollars)	Major-industry-group (signs of difference, state minus national rate-constant earning)							
		Agriculture, forestry and fisheries	Mining	Manufactures			Trade		
				Total	Durable goods	Non-durable goods	Total	Wholesale	Retail
Michigan	2,696	+	+	+	+	+	−	−	+
Ohio	2,638	−	−	+	+	+	−	+	+
Indiana	2,616	−	−	+	+	+	−	−	+
Connecticut	2,608	+	−	+	+	−	+	+	+
Illinois	2,605	−	−	+	+	+	−	+	−
New Jersey	2,603	+	+	+	+	+	+	+	+
D. C.	2,584	+	−	+	+	+	−	−	−
Utah	2,579	−	−	+	+	+	+	−	+
Pennsylvania	2,569	−	−	+	+	−	−	−	+
Kansas	2,554	−	+	+	+	+	+	−	+
Delaware	2,540	−	−	+	+	+	−	−	+
Oklahoma	2,538	−	+	+	−	+	−	+	+
Maryland	2,534	+	−	+	+	+	−	−	+
New York	2,534	−	+	−	+	−	+	+	−
Wisconsin	2,529	−	−	+	+	+	−	−	−
Massachusetts	2,520	+	−	−	+	−	−	−	−
Wyoming	2,511	−	+	+	−	+	−	+	−
West Virginia	2,508	−	−	+	−	+	−	−	−
Minnesota	2,502	−	+	+	−	+	+	−	−
Rhode Island	2,501	+	+	−	−	−	−	+	+
Missouri	2,500	−	−	−	+	−	+	+	+
California	2,497	−	+	+	+	+	+	−	−
Colorado	2,474	−	−	+	−	+	+	−	+
Washington	2,469	+	−	−	−	+	0	+	+
Texas	2,463	−	+	+	−	+	+	−	+
Nebraska	2,461	−	+	+	−	+	+	−	+
Iowa	2,457	−	−	+	+	+	+	−	+
New Mexico	2,442	−	+	−	−	+	−	+	−
Montana	2,424	−	+	−	−	+	−	+	−
Kentucky	2,414	−	−	−	−	0	−	−	−
Virginia	2,412	+	−	−	−	−	−	−	+
Louisiana	2,411	+	+	−	−	+	−	+	−
Nevada	2,401	−	+	0	−	+	−	+	−
Tennessee	2,381	−	−	−	−	−	+	−	+
New Hampshire	2,367	+	−	−	−	−	−	−	+
Idaho	2,364	−	+	−	−	+	−	−	−
Arizona	2,363	−	+	−	−	+	−	−	−
North Dakota	2,355	−	−	+	−	+	+	−	+
Oregon	2,354	+	−	−	−	+	+	+	−
Vermont	2,353	−	−	−	−	−	−	−	+
South Dakota	2,352	−	+	+	−	+	−	−	−
Maine	2,350	+	−	−	−	−	+	−	+
Alabama	2,329	−	−	−	−	−	−	−	+
Florida	2,275	+	−	−	−	−	−	−	−
Georgia	2,264	+	−	−	−	−	+	−	+
Arkansas	2,264	−	+	−	−	+	−	−	+
North Carolina	2,246	−	−	−	−	−	+	−	+
South Carolina	2,195	−	−	−	−	−	−	−	+
Mississippi	2,183	−	+	−	−	−	−	−	+

(Continued on next page)

TABLE 42 (Continued)

SIGNS OF WITHIN-MAJOR-GROUP INDUSTRIAL COMPOSITION, 1949, BY STATE

State (arrayed by rate-constant earning)	Major-industry-group (signs of difference, state minus national rate-constant earning)							
			Services					
	Utilities	Finance	Total	Business and repair	Personal	Entertainment and recreation	Professional	Public administration
Michigan	−	−	+	+	+	−	−	−
Ohio	+	−	+	+	+	−	−	+
Indiana	+	+	+	−	+	−	+	−
Connecticut	−	+	+	+	−	+	−	−
Illinois	+	−	+	+	+	−	+	−
New Jersey	−	+	+	+	+	−	+	−
D. C.	−	−	−	+	−	+	−	+
Utah	+	−	+	−	+	+	+	+
Pennsylvania	+	+	+	−	+	−	−	−
Kansas	+	+	+	−	+	−	−	−
Delaware	+	+	−	−	−	−	−	−
Oklahoma	+	−	+	−	+	+	+	+
Maryland	−	+	−	−	−	−	−	+
New York	−	−	+	+	+	+	−	−
Wisconsin	−	+	+	−	+	−	−	−
Massachusetts	−	+	+	+	+	−	−	−
Wyoming	+	−	+	−	+	−	+	+
West Virginia	+	+	+	−	+	−	+	−
Minnesota	+	+	+	+	+	−	−	−
Rhode Island	−	+	+	−	+	−	−	−
Missouri	+	−	+	−	+	−	−	+
California	+	−	+	+	+	+	+	+
Colorado	+	−	+	−	+	−	−	+
Washington	+	−	+	−	+	−	+	+
Texas	+	+	−	−	−	+	+	+
Nebraska	+	+	+	−	+	−	−	−
Iowa	−	+	+	−	+	−	+	−
New Mexico	+	−	+	−	+	+	+	+
Montana	+	−	+	−	+	−	+	−
Kentucky	+	+	−	−	−	−	−	+
Virginia	+	+	−	−	−	−	+	+
Louisiana	−	+	−	−	−	−	−	−
Nevada	+	−	+	−	+	−	+	+
Tennessee	−	+	−	−	−	+	−	+
New Hampshire	−	+	−	−	+	−	−	−
Idaho	−	−	+	−	+	−	+	−
Arizona	+	−	−	−	+	+	+	+
North Dakota	+	+	+	−	+	−	−	−
Oregon	+	−	+	−	+	−	+	−
Vermont	+	+	−	−	−	−	−	−
South Dakota	−	+	+	−	+	−	−	−
Maine	−	+	−	−	+	−	−	−
Alabama	+	+	−	−	−	+	+	+
Florida	+	−	−	−	−	−	+	+
Georgia	0	+	−	−	−	+	+	+
Arkansas	+	−	−	−	−	−	+	0
North Carolina	−	+	−	−	−	+	+	−
South Carolina	−	+	−	−	−	+	+	−
Mississippi	−	+	−	−	−	+	+	−

[a]Table 38.

Source: The state rate-constant earning for a major industry group was computed by multiplying the national average annual earning in a detailed industry (appendix C, table 68) by the number in the experienced labor force attached to the industry, summing over all industries in the major group, and dividing the sum by the total number in the labor force attached to the major group. These calculations were made by the Bureau of the Census as a special tabulation. The national rate-constant earning for a major group is the weighted mean of the state rate-constant earnings. For the national rate-constant earning, and the interstate range of rate-constant earnings, see table 39.

compositions, and the shift of one state from favorable to unfavorable composition. Though the compositional classification on the basis of the detailed categories and the telescoped categories differs for a smaller number of states than does the classification on the basis of the detailed wholesale-trade and population-census categories, there is enough evidence to indicate that many of the apparent differences between the 1948 and 1949 figures could be due to statistical differences in the two sources of data.

Governments

Although the population census provides four industrial categories, they cannot be made comparable with the three categories used by Schaller (above, table 37). Separate data are provided by the population census on postal workers and other employees of the federal government, and state government employees are separated from those of local governments, but government educational services at all levels are included with professional and related services rather than with public administration. The reported earnings of workers in government education services, while higher than those in private educational services, are below those reported by workers classified in any of the public administration categories. Schaller's estimates indicate that state and local government education employees had earnings above other state and local government employees. Moreover, the population census classified only 2.6 million wage and salary workers in public administration; other wage and salary government workers are scattered throughout numerous other industrial classifications.[56] Despite these large classificatory and earning differences in the two series relating to government employees, both show much the same pattern of interstate differentials. Four states—Maine, Rhode Island, Pennsylvania, and South Dakota—which on the basis of the more complete data in table 37 had 1952 rate-constant earnings which exceed the national average by less than 1.0 percent, had rate-constant earnings below the national average for public administration employees in the 1949 data. Two states—Florida and Ohio—according to these data had favorable compositions of government industries in 1949 and unfavorable ones in 1952. Florida's rate-constant earnings were 1.5 and Ohio's were 0.3 percent below the national average in 1952. It was pointed out above that the estimates underlying table 37 are too crude to support a confident

[56] A special "class of worker" code is assigned "wage and salary workers, government," but these workers were grouped with other wage and salary workers in the tabulation underlying table 38.

decision about even the direction of a state's composition when its rate-constant earning is very close to the national average.

All industries

Consistency may also be looked upon as the tendency for a state with a favorable composition of all industries to have favorable compositions in each industrial group.

The deviations of state compositions of manufacturing industries from the national composition computed from the manufactures census tend to be the same as those computed from the population census. The composition of the wholesale-trade industries is unfavorable in ten states and favorable in three states having composition of population-census industries in an opposite direction. Except for Utah, which has unfavorable compositions of both manufacturing and wholesale-trade industries but an over-all favorable composition, these states also deviate from the pattern for manufacturing.

Every one of the states has at least one major industrial group with a favorable composition and at least one with an unfavorable composition (table 42). It is, of course, possible for a state to have, for example, a favorable composition within each of the groups and, because of the distribution of its experienced labor force among the groups, to have an unfavorable over-all composition. This situation, as discussed above, is the result of three sets of forces: the composition of the state's industry in terms of detailed industries and major groups, the differences in the group average earnings, and the differences in the detailed industry earnings within each of the major groups. Although California has a favorable composition within all but the agricultural and finance major groups, the distribution of its experienced labor force among the major groups is, on the whole, unfavorable (table 43). Taking account of both the within-group and the between-group composition, it is found that the finance, insurance, and real estate (despite its unfavorable within-group composition), the business and repair services, the entertainment and recreation services, and the public adminstration groups contribute in the direction of a favorable industrial composition, but the contribution of these groups is more than offset by the contributions of the other groups in the opposite direction.

Table 42 is affected by the number of detailed industries in a major group. The construction group, which consists of a single "detailed" industry—that is, all construction industry employees are grouped under a single heading—provides no information to determine differing composi-

TABLE 43

INDUSTRIAL COMPOSITION OF THE EXPERIENCED LABOR FORCE, 1950, BY STATE[a]

State	Agriculture, forestry, and fisheries[b]	Mining	Construction	Manufactures		Transportation, communication, and utilities	Wholesale and retail trade
				Durable	Nondurable[c]		
New England							
Maine	5.3	.2	6.5	12.0	25.9	7.8	17.7
New Hampshire	2.6	.1	7.0	13.5	29.5	6.0	16.4
Vermont	7.6	1.6	6.8	16.7	11.7	7.8	17.8
Massachusetts	1.1	.1	6.1	16.1	22.3	7.1	19.6
Rhode Island	.8	.1	6.1	18.5	27.0	5.7	18.1
Connecticut	1.3	.1	6.4	29.5	14.5	5.4	17.3
Middle Atlantic							
New York	1.0	.2	5.8	13.5	17.7	9.0	21.6
New Jersey	1.2	.2	6.7	18.1	20.7	8.5	18.3
Pennsylvania	1.2	5.2	6.1	20.7	16.4	8.8	18.2
East North Central							
Ohio	1.4	1.1	6.0	27.4	11.9	8.4	19.6
Indiana	2.2	1.1	6.0	28.0	10.9	8.3	19.8
Illinois	1.6	1.3	5.5	21.2	13.3	10.1	21.0
Michigan	1.3	.7	5.6	36.5	7.8	6.7	18.7
Wisconsin	3.9	.3	6.2	22.1	14.6	7.6	20.7
West North Central							
Minnesota	4.0	1.8	7.4	9.8	10.9	10.6	25.1
Iowa	6.1	.5	7.6	10.3	10.2	9.4	25.9
Missouri	3.2	.8	6.9	11.7	14.6	10.6	23.6
North Dakota	10.7	.6	9.3	1.1	3.7	11.6	28.9
South Dakota	9.7	1.8	10.3	2.0	5.6	8.4	27.6
Nebraska	5.7	.3	9.2	3.9	8.8	12.7	26.3
Kansas	3.5	2.7	9.4	6.9	9.3	12.2	24.8
South Atlantic							
Delaware	3.8	.1	9.2	8.2	26.8	8.2	17.4
Maryland	3.0	.4	8.3	13.6	12.9	9.6	19.9
D. C.	.1	.0	6.6	2.1	5.3	7.2	18.1
Virginia	5.4	2.8	8.4	8.9	14.3	8.9	18.6
West Virginia	2.6	23.4	5.9	12.4	8.4	9.3	17.0
North Carolina	5.4	.3	7.7	9.4	26.7	5.7	18.3
South Carolina	7.2	.2	7.3	7.5	28.3	5.0	17.2
Georgia	6.4	.5	7.2	9.6	18.5	7.4	19.6
Florida	8.4	.6	10.0	4.8	6.7	8.3	25.6
East South Central							
Kentucky	5.5	9.6	7.6	10.2	10.4	9.9	20.1
Tennessee	4.4	1.6	9.1	9.9	16.6	8.3	21.3
Alabama	5.1	3.5	7.1	15.0	13.0	7.4	19.0
Mississippi	9.4	.8	8.6	10.9	9.5	6.9	21.4
West South Central							
Arkansas	10.7	1.6	8.6	11.7	8.0	8.1	22.4
Louisiana	6.3	3.2	9.1	6.6	11.1	10.2	22.5
Oklahoma	4.0	6.6	9.9	5.1	7.0	8.7	24.5
Texas	6.2	3.7	10.1	6.5	8.9	9.4	24.3
Mountain							
Montana	8.7	5.4	9.1	7.0	3.8	12.7	23.6
Idaho	8.4	3.3	10.3	8.1	4.4	11.5	24.3
Wyoming	8.5	9.5	10.5	1.8	5.3	15.1	20.2
Colorado	5.1	2.6	9.3	6.1	7.8	10.8	23.9
New Mexico	7.4	6.0	13.7	3.3	3.6	9.7	22.0
Arizona	9.1	4.8	9.8	5.1	4.5	9.6	23.8
Utah	3.6	5.9	8.7	6.9	6.8	10.7	22.8
Nevada	5.1	5.7	9.6	2.6	2.9	12.4	21.7
Pacific							
Washington	4.1	.5	9.4	15.4	7.9	10.0	22.3
Oregon	4.8	.3	8.9	18.6	6.7	9.4	22.6
California	4.6	.8	8.3	11.3	9.3	8.5	23.5
United States	3.4	1.9	7.2	15.5	13.6	8.7	21.0

(Continued on next page)

TABLE 43 (Continued)

INDUSTRIAL COMPOSITION OF THE EXPERIENCED LABOR FORCE, 1950, BY STATE[a]

State	Finance, insurance and real estate	Service industries				Public adminis-tration
		Business and repair	Personal	Entertain-ment and recreation	Professional and related	
New England						
Maine	2.2	2.8	6.4	.8	8.3	4.1
New Hampshire	2.5	2.6	6.1	.8	9.2	3.6
Vermont	2.8	3.2	7.9	.8	10.8	4.4
Massachusetts	4.2	2.4	5.3	.9	9.9	4.9
Rhode Island	3.0	2.2	4.7	1.0	7.6	5.2
Connecticut	4.7	2.4	5.2	.8	9.0	3.5
Middle Atlantic						
New York	5.8	3.1	6.8	1.4	9.6	4.6
New Jersey	5.0	2.7	5.8	.9	7.7	4.2
Pennsylvania	3.0	2.4	5.2	.8	8.1	3.9
East North Central						
Ohio	3.0	2.6	5.4	1.0	8.1	4.3
Indiana	2.9	2.4	5.4	.9	8.4	3.6
Illinois	4.1	2.9	5.6	1.0	8.4	4.0
Michigan	2.8	2.5	5.1	1.0	8.1	3.0
Wisconsin	2.9	2.8	5.0	1.0	9.3	3.6
West North Central						
Minnesota	4.0	3.6	5.8	1.1	11.5	4.4
Iowa	3.7	3.6	6.0	1.1	11.7	4.1
Missouri	4.0	3.0	6.7	1.0	9.3	4.8
North Dakota	2.9	4.7	5.8	1.2	13.5	6.1
South Dakota	3.1	4.4	6.2	1.3	13.5	6.1
Nebraska	4.7	3.8	6.4	1.2	11.6	5.5
Kansas	3.6	3.3	6.4	1.2	11.4	5.3
South Atlantic						
Delaware	3.4	2.4	7.8	.9	8.6	3.3
Maryland	3.7	2.4	7.3	1.0	9.1	8.9
D. C.	4.6	2.1	11.1	1.0	11.1	30.8
Virginia	2.9	2.2	8.7	.8	8.4	9.7
West Virginia	1.7	2.0	5.3	.8	8.2	3.0
North Carolina	2.1	2.3	9.5	.9	8.4	3.4
South Carolina	2.2	1.9	11.2	.7	8.1	3.2
Georgia	2.9	2.3	12.1	.9	7.9	4.7
Florida	4.0	3.0	13.2	1.6	8.5	5.5
East South Central						
Kentucky	2.8	3.0	7.3	1.1	8.7	4.0
Tennessee	2.8	2.6	9.3	.9	9.2	4.1
Alabama	2.6	2.1	11.3	.8	8.5	4.7
Mississippi	2.0	2.5	13.1	.8	9.9	4.0
West South Central						
Arkansas	2.4	2.7	9.5	1.0	9.6	3.8
Louisiana	2.8	2.7	10.4	1.2	9.4	4.4
Oklahoma	3.6	3.5	8.2	1.3	10.9	6.6
Texas	3.6	3.0	9.6	1.1	8.8	4.9
Mountain						
Montana	2.8	3.6	6.0	1.1	10.6	5.7
Idaho	2.9	3.8	6.7	1.3	10.2	4.8
Wyoming	2.3	3.4	6.4	1.1	9.9	6.0
Colorado	4.0	3.6	7.2	1.4	12.0	6.3
New Mexico	2.5	3.3	7.8	1.1	11.8	7.6
Arizona	3.2	3.3	9.1	1.3	10.6	5.7
Utah	3.5	3.0	5.3	1.4	10.9	10.4
Nevada	2.6	3.3	10.6	7.1	8.2	8.2
Pacific						
Washington	4.0	3.1	6.1	1.1	10.2	5.9
Oregon	3.6	3.6	6.2	1.1	9.6	4.5
California	4.6	3.5	7.1	2.2	9.7	6.5
United States	3.7	2.8	7.0	1.1	9.1	4.9

[a]Adjusted to exclude farm self-employed and the "industry not reported" group.
[b]Excludes farm self-employed.
[c]Includes manufacturing industries not specified.
Source: *Census of Population, 1950.* Detail may not add to 100.0 percent because of rounding.

tions of detailed industries for the states, and is omitted from the table for this reason. The agriculture, forestry, and fisheries group consists of only three industries, so that it provides no opportunity to reflect differences in the earning rates, skills, and length of work year which differentiate, for example, the Eastern hardwoods and Western softwoods forest operations. Since the average earnings of agriculture ($1,149) are lowest, of forestry ($2,031) next, and of fisheries ($2,277) the highest, a "favorable" composition within this group means only that a relatively larger proportion of the group's employees is engaged in forestry or fisheries. Much the same situation is found in the individual service groups. The group compositions have been retained in these cases, however, because of the additional information they provide on the industrial structure of the states. The trade group had been subdivided into wholesale and retail trade, not only to provide information directly comparable with the wholesale-trade data from the *Census of Business, 1948,* but also to provide information, not readily available elsewhere, on the retail trade subgroup. In addition to the group detail, subtotals have been provided for the manufacturing and service industry segments.

It is of some interest to note that the composition of nondurable manufactures in 10 states and of durable manufactures in 12 states has a sign differing from that for all manufactures.

There is some slight tendency for the states at each end of the array of rate-constant earnings to have conpositions within the groups predominantly in the direction of their over-all compositions. This tendency is more marked at the lower end of the array. Were all of the group compositions unfavorable, it would suggest that the available skills and other resources in the state operate to limit the range of services and goods that the state can produce. Conversely, a favorable composition in every industry group would suggest that a state's industrial composition is not limited by available skills or other resources and that it concentrates on those in which the terms of trade are more favorable. The fact that the within-group compositions are favorable (unfavorable) in the lowest (highest) income states does not negate such a suggestion, however, since the distribution of skills and resources may be more effective in determining the relative concentrations among groups than among industries within the groups.

1949 Earning-Rate Differentials

In the discussion of the compositional differences among the states, for all industries and within the major groups, the final column of table

38, which shows the differences in state and national earning rates for the industries found in each state, has escaped mention. Since the percentages in this column are based on the differences between the reported and the rate-constant earnings, much of what has been said about the limitations of the figures for rate-constant earnings is relevant here. To the extent that the rate-constant earnings fail to reflect adequately the differences directly associated with industry, the percentage differences in earnings will also be affected. This relationship was treated in detail with regard to the earning rates of government employees. It need only be emphasized here that limiting the number of industrial classifications can result in attributing too little as well as too much to composition, and hence too much or too little to earning rates. If, for example, a state's experienced labor force were concentrated in the lower-earning plants within one of the broad industrial categories provided by the population census, these employees would be attributed the earnings of the entire category. This would tend to increase the size of the state's rate-constant earning, and hence to attribute to composition rather than to earning rates the difference between the national average earnings for the type of plants in the state and the national average earnings of all the plants in the broad industrial category.

Because of the limitations of the basic data underlying table 38, the magnitudes of the percentage differences in earning rates do not command great confidence. It is possible that even the signs may be in error in a few of the states which have both compositions and earning rates which approximate the national average, although the signs are more reliable than the magnitudes to which they are attached. Since reported state earning data are available only for all industries combined, it is not possible to test whether the state-national differences in earning rates calculated for all industries tend to persist within each of the population-census major-industry groups. The signs are the same as those found for occupations in every state, and they differ from those found for 1947 manufacturing production-worker hourly rates in eight states, from those found for 1948 wholesale-trade average annual earnings in eight states, and from those found for 1952 government-employee average annual earnings in six states.[57] Since some states have earning rates in more than one in-

[57] The signs for all population-census industries differ from those for manufacturing, wholesale trade, and governments in Pennsylvania, Delaware, and Utah; from those for manufacturing and wholesale trade in Maryland and Idaho; from those for wholesale trade and government in Wyoming; from those for manufacturing alone in Massachusetts, Connecticut, and Wisconsin; from those for wholesale trade alone in Montana and Arizona; and from those for government alone in Indiana and Minnesota. Outside of the Mountain

dustrial segment which differ in sign from those of the population-census industries, only 13 states account for these 22 differences in signs. Moreover, the state and national earning rates differ in 11 of these 13 states by less than 5 percentage points. Of greater importance is the fact that in 35 states and the District of Columbia the signs of the percentage deviations due to rates are the same for the 146 population-census industries for 1949, the 458 manufacturing industries for 1947, the 244 wholesale-trade industries for 1948, and the 3 government industries for 1952.

The population-census industry data thus support the conclusion reached in the analysis of the 1949 occupational data (chapter 5) and the 1947 manufacturing data that the Southern and West North Central regions tend to be low-earning areas, the Middle Atlantic, East North Central, and Pacific regions tend to be high-earning areas, and that the remaining regions may be characterized as average-earning areas.

Relation of Composition and Earning Differentials

There is a marked tendency for states with unfavorable industrial compositions to have earning rates below the national average for their industries and, conversely, for states with favorable industrial compositions to have above-average earning rates. Fourteen states depart from this pattern for the 1947 hourly earnings of manufacturing production workers; 14 for the 1948 annual earnings of wholesale-trade employees; and 9 for the 1949 annual average earnings of population-census wage and salary workers reported by industry (10 when these workers are reported by occupation.) The only industrial distribution in which the relationship does not hold is that for government, where there are about an equal number of states with earning-rates difference signs which do or do not agree with the sign for compositional differences.[58] Except for governments, not only do the departures from average composition and average rates tend to be in the same direction for each state, but there is also a tendency for states with the extreme percentage departures in composition to have extreme percentage departures in the same direction for earning rates.[59]

---

states the magnitude of the deviating percentages was less than 3, with the exception of the Maryland and Pennsylvania entries for manufacturing and of the Maryland entry for wholesale trade.

[58] It is pointed out above that the signs for government composition and earnings are subject to some error largely because of the small numbers of "industries" for which separate data are available.

[59] The coefficients of determination between the percentage differences attributable to composition and to earning rates are: for manufactures (table 34, columns 5 and 6), .26; for wholesale trade (table 36, columns 5 and 6), .27; for the population-census industries (table

When the government data are set aside, composition and earning rates in 25 states differ from their national averages in the same direction in every set of data. Of the 23 states and the District of Columbia with one or more rate deviations which differ in direction from that for composition, the only clearly marked regional concentration is in the West, where unfavorable compositions were accompanied by above-average earnings in all but Colorado.[60] Outside the West the tendency is in the other direction—that is, for favorable compositions to be accompanied by below-average earning rates. Oregon and Nevada had unfavorable compositions and above-average earning rates in each body of data; Montana and Arizona showed a similar situation in all but wholesale trade, and Washington in all but occupations.[61]

The relationship between composition and earning rates, which persists throughout most of the available data, has consequences important both for the technical problem of measuring and understanding state income differentials and for their implications for public policy decisions taken with regard to these differentials.[62] They are, therefore, worthy of additional attention.

38, columns 5 and 6), .53; for the population-census occupations (chapter 5, table 24, columns 7 and 8), .77; and for government (table 37, columns 8-11), .00. All of the coefficients except those for government are significant at the .01 level.

[60] In the West the only two states without differing rate and composition signs are New Mexico and Utah. By region, the number of states with differing signs are: North, 3; Central, 6; South, 6; and West, 9.

[61] Oklahoma and Kansas are the only other states with differing signs in as many as three bodies of data. They have favorable compositions of manufacturing, and of population-census industries and occupations which were accompanied by below-average earning rates. There are eight states with differing signs in two bodies of data, and ten states with differing signs in a single body of data.

[62] The technical problems are discussed in appendix B. The type of interpretative problem encountered because of this relationship may be illustrated by reference to the question of whether unionization is one of the factors associated with state earning differentials. Leo Wolman, in *Thirty-Sixth Annual Report of the National Bureau of Economic Research,* New York, 1956, p. 46, provides state estimates of the percentages of nonagricultural employment in organized trade unions for 1939 and 1953. The more thoroughly unionized states tend to have higher per capita personal incomes (based on the average 1929-1954 incomes, the rank correlation coefficient is .65), but this cannot be interpreted causally since the higher-income states tend to have the more favorable industrial and occupational compositions and it may be that unions have concentrated on organizing the already-better-paid employees. Presumably, the percentages attributed to earning rates are net of the influence of composition, and these, too, are correlated with unionization (for 1947 manufactures the coefficient of rank correlation is .71). But the strong correlation between composition and rates renders this evidence ambiguous, since the rates, even when taken net of composition, are an indirect reflection of composition. Again, if unions are efficacious in obtaining differential increases in earnings, the larger increases in earnings would be expected in states with the larger increases in unionization. The larger increases in earnings have been noted for the states with lower earning rates. These tend to be the states with earning rates,

There are three possible explanations for this relationship, none of which can be tested with the data at hand: First, it may be that the relationship stems largely from the statistical framework in which the data were collected, classified, and compiled. The classificatory systems, designed as they were to serve many general uses, may not reflect adequately the many criteria which determine earning rates. It may be, for example, that the occupational classification "carpenter" does not reflect the basic differences in skills, experience, amount of supervision, specialization of function, and other factors needed to distinguish occupational from earnings characteristics. Such an explanation would seem more cogent if it related to only one of the classificatory systems. Before this explanation can be used to explain a relationship which persists in numerous bodies of data, it seems necessary also to hypothecate some regional distribution of the basic levels of skills. Firms operating in areas where only the lower skills were found would then find it necessary to organize their work flows so that only locally available skills were required. Types of businesses that were economically dependent upon skills not locally available might also be discouraged. The finding that states near the lower-earning limit of the distribution tend to have unfavorable compositions within each of the major occupational and major industrial groups lends some, though not conclusive, support to this hypothesis. It is not possible, however, to go behind the classificatory systems used in the available bodies of data, nor to introduce into them the further classificatory criteria which are needed to test this hypothesis adequately.

A second possible explanation is that the relationship reflects a competitive situation in which the demand for the higher skills differs from their potential supply. In an area in which low-earning industries predominate, the lack of enough high-earning jobs to absorb all those qualified to hold them would have a depressing effect on earning rates. Conversely, in areas with high-earning industries, the search for a qualified labor force may lead to the inauguration of training programs, upgrading, pirating, and other practices which inflate earnings. Moreover, in such an area, the low-earning industries might find it necessary to raise rates in order to attract and hold a labor force. Such an explanation does not depend upon a differential distribution of skills among regions. Migration from the lower- to the higher-earning areas presumably would operate in the direction of leveling out the earning differential between areas, but the barriers to migration at any one time are probably enough to maintain

net of composition, below the national averages for their industries. There is, however, no correlation between net earning-rate differentials and percent of increase in unionization.

regional differentials. The hypothesis outlined here is consistent with the often-noted tendency during recent decades toward smaller earning differentials within firms, industries, cities, and states.[63] Presumably a test of this hypothesis would require that the findings of many case studies of the experience of firms in obtaining and holding a labor supply, be pieced together with studies of the effects of expansion and changes in the composition of industries on earning rates within relatively small areas and of changes in the occupational characteristics of the labor force during inflationary and deflationary periods.

Finally, it may be that the observed relationship, rather than being purely economic in its origin and perseverance, reflects differentials that are primarily based on the historically developed work habits and desire for leisure of persons living in particular communities or sections of the country. Such a hypothesis depends on somewhat greater immobility of the labor force than do the other possible explanations, and, if the hypothesis is correct, it would generate many of the barriers to migration. The cumulative effects of failing to provide adequate education, to build and maintain highways, to provide the other public capital necessary for industrial growth, and of becoming complacent about existing living standards and consumption patterns, could create barriers to improvements in earnings at least in the states with lower earning rates.[64] A test of this hypothesis would require techniques not usually associated with economics.

Whatever the explanation of the relationship between composition and earnings, it is available to make composition a more powerful instrument for explaining interstate earning differentials. Too, the existence of this relationship probably makes less consequential our inability to separate cleanly compositional and earning-rate differences, although it does not operate in this way for government. Were the two variables uncorrelated, it would be more essential that the industrial categories be defined in such a way that variation within categories be held to a minimum. With a strong correlation between the variables, the effects of a failure clearly to differentiate compositional differences (and thus earning-rate differences) are only partially carried over into the use of compositional differences to ex-

[63] In addition to chapter 4, see Frederic Meyers, "Note on Changes in the Distribution of Manufacturing Wage Earners by Straight-time Hourly Earnings, 1941-1948," *Review of Economics and Statistics,* 32 (1950), 352; and Edwin Mansfield, "Wage Differentials in the Cotton Textile Industry, 1933-1952," *ibid.,* 37 (1955), 77, and the literature there cited.

[64] To be operative, however, such forces would have to make themselves felt on the competitive labor market. For this reason, this hypothesis should probably be considered a special case of the second hypothesis.

plain reported earning differentials. Thus industrial composition, together with the forces correlated with it, appears to explain up to 70 percent of the reported interstate earning differentials in the areas, other than governments, covered by the industrial series.[65] This percentage is smaller than that explained by occupational composition (chapter 5).

The independent effects of industrial composition are from slightly less to about three times as effective as those of occupational composition in explaining statistically the interstate variation in reported earnings. On the other hand, the explanatory effects of elements correlated with industrial composition are smaller than are those correlated with occupational composition, and industrial composition leaves more of the interstate variation in earnings unexplained. In terms of the distribution of variation among independent and correlated influences, the differences between the population-census industrial and occupational compositions are smaller than the differences between either of these and the industrial compositions within the manufactures and wholesale-trade segments. When the total explanatory values of the occupational and industrial compositions from the population census are compared, it is found that occupational composition accounts for about 46 percent of the interstate variation left unexplained by industrial composition.[66]

The independent influences of industrial composition based on the population, manufactures, and wholesale-trade censuses account for a significant proportion of the total interstate variation in earnings. This fact

[65] This measure is based on the coefficient of determination between the rate-constant and the reported earnings. The method is discussed in appendix B. The coefficients, and the distributions of the variation between independent and correlated effects, are:

	Coefficient of determination	*Independent effects*	*Correlated effects*	*Unexplained*
		(percentage of total variation)		
Population-census industry average annual earnings of wage and salary workers, 1949 (table 38)	72	9	63	28
Census of manufactures, hourly earnings of production workers, 1947 (table 34)	72	32	40	28
Business census average annual earnings of wholesale-trade employees, 1948 (table 36)	73	27	46	27

The coefficients for governments do not depart significantly from zero in either 1939 or 1952.

[66] Based on the proportion of the variation left unexplained by industrial composition which is explained by occupational composition. This views occupation as an independent classificatory variable capable of explaining some of the dispersion within industries, that is, as a coefficient of partial determination between rate-constant occupational earnings and reported earnings after account has been taken of the effects of interstate variation in industrial compositions.

alone lends support to the hypothesis that interstate earning differentials are to a significant extent reflections of interstate differentials in the types and kinds of industrial pursuits within the various states. The influences correlated with industrial composition are available to increase the explanatory power of industrial composition, although the economic content of these correlated influences is difficult to specify.

Chapter 7

DEMOGRAPHIC FACTORS

THE AGE, education, marital status, urbanization, crude fertility rates, and other demographic characteristics of the state populations provide measures of the state distributions of human resources. To the extent that persons and industries are mobile, it may be expected that economic considerations will operate in the direction of matching supply and demand for various levels of skills and other human resources. Consequently, a study of the state demographic differentials may be expected to reflect, though indirectly, some of the differentials found in the study of state occupational and industrial differentials. To some extent, however, the demographic differentials will tend to be independent and will help to explain the existence and persistence of the occupational and industrial differentials.

In this chapter attention will be devoted to two sets of demographic characteristics: First, the direct effects on the distribution of state per capita personal incomes of using several variants of age and labor-force population groups as the denominator in computing "per capita" incomes will be investigated. This portion of the study will be confined to the four decennial census years, 1920, 1930, 1940, and 1950, for which both census data and income estimates are available. Secondly, some attention will be devoted to the income differentials associated with the size of the city in which a family resides. This portion of the study will necessarily be confined to 1949, the only year for which reasonably complete data are available in the *Census of Population, 1950*.

POPULATION VARIANTS BASED ON AGE AND LABOR FORCE[1]

Five population variants have been singled out for intensive study. Three of these variants consist of age groups: persons 15 years old and

[1] An earlier version of this section appeared as "Age, Labor Force, and State Per Capita

older; persons 20 years old and older; and persons who have reached their 20th but not their 65th birthdays. The other two variants are based on more direct measures of participation in the labor force: the total labor force and the employed labor force. To some extent all of these variants attempt to measure, with varying degrees of precision, that part of the population which contributes or may be expected to contribute directly to the flows of personal income. Certainly, children under 15 years of age can hardly be expected to make more than a nominal contribution to income, and then largely as unpaid family labor. Somewhere between the ages of 15 and 20 are found most of the new recruits to the labor force.[2] The age of 20, therefore, may be viewed as near the upper age limit below which school or other preparatory work prevents entry into the labor force. As persons become older and unable to work, their contributions to income diminish. The choice of 65 as the age of retirement is purely conventional, however; it is the age at which those covered under the old age and survivors' benefit program become eligible for pensions.[3]

The *Census of Population, 1950* reports persons 15 years old and older are 73.1 percent of the total population, that persons 20 years old and older are 66.1 percent, and that persons 20-64 years old are 57.9 percent

Incomes, 1930, 1940, and 1950," *Review of Economics and Statistics,* 37 (1955), 63-69. The analysis which appeared there was based on the National Income Division's estimates of state income payments. In addition to making use of the recently available personal income series, this analysis has been extended to 1920 by making use of the income estimates for that year in Maurice Leven, *Income in the Various States, Its Sources and Distribution, 1919, 1920, and 1921,* New York, 1925.

[2] Harold Wool, *Tables of Working Life,* B. L. S. Bulletin No. 1001, Washington, 1950, p. 36, estimates that about 92 percent of the male accessions to the labor force are from the age groups under 20 years.

[3] Other variants, also designed to exclude those who can make only a limited contribution to income, might be devised. The institutional population or those who are partially or wholly incapacitated might, for example, be excluded. The former group, however, is small, and there are no reliable data for the latter. In 1950 only 1.0 percent of the population was in institutions. By states the percentages varied from .6 percent in Mississippi to 1.5 percent in Massachusetts and 1.6 percent in the District of Columbia. *Census of Population, 1950,* Bulletin P-B1, tables 59 and 69. Some attention might also be paid to the number of mothers who are prevented, temporarily at least, from participation in the labor force by the necessity of caring for their children. To some extent a count of children reflects this factor, although imperfectly. It is conjectural whether much would be added to our knowledge by some scheme which would, for example, take into account more explicitly the inability of the mother with children below the age of four to participate in the labor force. It is believed that the age criteria used here largely account for the differences in state per capita incomes, or are closely associated with other important variants.

TABLE 44

Percentage Differences between State and National Population Compositions, for Three Variants Based on Age, Decennial Census Years, 1920-1950[a]

State	Population 15 years old and older				Population 20 years old and older				Population 20 to 64 years of age			
	1920	1930	1940	1950	1920	1930	1940	1950	1920	1930	1940	1950
New England												
Maine	5.3	1.0	−1.4	−1.2	7.1	2.4	−1.5	−2.3	1.5	−3.2	−6.2	−6.3
New Hampshire	7.0	3.6	2.2	2.0	9.7	5.9	3.4	2.2	4.6	.2	−1.4	−2.1
Vermont	4.9	1.6	−1.0	−1.6	6.5	3.0	−.6	−2.6	.2	−2.6	−5.4	−7.0
Massachusetts	5.6	4.0	4.3	4.4	8.3	6.0	5.6	5.6	7.7	4.6	3.4	3.2
Rhode Island	4.4	2.1	3.9	4.6	5.7	3.0	4.2	5.4	5.6	2.5	3.4	4.9
Connecticut	2.6	2.4	5.1	4.2	5.0	3.0	6.3	6.2	4.9	2.6	5.9	5.9
Middle Atlantic												
New York	6.0	6.1	5.9	5.8	8.6	8.5	8.3	7.9	9.2	9.5	9.3	8.4
New Jersey	2.4	3.2	5.4	5.0	4.2	4.4	6.6	7.0	5.4	5.6	7.7	7.9
Pennsylvania	−.4	−.8	1.1	2.5	.2	−1.1	.7	3.0	.5	−1.0	.8	2.9
East North Central												
Ohio	4.9	2.7	2.9	1.4	7.0	4.3	3.8	2.6	6.0	3.2	2.6	1.6
Indiana	4.2	2.4	1.4	.1	5.3	3.8	2.0	.5	2.8	.9	−.4	−1.2
Illinois	3.8	4.8	4.6	3.9	5.4	6.4	6.5	5.6	6.0	6.9	6.7	5.4
Michigan	2.8	.5	.0	−.7	4.6	1.9	.5	−.4	4.0	2.3	1.5	1.1
Wisconsin	.9	.7	.2	−.2	.8	1.1	.6	−.0	−.3	−.8	−.8	−1.6
West North Central												
Minnesota	1.0	.7	.5	−1.0	.7	.9	.8	−1.0	.8	−.8	−.4	−2.7
Iowa	2.9	1.6	.6	−.1	3.3	2.4	1.0	−.1	1.1	−1.0	−2.4	−4.0
Missouri	3.6	3.7	2.2	2.6	3.9	5.0	3.3	3.2	2.8	3.1	.7	−.1
North Dakota	−10.3	−7.0	−6.2	−5.7	−12.8	−10.8	−8.5	−8.1	−10.8	−10.1	−8.3	−8.6
South Dakota	−4.2	−4.3	−3.6	−3.2	−5.5	−6.0	−5.2	−4.7	−4.8	−6.5	−5.9	−5.9
Nebraska	−.4	−.3	−.2	.8	−.8	−.7	−.4	.4	−1.5	−2.3	−2.5	−2.5
Kansas	1.0	.8	.8	.9	.6	1.1	1.0	.8	−1.6	−1.4	−2.1	−2.6
South Atlantic												
Delaware	4.4	3.5	3.1	1.5	6.1	4.9	4.5	2.4	5.0	2.5	3.6	2.5
Maryland	3.1	1.4	1.6	.2	3.4	2.4	2.1	.8	3.1	2.2	2.5	3.0
D. C.	16.5	11.9	9.6	9.3	21.1	17.1	14.1	12.4	22.9	18.4	16.8	16.0
Virginia	−5.8	−6.2	−4.8	−3.0	−8.7	−9.1	−7.3	−4.9	−8.8	−8.9	−6.3	−2.6
West Virginia	−7.9	−9.2	−8.3	−6.7	−10.3	−11.9	−11.7	−9.3	−9.6	−10.9	−10.4	−8.4
North Carolina	−12.5	−12.0	−10.0	−7.4	−17.0	−17.1	−14.4	−11.2	−17.0	−15.6	−11.9	−8.3
South Carolina	−13.2	−12.8	−11.6	−10.8	−18.4	−19.3	−16.9	−15.2	−17.3	−17.4	−14.5	−12.6
Georgia	−9.6	−7.5	−7.5	−6.5	−13.9	−12.1	−10.3	−9.4	−13.0	−10.6	−8.5	−7.6
Florida	−2.2	−.6	−.0	.9	−3.5	−.6	.6	1.7	−2.9	.3	.6	1.2
East South Central												
Kentucky	−4.9	−6.6	−7.1	−5.4	−7.1	−8.3	−9.6	−8.1	−7.7	−9.2	−10.4	−9.0
Tennessee	−6.2	−5.5	−5.8	−4.4	−9.3	−8.2	−7.8	−6.6	−9.5	−7.5	−7.1	−5.8
Alabama	−10.6	−9.2	−9.7	−7.9	−14.7	−13.4	−13.0	−11.2	−14.0	−11.7	−11.0	−10.0
Mississippi	−9.7	−8.5	−10.1	−9.7	−14.2	−12.6	−13.3	−13.6	−13.6	−11.0	−12.2	−13.6
West South Central												
Arkansas	−9.4	−7.7	−7.9	−6.9	−13.5	−11.3	−10.8	−9.7	−12.6	−10.0	−9.8	−10.4
Louisiana	−6.4	−6.0	−6.2	−6.3	−10.0	−8.4	−8.4	−8.2	−8.4	−6.0	−6.2	−6.6
Oklahoma	−8.4	−6.2	−5.6	−2.4	−12.0	−9.0	−7.8	−4.1	−10.3	−7.4	−7.6	−5.6
Texas	−5.2	−4.0	−4.0	−3.1	−8.7	−6.3	−5.4	−4.6	−7.3	−4.4	−3.5	−2.7
Mountain												
Montana	−1.1	−.4	−.4	−2.6	.9	−.4	−.1	−2.6	−3.9	.4	.5	−3.8
Idaho	−5.1	−4.8	−4.8	−6.6	−5.7	−6.5	−6.2	−8.2	−4.0	−6.4	−5.6	−8.1
Wyoming	.8	−1.3	−2.1	−3.1	3.1	−.8	−2.7	−4.4	7.3	1.9	.1	−1.8
Colorado	2.8	.7	−.8	−.8	4.1	1.1	−.5	−1.3	5.0	.2	−2.0	−2.4
New Mexico	−7.7	−10.3	−12.6	−10.9	−10.0	−13.2	−15.7	−14.1	−8.6	−11.9	−13.4	−10.4
Arizona	−2.2	−5.1	−7.7	−6.9	−1.8	−5.5	−9.2	−8.5	1.1	−2.8	−6.8	−5.8
Utah	−8.6	−8.8	−8.5	−9.1	−11.1	−11.8	−11.6	−12.0	10.0	−11.2	−10.6	−10.2
Nevada	10.3	7.4	3.3	1.4	16.1	11.5	6.6	3.2	17.8	12.9	8.5	5.9
Pacific												
Washington	6.5	6.3	5.2	.7	9.3	8.2	7.4	1.4	10.5	7.0	5.8	.3
Oregon	6.7	7.0	5.1	.4	9.3	9.2	7.2	1.5	8.7	7.1	5.2	.7
California	11.8	9.1	7.0	3.2	16.7	13.5	10.3	5.2	15.9	12.9	9.4	5.3

[a] Persons for whom age was not reported are included in each of these variants.

of the total population.[4] Corresponding percentages for each of the states vary considerably. In New York, for example, persons 15 years old and older are 77.4 percent of the total population. For this group the difference between the percentages for the United States and for New York, expressed as a percent of the United States percentage, is + 5.8 (the plus sign showing that the state percentage is the higher). Similar percentage differences may be calculated for each age group and each state (table 44).

The percentage differences shown in table 45, relating to the two labor-force variants, have been prepared in the same manner as those in table 44. The difference between the percent of the total state population and United States population in the labor force (or the employed labor force) has been expressed as a percentage of the United States figure.[5]

Absolute differences among states

The more heavily populated states in the Northeast and along the Pacific Coast tend to have larger percentages of their total population in the three age groups considered, while the Southern and Mountain states tend to have smaller percentages in these groups; conversely, the Southern and Mountain states have larger percentages in the groups *excluded*—that is, in the groups consisting of persons under 15 years of age, under 20 years of age, and under 20 years of age and 65 years of age and over. The geographic distributions found for the labor-force groups are similar. The largest positive percentage differences in 1950 are found in New York for the variants based on age, in Nevada for the total labor force, and in Connecticut for the employed labor force (although the District of Columbia, a city, had larger differences for all five variants). The 1950 largest negative percentage differences are found in New Mexico for the groups consisting of persons 15 years old and older and the employed labor force; in South Carolina for the group 20 years old and older;

[4] Comparative percentages for earlier years, for the United States, are:

	1920	*1930*	*1940*	*1950*
Persons 15 years old and older	68.2	70.6	75.0	73.1
Persons 20 years old and older	59.3	61.1	65.6	66.1
Persons 20-64 years old	54.6	55.7	58.7	57.9

[5] The United States percentages, as shown in the *Census of Population, 1950,* Bulletin P-B1, Tables 51 and 52, are:

	1920	*1930*	*1940*	*1950*
Percent of total population in:				
Total labor force	39.0	39.6	40.1	39.9
Employed labor force	n.a.	n.a.	34.1	37.3

For 1920 and 1930 the census data relate to gainful workers rather than to labor force. Data comparable with employed labor force were not collected prior to 1940.

TABLE 45

PERCENTAGE DIFFERENCES BETWEEN STATE AND NATIONAL POPULATION COMPOSITIONS, FOR TWO VARIANTS BASED ON LABOR FORCE, DECENNIAL CENSUS YEARS, 1920-1950

State	Population in total labor force[a]				Population in employed labor force	
	1920	1930	1940	1950	1940	1950
New England						
Maine	3.5	− 2.7	− 2.7	− 5.2	− 4.0	− 8.4
New Hampshire	11.6	4.1	5.0	2.4	4.4	1.8
Vermont	.7	− 1.3	− 1.8	− 3.3	1.5	− 2.6
Massachusetts	15.1	7.4	6.6	4.9	3.6	4.4
Rhode Island	16.7	8.7	12.5	9.2	8.2	3.0
Connecticut	9.6	6.0	12.4	10.2	16.1	10.5
Middle Atlantic						
New York	11.3	10.3	10.3	7.5	7.6	7.4
New Jersey	6.5	6.5	11.4	9.1	10.0	8.8
Pennsylvania	.7	− 2.8	.4	− .2	− 4.9	.3
East North Central						
Ohio	2.4	− 1.0	− .1	1.3	− 1.0	3.2
Indiana	− 2.4	− 2.9	− 3.1	.1	− 2.0	3.4
Illinois	3.9	4.9	6.2	7.4	6.1	9.1
Michigan	3.0	.1	.9	.0	1.2	.7
Wisconsin	− 3.0	− 3.4	− 2.4	2.2	− 1.4	5.7
West North Central						
Minnesota	− 2.6	− 2.6	− 1.6	− .0	− 2.8	2.8
Iowa	− 8.5	− 7.1	− 5.9	− 2.2	− .9	2.4
Missouri	− 1.0	1.0	.2	.1	− .1	3.1
North Dakota	18.2	−11.3	− 8.4	− 5.8	− 9.0	− 3.3
South Dakota	−12.9	−10.1	− 7.0	− 3.1	− 7.3	− .6
Nebraska	− 9.7	− 7.5	− 5.0	− .3	− 4.0	3.4
Kansas	− 9.7	− 7.2	− 7.2	− 2.7	− 5.5	− .5
South Atlantic						
Delaware	4.8	3.5	6.9	3.4	12.3	6.7
Maryland	6.6	3.7	5.0	4.2	10.6	2.3
D. C.	38.3	25.9	29.4	26.3	35.8	24.8
Virginia	− 8.3	− 8.6	− 3.9	− 1.3	1.6	− 7.1
West Virginia	−14.2	−17.0	−16.7	−17.4	−20.4	−16.1
North Carolina	−13.0	− 9.5	− 6.9	− 3.9	− 1.3	− 3.5
South Carolina	− 2.1	− .6	− 4.1	− 5.4	1.4	− 4.4
Georgia	− 3.9	.5	− 2.1	− 2.6	3.4	− 2.4
Florida	1.0	2.6	3.4	− .5	5.0	− 2.4
East South Central						
Kentucky	−10.6	−12.8	−12.5	−13.7	−13.2	−13.1
Tennessee	−10.8	− 7.9	− 8.3	− 8.6	− 5.8	− 7.6
Alabama	− 5.9	− 2.5	−10.4	−11.1	− 8.0	− 9.7
Mississippi	− 2.2	5.7	− 7.7	−12.8	− 2.9	−11.8
West South Central						
Arkansas	−10.9	− 9.4	−13.1	−14.9	−12.7	−13.6
Louisiana	− 4.6	− 2.4	− 6.7	−13.2	− 4.9	−12.6
Oklahoma	−15.1	−13.1	−14.1	−10.5	−17.8	− 9.6
Texas	− 7.6	− 4.7	− 4.6	− 3.3	− 2.8	− 4.2
Mountain						
Montana	.0	1.2	.3	− 1.4	− 3.3	− 1.0
Idaho	− 9.1	− 8.3	− 9.1	− 6.9	−11.9	− 6.2
Wyoming	7.5	3.0	− .1	3.2	.6	− .5
Colorado	− .2	− 2.2	− 6.4	− 2.8	− 9.2	− 3.6
New Mexico	−13.6	−15.3	−16.6	−15.3	−23.1	−18.8
Arizona	− .6	− 4.6	−10.0	−11.1	−12.3	−14.7
Utah	−15.2	−15.8	−17.8	−11.5	−21.1	−11.0
Nevada	24.4	18.4	8.6	11.2	9.6	6.5
Pacific						
Washington	9.3	6.9	2.9	1.0	2.0	− 5.4
Oregon	5.4	8.0	3.8	2.2	4.3	1.5
California	13.2	10.8	6.5	4.6	6.6	− 1.2

[a]Gainful workers used in 1920 and 1930.

in Mississippi for the group of persons 20-64 years old; and in West Virginia for the total labor force. The interstate range of percentage differences (excluding the District of Columbia), from largest positive to largest negative, tends to be smaller in 1950 than in earlier years, and it will be shown below that there is some narrowing of the differentials among the states.

The states with the largest percentages of persons under 15 years of age tend to be the ones which have the largest percentages under 20 years of age and under 20 and over 64 years of age, and also the largest percentages outside the labor force and outside the employed labor force. There is much concordance between the rank of a state by any one characteristic and the state's rank by the other characteristics (table 46).

TABLE 46

INTERSTATE RANK CORRELATION COEFFICIENTS BETWEEN POPULATION VARIANTS, DECENNIAL CENSUS YEARS, 1920-1950

Population variants	1920	1930	1940	1950
Persons 15 years old and older, and				
Persons 20 years old and older	.99	.99	.99	.99
Persons 20-64 years old	.92	.95	.96	.93
Persons in labor force[a]	.79	.74	.87	.87
Persons in employed labor force	n.a.	n.a.	.75	.84
Persons 20 years old and older, and				
Persons 20-64 years old	.94	.95	.97	.95
Persons in labor force[a]	.82	.73	.85	.89
Persons in employed labor force	n.a.	n.a.	.74	.85
Persons 20-64 years old and				
Persons in labor force[a]	.84	.79	.89	.93
Persons in employed labor force	n.a.	n.a.	.77	.82
Persons in labor force[a], and				
Persons in employed labor force	n.a.	n.a.	.93	.90

[a]Based on gainful workers for 1920 and 1930.
Source: tables 44 and 45.

To some extent this might be expected, since each variant is designed to help in measuring that part of the population which contributes or may be expected to contribute substantially to a state's income. The only difference between the variant which includes only persons 20 years old and older and the variant which includes only persons 15 years old and older is persons in the 15-19 age group. Similarly, the labor-force variant includes all persons in the employed labor-force variant; the only difference is the number of unemployed on the census dates. The coefficients in table 46 are slightly higher when both variants are based on age than when one variant is based on age and the other on labor force. The coefficients tend to be lowest when one of the variants is employed labor force. Not only is employed labor force an extreme variant in the sense that it attempts to exclude any who are not making a direct contribution to income in the current year, but it is also subject to considerable random error. Unemployment, measured as of a specific week, might vary erratically among states.[6]

As may be expected from the regional distribution of the states with relatively large percentages of children and/or persons over 65 years of age, they tend to be states in which agriculture is relatively important and employment in durable manufactures relatively low.[7] The tendency for the densely populated states in the Northeast to have relatively smaller percentages of children, and the association between agriculture and age composition, suggest that the larger ratios of children to total population are found outside urban areas.[8]

Since the variants based on labor force (table 45) are associated with those based on age composition, they display much the same regional distribution. The association with the percent of population employed in agriculture, in durable manufactures, or classified as urban is not as close as with the variants based on age composition. The variants based on employed labor force tend to show even less association with these factors than do the variants based on total labor force.[9]

Relative differences among states

The percentages in tables 44 and 45 show the extent to which the states depart from the average composition of the nation's population. The interstate dispersion of these percentage departures tends to be smaller at each succeeding census period (table 47).[10] The interstate differences

[6] This statement is supported by the low rank-correlation coefficient between 1940-1950 for this variant, .75. For all other variants, the 1940-1950 ranks yield rank-correlation coefficients of .94 or .95.

[7] The coefficients of rank correlation between the percent of the 1950 population employed in agriculture (ranked from the highest) and the percentage differences shown in table 44 (ranked from largest negative to largest positive) are from .69 to .76; for the percent of the 1950 population employed in durable manufactures (ranked from the lowest) the coefficients are from .47 to .50 for the three variants based on age.

[8] The coefficients of rank correlation between the percent of the 1950 population classified as urban and the three variants based on age are from .78 to .85.

[9] The coefficients of rank correlation for 1950 are:

	Labor force variant	
	total	*employed*
Percent of total population:		
employed in agriculture	.65	.46
employed in durable manufactures	.46	.42
classified as urban	.73	.60

[10] The interstate coefficient of variation (the standard deviation divided by the mean) is the usual measure of relative dispersion. Since the mean approches zero when signs are taken into account, the coefficients of variation become very large and meaningless. The

decreased by 11-19 percent from 1920 to 1930, by 4-9 percent from 1930 to 1940, and by 8-18 percent from 1940 to 1950. Over the 30-year period 1920-1950, the decreases ranged from 25 to 33 percent, with the largest decrease recorded for the group of persons 20-64 years of age. These decreases indicate a tendency for the state age and labor-force composition to become more like that of the nation.

The standard deviations shown in table 47 are weighted neither by population nor by income. It may be argued, and with some merit, that the reduction in the average differences for the labor-force variants is the result of increasing employment during the later periods. With a widespread increase in opportunities for employment, it may be expected that new entries into the labor force will be relatively more frequent in areas which have more potential manpower outside of the labor force.[11] However, such an argument is not available with regard to the variants based on age. For the age compositions of the states to become more alike, a series of decisions affecting birth rates, which require time for their efforts to be felt, and/or migration is required.[12] Since persons entering the labor force for the first time typically are freer to migrate to areas where opportunities appear greater, the migration which occurred as a consequence of the war and of postwar full employment could have operated to level out interstate differences.[13] The large numbers of men 18 and 19 years old who were in the armed services in 1940 and 1950, and thus excluded from the civilian population, could also account for some of the narrowing of the relative differences among states in the group of persons 20 years old and older.

To the extent that state per capita incomes are affected by disproportionate numbers of children and/or persons over 65 years of age, the tendency shown in table 47 for the differences in age composition among states to become smaller affords one independent explanation of why

---

standard deviations of the percentage differences for total labor force apparently did not change between 1930 and 1940, but this may be due to a lack of comparableness between gainful workers and total labor force.

[11] However, a greater percentage of the nation's population was in the labor force in 1940 than in any other year here studied. See above, note 5.

[12] Some information on the differential changes in state birth rates is available for the 33 states which maintained birth registration systems in both 1925 and 1935. The data for these states indicate that the greater declines in birth rates from 1925 to 1935 occurred in those states which already had the fewest children (the coefficient of rank correlation is .68). Such a differential change would operate to increase the differences in state population compositions by age group.

[13] Many of the requisite migration data apparently are available to test this statement. A test with sufficient precision to be worthwhile would carry the analysis beyond the scope of this study.

differences in state per capita incomes have become smaller (chapter 2). However, substantial percentage differences among the states still exist. In the next section the effects of these differences on per capita income will be considered.

TABLE 47

STANDARD DEVIATION OF THE PERCENTAGE DIFFERENCES BETWEEN STATE AND NATIONAL POPULATION COMPOSITIONS, BY VARIANT, DECENNIAL CENSUS YEARS, 1920-1950

Population variant	1920	1930	1940	1950
15 years old and older	6.3	5.5	5.3	4.4
20 years old and older	8.9	7.9	7.2	6.1
20-64 years	8.4	7.1	6.4	5.6
Total labor force[a]	9.5	7.7	7.7	7.1
Employed labor force	n.a.	n.a.	8.7	7.1

[a]Based on gainful workers for 1920 and 1930.
Source: tables 44 and 45.

Income effects

State per capita personal incomes are computed by dividing the personal income received by the residents of a state by the state's total population at midyear. This computation implicitly assumes that the denominator, total population, does not vary from one state to another in any important way. If only persons who were 15 years old and older, for example, were considered the appropriate population for each of the states, the per capita incomes computed from this population would be higher than those computed from the total population. The relative differences among the states would not be the same in the two series of per capita incomes, however, since all of the states do not have the same percentage of their total populations in the group 15 years old and older. This study is interested chiefly in the relative differences among states.

Each of the five populations used as variants in tables 44 and 45 has been used as the denominator in computing state "per capita" personal incomes for the four census years from 1920 to 1950. The coefficient of variation computed for these state "per capita" personal incomes affords a measure of the relative differences among states for each variant and for the total population (table 48).[14]

[14] Basically, the computations underlying table 48 are equivalent to computing a composition-constant per capita personal income for each state (appendix B), although the computed incomes have not been adjusted for level. They could be adjusted for level by multiplying each state per capita personal income (for a single variant) by the reciprocal of the ratio of the United States per capita personal income computed from total population to the United States per capita personal income computed from the population used as

TABLE 48

INTERSTATE COEFFICIENTS OF VARIATION OF "PER CAPITA" INCOMES COMPUTED FROM SPECIFIED VARIANTS, DECENNIAL CENSUS YEARS, 1920-1950

Population variant	Interstate coefficient of variation (percent)				Percentage reduction from total population variant			
	1920	1930	1940	1950	1920	1930	1940	1950
Total population	31.7	37.7	34.9	23.2	....	....	....	....
15 years old and older	27.2	33.6	30.6	20.1	14.2	10.9	12.3	13.4
20 years old and older	25.1	31.8	29.0	18.6	20.8	15.6	16.9	19.8
20-64 years old	25.0	32.1	29.3	18.5	21.1	14.9	16.0	20.3
Total labor force[a]	25.0	32.3	28.3	17.9	21.1	14.3	18.9	22.8
Employed labor force	n.a.	n.a.	28.7	18.5	....	....	17.8	20.3

[a]Data for 1920 and 1930 based on gainful workers.

Although table 47 shows that the states are becoming more closely grouped around the national population composition, the percentage reductions shown in table 48 are greater for 1950 than for 1940 and greater for 1940 than for 1930. This apparent inconsistency is due to the interrelations between the changes in income and the deviations from the national population composition. Although the deviations from the national population composition are becoming smaller, they continue to exist, and the states which have the lowest average incomes and are most sensitive to changes in the national level of income are the states which also have the largest relative numbers of children, aged persons, or persons not in the labor force. The larger increases in income, particularly during the 1930-1950 period, in the states with the lowest average incomes have served both to reduce the coefficient of variation for state per capita incomes (based on the total population) and to reinforce the direct effects of differences in population composition when these also are taken into account.

The final column of table 48 indicates that in 1950 some 13-23 percent of the relative interstate variation in per capita personal income is accounted for by differences in the relative numbers of children below productive ages, of persons 65 years old or older, or of persons who are in the labor force and thus contribute directly to income production. The largest difference is that associated with the total labor force. Since this is a direct measure of the contributors to income, rather than an approximation of their number, the large difference may be expected. The labor force excludes not only those too young or too old to work, but

the variant. But since multiplying a series by a constant does not change the coefficient of variation for the series, an adjustment for level is not necessary.

also those incapacitated for whatever reason, those who find it necessary to stay at home and care for their children, and those who are living in areas such as mining camps, which provide employment opportunities for only the male members of the family. But to pay exclusive attention to the labor force presumes that all who are able to work are either working or looking for work. The use of other measures, such as the age group from 20 to 64 years of age, while not excluding some who are unable to work for one reason or another, includes in the population relevant to the per capita personal income computation those who apparently prefer leisure or home-making to gainful employment.

While the differences among the variants are of significant size, the differences between the most conservative of these variants and total population are much larger and could have a substantial bearing on many problems to which the per capita personal income computation is appropriate.

By substituting total labor force for total population as the denominator in the per capita income computation, the relative interstate personal income differentials are reduced by 14 to 23 percent. This is an appreciable narrowing of the area in which explanations of the interstate income differentials are to be sought in terms of the composition of industry, of skills, and of resources. It also marks out the area in which explanations might best be sought in terms of differences among states in the time spent in schools, the relative status of women in the home and in gainful employment outside the home, patterns of migration from lower- to higher-productivity areas, urban-rural differentials among states, the average age of the mother when the first child is born, and similar demographic factors.

City Size[15]

A tendency for individual and family income to increase with city size has been observed repeatedly and has made the core of a number of explanatory hypotheses by students of the spatial distribution of income.[16]

[15] This section is based largely on Edwin Mansfield, "City Size and Income, 1949," in *Studies in Income and Wealth,* 21 (Princeton, 1957), 271-307; "Community Size, Region, Labor Force, and Income, 1950," *Review of Economics and Statistics,* 37 (1955), 418-423; "Some Notes on City Income Levels, 1949," *ibid.,* 38 (1956), 474-481; and on unpublished materials Mansfield prepared while he was a research associate with the Study of Differences in State Per Capita Incomes.

[16] Those who rely most heavily upon the association between income and city size apparently would be willing to use a sample of cities, drawn from differing regions but from the same size class, as the basis of regional studies. See Robert M. Williams, "Comment," *Studies in Income and Wealth,* 21 (Princeton, 1957), 179-185. Others suggest that the differences in city-size composition provide an explanation of the observed

Some of these hypotheses are relevant, either directly or tangentially, to the use of the 48 states as a regional framework. Consequently, the findings based on the *Census of Population, 1950,* the first comprehensive body of data reflecting consumer-unit income by the city-size characteristics of place of residence, are worthy of review in a study devoted primarily to state income differentials.

Although there is some tendency for income level to increase with city size, the dispersion within cities of similar size is also important (table 49). In general, the difference between one city-size group and the group immediately above it tends to be moderate. In two instances, the differences are negative, and the difference exceeds $200 in only one

TABLE 49
MEAN MEDIAN INCOMES, BY CITY SIZE, 1949

City size in 1950[a]	Number of cities	Mean median income[b]	Standard deviation
Urban places outside standard metropolitan areas			
2,500- 4,999	1,351	$2,409	$691
5,000- 9,999	779	2,372	611
10,000-24,999	500	2,546	594
25,000-49,999	156	2,558	593
Standard metropolitan areas			
50,000- 99,999	17	2,798	511
100,000-249,999	74	2,683	485
250,000-499,999	44	2,860	370
500,000 and over	33	3,027	327

[a]Size is designated in terms of number of inhabitants. An urban place is an incorporated city or town having 2,500 or more inhabitants, or an unincorporated place of like size located outside the urban fringe of another city, town, or metropolitan area. A standard metropolitan area is a county, or group of contiguous counties, which contains at least one city of 50,000 or more inhabitants and which is essentially metropolitan in character. See *Census of Population, 1950*, vol. 2, Introduction.

[b]The figures shown are the unweighted means of the median incomes of consumer units (in census terminology, "families and unrelated individuals") reported for the cities in the class. The 1949 median income of all consumer units in the United States was $2,619. The corresponding median incomes of the consumer units living in urban areas was $2,970; in rural nonfarm areas, $2,186; and in rural farm areas, $1,567.

Source: Edwin Mansfield, "City Size and Income, 1929," *Studies in Income and Wealth*, vol. 21, Princeton, 1956, p. 275.

income differences of two or more areas. See John L. Fulmer, "Factors Influencing State Per Capita Income Differentials," *Southern Economic Journal,* 16 (1950), 259-278; D. Gale Johnson, "Some Effects of Region, Community Size, Color, and Occupation on Family and Individual Income," in *Studies in Income and Wealth,* 15 (New York, 1952), 49-66; and Milton Friedman and Simon Kuznets, *Income from Independent Professional Practice,* New York, 1945. The central city of a large metropolitan area has been viewed as a nodal point which, together with the hierarchy of smaller cities and open country surrounding it, becomes the basis for defining a "region" which has some economic significance and is thus considered worthy of study. Although the nodal region is the subject for investigation, rather than an explanation of state differences, apparently state boundaries would bisect some nodal regions. See Rutledge Vining, "Regional Variation in Cyclical Fluctuations Viewed as a Frequency Distribution," *Econometrica,* 13 (1945), 183-213; "Location of Industry and Regional Patterns of Business-Cycle Behavior," *ibid.,* 14 (1946), 37-68; and "The Region as a Concept in Business-Cycle Analysis," *ibid.,* 14 (1946), 201-218. For citations of earlier works investigating the existence of the income and city-size association, see Mansfield, "City Size and Income, 1949," *loc. cit.*

instance, between the 25,000-49,999 and the 50,000-99,999 groups. It is when the two size classes being compared are widely separated that large and significant differences can reasonably be expected.

The maximum difference in the mean median incomes of two city-size classes, found between cities of 5,000-9,999 and standard metropolitan areas of 500,000 and more inhabitants, is $655. This difference is an impressive 22-28 percent of the mean median incomes for these groups of cities, and despite the large standard deviations within each group of cities, it is clearly significant.[17] The income level of the group of cities with 5,000-9,999 inhabitants, while lower than that found in cities with 2,500-4,999 inhabitants, differs significantly from that in the groups with 10,000 or more inhabitants. The two groups of cities with 10,000-49,999 inhabitants, however, have income levels which do not differ significantly from the groups with 50,000-249,999 inhabitants. The standard metropolitan areas with 50,000-99,999 inhabitants have a mean median income which differs significantly only from that of cities with fewer than 10,000 inhabitants. The data seem to indicate that fewer and broader classes would be required if all of the income differences among city-size classes are to be statistically significant.[18]

When a table is constructed showing data similar to those in table 49 for each of the nine census regions, the tendency for income level to increase with city size persists. In four of the regions the lowest mean median income in a city-size group differs from the highest by more than the $655 difference found for the nation. In only two regions is the range among city-size groups more than $100 lower than that figure.[19] Perhaps of more importance, the difference in the mean median incomes of the nine regions within each of the city-size classes is larger than the $655

[17] Based on a *t*-test and using the .05 level of probability. Other significant differences in income levels are found between cities with 2,500-4,999 and those with 10,000 or more inhabitants; cities with 5,000-9,999 and those with 10,000 or more inhabitants; cities with 10,000-24,999 or with 25,000-49,999 and those with 250,000 or more inhabitants; and among the groups of standard metropolitan areas with 100,000 or more inhabitants. *Ibid.*, table 4.

[18] Mansfield, *ibid.*, suggests four groups: 2,500-9,999; 10,000-249,999; 250,000-499,999; and 500,000 and more inhabitants. He presents some evidence that 175,000 might provide a better breaking point than 250,000 inhabitants.

[19] *Ibid.*, table 3. The range of mean median incomes among city-size groups, by region, is:

New England	$579	East South Central	$814
Middle Atlantic	570	West South Central	878
East North Central	687	Mountain	329
West North Central	644	Pacific	294
South Atlantic	787		

difference between the largest and smallest mean median income for the city-size classes.[20] Thus, the nine census regions provide a significant classification of the median incomes of cities of similar size.[21]

Large regional differences, with each regional mean median income accompanied by a relatively small standard deviation, could give rise to large standard deviations on a national scale. This explanation of the large standard deviations in each of the city-size groups is only partially available. The standard deviations for most regional and city-size mean median incomes, although smaller than those for corresponding national city-size groups, remain large.[22] Regional location, thus, explains only a small fraction of the dispersion within the median incomes of cities of similar size.

When cities are classified according to number of inhabitants and to whether they are more or less than five miles from another city, it is found that those within five miles of another city tend to have higher median incomes. Such a classification has meaning only for urban places with fewer than 50,000 inhabitants; the standard metropolitan area concept used for larger places is based on whole counties, and if there was evidence of a connection between two of these, presumably they would have been included in the same standard metropolitan area. The larger differences in median incomes are found for cities with fewer than 5,000 inhabitants. In part, these differences are reflections of the regional

[20] The regional range of mean median incomes within each city-size class follows:

2,500- 4,999	$1,051	50,000- 99,999	817
5,000- 9,999	977	100,000-249,999	1,059
10,000- 24,999	1,129	250,000-499,999	944
25,000- 49,999	1,164	500,000 and more	688

[21] This statement is based on a ranking of the mean median incomes within each city-size class by region. See Milton Friedman, "The Use of Ranks to Avoid the Assumption of Normality Implicit in the Analysis of Variance," *Journal of the American Statistical Association,* 32 (1937), 675. The East South Central region has the lowest mean median income in each of the city-size groups, except the one for cities with 50,000-99,999 inhabitants. While the concordance in ranks is not so uniform for other divisions, they may be grouped in ascending order as follows: South Atlantic and West South Central; West North Central; New England, Middle Atlantic, and Mountain; and Pacific and East North Central.

[22] When the unweighted averages of the regional standard deviations for each city-size class are computed, they are found to be 81 to 87 percent of the national figures shown in table 49 for the urban places outside of standard metropolitan areas. Because of the limited number of standard metropolitan areas in each region, similar comparisons of acceptable reliability cannot be made for them. Both the regional and national standard deviations would be reduced by excluding cities in which college students are 10 percent or more of the number of consumer units. Students, often with only nominal incomes, exert a strong downward pressure on the median incomes of the cities in which they are concentrated.

concentrations of cities more or less than five miles from other cities. When these regional effects are removed, the observed income differences are reduced by about one-fourth among cities with 2,500-4,999 inhabitants and by about two-fifths among cities with 5,000-24,999 inhabitants, but are unaffected among cities with 25,000-49,999 inhabitants.[23] When these data are further classified by census region, the tendency for income level to increase with city size can be discerned among cities more than five miles from other cities in all but the Pacific region; such a tendency is not easily discerned among cities within five miles of another city. Moreover, the differences among regions in either group of cities exceed the differences among city-size groups within regions.[24] There is, however, a marked tendency for the income level of cities within five miles of another city to be higher than that of cities of similar size which are more remote from other cities.[25]

The large standard deviations attaching to the median incomes in each city-size class are changed only slightly by separating the cities according to whether they are more or less than five miles from another city. Moreover, the changes are often in opposite directions.[26] Thus, while there are significant differences both at the national and regional levels in the mean median incomes of cities of similar size according to whether they are more or less than five miles from another city, this fact does not account for the large standard deviations attaching to the mean median incomes of all cities of similar size.

The evidence presented so far is sufficient to point up the problem of relating city size to state income differentials. The two pertinent char-

[23] The mean median incomes of cities within five miles of another city exceed those of more remote cities, by city size, as follows:

City Size	*Observed*	*Adjusted for regional location*
2,500- 4,999	$400	$299
5,000- 9,999	221	126
10,000-24,999	240	138
25,000-49,999	145	149

[24] These differences among regions are significant. The differences between the three Southern regions and the remainder of the nation, however, are much more marked than are the differences within these broad regional categories.

[25] On the 36 possible comparisons afforded by the nine regions and four city-size classes, this tendency is found in 27. Only in the Mountain states do neighboring cities have lower mean median incomes than isolated cities in as many as three city-size classes.

[26] Among cities more than five miles from another city and of less than 25,000 inhabitants, the standard deviations are as much as 7 percent lower than those shown in table 49. Among such cities of 25,000-49,999 inhabitants, the standard deviation is 11 percent larger. Except for those of 10,000-24,999 inhabitants, in which the standard deviation remains practically unchanged, the cities which are within five miles of another city show an opposite change in the standard deviation.

acteristics of this evidence are: (1) The observed tendency for income levels and city size to move together is very broad and subject to many limitations. The dispersion within cities of similar size is often great enough to cast doubt on the reliability of the income-level and city-size function. (2) The differences among regions within city-size categories tend to be larger and more persistent than differences among city-size categories. The full use of the observed differences in mean median incomes by city size to estimate regional income levels could at best provide some indication of rank order, and even here it is doubtful whether rank order would be reasonably reliable at the subregional (i.e., state) level. Even within the nine census regions, there is marked dispersion within the city-size categories.

It may be possible to classify cities further in such a way that the dispersion within classes is brought within reasonable bounds. The search for such classificatory criteria may be expected to take much the same road as that followed in seeking to understand state income differentials. To what extent do the higher-skilled industries tend to locate in larger cities? Are the higher average earnings found in larger cities due to the demand for higher average skills? Are higher rates paid in large cities for a given skill? Do workers migrate toward larger cities during their most productive years and away from them after their peak is past? Is there a greater tendency in larger cities for more members of a family to work, and, if so, is this due to their age distribution, to the availability of employment, or to a lack of facilities for making use of leisure? Clearly, answers to these and many similar questions must be at hand before city-size differentials can be understood, and such an understanding is essential to the use of the income to city-size function to explain state income differentials.

Some of the difficulties of obtaining answers regarding the sources of dispersion among the median incomes of cities of similar size may be illustrated by reference to those personal characteristics on which the census of population provides information. Although the census provides information on occupational and industrial attachments, detailed information is not available by city size. Consequently, only information on age, sex, participation in the labor force, education, family status, and industrial type of employment can be utilized. Moreover, these demographic characteristics often can be brought to bear on the problem only indirectly.

While cities of various sizes typically differ significantly with respect to a specific demographic characteristic, the difference between the city-size category with the smallest and that with the largest median value is often smaller than the interregional differences within a city-size category (table 50).[27] Existing studies indicate that the percentage of males

TABLE 50

RANGES OF CITY-SIZE AND REGIONAL DIFFERENCES FOR SELECTED DEMOGRAPHIC CHARACTERISTICS, 1950

Characteristic	Unit of measure	Average ranges[a]	
		Among city-size classes (average of nine census regions)	Among census regions (average of eight city-size classes)
Percentage of persons 14 years old and older in the labor force			
Males	percent	3.5	5.0
Females	percent	6.1	8.8
Percentage of employed labor force in manufacturing	percent	12.1	35.2
Number of persons in the labor force per hundred consumer units[b]	number	14	21
Median number of school years completed by persons 25 years old or older	year	1.5	2.5
Number of males per thousand females	number	72	123
Percentage of population 65 years old or older	percent	1.8	4.4
Median age	year	2.4	5.0
Percentage increase in population, 1940-1950	percent	18.7	40.7

[a]For each of the eight city-size classes (used in table 49) in each of the nine census divisions, Mansfield developed frequency distributions for each characteristic of the city values reported by the *Census of Population, 1950*. From these distributions the median value for each city-size and regional group of cities was ascertained. Tables were then prepared for each characteristic showing the median values by city size cross-classified by census region. From these tables the ranges among city-size groups for each region, and among regions for each city-size group, were then computed. Cells containing only one city were excluded in computing these ranges. The figures in the first column are the unweighted means of the ranges between classes according to size; those in the second column are the unweighted means of the ranges between regions.

[b]The number in the labor force divided by the number of families and unrelated individuals, multiplied by 100. The number of families and individuals is based on a 20 percent sample of the population.

or females in the labor force, the number of persons in the labor force per consumer unit, the median number of school years completed by persons 25 years old or older, and, less clearly, the percentage of employed labor force in manufacturing industries might be expected to be directly associated with income level. Similarly, an inverse association might be expected between the percentage of population 65 years old and older and income level.[28] To the extent that a differential increase in a city's population reflects a growth of economic opportunity sufficient to induce the necessary immigration, a large growth rate could be expected to be accompanied by a rising income level. The other categories included in table 50 are composites of diverse forces, and little may be said a priori

[27] Except for the percentage of males 14 years old and older in the labor force, the number in the labor force per consumer unit, and the number of males per thousand females, the situation is not adequately represented by the averages since the smallest interregional range in any city-size category exceeds the largest city-size range within any region.

[28] In addition to the evidence presented in the previous section of this chapter, see Herman Miller, *Income of the American People,* New York, 1955, and Fulmer, *op. cit.*

TABLE 51

RANKS OF CITY-SIZE CATEGORIES WITH RESPECT TO SELECTED DEMOGRAPHIC CHARACTERISTICS, 1950
(Rank of average ranks)[a]

City-size[b]	Percentage of persons 14 years old and older in the labor force		Percent-age of employed labor force in manufac-turing	Number in the labor force per consumer unit	Median number of school years complet-ed	Number of males per thousand females	Percent-age of popula-tion 65 years old and older	Median age	Percent-age in-crease in popula-tion, 1940-1950
	Male	Female							
2,500- 4,999	2	1	1	4	1	4	7	5	1
5,000- 9,999	1	2	2	2	2	3	6	2	2
10,000- 24,999	6	6	3	3	5	2	4	3	3
25,000- 49,999	4	7	4	1	6½	1	5	6½	4
100,000-249,999	5	4	6	7	3	6	1	1	7
250,000-499,999	3	3	5	5½	4	7	3	4	6
500,000 and more	7	5	7	5½	6½	5	2	6½	5

[a]From a series of tables, one for each characteristic, in which the median values for each city-size group were cross-classified by region (see table 50, note a), the city-size categories were ranked from the lowest within each region. The unweighted average of the regional rank with each city-size category was then computed. These average ranks for each city-size category were then ranked and the results entered in this table.

[b]Since there are no standard metropolitan areas of 50,000-99,999 inhabitants in the Middle Atlantic, South Atlantic, and Pacific regions, this city-size category was omitted from the analysis. The rank of city-size category thus is based on only seven categories.

about their relation to the income level of an agglomeration, such as a city. It has been shown elsewhere that earnings vary with age and occupation, but the relationship is a nonlinear one. Typically, earnings increase from entrance in the labor force to a peak or plateau some time in the middle years and then decline rapidly thereafter.[29] But median age, being a measure of central tendency, could hardly be expected to show a similar relationship. For a city, median age is probably affected more by the number of children under working age and by the number of super-annuated persons who have withdrawn from the labor force than by the average age of those persons in the active labor force. Similarly, a large number of males per thousand females may be accompanied by a higher participation in the labor force, a factor which would tend to increase median incomes, or it may be accompanied by a larger proportion of unattached persons and associated with somewhat lower income levels.

While the differences among city-size classes are significant with respect to most of the demographic characteristics, often the higher medians for the demographic characteristics do not occur in the city-size classes with the higher incomes (table 51).[30] The percentage of the em-

[29] A number of examples are provided in Miller, *op. cit.*

[30] When the median values for each characteristic for each census region and city-size category are ranked in each region from the city-size category with the lowest value to that with the highest value, all of the characteristics except the percentage of males 14 years old and older in the labor force differ significantly by city size. However, it is not necessarily the larger city-size groups which have the higher incomes. The rank order test in Friedman, *op. cit.*, was used.

ployed labor force in manufacturing and the percentage increases in population during 1940-1950 tend to increase with city size. The number in the labor force per consumer unit and the number of males per thousand females are somewhat smaller in the cities with fewer than 50,000 inhabitants, though the rank order of the latter characteristic within the four city-size groups is a descending one.[31] As expected, the percentage of population 65 years old and older tends to decrease as city size increases.

The distributions of these five characteristics afford limited insight into the sources of income differences by city size. The patterns for the other characteristics cannot be summarized easily. For example, the median number of school years completed by persons 25 years old and older is as high in many regions in cities with 25,000-49,999 inhabitants as it is in cities with 500,000 or more inhabitants, and in too many regions it is higher in cities with 10,000-24,999 inhabitants than it is in cities with 100,000-499,999 inhabitants. Such evidence is poor support for the hypothesis that variations in educational attainments help to explain the city-size income differentials. Rather, it is further evidence of great dispersion in income and in other characteristics of cities of similar size.

The differences among regions, when an incomplete account is taken of variations in their city-size composition, tend to be larger than the differences among city-size categories (table 52).[32] The three Southern regions, which tend to have the lower income levels, do tend to have fewer males per thousand females and lower educational attainments, but they also have smaller percentages of the population 65 years old and older. They occupy an intermediate position with respect to population growth and concentration in manufacturing. The Western regions, which occupy intermediate income positions, tend to have the highest educational attainments, the most rapid population growth, and the largest male-female ratio. On the other hand, they have low concentrations in manu-

[31] Mansfield has shown that in all but the South Atlantic, Mountain, and Pacific regions there is a significant relationship between city size and the number in the labor force per consumer unit. Rural nonfarm areas were included when determining these relationships. See his "Community Size, Region, Labor Force, and Income, 1950," *loc. cit.*

[32] The regions were ranked within city-size groups, and the rank order tested to see whether the differences among regions were significant. The interregional differences were significant at the .001 level for every characteristic. The test basically is one of whether the regional ranking tended to be the same in every city-size category. With the highly significant differences among regions, it is doubtful whether reweighting of the regions to adjust for differences in city-size composition would affect the results materially. Explicit account was not taken of city-size composition other than to work with each category separately.

TABLE 52

RANKS OF REGIONS WITH RESPECT TO SELECTED DEMOGRAPHIC CHARACTERISTICS, 1950
(Rank of average ranks)[a]

Census region (arrayed by income level from the lowest)[b]	Percentage of persons 14 years old and older in the labor force		Percentage of employed labor force in manufacturing	Number in the labor force per consumer unit	Median number of school years completed	Number of males per thousand females	Percentage of population 65 years old and older	Median age	Percentage increase in population, 1940-1950
	Male	Female							
East South Central	1	7	5½	6	1	1	2	1	6
West South Central	6	3	2	4	4	6	3	4	8
South Atlantic	9	9	5½	7	2	2	1	3	5
West North Central	3	5	4	2	7	5	9	7	3
Mountain	7	1	1	3	9	8	4	2	7
New England	5	8	9	9	6	3	8	8	1
Pacific	2	2	3	1	8	9	5	6	9
Middle Atlantic	4	6	8	8	3	4	7	9	2
East North Central	8	4	7	5	5	7	6	5	4

[a]From a series of tables, one for each characteristic, in which the median values for each city-size group were cross-classified by region (see table 50, note a), and the regions, within each city size category, were ranked from the lowest. The unweighted average of the city size ranks within each region were then computed. These average ranks were then ranked and the results entered in this table.

[b]Based on the weighted mean median incomes in each city-size and rural category. The weights were consumer units. See Mansfield, "City Size and Income, 1949," *loc. cit.*, table 15.

facturing, low female participation in the labor force, and an intermediate percentage of persons 65 years old and older. Apparently there is no relation between the number of persons in the labor force per consumer unit in a region and the region's income level. Only New England and the West North Central regions have as low a rate of population growth as do the high income East North Central and Middle Atlantic regions. Thus, while the interregional differences within city-size classes are large and significant, there is no marked concordance between the ranks of the regions with respect to income and their ranks with respect to the demographic characterics here reviewed.

In part, these disturbing findings result from the omission from the analyses of those persons living in rural territory, about 36 percent of the total population. Often the demographic characteristics of the urban and rural populations differ by more than do those of the smallest and largest cities. Thus it is possible for regional income differences to show considerably more association with a specific demographic characteristic when the entire population is accounted for than when the analysis is based on urban residents alone. Of course, it is possible to include rural residents in the analyses and still make full use of the income differences by city size. Such a tack, however, does not seem very promising. This dispersion among cities of similar size, and within the rural farm and rural nonfarm areas among the regions, still remains to becloud the effect of the demographic characteristic on regional income.[33]

To introduce city size as a composite summary of the interrelated demographic and economic forces in the investigation of regional income differentials carries aggregation to an almost meaningless extreme. Much more is likely to be learned if city size, as a classificatory variable, is ignored and if the many demographic and economic variables, in their most detailed available form, are related to regional income. Such an approach will leave us with the problem of untangling the interrelationships between age and education, between this relationship and the number of workers per family, and so on through all of the combinations of factors which may have an important association with income level. While such an approach obviously is an arduous one, is likely to involve many false and unrewarding starts, and will falter and stop for lack of appropriate data to test promising hypotheses, it seems preferable to grasping at the thin hope of finding some classificatory device, such as city size, which will adequately reflect the relevant income-connected relationships.

[33] The relative quartile—that is, the semi-interquartile range divided by the median—within each of the eight city-size classes ranged from 3.5 to 9.1 percent for median age; from 5.9 to 10.6 percent for median number of school years completed by persons 25 years old or older; from 12.3 to 29.2 percent for the percentage 65 years old or older; from 2.9 to 5.5 percent for the number of males per thousand females; and from 42.3 to 92.0 percent for percentage increase in population between 1940 and 1950.

Appendix A

REGRESSION AND DIFFERENTIAL CHANGE, 1919-1949

The detailed results of regression analyses of the changes in state per capita incomes between all possible pairs of years from 1929 to 1949, and between each of the years from 1919 to 1921, paired with each other and with 1929, 1933, 1939, and 1949, are presented in this appendix. The data for 1929-1949 are from the state income payments series prepared by the National Income Division of the Department of Commerce, a series which was replaced in September 1955 by the state personal income series; those for the 1919-1921 period are the Leven estimates.[1] The techniques used here and a summary of the results of these analyses have been given in chapter 2.

Correlation

How well the regression lines describe the relationship of the state per capita incomes of one year to those of another is indicated by the coefficients of determination. The coefficients are consistently high, ranging from .54 for the per capita incomes of 1948 and 1932 to .99 for 1932 and 1933 (table 53). Since the year-to-year changes in state per capita incomes tend to be small, relative to their absolute magnitude, high coefficients might be expected from even a superficial examination of the basic data.[2]

Except in periods of very rapid inflation, large relative changes in a state's per capita income seem unlikely to be accomplished in a year or two. Real changes in per capita incomes, based on a fuller employment of resources or a shift from less productive to more productive uses of resources, require time to become effective. Consequently, we may also expect less

[1] Maurice Leven, *Income in the Various States, Its Sources and Distribution, 1919, 1920, and 1921*, New York, 1925.

[2] The size of the coefficients may be attributed in part to autocorrelation. This difficulty might be reduced by correlating the paired changes from one year to the next; for example, the changes from 1947 to 1948 with the changes from 1932 to 1933.

TABLE 53

Coefficients of Determination, State Per Capita Income Payments, 1929-1949

Regression on year	Regression of (year in caption on year in stub)									
	1930	1931	1932	1933	1934	1935	1936	1937	1938	1939
1929	.98	.97	.93	.93	.93	.96	.96	.97	.97	.96
1930		.99	.94	.94	.92	.95	.95	.95	.97	.95
1931			.98	.98	.96	.98	.97	.96	.97	.96
1932				.99	.98	.97	.96	.94	.95	.93
1933					.98	.97	.96	.94	.95	.93
1934						.98	.98	.96	.96	.95
1935							.99	.98	.98	.98
1936								.99	.98	.98
1937									.99	.99
1938										.99

Regression on year	Regression of (year in caption on year in stub)									
	1940	1941	1942	1943	1944	1945	1946	1947	1948	1949
1929	.95	.93	.78	.81	.85	.85	.85	.73	.71	.86
1930	.93	.91	.80	.82	.83	.85	.83	.69	.72	.85
1931	.94	.91	.77	.79	.78	.80	.80	.67	.64	.80
1932	.92	.89	.71	.73	.72	.73	.69	.55	.54	.71
1933	.92	.89	.71	.73	.73	.73	.69	.56	.55	.71
1934	.94	.90	.73	.75	.75	.75	.71	.59	.55	.73
1935	.97	.94	.80	.81	.80	.81	.79	.66	.65	.80
1936	.98	.95	.81	.83	.82	.83	.80	.67	.65	.82
1937	.98	.96	.82	.85	.84	.85	.82	.70	.67	.85
1938	.98	.95	.82	.85	.84	.86	.83	.70	.69	.85
1939	.99	.96	.84	.86	.85	.86	.85	.72	.70	.87
1940		.97	.86	.88	.86	.88	.86	.74	.71	.87
1941			.89	.92	.90	.89	.86	.77	.73	.87
1942				.95	.91	.92	.88	.80	.75	.87
1943					.96	.92	.87	.80	.76	.88
1944						.97	.90	.86	.82	.90
1945							.97	.92	.88	.94
1946								.93	.94	.95
1947									.92	.91
1948										.91

correlation when the time-spread between the years correlated is extended. Not only do the coefficients tend to become smaller as the spread between the years is lengthened, but they tend to become more disperse (table 54). For contiguous years, the coefficients of determination are in the narrow range between .89 and .99, with an average of .97. As the period of time is lengthened, the average coefficient decreases and the relative range tends to increase, at least so long as there are as many as four or five coefficients available for averaging. The reverse tendency when there are very few coefficients available, shown near the bottom of table 54, may be due to peculiarities of the specific years treated (1929, 1930, 1948, and 1949). The fact that the coefficients for 1929-1953 and 1929-1954 are both .88 (chapter 2) suggests, however, that the correlations during the 1931-1947 period

TABLE 54

AVERAGE COEFFICIENTS OF DETERMINATION, REGRESSION OF EACH YEAR, 1930-1949, ON EACH EARLIER YEAR, 1929-1948

Number of years intervening between pair related	Number of coefficients used in average	Average coefficient of determination	Range of coefficients		Relative range (percent)
			Highest	Lowest	
0	20	.97	.99	.89	11
1	19	.95	.99	.86	14
2	18	.93	.98	.84	15
3	17	.91	.98	.80	19
4	16	.89	.97	.76	23
5	15	.88	.96	.75	24
6	14	.87	.97	.73	28
7	13	.85	.97	.71	30
8	12	.83	.97	.70	33
9	11	.81	.96	.69	34
10	10	.78	.95	.67	35
11	9	.76	.93	.65	37
12	8	.73	.82	.59	32
13	7	.72	.83	.55	38
14	6	.72	.85	.55	42
15	5	.72	.85	.54	43
16	4	.72	.84	.64	29
17	3	.75	.80	.72	11
18	2	.78	.85	.71	17
19	1	.86	.86	.86	..

were disturbed by the differential changes occasioned by the great depression and the mobilization for World War II, and that since 1947 the pattern of state per capita incomes is again becoming more like that of 1919-1921 and 1929.

Each year from 1929 to 1949 enters 20 regressions as either a dependent or independent variable. When viewed as only the dependent variable, the coefficients of determination are all above .88 for the years 1930-1941 (table 55). In 1942, the first full year of an all-out war effort, the coefficients average only .79. They were somewhat higher during 1943-1946 but dropped to .73 in 1947, the first year of full-scale post-war production. By 1949 the average coefficient had risen to .85. When treated as the independent variable, 1933 seems to have less relation to the later years.

Although high coefficients imply correspondingly low standard errors of estimate, there is some interest in the actual magnitude of these standard errors since they provide a measure of the dispersion around the regression line. The standard errors range from a low of $10 for 1932 and 1933 to a high of $191 for 1932 and 1948. Like the coefficients of determination, the errors tend to vary as the spread between the years correlated is increased (table 56).

Only a limited number of regressions on 1919-1921 were computed. In addition to the relations among the three years, these years were the

TABLE 55

AVERAGE COEFFICIENTS OF DETERMINATION, 1929-1949, BY YEAR

Year	When year is treated as: Dependent variable: Number of determination coefficients	Dependent variable: Determination coefficients: Average	Dependent: Range: High	Dependent: Range: Low	Independent variable: Number of determination coefficients	Independent: Determination coefficients: Average	Independent: Range: High	Independent: Range: Low
1929	0	...	...	...	20	.89	.98	.71
1930	1	.98	...	...	19	.88	.99	.69
1931	2	.98	.99	.97	18	.87	.98	.64
1932	3	.95	.98	.93	17	.82	.99	.54
1933	4	.96	.99	.93	16	.81	.98	.55
1934	5	.95	.98	.92	15	.81	.98	.55
1935	6	.97	.98	.95	14	.85	.99	.65
1936	7	.97	.99	.95	13	.86	.99	.65
1937	8	.96	.99	.94	12	.86	.99	.67
1938	9	.97	.99	.95	11	.85	.99	.69
1939	10	.96	.99	.93	10	.85	.99	.70
1940	11	.95	.99	.92	9	.85	.97	.71
1941	12	.93	.97	.89	8	.85	.92	.73
1942	13	.79	.89	.71	7	.87	.95	.75
1943	14	.83	.95	.73	6	.87	.96	.76
1944	15	.83	.96	.73	5	.89	.97	.82
1945	16	.84	.97	.73	4	.93	.97	.88
1946	17	.82	.97	.69	3	.94	.95	.93
1947	18	.73	.93	.55	2	.91	.92	.91
1948	19	.71	.94	.54	1	.91	...	...
1949	20	.85	.95	.71	0	...	...	...

independent variables in regression analyses in which the years 1929, 1933, 1939, and 1949 were the dependent variables. With four exceptions, all of the coefficients of determination were above .80.[3] However, the coefficients tend to be smaller than those found in the later period, even when the number of years intervening between the dependent and independent variables is taken into account. Among the contiguous pairs of years chosen from the 1929-1949 period, none has a coefficient as low as that of 1920-1919, and only six have coefficients as low as 1921-1920. Although the period of 1919-1921 was a period of postwar readjustments, the level of the coefficients suggests that the annual estimates of per capita income for 1919-1921 are not as consistent from year to year as those for 1929-1949. Indeed, the consistency in the National Income Division series

[3] The coefficients of determination for the 15 pairs of years correlated follow:

Independent variable	*Dependent variables* 1920	1921	1929	1933	1939	1949
1919	.88	.83	.78	.65	.77	.86
1920		.96	.88	.81	.87	.81
1921			.87	.84	.85	.78

TABLE 56
AVERAGE STANDARD ERROR OF ESTIMATE, REGRESSION OF EACH YEAR, 1930-1949, ON EACH EARLIER YEAR, 1929-1948

Number of years intervening between pair related	Number used in average	Average standard error of estimate	Range of standard errors of estimate		
			Highest	Lowest	Relative range (percent)
0	20	$ 37	$ 84	$ 10	200
1	19	48	94	18	158
2	18	55	102	21	147
3	17	63	122	22	159
4	16	70	135	29	151
5	15	76	142	29	140
6	14	82	147	25	149
7	13	89	149	27	137
8	12	98	154	26	131
9	11	107	157	33	116
10	10	116	161	41	103
11	9	126	167	55	89
12	8	137	181	115	48
13	7	140	188	108	57
14	6	137	189	96	68
15	5	140	191	97	67
16	4	143	170	100	49
17	3	136	146	118	21
18	2	127	148	106	33
19	1	98	98	98	..

is achieved only through a process of continuous revision, a process not available to investigators making a one-time study.

ARE THE REGRESSIONS LINEAR?

Regression is presumed linear unless there is clear evidence to the contrary.[4] What is the nature of this evidence? Probably the most clear-cut test is to fit a curve to the data and then test to ascertain whether the improvement in fit is greater than could be expected by chance. Since one degree or more of freedom is sacrificed in fitting the curve, a somewhat better fit may be expected. The test applied (analysis of variance) tells in probability terms whether the improvement in fit is smaller or larger than might be expected to result from chance alone when a curve is fitted to data which are truly linear.[5] The improvement in the fit, degrees of freedom considered, is more than can be reasonably attributed to chance, then we may conclude that the regression is nonlinear. Second-degree parabolas fitted experimentally to the data for several pairs of years often provided an even poorer fit than a straight line.[6] Straight

[4] Croxton and Cowden, *Applied General Statistics*, New York, 1939, p. 692; Frederick C. Mills, *Statistical Methods*, New York, 1938, pp. 502 ff.

[5] G. Udny Yule and Maurice G. Kendall, *An Introduction to the Theory of Statistics*, New York, 1950 (14th edition), pp. 519-520.

[6] A line of the type $Y = a + bX + cX^2$ often curves the wrong way at the lower end of the scale because of the positions of a few states.

lines fitted to the logarithms of state per capita incomes apparently yield a better fit than straight lines fitted to their dollar amounts.[7] The desirability of making the transformation to logarithms is discussed in the text.

Another test for linearity, somewhat less precise than analysis of variance, is based on the expectation that if the data are linear, the individual points representing particular states will be randomly distributed about the regression line. Such a random distribution would show up as a tendency for the states, as we move from lower to higher incomes, to be alternately above and below the regression line. Particularly, we would expect to find an absence of blocking—that is, for states in particular ranges (with respect to the earlier of the two years paired) to be consistently above or consistently below the regression line. If, for example, the "block" of 16 states with the lowest incomes and the "block" of 8 states with the highest incomes in 1929 were all below the 1945-1929 regression line, while the "block" of the remaining 24 states with middle incomes in 1929 were above it, we could use this evidence of blocking to conclude that the regression was nonlinear. Such an extreme example, given for purposes of exposition only, is not to be found in the data studied. Rather, an examination of the charts shows some scatter about the line throughout the range of the data. A somewhat more realistic description of the data, but still by way of example, would be for only 5 of the lowest 16 states and 2 of the topmost 8 states to be above the line of regression, while 8 of the middle 24 states were below the line of regression. A visual inspection of such a scatter diagram gives the impression of a lack of linearity.

The number of consecutive states in an array that are on one side of the regression line is called a run.[8] In a truly linear regression, the chances are about even that a specific state will be on a particular side of the regression line. But chance alone would be sufficient to provide runs greater than one, just as in flipping true coins, where chances also are even, we do not expect a true coin to alternate regularly between heads and tails. However, a run of three or more states would occur by chance alone only about 3 times out of 100; a run of four or more states less than 2 times out of 100; and a run of five or more states less than once in 100 times.

[7] The comparison is between two straight lines, one on natural scales, the other on log scales, and there is a question whether the transformation to logarithms involves the sacrifice of one or two degrees of freedom, or none.

[8] A run is terminated (in each direction) when the next consecutive state in an array is either on (actually, within approximately $10 of) the regression line or is on the opposite side. In counting the runs, a run was terminated when two states with the same per capita income lay on opposite sides of the regression line.

An examination of the 210 scatter diagrams to which regressions have been fitted for the 1929-1949 period reveals that 131 of the regressions contain runs of five or more states and 92 of these contain runs of six or more. On 80 of these 131 diagrams only one run of five or more was found; 40 contained two such runs, 10 contained three, and one, that for 1945 on 1937, contained four runs of five or more.

The presence of an improbable run cannot be interpreted as conclusive evidence that the regression in which it occurs is nonlinear. Account must also be taken of the position of the cluster of states composing the run, and of the distribution of the other states about the regression line. A single run of five or more states near the center of the distribution, in which the departures from the regression line are not marked, might well be consistent with linear regression. Even a long run near the end of the distribution might be found in a regression which otherwise appeared best described as linear. The presence of a run, however, makes the linearity of the regression suspect and warrants further tests. Particularly suspect are regressions with two or three runs of five or more states in which the runs near the ends of the distribution are in the same direction and opposite to the run near the center of the distribution.

Too, there is a lack of independence (each of the 21 years treated appears as either the dependent or independent variable in 20 diagrams) among the regressions. However, the large number of runs is imposing evidence of the prevalence of blocking, if not of the presence of nonlinearity. That the lack of independence is not crucial is indicated by the fact that runs or five or more states are found in the diagrams for all 21 of the years. The number of diagrams containing such runs range from six for 1934 and 1935 to 18 for 1942, 1947, and 1948. Although more runs might be expected for the years at or near the end of the period, since long periods could intervene between the years paired, the average number of runs, 10.6 for the middle five years, 1937-1941, was only slightly less than the average, 12.5, for the entire period.[9]

The use of runs, rigorously defined as they are, as a test of linearity may miss some fairly wide departures from linearity. It is possible to think of regression in which there are no runs of more than three states (that is, the runs found could be attributed to chance), while all but a few states at both ends of the distribution are below the line of regression and

[9] This count by year was obtained by counting each run twice: once for the year when it was treated as the independent variable and once for the year when treated as the dependent variable.

those in the center of the distribution are mainly above the line, a situation that is clearly nonlinear.

To some extent the problem last mentioned can be overcome by grouping states and using the position of the group average with respect to the regression line as a criterion. For convenience, class intervals of $100 have been used.[10] A review of the charts on which the class averages have been plotted and connected by straight lines seems to indicate that in most cases the $100 class intervals provide a reasonably satisfactory criterion for determining departures from linearity.

Of the 210 regressions based on 1929-1949 there were 36 that had as many as four consecutive $100 class averages on one side of the regression line. Twenty-two of these occurred in the regressions of 1947-1949 on earlier years. But 134 of the regressions contained runs consisting of as many as three classes (table 57). Most of these runs of three or more $100 class averages are in the center of the distribution and are positive, although about one-fourth of the runs include either the lower or the upper terminal class, indicating some tendency for the shape of the regression curve to be lower at each end and higher in the center. This conclusion is reinforced by the fact that the lowest class in 172 pairs of years and the highest class in 156 pairs of years are below the regression line.[11] However, the 210 regressions are not independent.[12] The lack of

[10] This method immediately raises the problem of the best way in which to group the states. One method would be to array the states with respect to their incomes in the earlier of the paired years, which is treated as the independent variable, and then to divide the array into 6, 8, or 12 equal groups. Such a method could assure enough states in each group to provide a meaningful average. It also involves the construction of 20 arrays, and some difficulty in pairing and computing averages for the year treated as the dependent variable. From a computational standpoint, it is somewhat easier to divide the states into groups according to class intervals with fixed limits. Such a method should give us results similar to those derived from classes equal in numbers of states, although it may be affected by the limits picked and extreme classes may have too few states to provide meaningful averages. The $100 classes used provide classes ranging from five in the depression years to ten during the late 1940's. Terminal classes with only one or two states were omitted from the analysis. Obviously, the use of a different interval—e.g., $50—would have yielded slightly different results. Similarly, the use of intervals of $100 with the limits falling on 25's, 50's, or 75's rather than on the even 100's used might also give rise to small differences.

[11] If the regressions were independent and truly linear, we might expect approximately half of the regressions to have averages for the terminal classes below the line, about half above, with a standard deviation of 3.46. As many as 116 pairs below the line would then exceed three standard deviations.

[12] There are 20 regressions based on 1929, 19 based on 1930, etc. For 1946-1948 there are only from one to three regressions in which these are the base years. Peculiarities of 1929 can therefore affect the 20 regressions for which it is the base year (treated as the independent variable). The peculiarities of the state per capita incomes in a year like 1941 affect some 8 regressions when it is treated as the independent variable and another

TABLE 57

POSITION OF RUNS OF THREE OR MORE CLASS AVERAGES FROM REGRESSION LINE, STATE PER CAPITA INCOME PAYMENTS, 1929-1949

Regression on (independent variable)	Total number of regressions	Regressions with runs of 3 or more consecutive ($100 interval) classes					
		Above regression line			Below regression line		
		Not including terminal class	Including: Upper class	Including: Lower class	Not including terminal class	Including: Upper class	Including: Lower class
1929	20	11	1	1	1		
1930	19	2	3	3	5		
1931	18	5	1		2		
1932	17	13					
1933	16	12	1				
1934	15	6	3				
1935	14	1					
1936	13	1	1			1	
1937	12	6	1		1		
1938	11	5			1	1	
1939	10	3	1				
1940	9	6					
1941	8	4				1	
1942	7	3	4				3
1943	6	4					
1944	5	2				2	4
1945	4						2
1946	3						1
1947	2	2			1		1
1948	1	1					
Totals	210	87	16	4	11	5	11

independence means that the totals over the several years may arise from the effects of only a few years, while the others may conform to what may be expected from a linear situation. A check of the regressions having the same year as the base eight or more times indicates that either the lowest or topmost class is below the regression line frequently enough to be at least two standard deviations beyond the half-way mark for 10 of the 13 base years. Of the remaining seven base years, all but two have the lowest class below the regression line for every year.[13]

To test further this inconclusive evidence, regression lines were fitted to the logarithms of per capita incomes for some 45 pairs of selected years.[14] Eighteen of the 45 regressions provide significantly better fits

12 when it is treated as the dependent variable. Nineteen forty-nine, never treated as the independent variable, is the dependent variable in 20 regressions.

[13] The standard deviation for seven regressions is 1.32, so that if all seven lower classes are below the regression line, it deviates from expectation by less than three standard deviations. Consequently, the behavior of the deviations can best be described in terms of uniformity.

[14] The years were selected, for the most part, on the basis of other evidence that the regressions were nonlinear. A few cases were included, however, when there was no previously developed evidence that the regressions were nonlinear.

than do the linear regressions fitted to the dollar amounts.[15] More than half of the cases in which the logarithmic regressions provided a superior fit had been indicated to be nonlinear by the other tests, but this is also the case when the logarithmic regression did not provide a superior fit. Furthermore, the logarithmic regressions seemed to yield a significantly better fit in a few cases in which there was no other evidence that regressions on the dollar amounts were anything but linear. Consequently, further efforts to fit linear regression lines to the logarithms were halted.

Only a limited analysis has been made of the 15 regressions in which one of the years from 1919 to 1921 is the base. Except for three pairs of years, 1929 and 1939 with 1920, and 1939 with 1921, all of the regressions contained at least one run of five or more states. Two pairs of years contained four such runs, and the three such runs in the regression of 1939 on 1919 are of a pattern that indicates curvilinear regression. An examination of the scatter diagrams for this group of regressions indicates that the evidence of nonlinearity is about of the same order as for the 1929-1949 period.

The voluminous, though partially conflicting, evidence of departures from linearity, is summarized in table 58. There is one case in which

TABLE 58

RESULTS OF VARIOUS TESTS OF LINEARITY

Category	Pairs of years for which regression lines were not fitted to logarithms	Pairs of years for which regression lines fitted to logarithms were		Totals
		Not significant	Significant	
1. No runs of 3 or more $100 classes or 5 or more states.	40	2	1	43
2. One run of 3 or more $100 classes but no runs of 5 or more states	29	4	3	36
3. No runs of 3 or more $100 classes but one run of 5 or more states	24	5	3	32
4. One or more runs of 3 or more $100 classes and one run of 5 or more states	37	6	5	48
5. No runs of 3 or more $100 classes but two or more runs of 5 or more states	12	3	0	15
6. One or more runs of 3 or more $100 classes and two or more runs of 5 or more states	23	7	6	36
Totals	165	27	18	210

the only evidence of nonlinearity is the significantly better fit provided by the logarithmic regression line. There are numerous cases in which the results of the tests based on $100 classes are inconsistent with the tests based on runs of individual states. More important, the data indicate that

[15] The .05 level of probability was used. In testing the significance of the fit, it was assumed that only one degree of freedom was sacrificed—i.e., that the test related to a simple curve without point of inflection on a natural scale.

the logarithmic regressions provided significantly better fits about as often when the simpler tests failed to indicate nonlinearity as when they did. Taken together, these three series of tests leave some, though not necessarily prevailing, doubt as to the linearity of all but 42 of the 210 regressions. At the same time, they provide no more than an indication of the shape of the regression for all but 18 of the 168 regressions for which there is some evidence of nonlinearity.

The inconsistencies among the various tests, the lack of independence among the regressions, and the fact that many of the departures from linearity occur near the lower extremes of the distribution suggest that a more meaningful interpretation may be found in the peculiarities of particular states than in a continued effort to test for linearity. If Arkansas, for example, which has one of the lower state per capita incomes, is low because of a set of circumstances particular to that state, these circumstances may exert a depressing effect and act as a barrier to the orderly growth of income over a long period; yet forces making for some regression toward the mean state per capita income may be at work. Of course, every state has circumstances particular to it. When these particular forces are stronger than the forces making for regression, there is likely to be a marked departure of the state from the regression line. We now turn to an examination of the departures of each of the states from the linear regression line.

If the forces responsible for the position of states on one side or the other of the regression line were temporary and soon gave way to other temporary forces or to the forces making for regression, we might expect the departures of each state from the regression line to be in one direction about as often as in the other. When, however, there is a tendency for the departure of a state to be markedly in one direction, either above or below the regression line, there is reason to believe that more persistent forces are affecting the state's development.[16] Eighteen states were below and 14 states above the linear regression line too frequently to be attributed to the operation of temporary forces (table 59).

[16] If each of the 210 regressions were independent, and the departures due to chance forces, we would expect a mean number of departures above (or below) or on the regression line to be 105, with a standard deviation of 7.25. As many as 124 departures in one direction would be expected to occur only once in 100 times. Although the criteria of independence and randomness are not met, we shall use 124 or more departures in one direction as evidencing the operation of persistent forces. However, in preparing the counts, use was made of scatter diagrams, and only clear departures—i.e., points clearly separated from the regression line—were counted. A separate count was prepared of points on the line. Because of the size of the points and the scales used, a state as much as $10 from the regression line would be counted as on the line.

TABLE 59

POSITION OF STATES WITH RESPECT TO LINEAR REGRESSION LINES

Region and state	Frequency with which a state's position was: Above the regression line	On the regression line	Below the regression line	Rank (from most above to most below regression line)
New England				
Maine	26	15	169	45
New Hampshire	34	16	160	40
Vermont	23	25	162	42
Massachusetts	26	12	172	46
Rhode Island	31	12	167	43
Connecticut	105	31	74	19
Middle Atlantic				
New York	46	13	151	34
New Jersey	32	28	150	33
Pennsylvania	30	50	130	31
East North Central				
Ohio	145	26	39	9
Indiana	164	18	28	3
Illinois	142	16	52	11
Michigan	138	18	54	13
Wisconsin	140	35	35	12
West North Central				
Minnesota	89	34	87	23
Iowa	145	18	47	10
Missouri	57	32	121	29
North Dakota	158	25	27	4
South Dakota	157	15	38	6
Nebraska	131	16	63	14
Kansas	123	26	61	15
South Atlantic				
Delaware	96	23	91	25
Maryland	109	28	73	18
Virginia	73	30	107	26
West Virginia	37	21	152	35
North Carolina	36	19	155	38
South Carolina	36	21	153	36
Georgia	24	26	160	41
Florida	81	42	87	24
East South Central				
Kentucky	11	25	174	47
Tennessee	33	36	141	32
Alabama	23	29	158	39
Mississippi	11	17	182	48
West South Central				
Arkansas	17	25	168	44
Louisiana	28	28	154	37
Oklahoma	51	41	118	28
Texas	90	57	63	22
Mountain				
Montana	174	15	21	1
Idaho	146	25	39	8
Wyoming	100	31	79	21
Colorado	101	35	74	20
New Mexico	49	49	112	27
Arizona	59	28	123	30
Utah	111	46	53	17
Nevada	158	16	36	5
Pacific				
Washington	155	20	35	7
Oregon	165	18	27	2
California	122	29	59	16

There is some tendency for the states with lower per capita incomes to be found below the line of regression more frequently than the states with higher per capita incomes, but there is an even greater tendency for the states in a region to follow a similar pattern.[17] The states most

[17] The coefficient of rank correlation between the position of the state with respect to the regression line, ranked from the one most frequently above to the one most frequently

frequently above the regression line are found only in the North Central, Northwest, and Far West regions. Among the eight states in the North Central region, all but Minnesota and Missouri are found above the regression line more frequently than can be attributed to chance. Similarly, five of the nine states in the Northwest region—Idaho, Montana, Nebraska, North Dakota, and South Dakota—and all but California among the four states in the Far West are frequently above the regression line. The regional grouping of states found below the regression line too frequently to be attributed to chance is even more marked. Except for Connecticut in the Northeast, Delaware and Maryland in the Middle East region, and Virginia and Florida in the Southeast region, all the states in these regions are in this category.

When the states departing with significant frequency from the regression lines are distributed by size of 1929-1950 average per capita income, the states most frequently below the regression line are concentrated in the lowest quartile, while the states most frequently above the regression line are concentrated in the third quartile (table 60). This pattern of de-

TABLE 60

STATES DEPARTING FROM REGRESSION LINE IN ONE DIRECTION TOO FREQUENTLY TO BE ATTRIBUTED TO CHANCE, DISTRIBUTED BY SIZE OF 1929-1950 AVERAGE PER CAPITA INCOME PAYMENTS

1929-1950 average per capita income	Number of states too frequently	
	Above regression line	Below regression line
Lowest quartile	0	10
Second quartile	3	2
Third quartile	7	2
Highest quartile	4	4
Totals	14	18

partures suggests that the regressions are concave downward rather than linear.[18]

The departures of the states from the 15 regression lines which include

below the line, and the state's 1929-1950 average per capita income ranked from lowest, is —.41.

[18] Tests made by plotting the regression line fitted to the logarithms of per capita incomes on a natural scale for several pairs of years when the improvement in fit was highly significant indicate that the counts in table 59 would be changed only slightly if departures had been counted from the logarithmic regression line. Apparently, a regression line which would greatly reduce the number of states departing in a single direction to a frequency that could be attributed to chance would have more curve in it than the logarithmic regression line plotted on a natural scale. As mentioned before, efforts to fit such a line have not been fruitful.

one of the years from 1919 to 1921 as the independent variable show a different pattern. Fewer of the states depart in one direction frequently enough to justify saying that the departures are not due to chance. Even when the rules are relaxed for deciding whether the departures are consistently in one direction, there are 27 states which appear to be randomly distributed about the lines, and the other 21 states are equally divided as to direction of departures.[19] Except for South Carolina, which tends to be below the line in both sets of regressions, all of the Northeastern and Southeastern states which showed a tendency to be below the 1929-1949 regression lines appear to be fairly well described by the 1919-1921 regression lines. Similarly, most of the Central, Northwestern, and Far Western states, which tended to be above the 1929-1949 regression lines, show no significant departures from the 1919-1921 regression lines. Five states show opposite tendencies on the two sets of regressions. New York and New Jersey, significantly below the 1929-1949 regression lines, are above those for 1919-1921. The change is in the opposite direction for Oregon, Idaho, and South Dakota. The differences between the 1919-1921 and 1929-1949 distributions of individual state departures could arise by chance as often as five times out of 100.

Although there was considerable evidence developed in the last section that the regressions were nonlinear, the linear regression lines may be used as a basis for describing the behavior of individual states. The fact that the position of a state, whose income over the period is below the mean state income, is consistently below the regression line shows conclusively that the state did not regress toward the mean as much as would be indicated by linear regression. It cannot, however, be interpreted as indicating that the state did not regress toward the mean as much as other states. The latter interpretation presumes that linear regression is the best description of the expected behavior of the states. The evidence developed that this presumption is not true, at least for certain pairs of years, makes such an interpretation of doubtful validity.

If nonlinearity prevents a classification of states as to whether they have fared better or worse than could be expected, we can gain further knowledge of the shape of the regression line which does describe the expected pattern of the differential behavior of the states for the period of 1929-1949.[20]

[19] The rules were relaxed in two respects: (1) two rather than three standard deviations were adopted as the criterion for significance, and (2) some account was taken of the number of states counted as being on the line, since states could vary from the line by as much as $10 without being counted as a clear departure.

[20] The behavior of a state can be described in terms of its departure from any specific

Nine of the 10 states having the lowest per capita incomes over the period are Southern states and tend to occupy positions below the linear regression line more frequently than can be attributed to chance.[21] These states would be described by a line which curved downward at the lower end of the distribution. At the other end of the distribution the picture is not so clear. Among the 10 states with the highest per capita incomes, three tend to occupy positions above and four below the regression line. However, for pairs of years when there is a marked reduction in the coefficients of variation, all of these 10 states tend to be below the line of proportional change. This evidence on the best position of the regression line at the upper end of the distribution is weak and inconclusive. Of the remaining 28 states in the middle of the distribution of per capita incomes, 11 tend to occupy positions above and 5 positions below the regression line. The tendency for the states to occupy positions above the regression line is most marked just above the median, in the third quartile of the per capita income distribution. Among the 12 states in the third quartile, 7 tend to occupy positions above, and 2 states positions below, the regression line; in this quartile, the linear regression line appears somewhat low.

A regression line that started somewhat below the linear regression line at the lower end of the distribution, rose somewhat more rapidly to somewhere within the third quartile, and leveled off to a position about the same as or slightly lower than the linear regression line among the states at the upper end of the distribution, would appear to reduce the number of states departing from it with excessive frequency in one direction.[22] Such a line, though its exact position is unknown, would appear to give a better description of the average pattern of observed changes from one year to another during the period 1929-1949.

Even though some nonlinear regression line had been used as the point of reference for the construction of a table, such as table 59, showing

straight line. Both the line of proportionality (passing through the origin and the intersection of the means) and the least-squares regression line seem to provide a meaningful base for descriptive statements.

[21] They tend to occupy a position above the line of proportionality and below the linear regression line. Although a line fitted to the logarithms of state per capita incomes would be below the linear regression line in this income range, these states would also tend to be below it.

[22] For many pairs of years this description of the regression line seems consistent with the results of a visual inspection of the scatter diagrams. For some pairs of years the path of straight lines connecting the average per capita incomes of states grouped into $100 class intervals (according to the income of the earlier year) might be described similarly; when this was the case it was used as evidence of nonlinearity.

the number of departures from the regression line, the size of the deviations of some states from the linear regression line would be sufficient to insure their persistent departure from the nonlinear line. The Dakotas and Nevada are cases in point. The very rapid rise in income in these states following 1940 places them well above the regression lines when these years are included. In part, the large counts obtained in table 59, however, stem from the lack of independence among the regressions. A sharp rise in 1940 in the relative income of a single state, sufficient to place the state well above the line describing the regression of 1940 on 1939, probably will also be sufficient to place it well above the lines describing the regressions of 1940 on each of the earlier years from 1929 to 1938. This one increase may, therefore, be the basis of a count of 11 years in which the state was above the regression line. Even though its gain in relative position on the scale of state per capita incomes is not fully maintained in the next year, 1941, so that its position on the 1941-1940 scatter diagram is below the regression line, the state may still have gained sufficiently to place it above the regression lines on the scatter diagrams relating 1941 to the earlier years from 1929 to 1939. A further relative gain in 1941 would, of course, reinforce this tendency. Similarly, a short-lived relative loss in position on the scale of state per capita incomes during an early year of the period—e.g., 1931—would move it to the left along the X-axis and thus be sufficient to account for the state's position above the regression line for all years in which 1931 appeared as the independent variable. Such a short-lived loss in position might be due to accidental forces, such as a flood, drought, or extreme temperatures. It is exactly such accidental forces which might be expected to be responsible for departures from the regression line, and if the regressions were independent such forces might be expected to operate as often in one direction as in the other. With the lack of independence, however, the results of accidental forces operating in a single year may enter the counts several times.

Despite this lack of independence, table 59 does show the frequency with which the various states have fared better, about the same, or worse than the states as a whole on the (doubtful) assumption that linear regression, fitted either to the dollar amounts or to the logarithms of the per capita incomes, adequately describes the average changes for the 48 states. It must also be remembered that a variety of bases have been used in computing the estimated incomes with which to compare the observed incomes.[23] It would be remarkable, indeed, if each of these

[23] This statement looks upon the regression line as an estimate of income in the latter year based upon the income of the year treated as an independent variable.

bases gave precisely the same answer. The coefficients of determination based on linear regression are all very high, ranging as they do from .54 upward, with most of them greater than .80, so that the results of the estimates obtained from varying bases are tolerably close together. Nonetheless, a state in a year such as 1947 may be above the income expected when 1931 is used as a base, below the income estimated from a 1937 base, and have about the income estimated from a 1942 base. In table 59 each situation would give rise to a frequency.

It cannot be said, however, because Mississippi, for example, had less income than that estimated (by using the linear regression line) from previous years' incomes in 182 out of 210 cases, that there is a downward trend in the state. The fact that Mississippi consistently lies above the line of proportionality indicates that its per capita income has been increasing relatively faster than that of the United States. All that can be said is that Mississippi income has not increased as rapidly as would be indicated by a least-squares linear regression line. This situation is consistent with considerable growth—that is, with an increasing utilization of its existing industrial resources and some substitution of industries of higher productivity for those of lower productivity.

Appendix B

SOME NOTES ON STANDARDIZATION PROCEDURES[1]

THROUGHOUT this study extensive use is made of state rate-constant and state composition-constant earnings. The methods of computing such figures have a long history.[2] Typically, the purpose of computing such standardized figures as state rate-constant earnings is to facilitate comparisons between the industrial or occupational composition of two states without the disturbing influences of differences in earning rates. Often, however, such comparisons are accompanied by a desire to partition the difference between two observed figures among two or more factors.[3] In this study the rate-constant earnings are used to approximate the extent to which state compositional differentials statistically account for the variation in state earnings.

The analogous methods found in the literature for dealing with the composition-constant figures, which are product sums, in an additive framework require viewing each state as a separate classificatory factor. Moreover, the difficulties are multiplied when chief interest centers in the rate-constant figures.

It is possible to conceive of the problem in terms of variation, rather than arithmetic differences, but when it is so conceived new methods must be used.[4] This appendix describes one possible method in terms of the range of problems encountered in this study. The exposition starts

[1] During the course of preparing this appendix, I have benefited greatly from the comments of George H. Borts, Paul Boschan, Gerhard Bry, Edwin Goldfield, A. J. Jaffe, Maurice Liebenberg, Edwin Mansfield, Howard G. Schaller, and Irving H. Siegel on earlier drafts. Any errors or mistaken notions which remain are my responsibility.

[2] A number of the papers dealing with various aspects of the method have been reprinted in A. J. Jaffe, *Handbook of Statistical Methods for Demographers,* Washington, 1951. Such computed figures are sometimes known as "standardized" figures, and one framework in which they are analyzed is often referred to as the method of expected cases.

[3] This case is treated in Irving H. Siegel, *Concepts and Measurement of Production and Productivity,* Bureau of Labor Statistics, 1952.

[4] The methods proposed draw heavily upon M. G. Kendall, *The Advanced Theory of Statistics,* London, 1948, vol. 2, chap. 24.

with an examination of the applicability to these problems of the more familiar methods and of the reasons these methods were not accepted. The alternative methods used as tentative and provisional "solutions" to an essentially insoluble problem are then outlined and some of their attributes examined.

Notation

The notation of index numbers, to which the standardized figures are closely analogous, is adopted. Let

p represent earning rates (in this study these will usually be averages for the workers in an industry or occupation in a state or the nation),

q represent the composition element in relative terms, that is, the number of workers or man-hours relative to their total (by taking $\Sigma q = 1$, averages are obtained directly without loss of generality),

1, 2, . . n (subscripts) represents a particular state, and

0 (subscript) represent the nation.

Subscripts to denote particular industries or occupations will ordinarily be omitted, and the summation will be understood to be over all categories.

The Binary Case

The most frequent use of standardized figures is for the comparison of two groups, for example, for comparing the earnings of two states. The difference between the earnings of states *1* and *2* can be written:

$$\Sigma p_1q_1 - \Sigma p_2q_2 = \Sigma p_2(q_1 - q_2) + \Sigma q_2(p_1 - p_2) + \Sigma(p_1 - p_2)(q_1 - q_2) \qquad (1)$$

The left-hand side is the difference between the reported earnings of state *1* and state *2*. The first sum on the right is the rate-constant particle;[5] the second sum is the composition-constant particle; and the final sum is the joint particle. The weights used are those of state *2*, which may be said to have been taken as "standard." If state *1* weights are desired, the difference may be written:

$$\Sigma p_2q_2 - \Sigma p_1q_1 = \Sigma p_1(q_2 - q_1) + \Sigma q_1(p_2 - p_1) + \Sigma(p_2 - p_1)(q_2 - q_1) \qquad (1a)$$

[5] Since state *2* weights are being used, the rate-constant earning for state *2* is its reported earning, Σp_2q_2. The rate-constant earning for state *1*, using state *2* weights, is Σp_2q_1, and the rate-constant particle is the difference between the two rate-constant earnings, $\Sigma p_2q_1 - \Sigma p_2q_2 = \Sigma p_2(q_1 - q_2)$.

The differences in the weights may be of considerable consequence. The joint particle, however, will have the same sign and magnitude since the signs of the parenthetical terms are changed simultaneously as the subscripts are interchanged in going from equation (1) to equation (1a).[6]

As long as there is any correlation between $(p_1 - p_2)$ and $(q_1 - q_2)$ at the industrial or occupational category level, a joint particle will be present. This has led some investigators to suggest that standardization procedures should not be used to assay the relative importance of rates and composition in accounting for the difference between two sums of products, if there is any correlation between the factors. Others have suggested one or another method of partitioning the joint particle between the rate- and composition-constant particles. The most frequently suggested method for accomplishing this is to divide the joint particle equally between the rate- and composition-constant particles. Such a method is the equivalent of the use of the Edgeworth type of cross-weights[7] and is perhaps the most nearly consistent with acceptable assumptions concerning the distributions of the underlying factors.[8] There can be little objection to this method when the joint particle is the product of a correlation which does not depart significantly from zero. Still other investigators suggest that the joint particle be retained as a reminder that the

[6] Consider the following numerical example, in which there are three occupational or industrial categories and two states, and all of the particles have been computed.

Category	1 Rates (p_1)	1 Composition (q_1)	2 Rates (p_2)	2 Composition (q_2)	(p_1-p_2)	(q_1-q_2)	(p_{1+2})	(q_{1+2})
A	1.12	.60	1.67	.10	− .55	.50	1.395	.35
B	1.30	.10	1.90	.60	− .60	−.50	1.600	.35
C	1.50	.30	2.50	.30	−1.00	.0	2.000	.30

Category	p_1q_1	p_2q_2	$p_2(q_1-q_2)$	$q_2(p_1-p_2)$	$p_1(q_2-q_1)$	$q_1(p_2-p_1)$	$(p_1-p_2)(q_1-q_2)$
A	.672	.167	.835	−.055	−.560	.330	−.275
B	.130	1.140	−.950	−.360	.650	.060	.300
C	.450	.750	.0	−.300	.0	.300	.0
Sums	1.252	2.057	−.115	−.715	.090	.690	.025

Computations based on the above example yield the following percentage distributions for the two sets of weights:

Particle	State weights 1	State weights 2
Rate-constant	11.2	− 14.3
Composition-constant	85.7	− 88.8
Joint	3.1	3.1
	100.0	−100.0

[7] The Edgeworth cross-weights may be expressed, $p_{1+2} = (p_1 + p_2)$ and $q_{1+2} = (q_1 + q_2)$. The difference between two reported earnings then becomes:

$$\Sigma p_1q_1 - \Sigma p_2q_2 = \Sigma p_{1+2}\,(q_1 - q_2) + \Sigma q_{1+2}\,(p_1 - p_2).$$

[8] Unpublished manuscripts made available to me by Edwin Goldfield and by Gerhard Bry and Paul Boschan investigate this problem and come to this conclusion. Both manuscripts deal with changes over time.

rate- and composition-constant particles do not exhaust the difference between two sums of products.[9]

Whether or not there is a joint particle, there are several difficulties worthy of mention in the use of the relative size of the rate- and composition-constant particles as measures of the two sets of factors. When the relative sizes of the two particles are used as measures, the measures are nonoperative. Their use as operators will give rise to another "joint particle." This difficulty may be illustrated by reference to the index of manufacturing production.[10] Average 1939-1947 weights were used in constructing the index, so that there is no particle representing the joint effects of production and price changes. If the production and price indexes[11] are used as operators to account for the changes in the value added by manufactures, we obtain the following results:

Value added by manufactures:	
—1947	$74.4 billion
—1939	24.4
—Differences to be explained	50.0
Increase accounted for by:	
Production index: (174-100) x 24.4	18.1
Price index: (175-100) x 24.4	18.3
Increase unaccounted for by both indexes	13.6

The joint particle which appears in the above computation is many times the size of the difference between the composition (production) and rate (price) constant particles. How this particle is partitioned will affect the relative importance of the increases accounted for by the particles as used as operators. In this example the relative importance of the two factors is so nearly equal that an equal allocation of the increase unaccounted for by them will not affect their ratio. Where the two factors differ markedly, an equal allocation might change the ratio greatly.

Too, there is a question whether the two particles provide suitable bases for measuring their relative importance. When relative composition is used, so that $\Sigma q_1 = 1$, $\Sigma q_2 = 1$, etc., as it is here, then if some $(q_1 - q_2)$ are positive, others must necessarily be negative, and vice versa. Yet all $(p_1 - p_2)$ may have the same sign. Since all p's and all q's entering the computation are positive, the sign of the rate- and composi-

[9] Siegel, *op. cit.*

[10] *Census of Manufactures, 1947: Indexes of Production,* Bureau of the Census, 1952, pp. 2-4.

[11] The price index is derived as the ratio of the index of the change in the value added by manufactures to the production index.

tion-constant particles for a particular state will be determined by the sign of the parenthetical differences. When the products are summed, these signs are taken into account. Consequently, the rate-constant particle necessarily will be a net figure derived from adding algebraically some positive and some negative figures.[12] The composition-constant particle, however, may be cumulative in one direction.

To make use of the absolute size of the rate and composition differences between industries or occupations in building up a state's rate- and composition-constant earnings would overcome this difficulty. It would also destroy the basic identity in equation (1). The sum of the absolute particles, when the sum is taken over all industries or occupations, would more than exhaust the sum of the absolute observed differences.

Variation in the Binary Case

Recent decades have seen a growing preference for the use of variation rather than deviations in measuring dispersion. The question may be formulated in terms of how much of the total variation in the difference between the reported earnings of two states is due to the variation in rates, how much to the variation in composition, and how much to the two changing simultaneously. We shall be dealing with the variation within a state (among industries). While it is found convenient to work with variation rather than with variance, their distributions are the same.

The variation to be analyzed is the sum of the squared deviations of the differences between the reported industrial earnings and their mean differences—i.e., the difference between the average industrial earnings of the two states. Symbolically, this is $\Sigma[(p_1q_1 - p_2q_2) - \overline{(p_1q_1 - p_2q_2)}]^2$. When the variation for the right-hand side of equation (1) is computed, there are three interaction terms as well as terms for the three particles.[13] Computation can be simplified by combining the three particles into two and by combining the interaction terms so that their sum may be obtained by subtracting the independent variation of the two terms from total variation. The convenient but arbitrary cross-weights may be used to achieve this combination. When this method is used, the order of the factors on the left-hand side of equation (1) is immaterial; the right-hand side of the equation, with the summation signs omitted, is the same for

[12] Maurice Liebenberg has pointed out to me that the rate-constant earning may be derived as the sum of the products of positive figures. Basically, his method ignores all frequencies that are in the same category in the two distributions, and treats the remainder as shifting in only one direction.

[13] This may be seen from the expansion, $(a + b + c)^2 = a^2 + b^2 + c^2 + 2ab + 2ac + 2bc$.

$p_1q_1 - p_2q_2$ and $p_2q_2 - p_1q_1$. This method yields the following distribution of the variation, with the example in note 6 used for the numerical results given here and in the subsequent discussion of variation:

Source	Formula	Variation	Percent of total
Composition	$\Sigma[p_{1+2}(q_1 - q_2) - \overline{p_{1+2}(q_1 - q_2)}]^2$	1.1230	97.7
Rates	$\Sigma[q_{1+2}(p_1 - p_2) - \overline{q_{1+2}(p_1 - p_2)}]^2$	.0066	.6
Interaction	$2\Sigma[p_{1+2}(q_1 - q_2) - \overline{p_{1+2}(q_1 - q_2)}]$		
	$[q_{1+2}(p_1 - p_2) - \overline{q_{1+2}(p_1 - p_2)}]$	.0194	1.7
Total	$\Sigma[(p_1q_1 - p_2q_2) - \overline{(p_1q_1 - p_2q_2)}]^2$	1.1490	100.0

This method attributes more to composition than to rates, as is the case with absolute deviations. Unlike deviations, where the use of cross-weights eliminates the joint particle, it is present and weighted by the cross-weights.

The right-hand side of equation (1) may also be reduced to two terms by making use of the fact that when the joint particle is combined with one of the others, the combination has the weight of the other group. Thus, if the rate and joint particles in equation (1) are combined,

$$\Sigma q_2(p_1 - p_2) + \Sigma(p_1 - p_2)(q_1 - q_2) = \Sigma q_1(p_1 - p_2), \tag{2}$$

and the observed differences between the earnings in an industry in two states may be written:

$$p_1q_1 - p_2q_2 = p_2(q_1 - q_2) + q_1(p_1 - p_2), \tag{1b}$$

$$p_2q_2 - p_1q_1 = p_1(q_2 - q_1) + q_2(p_2 - p_1), \tag{1c}$$

$$p_1q_1 - p_2q_2 = p_1(q_1 - q_2) + q_2(p_1 - p_2), \tag{1d}$$

$$p_2q_2 - p_1q_1 = p_2(q_2 - q_1) + q_1(p_2 - p_1). \tag{1e}$$

Gaps in data often force an investigator to use one of these formulas.[14] Consequently, they are worth additional attention.

Using the numerical example in note 6, the following distribution of variation is obtained for equations (1b) and (1d).

[14] The occupational data are a case in point. Composition is available for each state, but state-specific earning rates are not. Consequently only state-weighted composition-constant rates can be computed. Samuel A. Stouffer has investigated the conditions under which "indirect" approximations may be used. See his "Standardization of Rates when Specific Rates are Unknown" in *Handbook of Statistical Methods for Demographers,* Bureau of the Census, 1951.

Source	Variations (based on deviations from their respective means)	Amount	Percent of total
	Rate particle approximated from formula (1b)		
Composition	$p_2(q_1 - q_2)$	1.5953	139
Rates	$q_1(p_1 - p_2)$	.0438	4
Interaction	$[p_2(q_1 - q_2)]\,[q_1(p_1 - p_2)]$	−.4901	−43
Total	$p_1q_1 - p_2q_2$	1.1490	100
	Composition particle approximated from formula (1d)		
Composition	$p_1(q_1 - q_2)$	.7334	64
Rates	$q_2(p_1 - p_2)$	.0522	4
Interaction	$[p_1(q_1 - q_2)]\,[q_2(p_1 - p_2)]$	.3634	32
Total	$p_1q_1 - p_2q_2$	1.1490	100

Although the percent of variation attributed to composition differs greatly, it is consistently larger than that attributed to rate variations. In this it follows the average deviation rather than the usual summation method. Since, for state 2 weights, equation (1b) yields the exact variation in composition, equation (1d) the exact variation in rates, and both of them the total variation, we can make use of these data to obtain by subtraction the interaction.

	Variation	Percent of total
Composition (from formula [1b])	1.5953	139
Rates (from formula [1d])	.0522	4
Interaction (by subtraction)[15]	−.4985	−43
Total (from left-hand side of formulas [1b] and [1d])	1.1490	100

The above distribution indicates that compositional differences, weighted by state 2 weights, can more than account for the observed differences in the two groups and that when these weighted composition

[15] Although obtained by subtraction, it can be shown that the joint particle is twice the sum of the products of $p_2\,(q_1 - q_2)$ and $q_2\,(p_1 - p_2)$ taken as deviations from their means.

differences are taken into account, state *1* (rather than state 2) earnings would be the larger. This is partially offset by the interaction, which is available to both the composition and rate particles. The rate particle also contributes slightly to the explanation of the observed differences; but if it is combined with the joint particle, the observed differences would be increased. These results reflect the inverse relationship between the weighted composition and rate differences in the joint particle.[16]

Similarly, formulas (1c) and (1e) provide exact estimates of the state *1* weighted variations, which are all positive:

	Variation	*Percent of total*
Composition (from formula [1c])	.7334	64
Rates (from formula [1e])	0.438	4
Interaction (by subtraction)	.3718	32
Total	1.1490	100

In this example it happens that the estimated distribution obtained from formula (1b) closely approximates the exact distribution when state 2 weights are used; the distribution estimated from formula (1d) approximates the state *1* weighted distribution. With complete data it is possible to use both sets of computations to ascertain the weight pattern being reflected. If data considerations force the use of only one of the approximation formulas (1b) and (1d), how can one know which of the two sets of weights are in the results?

The interaction, while available to both particles, must be either partitioned or viewed as the range of approximation in these measures. Apparently, the adoption of some convention or the making of an arbitrary decision is necessary to effect such a partition. Since the measures so obtained are subject to the limitations of the convention or decision adopted, little is gained by partitioning.

Variation among All States

In this study interest centers not so much in the comparison of the earnings in a single pair of states as in accounting for the variation in

[16] This may be seen from the following alternative ways of writing the variances of the joint particle:

$$\sigma^2_{[p_2(q_1-q_2)+q_2(p_1-p_2)]} = \sigma^2_{p_2(q_1-q_2)} + \sigma^2_{q_2(p_1-q_2)} + 2r\sigma_{p_2(q_1-p_2)}\sigma_{q_2(p_1-p_2)}$$

The sign of the joint particle variation will be the same as the sign of r, the coefficient of correlation between $p_2(q_1-q_2)$ and $q_2(p_1-p_2)$.

reported earnings among all states. For the multiple comparisons which are implied, a common set of weights is needed, and the average annual earnings of all earners in an industry and the national relative distribution of earners among industries have been adopted.

Formally stated, we wish to use $\Sigma p_o q_o$ as the standard rates and the standard composition, both for comparing states among themselves and for comparing states with the nation, when

$$\Sigma p_o q_o = (Q_1 \Sigma p_1 q_1 + Q_2 \Sigma p_2 q_2 + \ldots + Q_{48} \Sigma p_{48} q_{48}) \div \Sigma \quad Q_n \qquad (3)$$

where Q is the total number of earners in the state whose subscript it bears.

If we are content to compare the earnings of a single state with those of the nation, a new problem does not arise; $\Sigma p_o q_o$ may be treated as any single state and the only change in equation (1) is in the subscripts:

$$\Sigma p_n q_n - \Sigma p_o q_o = \Sigma p_o (q_n - q_o) + \Sigma q_o (p_n - p_o) + \Sigma (p_n - p_o)(q_n - q_o). \qquad (1f)$$

If the desire is to compare two states in terms of the nationally weighted rates, it can be seen that

$$\Sigma p_1 q_1 - \Sigma p_2 q_2 = \Sigma p_o (q_1 - q_2) + \Sigma q_1 (p_1 - p_o) + \Sigma q_2 (p_o - p_2) \qquad (1g)$$

The first term on the right of (1g) is the difference in the nationally weighted rate-constant earnings of the two states, a figure which, presumably, would be useful in comparing the earnings of the two states without the distorting effects of rate variations. The other two terms are state-weighted differences in state and national rates, and since the two differences are not comparable, they are of interest only in describing each state separately. As a means of analyzing the observed difference in two states, this formulation is definitely inferior to that of equation (1). Yet if the interest is in a series of simultaneous comparisons, such as the comparison of each of the states with all other states, a common set of weights is essential.

Simultaneous comparisons based on national standards introduce one further complication. How is an average, or aggregate, of the effects noted for each state to be combined? Treating each as a separate category and using multiple standardization techniques are not available for the simple reason that the weighted sum of the groups is identical with $\Sigma p_o q_o$ and the difference to be explained would be nil. This is the old problem of measuring deviations from a mean. The two solutions which have been offered are the average (absolute) deviation and the variation.

The problem may be illuminated by considering the following series:

$$\Sigma p_1q_1 - \Sigma p_oq_o = \Sigma p_o(q_1 - q_o) + \Sigma q_o(p_1 - p_o) + \Sigma(p_1 - p_o)(q_1 - q_o)$$
$$\Sigma p_2q_2 - \Sigma p_oq_o = \Sigma p_o(q_2 - q_o) + \Sigma q_o(p_2 - p_o) + \Sigma(p_2 - p_o)(q_2 - q_o)$$
$$\cdot$$
$$\cdot \qquad (4)$$
$$\cdot$$
$$\Sigma p_{48}q_{48} - \Sigma p_oq_o = \Sigma p_o(q_{48} - q_o) + \Sigma q_o(p_{48} - p_o) + \Sigma(p_{48} - p_o)(q_{48} - q_o)$$

Equation (3) shows that the weighted average of the state earnings is equal to the national average earning. Similarly the weighted sum of the state rate-constant particles would be zero, since by definition p_o for each industry is the weighted average of all p_n's (n = 1, 2, . . . 48); that is,

$$P_{oi} = (p_{1i}q_{1i} + p_{2i}q_{2i} + \ldots + p_{48i}q_{48i}) \div \Sigma_1^{48} q_n \qquad (5)$$

where the subscript i denotes a particular industry and the q's are in absolute rather than relative terms. The sum of the nationally weighted composition-constant particle plus the sum of the joint particles would also be zero.

The absolute size of the state particle often has been used to obtain sums which were then compared. The logic of this method would be strengthened if the identity in equation (1) were abandoned and the absolute deviations within the industries were summed to obtain the particles.[17]

A superior method would be to compute the total variation to be explained from the left-hand side of (4), and then to allocate the variation among the particles on the right-hand side by the methods discussed in connection with the binary case. If the variation within industries were also available, the variation among states would complete the data needed for an ordinary analysis of variance. This would treat the states as a classificatory device and would permit some test of whether composition, rates, or the states were the more important determinant of the observed interstate variation. If only the state sums (shown in [5]) are available, the analysis will have to relate only to the variation among states.

The particular characteristics of the state industrial earning data (the

[17] As was discussed above, the rate-constant term, $\Sigma p_o(q_1 - q_o)$, is the net result of positive and negative $(q_1 - q_o)$'s, so that it provides an inappropriate base for measuring the relative importance of rates and composition. This led me to reject the relative sizes of the average deviations, used earlier, as a measure of the relative importance of rates and composition as an explanation of the observed variation. Compare my "Contribution of Manufacturing Wages to Regional Differences in Per Capita Income," *Review of Economics and Statistics,* 33 (1951), 18-28, and "State Wholesale Trade Earnings, 1948," *Southern Economic Journal,* 22 (1955), 212-220.

standards are the weighted averages of the state earnings in each industrial category, and the weighted average of the state rate-constant earnings is equal to the weighted average of reported earnings) permit the use of correlation techniques to provide a provisional allocation of the variation into meaningful categories.

FIGURE 1

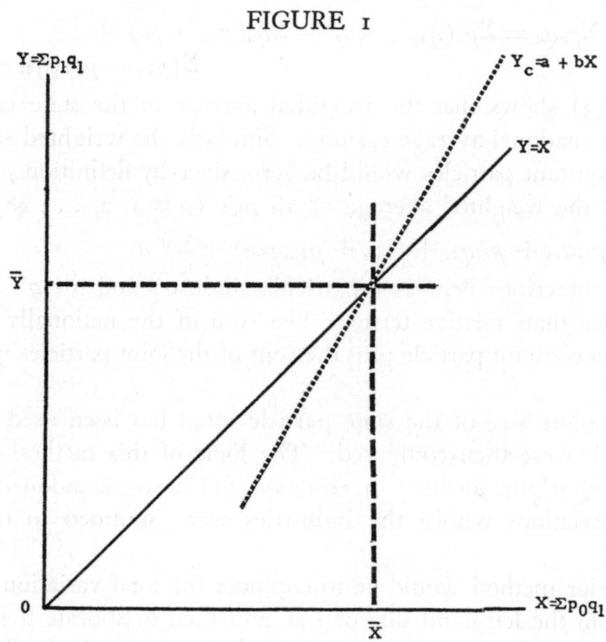

Let figure 1 represent a scatter diagram with state observed earnings ($\Sigma p_n q_n$) on the *Y*-axis and state rate-constant earnings ($\Sigma p_o q_n$) on the *X*-axis.[18] The weighted means of the two series will be identical and equal to the national average earning.[19] Two regression lines have been sketched: one has unit slope ($Y = X$), and the other represents a least-squares regression line ($Y_c = a + bX$). Each passes through the intersection of their means.

In terms of figure 1 the total variation in the observed series is $\Sigma(Y - \overline{Y})^2 = \Sigma y^2$. The variation in the rate-constant series is $\Sigma(X - \overline{X})^2 = \Sigma x^2$. The ratio of these two variations provides us with a measure of the independent effects of the rate-constant particle.

[18] I am indebted to George H. Borts for suggesting this approach.

[19] Because the means are identical and are equal to the national average, these observed earnings and state rate-constant earnings can be looked upon, in terms of equation (1f), as the deviation of the total and rate-constant particles from their respective means.

The remaining variation may be defined by $\Sigma(Y-X)^2$. The difference $(Y-X)$ is the difference between the reported and rate-constant earnings, and consists of the composition-constant and joint particles, as may be seen by adding $\Sigma p_o q_o$ to each side of equation (1f) and gathering the remaining terms as follows:

$$\Sigma p_n q_n - \Sigma p_o q_n = \Sigma q_o(p_n - p_o) + \Sigma(p_n - p_o)(q_n - q_o). \quad (6)$$

The problem is one of allocating $\Sigma(Y-X)^2$ into meaningful categories.

If there is no correlation between the rate- and composition-constant particles—that is, if the $(p_n - p_o)$ term is uncorrelated with the $(q_n - q_o)$ term in the joint particle in equation (6)—then a line of unit slope $(Y = X)$ would describe the relationship between $\Sigma p_n q_n$ and $\Sigma p_o q_n$. This must be so since both $(p_n - p_o)$ and $(q_n - q_o)$ are positive for some groups and negative for others, and it is impossible for all states to lie on one side of any line which passes through the intersection of their means.

When the least-squares regression line has a unit slope, the entire variation of $\Sigma(Y-X)^2$, which is $\Sigma y^2 - 2\Sigma xy + \Sigma x^2$, is attributable to the variation in the composition-constant particle. This may be seen from equation (6), since a unit slope implies that the joint particle would be zero and the remaining term on the right-hand side of the equation is the composition-constant particle. When Σx^2 is attributed to the variation in the rate-constant particle and $\Sigma y^2 - 2\Sigma xy + \Sigma x^2$ to the variation in the composition-constant particle, the remaining variation, $2(\Sigma xy - \Sigma x^2)$, is attributable to the interaction between the rate-constant and composition-constant earnings.

The percentage distribution of the variations will depend upon the coefficient of determination. If the unit-slope regression line passed through every point $(r^2 = 1)$, then $\Sigma y^2 = \Sigma x^2 = \Sigma xy$, and all of the variation would be attributed to the rate-constant earnings, which would be identical with reported earnings. When reported and rate-constant earnings differ, but a least-squares regression line between them has unit slope, the ratio $\Sigma xy/\Sigma y^2 = r^2$ becomes smaller, and the percentages attributable to the composition-constant earnings and to interaction become larger. It should be noted that when the interaction term is expressed as a ratio to the total variation, it consists of twice the differences between the coefficient of determination and the proportion of the total variation explained by the rate-constant earnings, that is, $2(r^2 - \Sigma x^2/\Sigma y^2)$. The interaction term thus includes the factors associated with rate-constant earnings other than differences in composition, which help to account for the total variation in the reported earnings. However, since it is an interaction term, it is available to increase the explanatory power of both the rate-constant and composition-constant particles.

Distributions in which rate and compositional differentials are uncorrelated are likely to be encountered only infrequently in economic data. We have seen that in the binary case the presence of a joint particle will lead to an identification problem which can be resolved only when complete data are at hand. A similar resolution of the identification problem has not been found for the case of multiple comparisons in which joint particles are present and the least-squares regression line departs from unity. The regression method does, however, provide a partial solution in this frequently found case.

Attention is now turned to the case in which the slope of the least-squares regression line (in figure 1) is not unity. The independent effects of composition can still be measured by the variation in the rate-constant earnings (Σx^2). The slope of the regression line will be used to allocate the remaining variation ($\Sigma y^2 - \Sigma x^2$) between the factors which are and which are not associated with the rate-constant particle.

The coefficient of determination is defined as the ratio of the explained variation to the total variation ($r^2 = b\Sigma xy/\Sigma y^2$). It thus provides a measure of the total statistical ability of the independent variable (rate-constant earnings) to explain the variation in the dependent variable (reported earnings). Part of this total explanatory power is attributable to the independent effects of the variation in rate-constant earnings (Σx^2). The remaining explanatory power of the rate-constant earnings is attributable to the correlation between the rate-constant particle and elements in the joint and composition-constant particles. In figure 1 these correlated effects would be represented by $\Sigma(Y_c - X)^2$. The source of these differences cannot be specified, but the magnitude of the variation to which they give rise can be measured by $b\Sigma xy - \Sigma x^2$. The remaining variation, which is unexplained, presumably would include all elements of the composition-constant particle, the joint particle, and interaction which are not correlated with the rate-constant particle.

The above method does not provide information on the effects of the composition-constant particle except in the infrequent case in which there is no joint particle in any of the states. The reason that it cannot be applied to the composition-constant particle is that there is no necessity that the weighted average of the composition for all states equal the national average. Indeed, it was shown above that it is the weighted average of the composition-constant particle plus the joint particle which equals the national average. These sums are the state-weighted composition-constant figures, and their variation among states would include the variation among the nationally weighted rate-constant particles, the variaation among the joint particles, and the interaction between them. The variation in the state-weighted composition-constant particles would thus overestimate the independent effects of the state variation in rates.

The problem may be illustrated by reference to the 1947 data on the hourly earnings of manufacturing production workers. It was found that the independent effects of the rate-constant particle accounted for 32 percent of the total interstate variation in hourly earnings. If the state-weighted composition-constant earnings are used to estimate the independent effects of the composition-constant particle, we get a figure of 35 percent. It has been shown that this is an overestimate of the independent effects of the nationally weighted composition-constant particle, though we have no way of telling how much of an overestimate it is. This leaves some 33 percent in the variation attributable to the interactions of thc ratc-constant particle with the composition-constant and joint particles. An unknown part of these interactions is available to increase the explanatory power of the rate-constant and composition-constant particles. The magnitude of these interactions exceeds the difference between the independent effects. Both because of the error necessarily involved in the estimation of the independent effects of rates and because of the large remaining interaction, a decision as to whether the compositional or rate differentials are the more important is not possible.

Appendix C

STATE PER CAPITA INCOME TABLES

In this appendix, tables have been gathered which show the per capita amounts of farm income and of the income components by state for each of the years from 1929 to 1954. These per capita amounts were computed by dividing the National Income Division estimates of the total amount of each of these types of income by the same population figures used in deriving state per capita personal income. For 1929-1940 and 1948-1954, midyear populations as estimated by the Bureau of the Census were used. For 1941-1947 the population figures are those estimated by the National Income Division by adding to the Bureau of the Census estimates of the midyear civilian populations the average number of military personnel stationed in a state as reported on a monthly or quarterly basis by the military services. The aggregate amounts of each type of income for 1954 are published and the items are defined in Charles F. Schwartz and Robert E. Graham, Jr., "State Personal Income, 1929-54," *Survey of Current Business* (September 1955), table 4. Similar data for 1929-1953 were supplied by the National Income Division in advance of their publication in *Personal Income by State since 1929.*

Farm income (table 61) consists of the net income of farm proprietors (table 66) and farm wages. The latter are not shown separately in these tables. Per capita nonfarm income may be derived by subtracting per capita farm income (in table 61) from per capita personal income (in table 1, chapter 2), for the corresponding year and state.

Tables 62-67 provide data on the per capita income components and subcomponents of personal income. These items have been defined in chapter 4.

TABLE 61

PER CAPITA FARM INCOME, 1929-1954, BY STATE

State	1929	1930	1931	1932	1933	1934	1935	1936	1937	1938	1939	1940	1941
New England													
Maine	$ 67	$ 68	$ 34	$ 20	$ 29	$ 31	$ 24	$ 50	$ 45	$ 36	$ 38	$ 39	$ 42
New Hampshire	32	39	24	20	21	19	27	28	27	28	27	20	29
Vermont	92	86	62	43	46	49	64	67	72	67	69	61	82
Massachusetts	12	11	9	7	8	6	10	9	9	9	8	8	11
Rhode Island	10	9	8	6	7	6	8	7	7	7	6	6	8
Connecticut	23	24	20	15	15	14	20	19	21	18	20	17	23
Middle Atlantic													
New York	18	18	13	9	9	9	13	12	15	13	11	13	16
New Jersey	15	14	12	9	11	9	13	13	14	13	12	12	15
Pennsylvania	21	16	15	9	11	11	17	15	19	15	15	15	19
East North Central													
Ohio	42	25	31	15	19	20	40	30	40	32	32	28	45
Indiana	64	45	43	23	26	30	64	44	75	49	52	42	76
Illinois	46	32	29	18	12	15	43	27	60	33	36	32	54
Michigan	35	30	25	16	19	18	35	31	36	31	29	32	36
Wisconsin	87	68	37	26	29	31	70	62	74	63	52	62	86
West North Central													
Minnesota	103	85	39	34	22	22	88	49	97	70	73	76	103
Iowa	164	122	62	43	34	16	147	69	183	132	128	145	186
Missouri	65	43	43	24	27	20	54	37	62	49	54	49	72
North Dakota	142	93	−13	24	5	3	82	11	96	61	98	120	261
South Dakota	176	125	28	23	−20	−15	105	8	80	77	97	105	181
Nebraska	188	139	70	47	42	−13	120	66	82	81	64	92	149
Kansas	117	92	72	18	29	29	83	63	89	63	57	77	122
South Atlantic													
Delaware	63	44	42	28	29	34	46	50	57	58	49	51	70
Maryland	40	24	29	16	19	21	26	27	31	26	25	26	32
Virginia	68	38	45	24	39	32	50	44	58	44	46	45	49
West Virginia	38	25	31	19	24	19	29	25	33	27	27	26	31
North Carolina	71	53	39	27	49	57	71	61	76	62	64	56	77
South Carolina	63	50	34	23	36	40	55	51	55	48	54	52	48
Georgia	71	51	33	23	35	40	54	50	55	49	47	51	50
Florida	44	47	40	30	23	31	37	37	46	35	42	34	47
East South Central													
Kentucky	81	45	50	30	31	33	48	44	81	54	51	52	64
Tennessee	74	42	44	26	33	33	44	44	64	48	42	49	62
Alabama	70	45	36	24	32	42	48	47	51	45	37	40	56
Mississippi	110	49	47	28	40	55	62	83	83	67	61	59	90
West South Central													
Arkansas	95	39	55	34	42	44	62	69	79	67	71	77	111
Louisiana	70	36	36	24	26	32	47	49	51	45	45	36	43
Oklahoma	82	38	33	19	36	30	60	30	65	51	51	66	77
Texas	93	60	46	32	42	41	60	51	72	56	60	65	80
Mountain													
Montana	87	76	18	60	35	35	102	36	60	101	101	121	217
Idaho	152	173	92	55	30	138	121	140	88	102	114	115	172
Wyoming	148	109	60	39	59	50	100	92	139	113	123	132	208
Colorado	85	84	43	15	40	14	54	69	56	59	47	59	86
New Mexico	116	66	52	23	37	36	60	62	71	54	65	73	96
Arizona	85	74	38	26	36	42	76	62	58	56	57	64	86
Utah	78	68	17	31	39	10	52	71	33	51	54	52	75
Nevada	92	118	− 7	39	34	−15	64	117	− 5	69	89	70	75
Pacific													
Washington	81	63	47	30	36	46	63	57	56	53	52	48	82
Oregon	83	67	52	36	41	59	50	70	61	61	66	63	102
California	74	69	47	28	38	44	55	59	59	49	44	55	74
United States	60	43	33	21	24	25	46	38	51	41	41	42	58

(Continued on next page)

TABLE 61 (Continued)

Per Capita Farm Income, 1929-1954, by State

State	1942	1943	1944	1945	1946	1947	1948	1949	1950	1951	1952	1953	1954
New England													
Maine	$ 73	$ 102	$ 97	$ 93	$ 122	$ 109	$ 130	$ 128	$ 96	$ 95	$ 142	$ 89	$ 51
New Hampshire	47	59	51	59	51	55	52	55	58	61	47	47	38
Vermont	124	150	139	157	158	149	147	121	121	144	122	92	92
Massachusetts	15	20	17	21	22	21	22	21	19	23	19	19	17
Rhode Island	11	10	11	12	13	14	15	15	13	16	15	14	11
Connecticut	26	35	33	42	42	43	42	43	39	44	38	38	33
Middle Atlantic													
New York	25	28	31	32	35	31	33	26	27	31	29	23	20
New Jersey	22	29	27	32	34	30	32	29	29	37	32	33	27
Pennsylvania	25	31	34	36	39	37	39	35	31	39	34	30	27
East North Central													
Ohio	65	67	59	76	72	68	89	62	59	69	70	63	69
Indiana	112	120	105	139	135	140	177	123	120	150	127	133	145
Illinois	69	83	78	84	102	93	150	85	91	112	99	84	96
Michigan	57	58	65	68	71	69	78	60	53	68	60	53	43
Wisconsin	129	157	154	178	187	182	189	153	141	192	169	134	123
West North Central													
Minnesota	178	192	178	209	220	236	307	194	180	236	200	178	188
Iowa	324	379	299	314	416	336	601	334	412	418	426	327	425
Missouri	117	122	127	115	161	133	201	144	158	165	140	127	129
North Dakota	356	546	573	522	485	837	674	365	471	465	318	282	253
South Dakota	369	355	445	471	487	578	720	328	425	575	330	385	382
Nebraska	267	305	293	324	338	373	501	322	422	380	407	293	338
Kansas	221	228	266	245	268	410	311	236	279	241	308	157	200
South Atlantic													
Delaware	98	105	88	111	94	83	106	111	107	121	95	84	62
Maryland	40	43	47	43	56	52	53	50	43	53	46	43	37
Virginia	62	64	75	79	98	91	109	88	92	105	92	68	81
West Virginia	42	51	48	57	59	57	63	52	47	59	53	43	49
North Carolina	118	119	153	156	181	167	165	139	151	186	157	149	151
South Carolina	78	89	117	114	147	125	135	101	95	141	114	109	77
Georgia	79	94	100	112	108	117	115	93	103	131	106	115	77
Florida	60	97	103	114	121	91	77	112	123	117	98	111	102
East South Central													
Kentucky	97	121	136	144	155	147	173	144	117	155	136	125	134
Tennessee	86	95	101	114	123	121	130	109	99	116	103	76	86
Alabama	68	89	96	97	105	116	131	95	92	111	105	111	77
Mississippi	134	128	161	146	136	191	250	144	166	182	202	199	167
West South Central													
Arkansas	138	129	181	152	206	198	276	195	187	213	191	189	174
Louisiana	68	85	84	89	86	101	118	98	91	111	107	99	81
Oklahoma	131	122	168	138	156	187	189	173	123	154	149	127	111
Texas	111	135	139	120	136	189	158	200	156	174	135	118	121
Mountain													
Montana	291	400	375	345	369	470	484	240	435	469	357	370	319
Idaho	254	308	320	327	341	367	362	292	277	315	351	269	230
Wyoming	226	278	243	250	325	348	279	235	264	428	254	198	152
Colorado	130	162	161	181	176	251	219	189	147	204	187	136	88
New Mexico	126	124	137	116	136	179	169	186	150	207	162	115	128
Arizona	130	121	130	144	160	173	191	211	213	331	299	248	231
Utah	96	126	124	135	124	152	122	117	107	143	114	82	77
Nevada	106	114	126	139	155	178	193	191	202	239	195	110	99
Pacific													
Washington	117	136	139	139	162	171	161	123	136	133	140	174	123
Oregon	134	164	155	172	178	171	177	138	145	161	127	129	113
California	108	134	133	130	150	131	123	112	116	142	149	110	100
United States	87	100	102	106	117	120	135	105	106	123	111	97	94

TABLE 62

PER CAPITA LABOR INCOME, 1929-1954, BY STATE

State	1929	1930	1931	1932	1933	1934	1935	1936	1937	1938	1939	1940	1941
New England													
Maine	$ 335	$ 317	$ 277	$ 216	$ 214	$ 244	$ 260	$ 282	$ 300	$ 279	$ 296	$ 314	$ 397
New Hampshire	437	408	355	259	263	302	310	325	355	334	353	369	466
Vermont	361	324	269	211	202	223	249	276	293	274	289	308	378
Massachusetts	567	519	462	365	340	382	412	448	473	437	471	506	620
Rhode Island	569	507	443	348	350	384	425	457	482	439	468	487	641
Connecticut	650	574	487	367	358	411	453	504	559	493	539	613	798
Middle Atlantic													
New York	671	605	514	391	366	403	435	484	513	491	515	546	642
New Jersey	598	549	464	369	332	377	406	465	505	471	507	569	689
Pennsylvania	489	457	373	282	268	313	336	397	429	373	400	440	541
East North Central													
Ohio	512	443	360	268	265	318	347	404	443	381	418	453	569
Indiana	394	337	273	202	199	244	267	318	382	308	340	373	483
Illinois	601	522	427	319	297	348	377	433	477	442	471	505	592
Michigan	501	424	341	268	244	325	369	425	487	395	438	483	604
Wisconsin	398	350	287	220	207	241	270	309	336	310	322	341	408
West North Central													
Minnesota	340	323	282	229	204	233	251	283	307	296	305	302	348
Iowa	272	256	223	173	155	174	188	210	223	221	228	235	279
Missouri	373	349	295	228	213	235	252	285	305	293	306	321	393
North Dakota	206	180	149	121	110	130	143	158	165	168	171	183	210
South Dakota	178	172	148	121	113	144	147	156	163	167	169	175	203
Nebraska	263	253	224	176	161	184	193	214	222	219	224	228	261
Kansas	271	250	215	171	157	180	190	207	222	213	211	225	282
South Atlantic													
Delaware	530	470	416	328	310	340	357	423	476	426	466	531	638
Maryland	447	422	368	298	280	313	333	375	412	388	421	459	592
D. C.	792	799	757	675	580	605	657	710	782	734	756	803	850
Virginia	263	251	227	187	179	210	223	247	267	254	282	315	413
West Virginia	317	286	237	178	183	231	243	278	301	261	276	297	365
North Carolina	181	167	143	112	116	138	145	166	178	168	183	199	256
South Carolina	152	140	120	98	106	127	132	150	164	153	167	197	269
Georgia	196	182	154	124	122	145	156	174	184	172	187	204	270
Florida	292	268	226	184	171	207	218	247	263	256	267	286	348
East South Central													
Kentucky	206	185	154	117	119	133	147	165	178	167	174	187	235
Tennessee	205	191	153	116	120	146	156	178	189	175	188	205	262
Alabama	178	156	126	95	95	118	122	142	155	144	155	177	237
Mississippi	112	102	79	63	61	75	77	91	94	92	100	109	157
West South Central													
Arkansas	136	122	99	81	78	91	96	114	120	113	121	126	163
Louisiana	231	218	183	144	139	160	167	187	207	208	214	224	286
Oklahoma	245	220	176	135	131	151	165	188	203	194	194	200	235
Texas	247	229	193	152	144	162	176	202	224	224	229	242	300
Mountain													
Montana	396	335	270	210	199	245	281	323	340	318	324	330	370
Idaho	271	250	205	158	151	185	209	239	256	247	243	259	309
Wyoming	421	388	319	253	236	274	308	342	360	341	339	337	429
Colorado	376	333	281	222	211	236	260	305	315	296	305	311	363
New Mexico	210	192	165	134	126	151	162	188	204	199	201	210	260
Arizona	373	326	270	208	191	235	240	280	320	297	297	303	388
Utah	345	315	256	199	190	225	249	282	306	285	289	306	365
Nevada	594	515	454	372	341	401	435	479	542	490	513	540	618
Pacific													
Washington	472	427	344	261	244	280	307	360	391	382	406	435	561
Oregon	412	380	313	240	224	268	294	333	358	338	358	383	498
California	549	512	434	348	325	360	393	440	476	461	473	500	613
United States	416	378	318	247	232	269	289	330	357	331	350	376	462

(Continued on next page)

TABLE 62 (Continued)

PER CAPITA LABOR INCOME, 1929-1954, BY STATE

State	1942	1943	1944	1945	1946	1947	1948	1949	1950	1951	1952	1953	1954
New England													
Maine	$ 560	$ 734	$ 748	$ 709	$ 677	$ 733	$ 775	$ 714	$ 742	$ 869	$ 960	$1011	$1014
New Hampshire	574	658	739	748	740	802	862	805	849	1013	1064	1083	1109
Vermont	452	560	590	621	625	690	732	699	732	849	911	969	949
Massachusetts	773	928	954	963	937	994	1063	1035	1138	1305	1342	1376	1349
Rhode Island	845	915	959	936	937	992	1069	997	1130	1268	1321	1353	1307
Connecticut	1026	1186	1196	1122	1079	1191	1251	1177	1314	1580	1677	1768	1687
Middle Atlantic													
New York	783	956	1074	1127	1121	1178	1236	1198	1271	1397	1461	1527	1523
New Jersey	876	1094	1195	1175	1082	1145	1212	1174	1286	1478	1571	1676	1634
Pennsylvania	676	832	915	906	856	950	1039	998	1072	1264	1343	1402	1280
East North Central													
Ohio	714	913	972	951	876	984	1063	1012	1124	1340	1404	1521	1427
Indiana	611	794	858	845	766	876	961	928	1051	1195	1263	1394	1284
Illinois	703	876	991	1022	1012	1122	1213	1167	1247	1412	1493	1580	1537
Michigan	763	1030	1050	942	899	1023	1114	1084	1225	1381	1466	1640	1522
Wisconsin	525	664	716	735	707	807	892	863	938	1106	1153	1205	1146
West North Central													
Minnesota	428	533	587	622	619	701	764	758	812	907	969	1041	1031
Iowa	332	426	473	502	490	559	624	627	660	751	785	823	829
Missouri	488	610	688	726	677	739	817	822	877	989	1094	1160	1147
North Dakota	258	336	366	369	389	447	529	520	527	582	609	631	653
South Dakota	266	342	373	414	381	443	516	516	524	574	611	640	654
Nebraska	366	493	566	595	521	575	644	648	685	790	836	874	890
Kansas	437	594	671	650	539	574	645	671	717	875	986	1053	1037
South Atlantic													
Delaware	766	937	990	949	917	1027	1112	1165	1312	1485	1588	1671	1601
Maryland	811	963	991	957	891	935	1025	1008	1104	1273	1389	1466	1418
D. C.	1004	1148	1179	1213	1187	1217	1329	1442	1475	1610	1648	1542	1499
Virginia	583	635	682	705	680	694	769	771	847	996	1076	1115	1096
West Virginia	449	549	625	659	633	750	852	765	794	911	924	957	873
North Carolina	349	454	483	507	479	523	570	562	617	691	742	781	779
South Carolina	377	456	499	501	448	484	564	542	567	697	775	787	752
Georgia	366	492	578	588	505	534	596	592	637	741	818	860	853
Florida	500	671	749	767	662	687	723	714	749	841	927	1005	1026
East South Central													
Kentucky	318	432	481	488	444	492	571	550	592	716	788	827	780
Tennessee	338	462	559	576	492	520	570	564	612	694	750	822	814
Alabama	346	449	512	529	438	480	524	501	539	645	724	761	750
Mississippi	229	316	365	358	300	311	337	340	365	420	453	486	500
West South Central													
Arkansas	246	315	382	422	331	343	394	392	401	483	533	562	566
Louisiana	392	541	618	601	502	541	617	635	665	742	812	875	881
Oklahoma	340	475	574	587	472	511	607	628	636	728	829	903	928
Texas	428	594	678	684	587	631	708	751	810	916	1001	1045	1053
Mountain													
Montana	457	572	607	631	627	710	787	799	803	914	993	997	998
Idaho	472	543	603	595	571	639	668	675	695	796	866	862	850
Wyoming	557	670	774	785	736	868	991	1006	987	1105	1201	1259	1224
Colorado	522	626	651	710	670	722	788	788	843	1039	1119	1109	1092
New Mexico	361	484	565	612	515	551	617	640	694	779	872	932	915
Arizona	587	697	715	743	651	707	733	742	760	879	995	1017	1011
Utah	584	770	715	753	667	727	793	796	833	972	1033	1071	1038
Nevada	1074	1052	1016	1071	1083	1086	1113	1098	1197	1385	1563	1682	1704
Pacific													
Washington	824	1045	1097	974	855	936	1023	1027	1051	1204	1284	1328	1316
Oregon	721	925	927	849	795	922	983	954	975	1098	1148	1156	1136
California	841	1057	1086	1051	1018	1062	1128	1100	1162	1343	1443	1504	1476
United States	600	757	826	827	779	846	920	900	966	1108	1184	1250	1217

TABLE 63

Per Capita Property Income, 1929-1954, by State

State	1929	1930	1931	1932	1933	1934	1935	1936	1937	1938	1939	1940	1941
New England													
Maine	$ 134	$ 133	$ 128	$ 106	$ 96	$ 97	$ 97	$ 106	$ 105	$ 95	$ 98	$ 103	$ 108
New Hampshire	143	131	121	110	99	104	98	108	117	102	111	111	116
Vermont	116	112	94	78	67	65	63	69	70	72	77	88	105
Massachusetts	241	234	216	192	165	164	156	173	172	149	162	171	165
Rhode Island	223	213	204	183	167	160	154	168	169	149	162	163	169
Connecticut	273	258	232	193	171	176	173	202	206	180	197	199	218
Middle Atlantic													
New York	340	311	263	218	195	191	183	203	208	182	188	187	195
New Jersey	219	215	195	166	139	130	138	148	152	140	148	147	141
Pennsylvania	190	178	154	121	103	107	101	114	118	100	108	110	116
East North Central													
Ohio	140	128	106	76	63	64	66	82	92	81	90	94	111
Indiana	85	77	63	48	39	40	41	53	57	54	60	65	75
Illinois	210	182	144	103	83	85	87	107	112	98	112	117	132
Michigan	174	138	110	69	48	60	67	85	88	72	82	84	91
Wisconsin	130	116	94	80	66	62	70	79	79	74	76	78	93
West North Central													
Minnesota	97	89	81	64	54	58	56	67	67	61	67	71	77
Iowa	84	77	62	48	39	42	42	48	49	49	55	58	63
Missouri	111	107	89	72	59	63	61	73	76	74	78	80	84
North Dakota	38	37	34	25	23	20	22	24	27	23	25	30	36
South Dakota	39	40	34	27	22	23	24	26	29	27	31	33	38
Nebraska	89	79	70	55	47	46	47	51	51	49	51	56	63
Kansas	84	70	60	48	39	41	42	49	54	51	52	56	66
South Atlantic													
Delaware	373	286	264	198	192	214	245	322	345	249	342	353	350
Maryland	213	207	181	158	129	134	130	139	149	143	136	139	140
D. C.	329	316	287	256	214	204	202	237	240	229	225	221	204
Virginia	65	62	59	50	43	46	44	52	55	50	53	58	59
West Virginia	65	60	51	38	31	32	33	41	43	39	43	42	45
North Carolina	44	40	35	28	24	25	26	30	32	30	32	33	37
South Carolina	33	31	28	22	19	20	20	22	24	24	27	27	31
Georgia	45	43	37	30	28	28	29	36	37	35	38	38	43
Florida	123	99	81	69	60	62	67	90	107	101	111	111	107
East South Central													
Kentucky	64	59	48	39	33	35	36	39	39	37	40	40	43
Tennessee	53	50	40	29	27	28	26	31	32	32	35	36	43
Alabama	43	38	32	24	21	21	22	24	27	25	26	28	33
Mississippi	29	24	20	17	15	16	16	18	19	17	18	19	21
West South Central													
Arkansas	37	31	24	19	18	19	19	21	22	22	23	23	25
Louisiana	71	67	60	46	39	40	40	45	50	50	52	49	53
Oklahoma	76	65	47	33	31	35	34	44	50	49	48	49	51
Texas	85	76	64	51	43	46	45	55	62	67	66	64	64
Mountain													
Montana	84	71	57	43	40	43	49	60	57	51	53	58	62
Idaho	53	44	34	30	27	27	25	27	28	27	33	38	46
Wyoming	80	64	58	56	51	50	53	57	62	59	68	72	81
Colorado	117	113	99	79	67	72	73	90	88	83	85	85	97
New Mexico	48	48	38	29	25	26	29	35	37	39	42	43	53
Arizona	86	75	68	48	44	40	44	54	60	56	63	62	68
Utah	85	79	61	50	44	44	46	54	55	51	52	55	62
Nevada	141	151	137	107	90	97	103	144	143	133	138	154	159
Pacific													
Washington	123	110	87	69	57	60	57	67	76	69	76	83	101
Oregon	103	96	78	61	56	57	56	62	64	62	68	73	90
California	260	219	185	143	124	120	119	149	147	145	141	146	162
United States	154	140	119	95	82	82	82	95	98	89	94	96	103

(Continued on next page)

TABLE 63 (Continued)

PER CAPITA PROPERTY INCOME, 1929-1954, BY STATE

State	1942	1943	1944	1945	1946	1947	1948	1949	1950	1195	1952	1953	1954
New England													
Maine	$ 120	$ 135	$ 130	$ 132	$ 139	$ 136	$ 154	$ 162	$ 169	$ 174	$ 191	$ 204	$ 212
New Hampshire	120	128	129	146	161	168	172	193	213	218	217	226	236
Vermont	108	110	115	130	136	127	152	172	177	182	187	196	210
Massachusetts	162	172	178	183	191	199	212	207	253	259	280	290	302
Rhode Island	153	137	147	157	179	195	208	212	229	238	229	237	250
Connecticut	248	233	224	224	240	244	257	262	313	330	358	371	383
Middle Atlantic													
New York	191	196	208	224	237	246	255	267	293	298	307	322	334
New Jersey	135	149	163	170	162	173	186	191	223	231	245	263	273
Pennsylvania	126	133	142	150	154	160	167	176	200	213	220	227	232
East North Central													
Ohio	126	132	136	142	150	158	175	184	201	215	215	226	232
Indiana	81	92	101	106	107	114	126	136	153	157	166	178	186
Illinois	127	134	145	155	169	186	199	205	233	237	237	248	257
Michigan	106	120	122	124	127	137	148	158	185	188	186	199	205
Wisconsin	109	108	111	117	130	133	147	162	179	190	191	202	207
West North Central													
Minnesota	86	93	102	112	121	126	139	147	164	169	173	184	192
Iowa	79	88	95	109	121	126	142	160	167	177	175	181	191
Missouri	97	104	116	122	128	143	155	161	176	182	193	201	212
North Dakota	36	46	57	63	74	81	96	111	113	125	121	125	131
South Dakota	45	56	60	63	82	89	97	105	109	120	126	132	138
Nebraska	79	85	95	103	114	128	144	161	165	179	178	185	195
Kansas	77	85	95	102	109	115	130	143	158	170	186	194	200
South Atlantic													
Delaware	310	296	291	301	333	350	375	437	518	462	456	470	477
Maryland	142	141	143	148	155	168	183	191	210	224	226	239	246
D. C.	202	186	188	207	230	248	280	307	351	352	342	350	365
Virginia	68	68	66	69	85	91	104	112	117	126	126	133	141
West Virginia	56	61	65	68	76	83	94	103	105	104	112	116	124
North Carolina	41	46	51	58	63	68	77	82	87	92	97	102	107
South Carolina	37	39	44	48	55	58	66	73	78	79	88	92	96
Georgia	53	57	63	67	75	79	87	92	102	105	113	120	126
Florida	106	109	116	123	149	157	176	170	197	200	211	226	230
East South Central													
Kentucky	52	56	59	62	69	77	84	85	92	99	102	108	114
Tennessee	50	58	68	70	72	77	80	90	105	104	107	116	120
Alabama	38	42	47	52	57	60	64	71	78	83	88	93	99
Mississippi	25	29	34	39	44	42	49	56	58	62	63	68	73
West South Central													
Arkansas	33	36	43	51	56	56	60	65	71	76	82	88	93
Louisiana	56	61	69	76	80	84	97	106	117	119	122	129	136
Oklahoma	63	70	81	87	98	105	118	130	135	134	147	158	167
Texas	74	85	94	101	114	122	133	145	159	164	170	178	184
Mountain													
Montana	76	85	92	97	117	134	148	165	160	172	183	189	197
Idaho	68	60	64	70	80	88	95	111	122	140	133	142	147
Wyoming	90	102	111	105	118	126	133	172	181	180	184	196	201
Colorado	110	110	109	122	133	140	158	175	192	218	221	226	229
New Mexico	71	69	71	76	89	97	113	116	121	128	131	140	144
Arizona	72	69	82	95	103	106	120	131	138	151	147	152	153
Utah	70	77	78	84	96	101	104	117	131	137	139	147	154
Nevada	135	118	151	159	194	230	225	230	277	289	287	294	295
Pacific													
Washington	111	116	118	116	125	142	161	168	179	192	198	211	217
Oregon	100	105	110	112	123	138	158	174	174	181	183	192	199
California	155	153	153	166	188	203	220	225	249	262	264	274	278
United States	109	114	121	129	139	148	160	169	187	194	200	211	219

TABLE 64

PER CAPITA TRANSFER PAYMENTS, 1929-1954, BY STATE

State	1929	1930	1931	1932	1933	1934	1935	1936	1937	1938	1939	1940	1941
New England													
Maine	$ 16	$ 15	$ 23	$ 19	$ 18	$ 16	$ 16	$ 27	$ 18	$ 24	$ 22	$ 24	$ 22
New Hampshire	14	14	22	19	17	18	20	29	20	26	23	25	24
Vermont	16	15	22	18	15	14	14	25	17	18	18	19	19
Massachusetts	15	15	28	25	27	23	23	35	26	33	32	36	32
Rhode Island	12	12	22	17	16	15	16	30	19	32	29	32	25
Connecticut	13	13	23	20	19	18	18	29	20	27	23	23	21
Middle Atlantic													
New York	18	19	29	25	26	29	31	39	29	35	35	36	35
New Jersey	12	12	22	18	19	22	25	30	20	20	24	23	23
Pennsylvania	13	13	22	19	20	22	28	30	22	30	30	28	25
East North Central													
Ohio	15	15	24	19	19	19	24	30	21	20	24	25	24
Indiana	15	15	24	18	16	15	15	25	17	23	22	22	21
Illinois	14	14	25	20	21	21	22	31	22	21	24	28	27
Michigan	12	12	22	18	18	17	18	26	16	26	24	22	21
Wisconsin	13	13	22	18	17	18	20	28	20	22	21	22	22
West North Central													
Minnesota	11	12	23	17	16	19	19	32	23	26	26	27	28
Iowa	13	13	22	16	13	12	13	27	17	18	19	20	20
Missouri	14	13	22	17	15	15	16	26	16	16	18	19	21
North Dakota	7	8	15	12	11	19	17	25	24	21	19	17	16
South Dakota	10	10	20	13	11	11	11	30	26	25	21	20	19
Nebraska	12	12	20	15	12	13	13	26	18	17	17	19	21
Kansas	16	15	23	17	14	12	13	25	15	15	18	19	20
South Atlantic													
Delaware	12	12	20	18	20	18	15	22	16	16	19	18	18
Maryland	12	12	22	17	16	21	20	28	19	25	22	22	22
D. C.	34	35	55	45	42	45	43	60	45	45	45	46	43
Virginia	8	8	16	11	10	9	9	19	10	12	12	13	12
West Virginia	8	9	16	12	11	11	11	19	11	18	13	13	14
North Carolina	6	6	12	9	8	8	7	14	7	10	9	9	10
South Carolina	5	6	12	9	8	8	7	15	7	8	9	9	10
Georgia	5	6	13	10	9	10	8	16	9	9	10	11	12
Florida	10	10	19	14	13	14	13	23	15	16	19	21	22
East South Central													
Kentucky	9	10	17	13	11	11	11	18	11	10	12	12	13
Tennessee	8	9	16	12	10	10	10	17	10	13	12	14	14
Alabama	6	6	12	9	8	9	7	14	8	10	9	10	10
Mississippi	6	6	13	10	8	8	7	14	7	7	7	9	13
West South Central													
Arkansas	9	9	17	13	12	11	10	18	10	8	9	11	13
Louisiana	7	7	16	11	10	9	9	19	11	12	13	15	16
Oklahoma	9	9	18	13	11	9	9	23	16	15	17	19	22
Texas	7	8	16	11	10	10	10	20	12	12	13	13	16
Mountain													
Montana	11	12	24	20	21	21	23	29	23	22	23	26	27
Idaho	10	10	19	14	13	12	16	26	17	16	19	20	22
Wyoming	11	12	27	18	15	14	15	35	19	17	22	23	22
Colorado	14	14	26	22	21	21	24	36	29	28	33	37	37
New Mexico	8	9	18	15	14	15	16	20	13	12	14	15	17
Arizona	10	11	24	20	19	21	23	29	20	26	26	28	32
Utah	9	9	19	15	15	15	18	26	19	24	24	26	30
Nevada	12	12	26	20	19	18	18	34	21	22	32	33	29
Pacific													
Washington	14	14	25	20	20	19	22	34	25	24	27	30	35
Oregon	15	15	27	20	19	19	19	33	21	26	26	27	27
California	16	16	28	22	21	22	26	37	28	34	38	44	40
United States	12	12	22	17	17	17	19	27	19	22	23	24	23

(Continued on next page)

TABLE 64 (Continued)

PER CAPITA TRANSFER PAYMENTS, 1929-1954, BY STATE

State	1942	1943	1944	1945	1946	1947	1948	1949	1950	1951	1952	1953	1954
New England													
Maine	$ 23	$ 23	$ 27	$ 45	$ 80	$ 81	$ 71	$ 79	$ 89	$ 82	$ 88	$ 97	$ 109
New Hampshire	23	25	30	51	82	83	75	88	99	88	92	99	111
Vermont	19	22	27	46	70	71	67	76	84	73	82	86	101
Massachusetts	32	31	36	61	120	108	98	110	124	115	117	120	131
Rhode Island	26	23	33	54	100	126	103	126	133	117	116	116	136
Connecticut	21	21	26	52	79	90	69	85	93	82	84	88	105
Middle Atlantic													
New York	35	30	35	57	99	95	105	99	112	97	100	104	116
New Jersey	23	21	26	52	88	77	65	74	90	75	79	87	106
Pennsylvania	23	23	28	49	92	84	75	90	133	89	93	94	115
East North Central													
Ohio	24	24	28	46	74	73	88	80	90	75	79	84	100
Indiana	22	21	24	42	66	63	58	63	75	69	78	95	92
Illinois	29	28	32	53	84	90	91	80	94	80	79	83	97
Michigan	25	20	24	54	81	98	66	73	82	72	77	78	97
Wisconsin	22	21	25	40	63	62	56	63	73	66	72	80	93
West North Central													
Minnesota	27	26	30	48	80	78	71	79	100	74	77	82	93
Iowa	20	20	25	42	67	65	60	80	76	66	70	75	89
Missouri	21	23	28	46	86	87	81	86	98	84	89	94	106
North Dakota	16	16	21	35	58	62	57	82	77	64	64	66	69
South Dakota	19	18	22	35	60	60	51	67	77	60	62	63	67
Nebraska	20	20	23	38	65	68	59	60	74	65	66	68	76
Kansas	21	20	24	41	71	68	59	62	80	68	72	80	87
South Atlantic													
Delaware	18	17	20	37	65	63	56	62	81	64	69	74	86
Maryland	21	20	25	42	73	69	61	71	89	73	72	77	89
D. C.	40	41	53	74	123	142	144	166	194	165	168	173	183
Virginia	12	11	15	27	51	54	49	52	75	55	57	62	69
West Virginia	16	15	20	37	78	67	55	64	76	65	100	83	104
North Carolina	10	10	13	27	53	60	53	58	71	56	55	57	65
South Carolina	10	10	14	26	52	59	55	63	74	58	55	57	63
Georgia	13	12	16	31	60	65	59	65	80	66	66	69	77
Florida	22	19	24	40	71	84	80	85	105	90	91	99	107
East South Central													
Kentucky	14	14	19	34	71	65	59	66	80	68	72	77	90
Tennessee	15	15	19	35	74	75	68	77	88	70	68	72	84
Alabama	10	10	14	30	67	69	63	70	80	68	68	69	78
Mississippi	11	9	13	27	61	65	59	66	78	61	59	62	69
West South Central													
Arkansas	13	13	17	32	75	75	69	75	87	72	72	76	84
Louisiana	16	15	19	34	65	67	72	117	113	95	90	88	93
Oklahoma	23	22	29	50	96	103	94	99	105	89	95	106	110
Texas	18	17	21	38	72	77	67	69	88	67	66	71	76
Mountain													
Montana	26	25	31	48	81	78	70	75	91	82	106	88	95
Idaho	22	20	24	39	67	76	67	71	83	73	76	80	87
Wyoming	21	20	23	40	60	68	61	65	88	71	73	76	87
Colorado	37	37	42	58	88	105	105	107	125	112	111	114	117
New Mexico	17	17	21	37	67	74	67	68	87	66	67	71	80
Arizona	29	24	28	46	73	80	72	81	94	78	79	86	91
Utah	26	24	30	47	87	88	79	81	91	75	78	82	96
Nevada	23	21	25	41	68	76	64	73	94	77	79	83	95
Pacific													
Washington	35	32	36	56	97	101	93	112	149	106	110	119	127
Oregon	25	23	28	48	83	85	78	90	102	85	119	107	112
California	34	31	36	55	92	102	97	115	135	112	112	116	125
United States	23	22	26	46	80	82	77	83	99	81	84	89	100

TABLE 65

PER CAPITA PROPRIETORS' INCOME, 1929-1954, BY STATE

State	1929	1930	1931	1932	1933	1934	1935	1936	1937	1938	1939	1940	1941
New England													
Maine	$ 116	$ 110	$ 63	$ 38	$ 46	$ 56	$ 55	$ 85	$ 82	$ 72	$ 77	$ 82	$ 99
New Hampshire	96	95	62	42	40	53	67	74	73	72	72	74	101
Vermont	134	118	83	53	55	68	83	92	98	88	96	92	127
Massachusetts	90	76	61	40	38	47	55	62	64	58	62	71	85
Rhode Island	67	55	43	28	28	37	44	51	53	50	54	61	86
Connecticut	93	81	63	41	39	49	60	69	74	69	75	82	105
Middle Atlantic													
New York	130	108	80	47	47	61	74	84	89	84	87	101	123
New Jersey	102	83	64	39	39	49	59	70	73	69	72	83	107
Pennsylvania	83	68	53	29	30	40	52	58	65	59	61	70	89
East North Central													
Ohio	114	85	78	41	43	56	82	81	95	83	87	93	125
Indiana	118	90	79	43	43	58	96	84	89	89	97	93	147
Illinois	132	98	79	47	41	54	89	81	120	89	98	104	144
Michigan	106	85	67	39	39	50	74	80	91	79	80	90	111
Wisconsin	141	116	71	46	46	59	103	103	118	106	98	113	152
West North Central													
Minnesota	150	128	72	53	37	48	121	88	138	111	119	126	164
Iowa	208	161	91	58	47	40	174	102	219	167	167	188	245
Missouri	130	100	89	51	51	55	93	84	111	95	104	104	148
North Dakota	124	80	−16	18	1	8	84	22	103	66	99	120	260
South Dakota	190	136	37	27	−17	1	118	28	101	97	119	131	210
Nebraska	226	173	96	60	56	12	148	99	118	117	103	136	203
Kansas	164	133	101	32	41	52	112	100	130	103	99	126	184
South Atlantic													
Delaware	102	81	69	44	43	56	73	83	92	91	89	102	135
Maryland	105	78	69	38	40	53	62	75	84	77	82	92	119
D. C.	118	112	99	75	64	67	72	88	95	88	91	100	108
Virginia	99	63	66	34	51	49	69	68	85	71	75	80	97
West Virginia	72	56	54	30	35	37	50	51	61	53	55	55	71
North Carolina	103	80	58	38	59	74	91	85	104	88	92	87	123
South Carolina	80	64	44	28	41	50	67	66	72	64	70	74	82
Georgia	104	77	52	35	45	57	74	75	81	74	75	87	99
Florida	96	87	69	47	40	56	69	80	91	79	89	95	120
East South Central													
Kentucky	112	71	70	41	42	50	68	68	106	78	77	81	101
Tennessee	111	75	66	40	47	56	68	74	97	78	73	84	114
Alabama	97	66	52	33	41	57	64	68	72	64	60	67	95
Mississippi	138	71	62	36	47	66	75	99	100	84	80	81	122
West South Central													
Arkansas	123	61	69	42	47	56	76	86	95	83	89	96	137
Louisiana	106	66	59	38	38	51	70	74	80	76	78	75	94
Oklahoma	124	74	58	35	49	52	85	62	100	85	86	105	126
Texas	139	98	73	48	56	66	87	86	110	93	101	113	144
Mountain													
Montana	104	85	32	64	39	52	120	65	93	123	130	156	256
Idaho	169	193	112	68	37	154	143	169	117	131	139	147	217
Wyoming	165	120	72	47	63	65	113	108	160	136	156	176	251
Colorado	130	120	68	33	56	40	85	107	99	100	93	113	151
New Mexico	141	84	66	31	44	51	79	90	100	83	95	107	141
Arizona	122	102	62	39	46	57	99	91	92	89	91	104	140
Utah	120	102	42	45	51	30	79	103	70	90	97	100	146
Nevada	131	148	32	43	50	15	94	165	42	117	158	149	169
Pacific													
Washington	141	114	82	53	57	80	103	107	108	111	108	114	174
Oregon	153	129	95	63	64	95	95	126	121	118	130	140	223
California	170	142	99	61	71	90	113	134	135	124	123	150	194
United States	121	94	70	42	44	55	82	82	99	85	89	99	131

(Continued on next page)

TABLE 65 (Continued)

PER CAPITA PROPRIETORS' INCOME, 1929-1954, BY STATE

State	1942	1943	1944	1945	1946	1947	1948	1949	1950	1951	1952	1953	1954
New England													
Maine	$ 147	$ 195	$ 186	$ 181	$ 221	$ 200	$ 229	$ 220	$ 192	$ 198	$ 246	$ 189	$ 157
New Hampshire	132	156	150	161	162	155	160	158	162	172	158	152	149
Vermont	178	210	198	216	227	211	219	175	184	206	181	149	148
Massachusetts	107	130	132	144	150	133	140	138	145	156	148	142	140
Rhode Island	110	109	122	120	133	123	133	129	137	146	142	136	130
Connecticut	122	150	155	170	180	168	175	175	183	199	204	196	186
Middle Atlantic													
New York	160	197	219	236	234	196	202	192	203	214	209	197	190
New Jersey	136	168	179	194	197	175	187	183	197	217	212	213	205
Pennsylvania	117	145	155	163	171	154	165	158	161	181	179	170	158
East North Central													
Ohio	164	190	186	210	211	197	226	196	201	225	228	219	224
Indiana	199	225	215	255	254	250	295	237	243	281	261	269	272
Illinois	180	220	224	240	265	238	306	238	252	284	272	257	264
Michigan	153	177	191	199	211	190	214	189	192	219	212	207	193
Wisconsin	216	260	263	294	309	292	307	273	270	332	310	275	260
West North Central													
Minnesota	255	283	279	318	354	351	430	314	316	374	339	317	328
Iowa	394	461	391	416	529	440	721	453	539	556	563	460	558
Missouri	203	225	241	240	295	252	331	275	293	311	295	277	282
North Dakota	344	529	558	542	525	856	701	423	538	539	399	361	333
South Dakota	412	400	495	535	560	640	787	406	510	662	423	476	473
Nebraska	346	395	388	427	451	472	616	436	544	514	544	427	474
Kansas	314	335	374	366	397	531	443	369	423	403	475	326	365
South Atlantic													
Delaware	173	188	182	220	218	194	223	232	239	259	242	233	208
Maryland	146	168	172	171	194	178	189	183	187	203	202	197	187
D. C.	118	133	141	141	149	141	152	163	171	177	181	176	173
Virginia	119	125	135	145	174	163	190	166	176	196	187	163	174
West Virginia	92	113	112	126	134	129	145	130	123	140	138	129	131
North Carolina	175	181	218	229	263	243	244	217	236	279	251	241	239
South Carolina	116	134	167	168	208	178	194	160	158	211	190	186	152
Georgia	139	164	178	196	204	206	206	183	198	234	211	221	181
Florida	141	186	201	221	255	215	205	234	254	251	238	255	247
East South Central													
Kentucky	149	187	200	210	227	216	251	220	196	244	231	223	232
Tennessee	152	182	210	221	218	204	217	194	192	217	207	215	194
Alabama	121	150	162	169	182	185	205	168	171	198	197	198	164
Mississippi	175	174	215	203	200	244	308	205	228	250	269	262	231
West South Central													
Arkansas	179	177	230	217	267	245	324	248	243	275	261	255	236
Louisiana	129	167	173	181	182	189	216	201	194	222	217	212	192
Oklahoma	198	207	260	243	273	296	311	298	251	286	289	272	261
Texas	192	235	245	228	255	298	280	318	284	313	281	261	261
Mountain													
Montana	337	446	438	415	453	535	593	351	548	588	481	494	439
Idaho	342	381	389	410	451	448	451	382	375	429	474	391	349
Wyoming	276	350	321	328	426	426	369	345	366	530	372	312	267
Colorado	222	257	261	293	304	371	343	315	289	370	358	301	248
New Mexico	179	188	212	201	235	266	279	289	263	319	278	236	248
Arizona	210	196	211	223	256	256	291	291	303	447	418	342	327
Utah	210	261	235	244	244	262	243	230	226	269	236	203	195
Nevada	315	302	285	314	372	340	348	357	370	438	415	331	320
Pacific													
Washington	233	280	284	279	318	318	323	280	298	304	313	302	289
Oregon	294	348	350	372	395	373	390	344	356	385	364	339	310
California	251	299	307	308	356	311	305	285	304	338	319	300	283
United States	177	209	221	232	251	240	263	230	239	266	255	240	234

TABLE 66

PER CAPITA FARM PROPRIETORS' INCOME, 1929-1954, BY STATE

State	1929	1930	1931	1932	1933	1934	1935	1936	1937	1938	1939	1940	1941
New England													
Maine	$ 53	$ 55	$ 23	$ 12	$ 23	$ 23	$ 16	$ 40	$ 34	$ 27	$ 29	$ 28	$ 27
New Hampshire	22	30	15	14	15	13	21	22	20	20	19	12	20
Vermont	72	65	45	30	34	36	48	50	54	46	50	41	59
Massachusetts	7	6	5	4	5	4	7	6	6	5	5	4	6
Rhode Island	6	5	5	4	5	4	5	5	4	3	3	3	5
Connecticut	14	15	12	9	10	9	14	13	14	11	13	10	14
Middle Atlantic													
New York	13	13	9	6	7	6	11	9	11	9	8	9	11
New Jersey	9	8	7	5	8	6	10	9	9	9	8	7	10
Pennsylvania	16	12	12	6	9	8	14	12	15	12	11	12	15
East North Central													
Ohio	36	20	29	12	16	17	37	26	35	28	27	24	39
Indiana	56	38	40	20	22	27	59	39	40	43	46	35	69
Illinois	38	25	26	14	10	11	39	22	55	28	31	26	47
Michigan	29	24	22	13	16	14	31	27	31	26	24	27	31
Wisconsin	71	55	26	19	23	24	61	52	63	53	42	51	73
West North Central													
Minnesota	84	70	26	25	13	13	79	38	84	58	61	65	88
Iowa	141	101	45	32	24	5	132	53	166	115	111	126	164
Missouri	57	36	39	20	23	16	50	33	57	43	49	42	64
North Dakota	85	47	−41	3	−12	−14	59	− 8	72	34	66	81	209
South Dakota	144	95	5	10	−31	−23	91	− 4	66	62	82	88	156
Nebraska	161	114	51	34	32	−23	108	53	70	69	53	80	133
Kansas	93	72	56	6	19	18	72	52	77	52	47	66	105
South Atlantic													
Delaware	37	30	29	17	19	23	35	37	41	44	35	37	51
Maryland	24	11	19	7	11	13	16	17	20	16	16	16	21
D. C.	....	....	....	....	....	....	....	....	....	....	....	....	....
Virginia	57	28	38	18	34	26	42	36	49	36	37	36	40
West Virginia	33	21	28	15	21	16	26	23	30	24	25	22	27
North Carolina	66	49	35	25	46	53	67	56	71	57	59	50	70
South Carolina	56	43	28	19	32	36	50	45	49	41	46	45	42
Georgia	65	45	28	20	31	35	48	44	48	43	40	45	43
Florida	30	33	28	20	14	19	25	24	32	22	29	23	33
East South Central													
Kentucky	75	40	47	27	28	30	45	40	76	49	46	46	57
Tennessee	70	38	41	24	31	31	41	40	60	44	38	45	57
Alabama	66	42	34	23	31	40	45	44	47	41	34	37	52
Mississippi	106	45	44	26	38	52	59	79	78	63	56	53	83
West South Central													
Arkansas	89	33	50	30	37	39	57	63	71	60	64	68	99
Louisiana	62	29	30	20	21	27	42	42	43	38	38	29	36
Oklahoma	68	28	27	15	31	25	54	24	58	45	44	59	67
Texas	79	48	37	26	36	35	52	42	61	45	49	54	67
Mountain													
Montana	45	37	− 6	41	20	18	81	17	41	75	75	95	181
Idaho	114	141	69	40	16	121	102	116	61	76	88	89	137
Wyoming	100	65	31	18	39	26	68	56	104	80	92	106	163
Colorado	59	62	24	5	30	3	42	54	41	44	33	46	68
New Mexico	98	48	38	12	27	26	50	51	58	43	54	61	79
Arizona	60	51	19	13	20	24	58	42	37	36	37	45	62
Utah	64	55	8	24	30	− 0	42	57	22	40	45	43	65
Nevada	24	60	−44	− 4	8	−45	25	80	−53	29	56	35	34
Pacific													
Washington	57	41	30	21	28	38	53	46	43	43	38	33	65
Oregon	60	47	34	25	30	45	35	52	43	43	49	46	81
California	46	41	25	14	25	30	40	44	39	31	25	37	54
United States	49	34	25	15	19	19	40	31	44	33	33	35	49

(Continued on next page)

TABLE 66 (Continued)

Per Capita Farm Proprietors' Income, 1929-1954, by State

State	1942	1943	1944	1945	1946	1947	1948	1949	1950	1951	1952	1953	1954
New England													
Maine	$ 55	$ 78	$ 69	$ 61	$ 90	$ 77	$ 101	$ 100	$ 70	$ 63	$ 107	$ 47	$ 11
New Hampshire	36	45	36	41	32	36	32	36	36	35	20	18	8
Vermont	97	113	99	112	112	100	101	64	70	85	57	24	24
Massachusetts	10	14	11	15	16	14	15	13	11	14	10	10	7
Rhode Island	7	7	7	8	9	10	12	11	9	11	11	9	7
Connecticut	15	23	20	29	30	29	29	28	25	27	23	21	13
Middle Atlantic													
New York	19	21	23	23	26	21	24	19	19	22	20	14	12
New Jersey	15	20	18	23	25	20	22	20	20	28	22	23	17
Pennsylvania	20	24	27	28	30	28	31	26	22	29	24	20	17
East North Central													
Ohio	59	60	52	69	64	60	80	53	50	60	61	52	59
Indiana	104	110	94	127	122	127	163	110	108	136	112	119	126
Illinois	61	74	68	74	92	81	137	74	81	101	87	74	85
Michigan	51	49	56	60	63	60	68	50	43	57	48	41	31
Wisconsin	112	137	130	154	163	158	162	130	121	109	146	111	102
West North Central													
Minnesota	159	168	153	184	205	210	280	168	162	212	176	154	165
Iowa	297	343	265	281	381	300	565	301	382	388	394	294	392
Missouri	107	110	114	102	146	114	182	128	140	149	123	109	113
North Dakota	279	446	467	445	411	748	575	298	413	404	263	228	198
South Dakota	336	313	394	427	438	522	651	272	376	522	279	332	329
Nebraska	244	275	261	292	304	334	461	287	388	343	370	256	302
Kansas	199	201	238	220	241	382	281	210	256	218	282	134	176
South Atlantic													
Delaware	78	75	59	93	76	63	86	89	85	98	75	65	44
Maryland	26	28	32	30	42	37	37	36	28	38	32	29	23
D. C.	....	....	....	....	....	....	....	....	....	....	....	....	....
Virginia	52	54	63	68	83	74	92	71	76	89	76	53	65
West Virginia	37	45	42	51	53	50	56	44	40	51	45	35	42
North Carolina	109	108	140	143	167	151	147	123	136	171	141	133	134
South Carolina	68	76	103	100	131	108	115	84	80	125	98	94	61
Georgia	70	84	89	98	94	103	95	77	87	114	88	97	60
Florida	43	78	82	89	93	63	47	84	97	88	69	79	69
East South Central													
Kentucky	88	110	123	131	141	132	158	128	104	141	120	110	119
Tennessee	80	88	94	105	113	110	117	96	88	105	92	95	74
Alabama	63	82	88	89	96	106	119	83	81	98	90	95	62
Mississippi	125	118	149	131	117	168	224	120	143	157	174	167	137
West South Central													
Arkansas	122	110	159	128	179	165	234	159	153	174	154	152	137
Louisiana	58	73	70	73	69	84	99	81	74	96	89	81	61
Oklahoma	115	104	146	119	138	168	165	151	106	135	129	106	92
Texas	92	112	112	90	104	151	117	159	118	138	101	83	87
Mountain													
Montana	241	333	310	279	305	393	413	179	379	407	290	306	253
Idaho	207	248	256	262	281	291	291	229	219	259	298	217	181
Wyoming	173	221	179	178	251	256	181	161	191	348	179	120	79
Colorado	105	131	126	143	139	214	173	150	113	168	152	107	62
New Mexico	102	96	107	83	103	144	132	146	117	172	127	83	97
Arizona	101	89	91	87	100	112	138	153	158	275	234	182	169
Utah	83	109	102	111	101	124	97	92	83	118	86	56	50
Nevada	68	72	86	88	91	106	124	148	155	185	148	65	55
Pacific													
Washington	91	105	105	106	130	139	128	95	111	106	112	104	94
Oregon	109	134	121	136	137	126	138	102	112	129	114	96	80
California	81	101	98	94	112	90	81	73	82	106	90	73	65
United States	74	84	86	89	99	101	115	86	88	104	91	77	74

TABLE 67

PER CAPITA NONFARM PROPRIETORS' INCOME, 1929-1954, BY STATE

State	1929	1930	1931	1932	1933	1934	1935	1936	1937	1938	1939	1940	1941
New England													
Maine	$ 63	$ 55	$ 40	$ 26	$ 23	$ 33	$ 39	$ 45	$ 48	$ 45	$ 48	$ 54	$ 72
New Hampshire	74	65	47	28	25	40	46	52	53	52	53	62	81
Vermont	62	53	38	23	21	32	35	42	44	42	46	51	68
Massachusetts	83	70	56	36	33	43	48	56	58	53	57	67	79
Rhode Island	61	50	38	24	23	33	39	46	49	47	51	58	81
Connecticut	79	66	51	32	29	40	46	56	60	58	62	72	91
Middle Atlantic													
New York	117	95	71	41	40	55	63	75	78	75	79	92	112
New Jersey	93	75	57	34	31	43	49	61	64	60	64	76	97
Pennsylvania	67	56	41	23	21	32	38	46	50	47	50	58	74
East North Central													
Ohio	78	65	49	29	27	39	45	55	60	55	60	69	86
Indiana	62	52	39	23	21	31	37	45	49	46	51	58	78
Illinois	94	73	53	33	31	43	50	59	65	61	67	78	97
Michigan	77	61	45	26	23	36	43	53	60	53	56	63	80
Wisconsin	70	61	45	27	23	35	42	51	55	53	56	62	79
West North Central													
Minnesota	66	58	46	28	24	35	42	50	54	53	58	61	76
Iowa	67	60	46	26	23	35	42	49	53	52	56	62	81
Missouri	73	64	50	31	28	39	43	51	54	52	55	62	84
North Dakota	39	33	25	15	13	22	25	30	31	32	33	39	51
South Dakota	46	41	32	17	14	24	27	32	35	35	37	43	54
Nebraska	65	59	45	26	24	35	40	46	48	48	50	56	70
Kansas	71	61	45	26	22	34	40	48	53	51	52	60	79
South Atlantic													
Delaware	65	51	40	27	24	33	38	46	51	47	54	65	84
Maryland	81	67	50	31	29	40	46	58	64	61	66	76	98
D. C.	118	112	99	75	64	67	72	88	95	88	91	100	108
Virginia	42	35	28	16	17	23	27	32	36	35	38	44	57
West Virginia	39	35	26	15	14	21	24	28	31	29	30	33	44
North Carolina	37	31	23	13	13	21	24	29	33	31	33	37	53
South Carolina	24	21	16	9	9	14	17	21	23	23	24	29	40
Georgia	39	32	24	15	14	22	26	31	33	31	35	42	56
Florida	66	54	41	27	26	37	44	56	59	57	60	72	87
East South Central													
Kentucky	37	31	23	14	14	20	23	28	30	29	31	35	44
Tennessee	41	37	25	16	16	25	27	34	37	34	35	39	57
Alabama	31	24	18	10	10	17	19	24	25	23	26	30	43
Mississippi	32	26	18	10	9	14	16	20	22	21	24	28	39
West South Central													
Arkansas	34	28	19	12	10	17	19	23	24	23	25	28	38
Louisiana	44	37	29	18	17	24	28	32	37	38	40	46	58
Oklahoma	56	46	31	20	18	27	31	38	42	40	42	46	59
Texas	60	50	36	22	20	31	35	44	49	48	52	59	77
Mountain													
Montana	59	48	38	23	19	34	39	48	52	48	55	61	75
Idaho	55	52	43	28	21	33	41	53	56	55	51	58	80
Wyoming	65	55	41	29	24	39	45	52	56	56	64	70	88
Colorado	71	58	44	28	26	37	43	53	58	56	60	67	83
New Mexico	43	36	28	19	17	25	29	39	42	40	41	46	62
Arizona	62	51	43	26	26	33	41	49	55	53	54	59	78
Utah	56	47	34	21	21	30	37	46	48	50	52	57	81
Nevada	107	88	76	47	42	60	69	85	95	88	102	114	135
Pacific													
Washington	84	73	52	32	29	42	50	61	65	68	70	81	109
Oregon	93	82	61	38	34	50	60	74	78	75	81	94	142
California	124	101	74	47	46	60	73	90	96	93	98	113	140
United States	72	60	45	27	25	36	42	51	55	52	56	64	82

(Continued on next page)

TABLE 67 (Continued)

PER CAPITA NONFARM PROPRIETORS' INCOME, 1929-1954, BY STATE

State	1942	1943	1944	1945	1946	1947	1948	1949	1950	1951	1952	1953	1954
New England													
Maine	$ 92	$ 117	$ 117	$ 120	$ 131	$ 123	$ 128	$ 120	$ 122	$ 135	$ 139	$ 142	$ 146
New Hampshire	96	111	114	120	130	119	128	122	126	137	138	134	141
Vermont	81	97	99	104	115	111	118	111	114	121	124	125	124
Massachusetts	97	116	121	129	134	119	125	125	134	142	138	132	133
Rhode Island	103	102	115	112	124	113	121	118	128	135	131	127	123
Connecticut	107	127	135	141	150	139	146	147	158	172	181	175	173
Middle Atlantic													
New York	141	176	196	213	208	175	178	173	184	192	189	183	178
New Jersey	121	148	161	171	172	155	165	163	177	189	190	190	188
Pennsylvania	97	121	128	135	141	126	134	132	139	152	155	150	141
East North Central													
Ohio	105	130	134	141	147	137	146	143	151	165	167	167	165
Indiana	95	115	121	128	132	123	132	127	135	145	149	150	146
Illinois	119	146	156	160	173	157	169	164	171	183	185	183	179
Michigan	102	128	135	139	148	136	146	139	149	162	164	166	162
Wisconsin	104	123	133	140	146	134	145	143	149	163	164	164	158
West North Central													
Minnesota	96	115	126	134	149	141	150	146	154	162	163	163	163
Iowa	97	118	126	135	148	140	156	152	157	168	169	166	166
Missouri	96	115	127	138	149	138	149	147	153	162	172	168	169
North Dakota	65	83	91	97	114	108	126	125	125	135	136	133	135
South Dakota	76	87	101	108	122	118	136	134	134	140	144	144	144
Nebraska	102	120	127	135	147	138	155	149	156	171	174	171	172
Kansas	115	134	136	146	156	149	162	159	167	185	193	192	189
South Atlantic													
Delaware	95	113	123	127	142	131	137	143	154	161	167	168	164
Maryland	120	140	140	141	152	141	152	147	159	165	170	168	164
D. C.	118	133	141	141	149	141	152	163	171	177	181	176	173
Virginia	67	71	72	77	91	89	98	95	100	107	111	110	109
West Virginia	55	68	70	75	81	79	89	86	83	89	93	94	89
North Carolina	66	73	78	86	96	92	97	94	100	108	110	108	105
South Carolina	48	58	64	68	77	70	79	76	78	86	92	92	91
Georgia	69	80	89	98	110	103	111	106	111	120	123	124	121
Florida	98	108	119	132	162	152	158	150	157	163	169	176	178
East South Central													
Kentucky	61	77	77	79	86	84	93	92	92	103	111	113	113
Tennessee	72	94	116	116	105	94	100	98	104	112	115	120	120
Alabama	58	68	74	80	86	79	86	85	90	100	107	103	102
Mississippi	50	56	66	72	83	76	84	85	85	93	95	95	94
West South Central													
Arkansas	57	67	71	89	88	80	90	89	90	101	107	103	99
Louisiana	71	94	103	108	113	105	117	120	120	126	128	131	131
Oklahoma	83	103	114	124	135	128	146	147	145	151	160	166	169
Texas	100	123	133	138	151	147	163	159	166	175	180	178	174
Mountain													
Montana	96	113	128	136	148	142	180	172	169	181	191	188	186
Idaho	135	133	133	148	170	157	160	153	156	170	176	174	168
Wyoming	103	129	142	150	175	170	188	184	175	182	193	192	188
Colorado	117	126	135	150	165	157	170	165	176	202	206	194	186
New Mexico	77	92	105	118	132	122	147	143	146	147	151	153	151
Arizona	109	107	120	136	156	144	153	138	145	172	184	160	158
Utah	127	152	133	133	143	138	146	138	143	151	150	147	145
Nevada	247	230	199	226	281	234	224	209	215	253	267	266	265
Pacific													
Washington	142	175	179	173	188	179	195	185	187	198	201	198	195
Oregon	185	214	229	236	258	247	252	242	244	256	250	243	230
California	170	198	209	214	244	221	224	212	222	232	229	227	218
United States	103	125	135	143	152	139	148	144	151	162	164	163	160

TABLE 68

AVERAGE ANNUAL EARNINGS OF WAGE AND SALARY WORKERS REPORTING INCOME, UNITED STATES, 1949, BY INDUSTRY AND SEX

	Industry	All workers	Males	Females
	01 AGRICULTURE, FORESTRY AND FISHERIES			
105	Agriculture	$1,149	$1,197	$ 634
116	Forestry	2,031	2,051	1,804
126	Fisheries	2,277	2,334	880
	02 MINING			
206	Metal mining	3,059	3,073	2,400
216	Coal mining	2,496	2,498	2,279
226	Crude petroleum and natural gas extraction	3,672	3,737	2,534
236	Nonmetallic mining and quarrying, except fuel	2,649	2,664	2,191
246	03 CONSTRUCTION	2,637	2,653	2,059
	04 DURABLE MANUFACTURED GOODS			
	Lumber and wood products, except furniture			
306	Logging	1,799	1,800	1,598
307	Sawmills, planing mills, and mill work	1,946	1,952	1,783
308	Miscellaneous wood products	2,118	2,272	1,367
309	Furniture and fixtures	2,407	2,544	1,685
	Stone, clay, and glass products			
316	Glass and glass products	2,795	3,095	1,829
317	Cement, and concrete, gypsum, and plaster products	2,770	2,804	2,072
318	Structural clay products	2,560	2,655	1,705
319	Pottery and related products	2,401	2,833	1,606
326	Miscellaneous nonmetallic mineral and stone products	2,973	3,179	1,879
	Metal industries			
336	Blast furnaces, steel works, and rolling mills	3,151	3,163	2,222
337	Other primary iron and steel industries	2,282	2,933	2,014
338	Primary nonferrous industries	2,994	3,101	2,108
346	Fabricated steel products	2,983	3,188	1,978
347	Fabricated nonferrous metal products	2,871	3,145	1,783
348	Not specified metal industries	3,055	3,328	1,777
	Machinery, except electrical			
356	Agricultural machinery and tractors	3,047	3,145	2,219
357	Office and store machines and devices	3,336	3,700	2,178
358	Miscellaneous machinery	3,198	3,369	2,043
367	Electrical machinery, equipment, and supplies	2,923	3,467	1,880
	Transportation equipment			
376	Motor vehicles and motor vehicle equipment	3,226	3,358	2,261
377	Aircraft and parts	3,392	3,548	2,318
378	Ship and boat building and repairing	3,053	3,091	2,415
379	Railroad and miscellaneous transportation equipment	3,216	3,329	2,219
	Professional and photographic equipment, and watches			
386	Professional equipment and supplies	2,983	3,442	1,942
387	Photographic equipment and supplies	3,425	3,911	2,219
388	Watches, clocks, and clockwork-operated devices	2,620	3,282	1,882
399	Miscellaneous manufacturing industries	2,487	3,027	1,612
	05 NONDURABLE MANUFACTURED GOODS			
	Food and kindred products			
406	Meat products	2,767	2,988	1,895
407	Dairy products	2,760	2,968	1,694
408	Canning and preserving fruits, vegetables, and sea foods	1,900	2,482	1,090
409	Grain-mill products	2,807	2,922	2,068
416	Bakery products	2,784	3,100	1,689
417	Confectionery and related products	2,268	3,003	1,554
418	Beverage industries	3,050	3,205	1,959
419	Miscellaneous food preparations and kindred products	2,572	2,857	1,596
426	Not specified food industries	2,994	3,603	1,840
429	Tobacco manufactures	1,940	2,484	1,476
	Textile mill products			
436	Knitting mills	2,084	3,023	1,527
437	Dyeing and finishing textiles, except knit goods	2,870	2,968	1,852
438	Carpets, rugs, and other floor coverings	2,876	3,202	1,970
439	Yarn, thread, and fabric mills	2,200	2,540	1,704
446	Miscellaneous textile mill products	2,481	2,975	1,652
	Apparel and other fabricated textile products			
448	Apparel and accessories	1,999	3,217	1,548
449	Miscellaneous fabricated textile products	2,080	2,778	1,561

(Continued on next page)

TABLE 68 (Continued)

AVERAGE ANNUAL EARNINGS OF WAGE AND SALARY WORKERS REPORTING INCOME, UNITED STATES, 1949, BY INDUSTRY AND SEX

	Industry	All workers	Males	Females
	Paper and allied products			
456	Pulp, paper, and paperboard mills	$2,970	$3,104	$1,953
457	Paperboard containers and boxes	2,643	3,102	1,750
458	Miscellaneous paper and pulp products	2,790	3,322	1,801
459	Printing, publishing, and allied industries	3,165	3,554	2,032
	Chemicals and allied products			
466	Synthetic fibers	2,918	3,148	2,178
467	Drugs and medicines	3,316	4,239	2,065
468	Paints, varnishes, and related products	3,221	3,451	2,088
469	Miscellaneous chemicals and allied products	3,317	3,558	2,129
	Petroleum and coal products			
476	Petroleum refining	4,104	4,279	2,676
477	Miscellaneous petroleum and coal products	3,208	3,267	2,265
478	Rubber products	3,011	3,348	1,971
	Leather and leather products			
487	Leather: tanned, curried, and finished	2,750	2,900	1,834
488	Footwear, except rubber	2,010	2,486	1,513
489	Leather products, except footwear	2,137	2,754	1,455
499	Not specified manufacturing industries	2,742	3,169	1,815
	07 TRANSPORTATION, COMMUNICATION, AND OTHER PUBLIC UTILITIES			
	Transportation			
506	Railroads and railway express service	3,188	3,219	2,650
516	Street railways and bus lines	3,043	3,131	1,973
526	Trucking service	2,804	2,853	2,014
527	Warehousing and storage	2,486	2,624	1,661
536	Taxicab service	2,021	2,052	1,425
546	Water transportation	3,072	3,116	2,288
556	Air transportation	3,786	4,067	2,427
567	Petroleum and gasoline pipe lines	3,771	3,828	2,500
568	Services incidental to transportation	2,968	3,170	2,054
	Telecommunications			
578	Telephone (wire and radio)	2,794	3,890	2,143
579	Telegraph (wire and radio)	2,938	3,140	2,575
	Utilities and sanitary services			
587	Gas and steam supply systems	3,095	3,227	2,213
588	Electric-gas utilities	3,302	3,476	2,210
596	Water supply	2,725	2,781	2,104
597	Sanitary services	2,367	2,376	1,899
598	Other and not specified utilities	2,986	3,146	2,302
	08 WHOLESALE AND RETAIL TRADE			
	Wholesale trade			
606	Motor vehicles and equipment	3,240	3,505	2,032
607	Drugs, chemicals, and allied products	3,251	3,772	2,005
608	Dry goods and apparel	3,719	4,665	2,184
609	Food and related products	2,729	3,045	1,550
616	Electrical goods, hardware, and plumbing equipment	3,351	3,715	2,038
617	Machinery, equipment, and supplies	3,638	3,978	2,126
618	Petroleum products	3,547	3,743	2,318
619	Farm products—raw materials	2,841	3,047	1,715
626	Miscellaneous wholesale trade	3,230	3,525	2,004
627	Not specified wholesale trade	3,195	3,604	2,251
	Retail trade			
636	Food stores, except dairy products	2,109	2,404	1,361
637	Dairy products stores and milk retailing	2,912	3,139	1,427
646	General merchandise stores	2,070	3,120	1,571
647	Five and ten cent stores	1,354	3,065	1,017
656	Apparel and accessories stores, except shoe stores	2,200	3,332	1,582
657	Shoe stores	2,577	3,015	1,474
658	Furniture and house furnishings stores	2,687	2,990	1,689
659	Household appliance and radio stores	2,616	2,840	1,639
667	Motor vehicles and accessories retailing	3,116	3,278	2,005
668	Gasoline service stations	1,947	1,963	1,390
669	Drug stores	1,858	2,456	1,225
679	Eating and drinking places	1,525	2,059	1,080
686	Hardware and farm implement stores	2,469	2,657	1,605
687	Lumber and building material retailing	2,812	2,929	1,903
688	Liquor stores	2,544	2,705	1,574

(Continued on next page)

TABLE 68 (Continued)

AVERAGE ANNUAL EARNINGS OF WAGE AND SALARY WORKERS REPORTING INCOME, UNITED STATES, 1949, BY INDUSTRY AND SEX

	Industry	All workers	Males	Females
689	Retail florists	$1,817	$2,161	$1,316
696	Jewelry stores	2,588	3,192	1,667
697	Fuel and ice retailing	2,540	2,619	1,927
698	Miscellaneous retail stores	2,412	2,842	1,520
699	Not specified retail trade	2,156	2,934	1,498
	09 FINANCE, INSURANCE, AND REAL ESTATE			
716	Banking and credit agencies	2,967	4,003	1,945
726	Security and commodity brokerage and investment companies	4,128	5,236	2,204
736	Insurance	3,140	4,246	1,927
746	Real estate	2,339	2,691	1,629
	10 BUSINESS AND REPAIR SERVICES			
806	Advertising	3,907	4,823	2,361
807	Accounting, auditing, and bookkeeping services	3,228	3,832	2,125
808	Miscellaneous business services	2,771	3,267	1,885
816	Automobile repair services and garages	2,442	2,466	1,765
817	Miscellaneous repair services	2,501	2,561	1,730
	11 PERSONAL SERVICES			
826	Private households	792	1,226	727
836	Hotels and lodging places	1,614	1,969	1,218
846	Laundering, cleaning, and dyeing services	1,780	2,473	1,273
847	Dressmaking shops	1,133	2,273	913
848	Shoe repair shops	1,637	1,646	1,549
849	Miscellaneous personal services	1,888	2,205	1,502
	12 ENTERTAINMENT AND RECREATION SERVICES			
856	Radio broadcasting and television	4,071	4,674	2,195
857	Theaters and motion pictures	2,783	3,463	1,529
858	Bowling alleys, and billiard and pool parlors	1,180	1,176	1,240
859	Miscellaneous entertainment and recreation services	2,164	2,365	1,463
	13 PROFESSIONAL AND RELATED SERVICES			
868	Medical and other health services, except hospitals	2,067	3,135	1,775
869	Hospitals	1,911	2,444	1,679
879	Legal services	2,687	4,655	2,043
888	Private educational services	2,224	3,052	1,575
889	Government educational services	2,538	3,033	2,259
896	Welfare and religious services	1,997	2,317	1,510
897	Nonprofit membership organizations	2,724	3,305	1,841
898	Engineering and architectural services	3,873	4,259	2,196
899	Miscellaneous professional and related services	3,482	4,086	2,293
	14 PUBLIC ADMINISTRATION			
906	Postal services	3,099	3,211	2,179
916	Federal public administration	3,202	3,497	2,535
926	State public administration	2,793	3,156	2,183
936	Local public administration	2,834	3,023	2,093
	15 INDUSTRY NOT REPORTED	1,629	1,809	1,199

Source: Computed from an unpublished tabulation, identified as D-9, of 3.3 percent of the *Census of Population, 1950* returns. It provided a frequency distribution of wage and salary workers by $500 intervals over the range $1-4,999; by $1,000 intervals over the range $5,000-6,999; $7,000-9,999; $10,000 and over; no income reported; and income not reported. In computing the averages the sum of the products of the midpoints of the class intervals times the number in the class were summed and divided by the total number reporting wage and salary income. The midpoint of the $10,000 and over class was assumed to be $17,500, a figure arrived at by averaging and rounding the average wages and salaries reported in amounts of $10,000 in *Statistics of Income* for several years. The major-group earnings are averages of the detailed industries weighted by the number of wage and salary workers reporting income.

INDEX